What God Wants You to Know

Daily Reflections from Genesis to Revelation

Lele Beutel

Paperback ISBN: 979-8-9902359-7-7
Ebook ISBN: 979-8-9902359-8-4

Contents

This book is dedicated to all those
who seek to know Him Who loves them.

Introduction

I came to know Him when I was 16. At the prompting of a Young Life leader named Jack Carpenter, who shared an inspiring message of hope to a group of teens at Pioneer Ranch in Colorado, I climbed up to the top of a mountain and prayed. "Jesus," I said, "I don't know You. But I want to. Will You come into my heart and be a part of my life?" And that was the beginning of a quest that will never end.

From the age of 19, I became an avid Bible student because I realized how desperately I needed His "armor" to protect and guide me. I spent many years studying the Bible, seeking life as a missionary, and attending Bible classes. I was even awarded an associate in theology degree. But after spending countless hours searching, and researching His Word, I still had so many questions, and I knew I was missing something—some hidden key that would unlock the scriptures' meaning for me.

My answer came when a pastor friend gave me a book that changed my life. In *Dining at the Master's Table* by Paul Norcross, I began to understand how to fill a gap in my life. "Go to your prayer closet," the author explained. "Spend time listening for His voice. Get to know Him personally and find out what He seeks for you." This was the key I'd missed for so many years.

With that information, I began to practice just listening. I set aside time each morning, and, for the next 20 years, sought His voice as I read the Bible, not just during my special morning quiet time, but throughout the day. As I read and reread the scriptures, and listened for His direction, He began to reveal things to me—things I'd never seen before. His Holy Spirit showed me how verses fit with other verses. He showed me where to look when a passage seemed obtuse, and the meaning avoided me. He enlightened me on the history and prophecy He'd inspired men to write down so many years ago. All for me and for you.

As I read and reread the scriptures from Genesis to Revelation, I asked questions, and He led me to sources for understanding. Often, He'd show me where to look outside the verses for the explanation of things I didn't understand. My eyes were opened to so many things! I began to write down what I discovered as I read. This took me years. Then I segmented the study into 365 days, with each day focusing on equal amounts of reading from the Bible and one or more pages of explanation. This was helpful to me as I created my own year-round study of the whole Bible. What I focused on in each summary was His heart regarding that section. What did He really want me to know and understand about these specific passages of scripture? I spent time putting it all together. And this book is the result. As you read it, imagine God speaking to you. That way, the message becomes more personal for you.

I hope you find this devotional as rewarding to read as it has been for me to write. In your quest for understanding who God is, who His Son is, and what their heart and hope is for all people, my desire is that you come to a greater knowledge of the truth and the ability to apply it in your own life. But, most importantly, I hope you discover how your life fits into the greater scheme of things, including God's plan for you and for all of us.

God's richest blessings on your life,
Lele Beutel 2024

Day 1

Once there was another earth

*"In the beginning God (prepared, formed, fashioned,
and) created the heavens and the earth."*
—Genesis 1:1

Genesis 1-2

A different earth existed before this one. It was similar in some ways but not the same. It had living creatures and plants and atmosphere, but they were different from those today.*
Long ago, I gave an assignment to another. He was My first Morning Star, and, when I created him, he knew his purpose—to glorify Me through what he did. I asked him to make a place that would bring Me joy, a place filled with creatures who could be part of a family—My family—and could communicate with Me through what I am: Spirit. To be able to do this, they must be able to understand and believe in Me.

What he made was hideous. The creatures that inhabited this first earth were destructive, vicious, and territorial. The "humans" were mere beasts unable to know or love Me. They were brutes who could not conceive of Me or receive My Spirit. I was disappointed and dismayed, and Lucifer knew it. But he did this on purpose. His creation served a purpose—to oppose and resist Me. He wanted to rebel against all that I am, and this was just the first step. It was all a slap in My face. I was angry, and I confronted him. But instead of undoing his rebellious feat, he summoned a third of the angels to side with him against Me. He wanted My power. He wanted to rule the universe. A war in heaven ensued, and I won with two-thirds of the angels. Lucifer and his followers were thrown from heaven to earth. In a cataclysmic event, he fell like an asteroid and disrupted the earth's atmosphere. His creation was demolished. What he'd made could not survive. He was furious and vowed to fight against Me and destroy all I would form in the future.

And so, I began again. But, this time, with the help of another, a new Morning Star Who came from My Word and My Light: My own beautiful Son. Using the "waters" or life-giving "juices"—matter I'd created, He helped Me to create what I'd always desired. He fulfilled the ancient assignment and made a new and glorious planet with light from the heavens to sustain life—the plants and creatures that inhabited it. All were for the benefit of the people He made—the culmination of His work. And, this time, they'd be able to know and worship Me as Creator over all because they could recognize My voice and receive My Spirit. I was pleased with My Son's work, and I approved it.

But Lucifer was not finished, and so the battle began.

3

Day 2

The same old story

"I will put enmity between you and the woman, and between your offspring and her Offspring; He will bruise and tread your head underfoot, and you will lie in wait and bruise His heel."
—*Genesis 3:15*

Genesis 3-5

It's the same old story, isn't it? Though I bestow so much and give to people more than they could ever need to live a wonderful life, they still turn away and follow their own inclinations. They heed voices besides Mine. And the voices, not having their best interest at heart, lead them far away from Me into lives of lack, sickness, and death. When they were created, Adam and Eve were equal in My eyes. I saw them the same. Their role was to simply walk with Me in the garden, share an intimate relationship with Me and enjoy all the bounty available to them.

But Eve was drawn away by her senses. Instead of looking to Me and trusting what I said, she heeded what seemed appealing to her at the time. Then she led Adam away with her, indulging in seductive "fruit." Because of this, I had to take them to another place apart from My presence.

After their choices, they experienced unexpected hardships. Far from the garden, they encountered thorns, thistles, and afflictions. There, Eve received her name, because life must spring from her to one day produce a Savior. Goodness and evil came from her children. Abel represented the goodness that comes from a life devoted to Me. He offered the first fruits of his labor and honored Me in all he did. Cain did not. He wanted his success to be his own and did not choose to honor or acknowledge Me by offering Me his best. Whenever people think I am not pleased with them, they attack those I've blessed because of their trust in Me. Hatred often leads to murder and death. My intention was never that people die, but destruction comes through disobedience and a turning to self. The result is disaster. With Abel gone, another had to come who would seek Me and bring a needed Savior. Seth was this one. From him came godly descendants, like Enoch, who walked with Me. From Enoch came Noah. Do you see how a family's lineage can bring goodness and godliness or evil and disobedience? Look back at your own family tree. What do you see?

As a believer in Me, you will find ancestors who also trusted, and your own progeny will be blessed because of them and because of you.

Day 3

I didn't want to start over again

"God looked upon the world and saw how degenerate, debased, and vicious it was, for all humanity had corrupted their way upon the earth and lost their true direction."
—Genesis 6:12

Genesis 6-9

I didn't want to start over again. I liked what My Son had made in its original state. It was His gift to Me. But Lucifer, later called Satan, had begun to corrupt it beyond recognition. He had lured people into degradation so that their every imagination and intention was continually evil. And the land was filled with violence: desecration, outrage, assault, and lust for power. As part of his plot to destroy what My Son had made, he invented a scheme. Seeing how he deceived Eve with his lies, he convinced other women to accept the "seed" of his "angels," those who had followed and fallen with him.* Using My created material, they impregnated some with their warped sperm to bear giants, who would roam and destroy the earth. These were the "men of renown" written and spoken of by the Greeks and Romans. Their purpose was only evil through a reign of terror on the earth. But I couldn't allow this. So I sent rain to wash away this pollution and cleanse the earth from evil.

Remember, I still needed a Savior to be born—One Who could redeem My people and bring them back to Me. Even then, I began to prepare for another earth that would later be filled with people who would worship Me. But they must originate from My Son's creation. Only Noah could provide what was needed because he listened to Me and did all that I commanded him. From him I would raise up a few who believed to bring a special line to the Messiah.

It had never rained before the flood. The earth was watered by a mist. (Genesis 2: 5-6.) That's why people thought Noah was crazy. Before the flood, plants and fish provided all the sustenance needed. But, after the flood, due to the sparsity of plants, I instructed Noah to kill and eat the "clean" creatures, who wouldn't further corrupt their bloodstream. These were included on the ark in groups of seven for this purpose. They were used for sacrifice to Me because I required an "accounting" for every life taken. The rainbow appeared for the first time after the flood. Its seven colors stood for My perfection and My promise to never allow such a flood again.

It also signified a greater promise—that a Savior would come one day to earth.

Day 4

And I will bless you

"Go for yourself [for your own advantage] away from your country, from your relatives and your father's house, to the land that I will show you."
—Genesis 12:1

Genesis 10-13

It's hard to move away from your family and all you've ever known. But Abraham did it out of obedience to Me. Why did I ask him to do this? Because I had something greater in mind for him and for his descendants.

Abraham descended from Shem, whose descendants were called Semites. Eber, another of his ancestors, produced the Hebrews. And, from Aram, came their dialect known as Aramaic. Ham's descendants from Canaan were cursed because he "saw the nakedness of his father," or had intercourse with his mother. (See Leviticus 18:7-8; 20:11.) Ham's descendants were the Philistines, Canaanites, and those of Babel, Sodom, and Gomorrah.

Abraham and his descendants would always be blessed. Why? Because, out of all the earth's people, he alone chose to follow My lead. So those who blessed him and his descendants would be blessed, while those who cursed him and his descendants would be cursed. I promised him a land and a great nation of people as an inheritance and a name above any other. I honored My promises to him, even when he misrepresented his wife as his sister. He hadn't completely misled Pharoah, since she was his half-sister. Though he wandered away from the land I'd promised to him, I stuck with him and led his family back to it once again.

Do you see how I uphold every promise I make, even when people don't always heed My voice? When you wonder why My promises to you are not yet fulfilled, as Abraham sometimes did, I will remind you, with angels and messengers if I must, to pull you back and assure you that I have not forgotten you and never will. Abraham wandered from Me at times, but I always pulled him back. When he reentered the promised land, he gave Lot a choice, and his nephew chose what seemed to be the best. But appearances can be deceiving. His land became a wasteland, due to the evil in it, while Abraham's inheritance grew ever more prosperous because he was in it.

You may at times think you have made bad choices, but, when you come to Me and follow My lead, I will always make something beautiful out of your "ashes."

I will honor and bless you, even when others won't.

Day 5

Be patient with My promises

"He [Abram] believed in (trusted in, relied on, remained steadfast to) the Lord, and He counted it to him as righteousness (right standing with God).
—*Genesis 15:6*

Genesis 14-17

I honored My promises to Abraham. Why? Because he honored Me. When he went to rescue his nephew Lot, who was captured by a conquering king, Abraham ended up with lots of loot. He could have lusted for more, but he never did. He gave one tenth of what he had to My priest and King of Salem, Melchizedek. And he was blessed for his giving.

In a vision, I came to Abraham and said, "I am your Shield, your abundant compensation, and your reward shall be exceedingly great." This is My promise to all who trust in Me.

Another promise I made to Abraham was that he would have descendants that would number as many as the stars in heaven. And, as he aged, I reminded him of this promise. He believed and continued to trust Me, and for this I counted him as righteous. I showed him the land his progeny would inherit one day and promised that they would reign as kings. But they must come from Sarai. Though she herself sometimes doubted that she could conceive and gave her handmaid Hagar to Abraham as a concubine, I worked with her because she honored her husband. When I changed her name from Sarai to Sarah, and Abram's name to Abraham, I added the fifth letter from the Hebrew alphabet, "hey," or "H" in English, which signified My grace and divine favor to them.* The meaning of the name Sarah was "princess"—I wanted her to know how I saw her.

Abraham's fathering of another child through Hagar resulted in a generational challenge to the descendants of Isaac. The number 13 signifies rebellion, apostasy, defection, and revolution. Ishmael was circumcised when he was 13. He became "a wild ass among men," and "his hand would be against every man and every man's hand against him." He would always be at odds with Isaac and with Me, and his children would always threaten the borders of Israel. I established circumcision as a token of My covenant with Abraham, a sign of My promise to him that his descendants would always be special and "set apart" for Me. This was because he believed in Me, was patient with My promises, and walked habitually with Me. As a result, I saw him as perfect and blameless, even when he made mistakes.

I see everyone who loves Me in this same way.

Day 6

Be patient with My promises

"Is anything too hard or too wonderful for the Lord?"
—Genesis 18:14

Genesis 18-20

I look at your heart. Though you may laugh, like Sarah, at My unfulfilled promises that seem too good to be true, I see what's in you, and I have hope for you and your future. Don't give up on Me or My promises. See My heart as I see yours.

Abraham pleaded for the lives of a few—those he knew and loved, and My Son now pleads with Me for your life and many others. To spare a few—some who will believe later, I hold off the time of judgment until all who choose Me can come. I wait patiently and need you to do the same. One day, My Son's time will come, and He will return to earth to judge between good and evil. But this time is held in abeyance until more can come along in their belief.

In the past, I used My angels as messengers to warn people of impending doom. I sent two to Lot. They looked like ordinary men. And they understood the inherent evil in Sodom, as the inhabitants sought to assault and abuse these "strangers." I see some of this in the world today, and I'm dismayed as it grows more prevalent, and the world grows ever darker. But I wait.

As I did with Lot and his family, I always warn people before any disastrous event occurs. In his time, I sent angelic messengers to warn them of impending doom. But now I work through people with whom I can communicate via My Spirit in them. Some, like Lot's sons-in-law and his wife, will never heed the warnings. Sadly, they will suffer the consequences.

You can plead with Me for mercy, even for those who don't deserve it, and I will listen to you, just as I listened to Abraham, because you have an Intercessor. And I will work out My plan for you and for others, in spite of wrong done or mistakes made, just as I did for Lot, his daughters, and for Abraham. I even warn those who aren't My own, who reject Me, and I can cause good to come out of their fear-based mistakes. I protected Sarah and Abraham from harm because they were part of My plan to bring My Son to earth.

Through My Son, I'd save to the uttermost those who believed and would one day occupy a new planet.

$\mathcal{D}ay$ 7

Abraham understood My promise

*"In your Seed shall all the nations of the earth be blessed and [by Him]
bless themselves, because you have heard and obeyed My voice."*
—Genesis 22:18

Genesis 21-23

I honored Abraham for his trust in Me, and I blessed him above any man on earth. I promised him that his descendants would be like the sand on the seashore and the stars in heaven, and they would possess the gates of My enemies. Through him, and the One who descended from him, all nations of the earth would be blessed. Others recognized this blessing and wanted to be a part of it, because they saw that I was with him.

Abraham knew of My promise to bring forth the Messiah through his lineage. He also believed in a promised "Lamb." So when I asked him to offer his son to Me as a burnt offering, he thought I might be requiring the sacrifice of his son Isaac as the Lamb, the One Who would take away the sins of the world. He'd also seen others sacrifice their own children to their gods, including his own family members in Ur of the Chaldees.[1] But when I told him to offer Isaac, I never required that his son be burned. Why would I? From him must come the Promised Seed. I did want Abraham to *dedicate* his son to Me as a living sacrifice. I would provide the burnt offering for sin. I also wanted Abraham and others to see the significance of what I and My Son must endure later to save mankind. Like Abraham, I would be willing to sacrifice My only Son. Like Isaac, My Son would carry wood as the device used for His death.[2] On the same Mount Moriah, He'd be tied up to die. I would provide the Lamb for the sacrifice, as I provided the ram to Abraham. But My Lamb would be tried and killed in your rightful place of judgment.[2]

When I called out to him, "STOP!" Abraham listened and heeded the warning. He proved himself faithful, even to the point of being willing to give up his own son for Me, and I counted this toward his righteousness. But I never willed Isaac's death. I needed Isaac to live and produce a people through whom My Son could come!

I never desire the death of anyone, especially of those who love and serve Me. People will see your faith—how you are blessed—and, as they did with Abraham, want to participate in your blessing. Turn to Me, and I will guide you in your choices.

And I will never lead you astray.

Day 8

Life may not turn out as you expected

"[Two] children struggled together within her; and she said, If it is so [that the Lord has heard our prayer], why am I like this? And she went to inquire of the Lord."
—*Genesis 25:22*

Genesis 24-25

Abraham saw that his son needed a wife. But he didn't want Isaac to marry a Canaanite. Why? Because Canaanitish blood was tainted by unbelief, degradation, and idolatry. So, Abraham knew he must find his son a wife from among his own family to maintain a godlier line to produce the Messiah. And she must be willing to accept his son and his God.

He sent his servant, just as I sent My Spirit through messengers to a willing people. And his servant prayed that I would prepare a way for him to find a wife for Isaac. He asked for a sign, and I answered his prayer. He found Rebekah, Abraham's great niece—daughter of Bethuel, son of Abraham's brother Nahor—at the well. I came through for him, as I will always come through for you. I sent a messenger, a representative of My Spirit, to prepare a way and find a bride for Abraham's son. In much the same way, I prepared the way for My Bride, working through inspired and willing messengers to seek Her out.

Rebekah came willingly. She answered the call. And, as Isaac's bride, she produced sons. She had two, but only one could be the rightful heir, so she asked Me, "Why twins?" And I answered her question: "Two nations of people would come from her sons, but the older would serve the younger one." Jacob would be My Son's ancestor.

They were different, these twins. Esau was hairy and bold and passionate—an outdoorsman. Jacob was contemplative and shrewd—a homebody. Jacob loved his mother, and she loved him. Isaac favored Esau's zeal, and he enjoyed eating his son's captured game.

Life often doesn't turn out as you might expect. You may wonder why some people end up on My path, while others don't. Your own children will surprise you. They may not turn out as you thought they would. But never give up on them! I had called Jacob, and his mother knew it. Though he was a "supplanter," a "trickster," I chose him to bring My heir, contrary to Isaac's expectation.

Ask Me "Why?" and I will always answer you, just as I did Rebekah.

Day 9

My purposes always move to the forefront

*"Behold, I am with you and will keep you wherever you may go, and I will bring you back
to this land; for I will not leave you until I have done all of which I have told you."*
—Genesis 28:15

Genesis 26-28

People often think that they can control their own and others' destinies. Rebekah believed
that she had to take matters into her own hands so that Jacob would receive Isaac's blessing,
instead of their eldest son Esau. She told Jacob to dress in his brother's clothes and to mask
his smooth skin with lambskins so that he'd seem to be his brother. She even cooked a lamb
to taste and smell like the wild game Esau hunted then gave it to Jacob to bring to his father.
Did she know that, one day, My own Lamb would come from her son Jacob's descendants
to be sacrificed for My people?

She was not thinking of this then but schemed to make sure her favorite son would be
the heir. Was she directed by Me to do this? Or was this her own plan? I never lead people
to lie or deceive to achieve My desired results. But I can use the actions of people, though
ill-conceived, for My purposes. Rebekah's plan worked, and Jacob received Isaac's blessing.
But there was a cost. When people try to do My work for Me, they always pay a price. Just
as Sarah and her progeny suffered later, after she asked Abraham to produce a child through
Hagar, Rebekah's scheme brought great dissension between brothers, and Jacob had to leave
home to escape his brother's wrath. Rebekah never saw her son again.

From Esau would spring a group of people, as I promised him, but tension would always
exist between his offspring, the Edomites, and Jacob's descendants, the Israelites. Still, I can
use any situation for good, and My purposes will move to the forefront of any family feud.
Even when others think circumstances can only bring about bad outcomes, I can use them
for My beneficial purposes. When you see dissension in your own family, or in your nation,
and when people don't end up doing what you wanted them to do, just realize that out of
every misfortune or misappropriation, I can still produce good.

And every person serves a purpose. Jacob came to know Me when he left home. On his
way to Haran, he had a dream. In it, he saw an opening between heaven and earth, and he
realized that I wanted to be his God. He made a pact with Me, and, though he supplanted
his brother's inheritance, I still worked with him.

Even through your shortcomings or "failings,", I will work for you, as I did for Jacob.

Day 10

I will always come through for you

*"You had little before I came, and it has increased and multiplied abundantly;
and the Lord has favored you with blessings wherever I turned."*
—Genesis 30:30

Genesis 29-30

Superstitious beliefs have always played a part in the lives of those who don't know or understand Me. Even today, people use horoscopes, talismans, charms, mediums, and soothsayers to "change the dial" or determine what lies ahead so they can control life. But only I can predict or change the future. Only I can control events or work them out as part of My plan. And when people come to Me for guidance, protection, advice, or blessings on their lives or labors, only then will they see how I work on their behalf. Sometimes, as in Jacob's case, I must work despite peoples' superstitions, and they see later how I was involved.

Rachel wanted children, but remained barren for many years. Out of her impatience and desperation, she vied for Leah's son's mandrakes, thinking they would bring her the desired result—fertility. Some believed superstitiously in the power of the roots of this plant, which were shaped like a human body with outstretched arms and legs. They thought that if one kept them close at hand, they would promote conception.[1] Rachel embraced this superstition, but it wasn't because of the mandrake that she conceived.

Jacob latched onto middle eastern customs to try to determine the types of progeny produced in his care. When his father-in-law tried to slight him, Jacob set up stripped rods to "make sure" Laban's goats and sheep bore streaked, speckled, and spotted offspring, which were his agreed-on share of the herds. Despite Laban's chicanery in removing the streaked, speckled, and spotted goats at the beginning, to ensure that Jacob would always have less, Jacob ended up with more. Later, he realized that it was I Who had supplied his needs all along. It was I Who kept multiplying the sheep and goats for him. It was never the rods, or his own manipulations, that brought Jacob abundant blessings and prosperity.[2]

People may try to deceive you. They may even try to steal your blessings.

But I will always come through to reward you with the blessings that were meant for you.

Day 11

Why I contended with Jacob

"He said, Your name shall be called no more Jacob [supplanter], but Israel [contender with God]; for you have contended and have power with God and with men and have prevailed."
—Genesis 32:28

Genesis 31-32

Jacob was a schemer. He manipulated his own family members to make things happen. Even while he often saw My hand in his life, he still doubted My ability to do things without his intervention. He struggled, as you do, to trust Me and My promises to him. But what was unique about Jacob, as it was for his father and grandfather, was that he worshipped only Me. That is why I loved Jacob, despite his lack of trust at times. I can work through idolaters, like Laban, to bring My desired results, and ultimately bless My people, but My real desire is for all people to come to Me alone for their needs.

You will see patterns of behavior in every family. Jacob's bent toward deception was learned from others. Abraham and Isaac misled others about their wives; Rebekah and Laban manipulated situations to suit their own designs and desires. Rachel hid her father's idols in her saddlebag. Why did she do this, and why was Laban so intent on finding them? Laban stormed after them because, in his culture, whoever possessed these household images bore the rightful claim to the family's property and assets. Laban worried about his "stuff," and did not want Jacob to eventually claim all that he had. That is one reason for the pact between them at Galeed. Rachel stole the images because she was disgusted with her father for the many times he had deceived her husband. She was also angry that he had not left her or Leah any inheritance. But this act of hiding her father's treasures in a saddle bag did not promote her blessing for a long life and was repeated later by her son, Joseph, when he hid valuables in his brothers' bags to implicate them.

All his life, Jacob struggled to trust Me because he'd seen so much distrust in his own family. When I sent My Messenger to contend with him, it was for his heart. Jacob had always struggled with fears and now feared for his life and his family's. It was time for him to realize that he might have earthly—flesh and blood—fears, but his real contention would always be with Me.

Would he trust Me to support him and fulfill My promises to him by working all things for his good?

Or not?

Day 12

You can't control what your children do

> *"Jacob said to Simeon and Levi, You have ruined me, making me infamous and embroiling me with the inhabitants of the land.... And we are few in number, and they will gather together against me and attack me; and I shall be destroyed, I and my household."*
> —Genesis 34:30

Genesis 33-36

You can't control your children's actions. They will do what they choose, and sometimes, their actions will be contrary to your desires for them.

After leaving Laban, Jacob traveled back to the land of his father and his grandfather, Abraham. Despite an unexpectedly joyful reunion with his brother, Esau, and an invitation to settle near him, he went in the direction I intended for him—Canaan. Before getting to Bethel, where he had once dreamed of a ladder leading to Me, his daughter, Dinah, was seized and raped by a young man named Shechem, who wanted to marry her. His father, Hamor, approached Jacob to make a pact between their tribes. He promised Jacob and his family peace and safety, if they settled nearby, and encouraged marriage between their families. Jacob wanted to establish a good name for himself in the area and agreed, but only if the males of the tribe were circumcised. They would, in effect, be making a covenant with Me by receiving this sign of My lordship, and they would become integrated into the tribe of Israel. But this never happened. Though Hamor and his son agreed to the terms and circumcised every male, two of Leah's sons decided to attack and kill the men of Shechem when they were most vulnerable because Shechem had violated their sister. Jacob's other sons finished the job by looting their town.

Jacob was very distraught by their actions. He feared his reputation was besmirched in the land and was concerned that other tribes would attack them defensively. Instead, the people of Canaan were intimidated by Jacob and his sons. But Jacob was even more upset when his eldest son lay with his concubine and lost the inheritance he intended for him.

Jacob had many fears for himself and the survival of his family. Most parents do. But I reminded him of My promises. After his father Isaac died at Mamre, I showed him that I would ensure that from him would come a great nation of people, and that kings would come from him.

In spite of your fears and concerns for your children and grandchildren, My promises to bless you and them will prevail because of your belief in Me.

Day 13

When others mean evil for you

"But the Lord was with Joseph, and showed him
mercy and loving-kindness and gave him favor."
—*Genesis 39:21*

Genesis 37-39

Those who are favored by Me are never treated or thought of well by those who are not. When you are one of Mine, I bless your every endeavor and cause good fruit to flourish in your life, even when others intend evil for you, because you believe in Me.

It was this way with Joseph. His father loved him as a child of his old age and one of his deceased wife's offspring. Rachel was his favorite wife. The whole family knew that. But favorites in families are not treated or looked upon favorably by the other members. Joseph's brothers conspired to kill him! Only because of Reuben and Judah did he end up being sold as a slave instead of being killed and flung into a pit. How could his own brothers be so cruel? Remember, these are the ones who killed and looted an entire town of people who wanted to befriend them. And they hated Joseph, and thought evil of him, because he was their father's favorite. Joseph had given a bad report of them to Jacob and revealed two dreams where they bowed down to him. Because of these things, their evil thoughts festered, multiplied, and developed a life of their own. They had to be talked into selling their brother as a slave for 20 pieces of silver instead of killing him outright.

Whenever evil thoughts grow in those who hate, their loathing never originates from Me. These brewing notions often foment to produce evil deeds that result in destruction and death. Those who are not favored want the blessings they see in others' lives, and they may try to "steal" them. But, even when some conspire against those I've chosen, I always work things out for good, especially for those who are graced by Me. When Joseph was blamed for another person's lack of integrity and thrown in prison, I began to work in his situation to bring about good for him and for many.

I use every situation for My ends, which are always good. When you look at some in your family and sigh because you don't see any good results coming from them, remember this: With Me, nothing is lost.

I can use all things to bring about the benefits of My plan for your family.

Day 14

I work through those who work with Me

"Joseph answered Pharaoh, It is not in me; God [not I]
will give Pharaoh a [favorable] answer of peace."
—Genesis 41:16

Genesis 40-42

Do you see how interwoven My plan is for your life? As with Joseph, I work through every detail. Nothing is ever wasted of what you do or say or of what others do to you. I loved Joseph, as his father Jacob did, and I wanted the best for him. But sometimes what is best comes with a price. Joseph was imprisoned for several years, but I worked in his situation to bring him up and out. I even worked through the dreams of those who didn't know Me!

My heart breaks to see My people living in hardship. If they will trust Me, I can use their hard times to bring ultimate good to them and others. I use situations to build strength of mind in those who trust Me, and I can lift them up and out of the tough places into places where they can use their gained strengths to help others who go through hardship later. The people who disown, displace, or cause harm to My people will suffer later, when they realize how their actions caused so much harm, even to themselves. Why did Joseph treat his brothers so harshly when they came to Egypt? Think of the years he'd suffered, away from his family, his brother Benjamin, and his father Jacob. He wondered at times why none had sought him out. Mostly, he wanted to know if his brothers regretted what they'd done to him. I made sure he heard them discuss this and understood the regret they felt. This is why he wept.

Because Joseph acknowledged his dreams from the time he was young, I could use this ability and willingness to discern others' dreams. He understood that dreams may be from Me and may mean something, and their meaning could only be interpreted by Me. He might have become arrogant, or self-important, being the favored son of his father, but he grew in humility through imprisonment. He saw how the ultimate control of the outcome of his life came only from Me. Because of his humble acknowledgement of how I could help him, I was able to raise him up and make him a supreme leader in Egypt.

In hardship, he had learned how to lean on Me for life itself.

Day 15

What Joseph learned

"God sent me before you to preserve for you a posterity and to continue a remnant on the earth, to save your lives by a great escape and save for you many survivors."
—Genesis 45:7

Genesis 43-45

How could Joseph resist telling his brothers that it was him? Why didn't he reveal himself to them right away? Remember what he'd endured. He'd learned discipline and patience—how I could work with him to get him out of prison and the situation he'd ended up in if he was patient. Mostly he'd learned endurance. So, when he saw his brothers, he was not in a hurry to show them who he was. Would they believe it anyway?

The trickery of putting his silver cup in Benjamin's saddlebag was learned from his mother, Rachel, but he had a purpose in it. He wanted to see his brothers again. So he'd bide his time in revealing how I worked their evil schemes into good. Imagine the emotion he felt, and the self-control he exerted, when he saw his brother Benjamin again and heard that his father was still alive.

Judah was My forerunner because he understood integrity. He put his own life on the line and was willing to be the surety for his half-brother, Benjamin, knowing that this was Jacob's favorite son. To spare his father's life, he was willing to stake his own. He went before Another who would one day come from his descendants to be a surety for all. Jesus, like Judah, would stake his own life so others could live.

Joseph is a pattern for forgiveness. What he displayed to all showed how to forgive even the worst cruelty. He exhibited how, after being terribly mistreated by his enemies, even his own family, one can survive and rise above it all to become strong and whole to the point of helping many. Joseph learned patience and how to abide in Me, and he was able to use these acquired skills to save nations.

He never gave away the grain he'd accumulated because he understood discipline and reliance on Me. He sold it. Nothing is of value to people when they are unwilling to earn or work or trust Me for it. When nations give away the prosperity they've fought and died for, and accumulated by discipline and hard work and faith, to those who don't appreciate the effort made to produce it, they can't be blessed in return. And those who receive it aren't advanced when they take it, because it is of little value to them.

They don't appreciate it.

Day 16

I go before you

*"And Israel said to Joseph, Behold I [am about to] die, but God will
be with you and bring you again to the land of your fathers."*
—Genesis 48:21

Genesis 46-48

As Jacob lay dying, he blessed Joseph's two sons before he closed his eyes. And Joseph bowed down to Me in thanks for seeing his father again. Neither of them thought they'd ever see the other again, yet I had worked it out, and they both acknowledged this.

I go before you to prepare a way, just as I prepared a way for the descendants of Abraham, because I love you just as I loved them. Though people may intend harm for you, even deceive and betray your trust and try to swindle what's meant for you, know that I will always turn things around so that your life is blessed, just as I did for Joseph and Jacob. Jacob acknowledged, in the end, that I had redeemed him from evil, though he told Pharaoh at first that "few and evil have the days...of my life been."

Why had the life of this one I loved been "few and evil?" Because he, like you, lived in the world, and not everyone in the world believes in Me. Jacob's wives and concubines were not raised to trust in Me. You can see how the wives' father, Laban, schemed and worshipped idols and relied on superstitions. It was Jacob who led his family to acknowledge a belief in Me, the one true God.

But his children were still surrounded by idolatrous practices and did not always honor their own or others' commitments or pacts. Jacob taught them My ways, the ways of his father and grandfather, but, like your own children, they didn't always heed him.

Yet, I still called them. I still gave them what was needed to live, survive, and thrive. I worked out goodness from evil intent because I loved them. Jacob saw this truth as his "lost" son bowed before him and brought his own progeny to be touched by him. The ones I choose are not always the "right" ones in the world's eyes, because I see inside people and know who they are.

Pharaoh listened to Joseph and acknowledged him as a leader directed by My Spirit. And Jacob blessed Pharaoh twice when he stood before him.

And because Pharaoh acknowledged Joseph's role, I was able to show favor to, not only Egypt, but the lives of multitudes of people during a severe famine.

Day 17

A father speaks into his children's lives

"Jacob called for his sons and said, Gather yourselves together [around me],
that I may tell you what shall befall you in the later or last days."
—*Genesis 49:1*

Genesis 49-50

You may think a lot has changed since the times of Abraham, Isaac, Jacob, and Joseph. But
it hasn't. People still marry, have children, and see the results of both evil and good in their
lives. Notice how I work through every family situation to bring needed results. I can even
speak to parents, or grandparents, and show them how I will work in their own children's
lives later.

Jacob's prophecies for his children unfolded over time. From Judah came the "cub of a
lion"—the great Lion of Judah. (See Revelation 5:5.) A ruler and leader would come out
from him and his descendants: Shiloh, the Messiah, Who would one day wash His garments
in the blood of grapes. (See Isaiah 63:1-3 and Revelation 19:11-16.) This One would bind a
donkey's colt to "the choice vine" of My Truth. (See Zechariah 9:9, John 12:15 and 15:1.)

Because he betrayed his father's trust by lying with his concubine, Reuben lost his
inheritance among the tribes of Israel. And his portion went to Joseph's sons, Ephraim and
Manasseh. Simeon and Levi had broken a pact and killed honorable men in Shechem, so
their inheritance was lessened. Simeon inherited very few cities in Israel, and Levi assumed
no land, though I allowed a priestly line to come from him. From Zebulun came a sea-faring
people, who lived by the Mediterranean Sea and the Sea of Galilee. Issachar inherited a
land good for farming and shepherding. Mighty judges came to rule from Dan, including
Samson. But, like a rider falling backward in the saddle, some of Dan's descendants would
fall to worshipping idols. From Gad came soldiers—men who fought and defended kings
later. Naphtali's descendants were peace-loving citizens, while Benjamin's were warriors and
leaders, with examples like Ehud, Saul, Jonathan, and the Apostle Paul.

Joseph received many blessings from his father because he endured and overcame the
most. From him, fruitfulness abounded through his faithfulness to Me. Though evil was
intended for him, I brought great good to many because of his dependence on My strength.

As I did with Joseph, I will help you in every situation and increase your blessings so that they
run over, if you depend on Me.

Day 18

How to lead others out of bondage

"Moses said to God, Who am I, that I should go to
Pharaoh and bring the Israelites out of Egypt?"
—*Exodus 3:11*

Exodus 1-4

Whenever people who believe in Me are imprisoned by slavery, but still seek Me and My will, I always work to release them from bondage. You can see this throughout history. I did this for the Israelites, who suffered under the hand of an Egyptian Pharaoh. And there have been many others whom I have freed.

Rulers can be cruel. Out of fear of losing power, they may dictate treacherous ways of subduing, or even eradicating, those I want to bless. They may see the prosperity and fruitfulness of a group, or an individual, and grow jealous and afraid of losing their own control over them. But slavery and manmade controls over others were never My purpose or desire. And I will always provide a means to freedom for those who trust Me.

It took great faith for Jochebed to release her son in an ark onto the water. Like Hannah and Mary later, she committed her son to Me and trusted that I would take care of him. Ruth also exhibited great faith when she followed her mother-in-law Naomi to an unknown land out of love and devotion. These are excellent examples of women who leaned on Me above their own desires and fears and brought great blessings to many.

Jochebed's son, Moses, eventually led an entire nation to freedom—to a land flowing with milk and honey. Hannah's willingness to honor her promise to Me enabled Samuel to become a great prophet and to later anoint David as a king who led Israel back to Me. Ruth birthed Boaz, whose lineage led to the Messiah. And Mary bore the Son of My love for you!

Moses doubted his ability to lead the Israelites to freedom, but he was willing to trust Me for support and follow My lead. Do you see how I provide a way through your fears to do My will and bring many to needed freedom?

If you just trust Me, you can be the conduit to a better life for many, who can also live lives of freedom through Me.

Day 19

How to succeed when others mistrust you

*"But Moses said to the Lord, Behold, [my own people] the Israelites
have not listened to me; how then shall Pharaoh give heed to me,
who am of deficient and impeded speech?"*
—Exodus 6:12

Exodus 5-8

Delivering people from bondage never comes easy. Many, when they don't receive an immediate answer or see a quick result, give up on prayer. But bringing about what is wanted and needed takes time and patience. Do you see how quickly the Israelites gave up on Moses? At the first sign of hardship, they turned away from him out of "impatience and anguish."

Moses asked Pharaoh to let My people go into the wilderness to sacrifice to Me. But Pharaoh, not knowing Me or Who I was, decided instead to increase the Israelites' workload. He ordered that they not be given any straw; they'd have to find it themselves. The water from boiled straw was mixed with clay to make durable bricks. Without needed straw, it was harder to make as many bricks as possible each day. The Israelites complained and rejected Moses in his mission to lead them to freedom.

Whenever a great work is pursued—one that potentially could bring deliverance to many people, the world always offers great resistance. Often, people turn their backs on the one trying to lead the effort out of fear. Though its accomplishment could result in greater freedom from hardship, many resist, especially if they are subjected to undue pressure from others. As a result, they miss out on the freedom I intended for them.

I desire that every person who lives as a slave—whether it be to drugs or work or sickness or other people or life itself—be freed and able to live as I intended—in prosperity and in health. (III John 2.) "The thief comes to steal, kill and destroy," but My Son came to give you an abundant life. (See John 10:10.) Abundant in what? Joy, peace, love, contentment, having all you need to be fulfilled and able to give to others.

At the first sign of hardship, the Israelites caved in. It was the determination of just one man that brought about the fulfillment of My plan. I chose Moses because he would listen to Me and carry out My instructions. And I can work with you to fulfill your dreams and Mine if you will hear Me and persevere. Like Moses, you'll encounter resistance because you live in the world.

But what will determine your own success is patience, persistence, and endurance.

Day 20

What happens when rulers rebel against Me

*"So Pharaoh's heart was strong and obstinate; he would not
let the Israelites go, just as the Lord had said by Moses."*
—Exodus 9:35

Exodus 9-11

*Do you see how the people of a nation suffer at the hands of a stubborn, arrogant, and
self-serving leader?* When rulers resist My words and defy those I send with messages of
direction and hope for My people, so they can live in relative peace and prosperity, you can
see the results.

In the case of Moses, I had to use supernatural means to force the hand of a defiant leader.
I needed a way to bring the Israelites back to their own land. Why was this so important?
Because I'd made a promise to Abraham, Isaac, and Jacob that this land would always be
theirs. And, from them, in this promised land, would come a Messiah. He'd be the One
Who'd lead people back to Me and redeem those who believed in Him. I had to fulfill My
promises. I always do. So I chose Moses to help Me bring the Israelites back to this place.
I picked him, because I knew he'd follow My directions. I also knew that Pharaoh would
resist him, so I had to be creative in how we could convince him to let My people go!

My desire was always that people be surrounded by natural beauty, having weather and
circumstances that benefitted and brought them bounty. Strong forces of nature can cause
great harm to people who won't listen to Me or heed My warnings. I try to alert people
of impending doom, just as I did the Egyptians. How many times did I warn Pharaoh of
coming disasters and destruction? I never desire hardship or devastation for any people. I
forewarned them, through Moses, of what would happen before each catastrophe came.
But, because they had a hard-headed and hearted ruler, they suffered.

It still happens today. When the people of a country live in extreme poverty, despair,
and hardship, or suffer horrible environmental destruction, it's almost always because of a
corrupt and self-serving leader or group of leaders.

When rulers come and worship Me, leading others to Me, their nations are greatly blessed.

Day 21

What the Passover means to you

"The Lord will fight for you, and you shall hold your peace and remain at rest."
—Exodus 14:14

Exodus 12-14

Do you see what I can do for those who allow Me to fight for them? Yet, people lose faith and trust so easily. Because I could have a dialogue with Moses—I could talk to him honestly and depend on him to do exactly as I told him—I was able to bring great victory to the whole nation of Israel, even as their enemies pursued them.

It's the same today. When people trust in Me, lean on My every word confidently, and do as I tell them, I can accomplish amazing and mighty acts through them. They become My hands and feet among the earth's people. But, sadly, most people give up quickly and want to "go back to Egypt" when any threat arises. Fear motivates most people, and, because of their fear, they remain imprisoned and in bondage to whatever and whoever they serve. It takes faith and patient trust to gain freedom. Moses had both. But this is rare among people.

The Passover was meant to be celebrated as an annual remembrance of what I did for Israel to free them from the Egyptians. This memorial was actually a forerunner of what would come later—when My Son would become the last Passover Lamb. His body would be slain to bring freedom from sin and death and redemption from any bondage in this world. The last supper Christ ate with His disciples was the final Passover meal. It was the last one anyone would ever need to eat, because of His sacrifice. But many still remain as slaves to this world, because they don't choose to come and eat the Passover Lamb or partake of the blessing and deliverance He offers.

What did the parting of the Red Sea represent to the Israelites, and what does it mean to you now? It shows the separation and salvation of those who follow Me. It symbolizes the complete deliverance of My people from the devastation that will overcome this world in the last days.

None of these things could be accomplished without My Son's blood that would one day be shed for them and for you.

Day 22

Moses saw Me

"Who is like You, O Lord, among the gods? Who is like You,
glorious in holiness, awesome in splendor, doing wonders?"
—Exodus 15:11

Exodus 15-18

Moses saw Who I am. And he began to understand what I could do. He saw Me first as Jehovah, or Yahweh in Hebrew: "I Am that I Am." Then he saw Me as El-Shaddai: "God Almighty." He learned that I am Jehovah Rapha: "The Lord Who heals," and Jehovah Nissi: "The Lord our Banner." Why was it so important for him and the Israelites to understand these things about Me? Because of what I needed them to accomplish. They would need to trek across a desert, where provisions were limited and sparse compared to those in Egypt, and they must understand My power and ability to provide for them. Getting to the promised land would require great effort, endurance, and patience on their part. And, because they wouldn't have access to different foods or plenteous water, they needed to see how I could give them all they needed along the way. This required trust.

So, I showed them miracle after miracle. Through the trusting hand of Moses, I healed the water at Marah, produced water from a rock in Meribah, provided manna each morning and quail each evening, and I brought victory over the Amalekites. But, even after the Israelites experienced so many supernatural events, and sang songs of praise to acknowledge My strength and salvation, and saw that I was a God Who fought for them, they still complained bitterly, disputed My ability, and even turned away from Me. Many still doubted that they would ever enter the promised land.

Even today, people will see My miracles and still question My promises.

Moses's father-in-law, Jethro the Midianite, heard what I had done for the Israelites and came to see for himself. He acknowledged that My power was greater than any god he'd ever known. But when he saw Moses ministering day and night to so many hundreds of people, he pointed out that he couldn't keep doing it all by himself. Moses needed the help of others who were qualified to counsel and lead this stubborn group of people. Jethro had Moses select elders from each tribe and set them over groups of 1,000, 100, 50 and 10. These elders would advise those who sought help.

This example of organized leadership set a pattern for use later.

Day 23

What was always My emphasis?

"But showing mercy and steadfast love to a thousand generations
of those who love Me and keep My commandments."
—Exodus 20:6

Exodus 19-22

What did I always emphasize to those who would listen? Wasn't it that when people choose to worship and serve only Me, they will be blessed beyond measure?

My first commandments to the Israelites were these: Don't worship other gods, and don't use My name disrespectfully. Why? Because My name is holy, and it brings power to those who believe in Me. Set apart one day each week for rest, trusting Me for your provision, as the Israelites did in the wilderness. Know that I will make up for that one day if you will devote it to Me and depend on Me for your sufficiency. Honor your parents and heed them. Then your own life can be long. Don't murder or commit adultery or falsely accuse others. Don't covet or crave what belongs to others.

Do you believe that I can provide what you need? If you know this, you will never need to make anything more important to you than Me. My laws were set forth to protect My people—to give them a basis for right choices in every situation. People were bought and sold as servants, not because I desired it, but because of debt and theft. When people fail to trust Me to provide for them, they end up owing more than they can repay. They may steal out of frustration and fear, thinking they have no other way out of their pit of poverty. It's the same today. People are enslaved to what and who they owe more than they can pay. But, I can always provide a way out of servitude.

My promise to those who kept My laws was this: "If you will obey My voice in truth and keep My covenant, then you shall be My own peculiar (unique) possession and treasure from among and above all peoples; for all the earth is Mine." And, I show "mercy and steadfast love to a thousand generations of those who love Me and keep My commandments."

What laws or rules should you obey today? What is most important to Me now? It's simple. "You shall love the Lord your God with all your heart and with all your soul and with all your mind."

You can do this when you are guided by My Spirit, which you receive when you believe in Me and what My Son accomplished for you.

Day 24

What was most important

*"Behold, I send an Angel before you to keep and guard you
on the way and to bring you to the place I have prepared."*
—Exodus 23:20

Exodus 23-25

*The words I spoke to Moses established a blueprint for survival on the earth, which was lost
when Adam and Eve rejected Me.* The hidden knowledge of how life should be lived was
revealed once again to Moses. My greatest desire was that My people be able to maintain
lives of health and prosperity so they could survive and thrive. Adam and Eve didn't need
to worry about eating harmful things, except the fruit from one forbidden tree. That was
because I could communicate with them and help them avoid anything hurtful. But they
resigned that ability when they lost that spiritual part of them. Then, their descendants,
without a connection with Me, were confronted with choices and often unable to discern
what was best for them. Without knowing Me, they were often misled.

After Adam and Eve's loss, most people were unable to gain access to My Spirit until the
return of My Son. Only a few prophets and leaders were blessed with My Spirit on them.
But its availability was contingent on their submission to Me. Because of this, I had to send
an angel to guide the Israelites on their journey. But now, you have access to your own special
Messenger—My Spirit in you, Who keeps and guards you and brings you to a place prepared
for you. If you listen and heed the voice of My Spirit, I can protect you from those who will
harm you, just as I did the Israelites when they heeded Moses. I can bless the food you eat, the
water you drink, and remove sickness from you. I can bless your children beyond anything
you might imagine and increase your blessings through them. Little by little, I honor My
promises to you for a fulfilling life. But you must refrain from worshipping other gods.

What did I think is most important? Besides the 10 commandments, I showed Moses
that raising false reports or joining with others as a false witness was harmful to oneself and
others. Following a crowd to do evil, siding with a multitude to pervert justice, or being
partial to the poor, were unjust practices. It was important to avoid what is false and never
condemn the innocent and righteous. I wanted all My people to realize that acquitting or
justifying the wicked—those who subvert what is right—would produce corruption. It is
never right to oppress temporary residents. And helping the poor brings blessings. Moses
wrote down My words to help people survive if they would just listen. Yet they turned away
when Moses lingered on the mountain. How quickly people forsake My promises!

Even now, listen to Me so I can surround you with My peace and help you survive.

Day 25

I love to work within the details of life!

"You shall erect the tabernacle after the plan of it shown you on the mountain."
—Exodus 26:30

Exodus 26-27

How I love the intricate details of life! As an example, the earth contains many diverse life forms and forces. I incorporated multiple meaningful symbols and details into My instructions on how to build the tabernacle. This temporary structure represented My presence among the people. It housed the sacred objects used in worship, and many parts of it symbolized the fulfillment and atonement that would come through My Son.

Every color stands for something. Blue symbolizes heaven and the revelation of Me through My Son. Purple stands for My majesty and He Who will be Lord of Lords. Red is the color of fire, which, like sin, could consume mankind if left unchecked. It also indicates the atonement of sins that My Son would bring by shedding His own blood.[1] The numbers of things is also symbolic: one means unity; two can show union and division; three is divine completeness; four denotes My creation; five means divine grace; six represents humanity—the people I created; seven shows spiritual perfection; eight stands for a new beginning; nine means divine completeness and fruit of the spirit; 10 is testimony, law and responsibility; 11 means judgment and disorder; 12 is governmental perfection and divine power; and 13 represents depravity and rebellion.[2]

The horns and the altar represented a holy place of consecration and refuge, where atonement for sin was accomplished. A veil, or curtain, separated the Most Holy Place from the place of worship. This sacred room could only be entered by a designated high priest and held the ark of the covenant, which represented My presence. Made of linen and fine yarn, the veil was embroidered with cherubim—spirits who serve Me and guard My throne. Pure olive oil was burned continuously, symbolizing the presence of My Holy Spirit, which would come to those who believed in My Son later. Four layers covered the tent of the tabernacle. The innermost layer of fine linen stood for divine truth and was embroidered with blue, purple, and scarlet. The second layer was made of black goats' hair and stood for sin and the separation it caused. Next, a layer of rams' skin dyed red represented sacrifice and Jesus's shed blood. The outermost layer was the skin of an unclean animal. It showed that the beauty of the tabernacle lay within, beneath the layers.

I wanted everyone to know that, if they entered My presence, the defiled layers of their lives would be penetrated to reveal what is most important and beautiful.

Day 26

What the priests wore and why

"So Aaron shall bear the names of the sons of Israel in the breastplate
of judgment upon his heart when he goes into the Holy Place,
to bring them in continual remembrance before the Lord."
—Exodus 28:29

Exodus 28-30

What was the significance of the priests' vestments? As with all things, I have reasons for every detail. The high priest wore a white turban with a gold plate reading: HOLY TO THE LORD. And over his white long-sleeved linen garment, he donned a sleeveless blue robe, the hem decorated with blue, purple, and scarlet pomegranates. These reminded him to exalt Me.[1] Gold bells sewn between the pomegranates alerted those outside the Most Holy Place if the high priest fell or died. Over both robes, he wore a special vestment made of woven scarlet, blue, gold, and purple linen. Called an ephod, it hung in front and back, and was held together at the shoulders by straps. On each strap sat an onyx stone set in a rosette of gold and engraved with the names of the 12 tribes, six on each side. The stone's translucent surface was like My protective covering over My people within each tribe, and the underlying reddish layer represented their flesh.[2] Attached to the front of the ephod by gold chains and rings was a breastplate with 12 stones in four rows, representing the tribes. Each stone and tribe pointed to the coming Messiah and what He would accomplish for My people. In the top row was a *sardius* stone, representing Reuben, which means "See, a son" (as I would announce My Son's coming to earth one day). The next stone was a *topaz* for Simeon, meaning "Hearing" (or hear My Son and His good news). Next was a *carbuncle* for Levi, meaning "Joined" (referring to My Spirit that would make you one with My Son). In the second row, an *emerald* represented Judah, or "Praise" (the response of the redeemed when joined to the Son). A *sapphire* stood for Dan with "Judgment" (showing how you pass from judgment to life through My Son's atoning blood). Next, a *diamond* for Naphtali with "Wrestling" (indicates the believer's struggle against the world while trying to walk righteously). In the third row, a *jacinth* for Gad, the "Troop, Company" (how believers in the household are part of a fellowship of faith). An *agate* for Asher means "Happy am I" (we experience real joy through the Spirit). An *amethyst* for Issachar with "Hire" (we are equipped for service in the kingdom). In the fourth row, a *beryl* for Zebulun means "Dwelling, Exalt, Honor" (while we dwell here, we honor and exalt Him). Next, the *onyx* for Joseph is "Adding" (through outreach, we add to the Body and receive rewards for our efforts). And, finally, a *jasper* for Benjamin, who is the "Son of My Right Hand" (the Son sits at My right hand, interceding for you).[3]

Wearing these, the priest stood for My coming Son.

Day 27

Come and sit beside Me

"And the Lord spoke to Moses face to face, as a man speaks to his friend."
—Exodus 33:11

Exodus 31-34

I need men and women who trust Me—people who will plead for the lives of those who are separated from Me and "stand in the gap" for them. I loved Moses. Why? Because I could talk with him face to face as a friend who has nothing to hide. I could do this because he came to Me and sat with Me and listened to My words. He honored Me and was willing to do what I suggested. He sought no other gods besides Me. He wanted to see Me, and I was able to show part of Myself to him. When he looked, his face shone, because he beheld My light.

Those who seek Me diligently, as Moses did, find favor and loving-kindness and mercy. I can know them personally, and they can know Me. I can give them special names, like I did Abraham and Jacob. My goodness went before Moses, and I made known My special names to him. As Elohim, I created all things through My strength and power. I can order all things and see all things, and I desire worship and recognition for what I've done. As Jehovah, I keep My covenants and promises, and I am gracious in My relationships. I am the One Who WAS, IS and IS to come. I am merciful, slow to anger, and abundant in love, revealing what is true to those who seek truth. I am a jealous God. Why? Because I created you and others to have a relationship with Me, not with other man-made gods. I want to speak with you, like I did with Moses—face to face. When people turn from Me to worship other things, I must turn from them, because of My pain.

I promised the Israelites that I would work wonders like nothing anyone had ever seen before on earth. They'd see My handiwork and be awed by it. I'd perform miracles and help them to occupy the land I promised to Abraham. Yet, they still turned away, even after they'd seen My mighty works. They doubted Me, dug in their heels, and made other gods just at the edge of the fulfillment of My promise to them. I desire more people like Moses, who will come to Me and want to see Me and sit with Me, whose hearts turn toward Me to believe and receive what I promise. I am Almighty God—a God of power. Yet so many still doubt My power and never receive what I want to give them.

Come out from among those who are afraid, and sit beside Me in the place I have prepared just for you.

Day 28

Special talents for sacred purposes

*"And Moses called Bezalel and Aholiab and every able and wisehearted
man in whose mind the Lord had put wisdom and ability, everyone
whose heart stirred him up to come to do the work."*
—*Exodus 36:2*

Exodus 35-37

Every person has unique gifts. And I can show you how to best use your special abilities
to excel and promote My kingdom. Bezalel, whose name meant "in the shadow of God,"[1]
had several talents, which he operated in and through My Spirit. He was a master carpenter,
weaver, and embroiderer. He also worked with metals and gems. He trained others to do this
work, including Aholiab, whose name meant "Tent of the Father."[2] Their work beautified
the tabernacle, My temporary abode. And every metal used was symbolic. To build the
tabernacle, they worked with bronze for the sacrificial altar, the washing-laver, and the
utensils outside the Tent of Meeting. This metal symbolized how I dealt with sin so that
people could enter My holy presence. Bronze is composed of tin and copper. Tin was a
foreign-mined metal found in combination with inferior metals and waste substances.[3] It
represented the sins of mankind, like dross consumed by the fire of the smelting furnace
(Ezekiel 22:18-22). Copper, native to Israel, was combined with tin to make bronze and
was as precious as gold (Ezra 8:27). One day, the Messiah would act as copper to refine and
perfect what once was considered as scum.

Inside the Tent of Meeting, most things were made of gold, which stood for My perfection, glory, and the holy place of My presence.[4] The gold lampstand held six branches on
each side and one branch in the middle. Six represents humanity; seven means perfection.[5]
In spite of the tendency for humans to sin, I make people righteous if they turn to Me. The
gold cups on the branches designed as almond blossoms represented My watchfulness and
presence. Since almond trees blossom while it's still winter, before spring arrives when things
are bleak, they exemplify how I am ever-present, watching and preparing, even when things
seem desolate. The lamp, or menorah, was lit day and night, showing My continual presence
amid the tabernacle. Also, inside the tent, stood a golden altar, where incense was burned to
represent the peoples' prayers. Separated by a veil, the ark of the covenant stood within the
Holy of Holies, the sacred, innermost room of the tabernacle tent. Made of acacia wood,
which resists decay, the ark was covered with gold. On its top, two cherubim faced each
other, their wings spread over the mercy seat. Gazing down, they represented My judgment
averted.

My mercy seat was where I appeared and spoke to the priests.

Day 29

What was it like to enter My tabernacle?

*"Then the cloud [the Shekinah, God's visible presence] covered the
Tent of Meeting, and the glory of the Lord filled the tabernacle!"*
—*Exodus 40:34*

Exodus 38-40

The tabernacle was a special place of honor. It represented "a tented palace for Israel's divine king."[1] It was My house among the Israelites, and My dwelling in it was a step toward the restoration of paradise, which will be completed in the new heaven and earth.[1] Approaching it, you first walked through an opening on the east side into a courtyard. This "door" in the fabric represented Christ as the way through which you could approach Me in worship.[2] The gate to the Garden of Eden was on the east side, the sun rises in the east, and Jesus' triumphal entry into Jerusalem would be through the Eastern Gate.[3] This opening to the tabernacle was a curtain made of blue, purple, and scarlet woven linen. Blue represents My divinity, purple stands for My royalty, and scarlet speaks of sacrifice and suffering.[3]

On both sides of the entrance, a seven-foot-high barrier extended to surround the 75 by 150-foot courtyard. This "wall" was made of linen hangings upheld by pillars, which stood for strength and solidarity, to remind you that you needed a mighty Savior.[4] The pillars were made of brass with silver capitals. The silver showed atonement and the price to be paid. Israelite men were required to pay a half shekel of silver as a ransom for their soul (Exodus 30:11-16). The brass (or copper) meant strength and judgment.[5]

After entering, you encountered the brazen altar, made of acacia wood covered with bronze. The wood came from the thorn-covered branches of the acacia trees, and it represented the humanity of Christ[6] and the thorny crown He would one day wear. Bronze stood for My judgment in dealing with sin so that people could enter My presence.[7] All must come to the sacrificial altar before approaching the Tent of Meeting, where My presence could be found. This was because, without the shedding of blood, there was no remission of sin (Leviticus 17:11, Hebrews 9:22). One could not approach Me without releasing this brokenness first. At the altar, the priest laid his hands on your offering and accepted it as your atonement, allowing your sins to be transferred to it. The altar was five cubits square and three cubits high, each cubit being one-and-a-half feet in length. Five represented My divine favor, and three meant that remission of sin would be completed.[8] Through Christ's sacrifice, this work would one day be accomplished, and no other sacrifice would ever again be required to remove sin.

The four horns on the altar's corners reminded you that this was the place where you were consecrated—spared the devastation of sin. The horns were a metaphor for physical strength or spiritual power (Deuteronomy 33:17; II Samuel 22:3; Psalm 18:2). The Hebrew

31

word for horn means "horn, hill or ray," and it describes the rays of light emanating from the face of Moses after his encounter with Me (Exodus 34:29). They stood for the Strength of salvation, Who would one day shed His blood for His people. Why four horns? Because they stood for the four Messianic attributes, like the four colors used throughout the tabernacle: scarlet for His humanity, purple for His kingship, blue for His divinity, and white for His sinlessness or righteousness.[9]

Leaving the brazen altar, you came to the laver. Halfway between the altar and the Tent of Meeting, it was a large bronze bowl filled with water. The bronze was made from the mirrors of the women who served at the door of the tent.[10] It represented the freedom from the shame of self-focus you received when you were washed from sin and your newfound, God-given ability to now devote yourself to Me. At the laver, the priests washed their hands and feet before entering the Tent of Meeting and the Holy Place. Here, they were reminded that they needed to be cleansed before they could approach Me. This physical act of washing was spiritually completed in Christ, Who was baptized for you and offered you wholeness physically, mentally, and spiritually through his cleansing blood.

Next, you came to the Tent of Meeting. Entering the first room of the tent, called the Holy Place, you could look to the left, or south, side of the room and see the golden lampstand, or menorah. Proffering six curving branches on each side, a seventh branch pointed straight up the center to show My unbending perfection amid sinful humanity, whose path to Me is never straight. Cups on the branches were filled with oil and lit continuously to symbolize My presence. The only source of light, the lampstand allowed the priests to fellowship with Me, even in darkness. Made of pure gold, it stood for My deity and holiness.[11]

On the right, or north, side of the Holy Place was the table of showbread. Made of acacia wood covered with gold, it measured two by one cubit and was one and a half cubits high. The number two represented the differences that existed, in this case between Me and mankind.[8] This divide between us would be made whole, or reconciled, one day through My Son. The table held 12 loaves of bread, one for each tribe of Israel. Made of fine flour, they lay in two rows of six and were replenished every Sabbath day. Beside each row stood a bowl of pure frankincense, representing the truth that brings spiritual good.[12] It must be pure, because it signified what would be clarified from the falsity of evil, and could be handled only by the priests. The bread, for their benefit, was eaten in the Holy Place because it was holy—dedicated to Me. Called "the bread of the presence," it symbolized the "Bread of Life" that would come one day, mankind's dependence on Me, and My desire to commune and share fully with My people.[13]

In the middle of the Holy Place, in front of a curtain, sat the golden altar. Smaller than the brazen altar, it was one cubit square and two cubits high. Made of acacia wood, it was also covered with pure gold. Four horns jutted out from its four corners and incense was burned on it every morning and every evening, as the daily burnt offerings were accepted at the brazen altar outside. Incense symbolized the prayers of the people—their intercession to Me as a sweet fragrance.[14] It also represented My desire for people to be able to approach Me in any place.

A curtain, or veil, divided the Holy Place from the Holy of Holies, or Most Holy Place, which was an inner room inside the tent. The veil separated My holiness from the sin of the people. The Holy of Holies was My special dwelling place among the people. Its dimensions were 20 by 10 cubits, and its height was 10 cubits. The veil was embroidered with cherubim—spiritual beings who serve, worship, and praise Me and guard My throne.[15] Only the high priest could enter My presence once a year on the Day of Atonement. When Jesus was crucified, this veil was torn in half, because He removed what separated Me from My people—sin. Inside the Holy of Holies lay the ark of the covenant—the only place in the world where atonement could take place.[16] Made of acacia wood covered with gold, it held Moses' stone tablets, the golden pot of manna, and Aaron's rod. The ark was a picture of the Person and saving work of Christ.[17] The manna showed My mercy revealed, because, even when the Israelites complained against Me in the wilderness, I still provided for them. The rod stood for My authority and ability to do miracles, even when some rejected Me. The tablets displayed My great grace. Even when people turn against Me, I provide a way so that they can stand in My presence. The mercy seat on top of the ark represented the atoning blood of My Son.[17] When the blood of the sacrifice was sprinkled on the seat, My glory appeared.[17] This was My throne among the people and a symbolic foreshadowing of the ultimate sacrifice for sin—the blood of My Son shed on the cross for remission of sins.

This final sacrifice was made available through the grace-filled willingness of My Son, Who died to remove sin once and for all.

Day 30

What were the different sacrifices?

"When a man is guilty in one of these, he shall confess the sin he has committed."
—*Leviticus 5:5*

Leviticus 1-5

Leviticus describes five different sacrifices: the burnt, grain, peace, sin, and trespass o-fferings. Each involved an animal or grain and had specific purposes. Portions were split between Me, the priests, and, sometimes, the person making the offering. I forbade the drinking or eating of the blood or fat of the animal, which represented the life and abundance I alone can give. Some sacrifices were voluntary; some were mandatory.

The three voluntary offerings were: First, the burnt offering to express devotion to Me and atonement for unintentional sins. This sacrifice involved unblemished bulls, male or female sheep or goats, and pigeons or turtledoves, which symbolized love and devotion. Sacrifices were killed on the north side of the altar; Jesus would be crucified on the north side of the temple. The second voluntary offering was a grain offering using unleavened cakes or bread made from flour, oil, and salt. The oil represented My Spirit, and the frankincense used with the offering emitted a fragrance that stood for the prayers going up to Me. Salt symbolized preservation and covenants made with Me. The grain in this offering was never mixed with leaven or honey, because they cause fermentation—a type of corruption. Accompanied by a drink offering of wine poured into the fire, this offering expressed recognition of My provision.

The third voluntary offering was the peace offering of an unblemished male or female animal or grain. Also called a vow, thanksgiving, or free will offering, the participant could partake in this sacrifice of thanksgiving, often for the fulfillment of a vow. The high priest took the breast of the animal, and the officiating priest received the right foreleg as a "wave" offering, because the priests waved them over the altar before partaking. The fat, kidneys, and liver were burned for Me, while the remainder of the animal was eaten by the participant.

The two mandatory offerings were called the sin and the trespass offerings. The sin offering atoned for sin. Possible sacrifices were: a young bull, a male or female goat, a turtledove or pigeon, or fine flour, depending on the person's financial ability. The trespass offering required that a ram be offered to atone for unintentional sins. The flour used was mixed with oil or frankincense.*

These sacrifices all represented what Christ would accomplish later.

34

Day 31

What were the priests responsible for?

"And the priest shall make atonement for him before the Lord, and he shall be forgiven for anything of all that he may have done by which he has become guilty."
—Leviticus 6:7

Leviticus 6-8

Once the tabernacle was set up in the wilderness, I needed priests from the tribe of Levi to man it. I had designed it to be a holy place, where the Israelites could come to meet Me, but the only way they could approach Me was through the priests. As My representatives, the priests must be consecrated and cleansed from their own sins before they could deal with others' sins. So, I instructed Moses on how the elders should come to stand for the Israelites at the court of the tabernacle, and how they should witness the consecration and ordination of the priests, who could then serve the people. This special ceremony required witnesses to a solemn transaction between Me and Israel. Through it, the priests would be ordained in things pertaining to Me, like communication and negotiations between Me and the people. All present must "own" the priests' appointment at the door of the Tent of Meeting. By witnessing this ordination, with its ceremonial veneration for the priests, including special vestments and instructions on how to perform each sacrifice or offering, the people would understand the solemnity and importance regarding each aspect of what must be done to remove their sins.

One thing I wanted them to remember was how Moses' face had shone when he came down from the mountain, after beholding that part of Me I revealed to him. He was My first minister, and I wanted this scene to be imprinted into their hearts through every rule regarding their sacrifices with fire, so they would never again argue with Moses or Aaron about their importance to Me or doubt what the priests were doing for them or Who they represented. I wanted the people to know that those who minister on their behalf would always have their eyes on Me as they ministered.

The priests who were ordained remained at the door of the Tent of Meeting for seven days, the number of days needed to attain "perfection." Each day, they sacrificed a bull as a sin offering and two rams, one for a burnt offering and one for consecration and ordination as a wave offering, with a basket of unleavened bread. As part of the consecration and ordination into priesthood, the priests were washed, dressed in white linen robes, and anointed with oil. Then the sin and burnt offerings were made.

Each day for seven days this was done, followed by a ceremonial feast.

Day 32

What was the significance of the offerings?

"Then Moses said to Aaron, This is what the Lord meant when He said, I [and My will, not their own] will be acknowledged as hallowed by those who come near Me, and before all the people I will be honored. And Aaron said nothing."
—*Leviticus 10:3*

Leviticus 9-11

What was the significance of each offering made under the Mosaic Law? The sin offering was a purification offering used for atonement of sin. Literally a "fault offering," it was made for sins committed in ignorance—unintentional sins where a person broke a commandment and then realized guilt. The method and sacrifice used depended on the status of the sinner. Unlike other offerings, this one was not eaten. It was a picture of the sacrifice of Christ—a lamb without blemish, whose blood was spilled and whose body was laid "outside the camp." The blood made atonement for the sins of those who realized their fault and asked Me for forgiveness. The literal meaning of the burnt offering was "to ascend" or "go up in smoke." The smoke from the sacrifice ascended to Me as a soothing aroma. This sacrifice was completely burned up, except for the hide.

Each type of burnt offering symbolized something and could be offered at any time as an acknowledgment of sin and a request for renewed relationship with Me, though the priests had set times to give burnt offerings for the Israelites as a whole. Before all parts were consumed by fire, the intestines and legs of the sacrifice were washed. This represented the washing of all that is inside a person and the means for committing sin. Remember, Christ on the cross was pierced by a sword to spill what was in Him for us, and his legs were unbroken, so that we could walk with Him, our feet placed in His steps.

The peace offering was "a propitiatory, conciliatory gift" given to please, placate, or pacify Me. It was a voluntary offering used to thank Me for My mercy and generosity, and it was a way to praise Me for My goodness, for a vow fulfilled, or for deliverance. The grain offering involved the giving of uncooked or cooked ground grain mixed with salt and oil. No yeast or honey was added, and a portion of it was offered with frankincense. Presented after a burnt offering, it was for worship and acknowledgement of Me for My provision. Grain was scarce during the 40 years in the wilderness, so this offering was considered precious. It exemplified the Israelites' dependence on Me.

Because I wanted them to respect My words to them through Moses, I demanded strict adherence to the ways sacrifices were performed.

Day 33

How does the law of leprosy apply to you?

"The priest shall offer the burnt offering and the cereal offering on the altar;
and he shall make atonement for him and he shall be clean."
—Leviticus 14:20

Leviticus 12-14

You may read about leprosy, and the laws regarding it, and you may wonder, "How does this apply to me now?" Those who heard Moses speak about the pervasive disease understood the seriousness of it, because they'd seen how it destroyed both body and soul. They saw the separation it caused. But what does it mean to you today? Believe it or not, a lot.

Leprosy was contagious and destructive, like sin in a person's life. People who displayed signs of it were removed from the community to prevent further contagion. If the diseased or affected areas showed significant improvement, or were healed, then the affected ones could go to the priest to be examined outside the camp. If approved, they offered a sacrifice of two live, clean birds. The first one, killed in a clay pot over fresh running water, symbolized the body of Christ offered up to give you living water. The other bird, along with cedar wood, scarlet yarn, and hyssop, was dipped into the clay pot containing the other bird's blood and the water. The water-blood mixture was sprinkled over the diseased person for purification, and this bird was set free to show the freedom from sin attained when a relationship with Me is restored. The second bird also represented Christ's resurrection.[1]

Turtledoves were used for this offering, because they were clean (Leviticus 5:7), an emblem of purity (Psalm 68:13), and a symbol of the Holy Spirit (Matthew 3:16).[2] The scarlet yarn represented blood shed to remove sin;[3] the hyssop's cleansing ability signified My desire for My people to be purified.[4] The cedar's strength, durability, and fragrance, reminded them of the Messiah, Who would be offered up as a sacrifice on a cross for the cleansing of their bodies—their "homes" for the Holy Spirit.[5]

Sin is pervasive, like leprosy. Like the disease, it can be halted in its progression through repentance, and a person can be cleansed—washed by the "living water." Repentance means recognizing wrong and turning from it, so the mind and heart and actions can change. The Israelites saw the degradation caused by turning from Me. Today, you can see what happens when people turn away or worship what the world offers.

And the resulting corruption can be pervasive like leprosy.

Day 34

The significance of the Day of Atonement

"And Aaron shall lay both his hands upon the head of the live goat and confess over him all the iniquities of the Israelites and all their transgressions, all their sins; and he shall put them upon the head of the goat [the sin-bearer], and send him away into the wilderness by the hand of a man who is timely (ready, fit)."
—Leviticus 16:21

Leviticus 15-17

The special Day of Atonement, or Yom Kippur, was the day set aside to symbolize the cleansing of the people from sins, so they could approach Me. It was the most solemn religious fast of the year, and the last of 10 days that began with Rosh Hashanah. On this day, the high priest entered the Holy of Holies to atone for the people. A whole bull was offered for the priest's sins, a male without blemish, and represented the Messiah, Who would one day be sacrificed to bear their burdens.[1] Two goats chosen stood for the abomination of sin, which separated people from Me. One was offered as a sin offering to remove the sins of the people; the other was given as a burnt offering, but not burned at all. Remember how Isaac was to be offered as a "burnt" offering, but never was? The word used for this offering, in Hebrew, is "olah," which means "whole burnt offering and ascent, stairway, steps."[2] In this offering, the entire animal was presented, and no part was shared with the one who is offering it, because it was all intended for Me. "Olah" was differentiated from other sacrifices because of the wholeness of the oblation. It was a devotional homage, a "soothing aroma" representing complete surrender to Me.[3] It was the only offering that could be made by non-Jews. Remember, Abraham was not a Jew; the Jews descended from Israel and his sons.[4]

The goat chosen as a burnt offering must be free from disease or blemish. It was set aside until the hands of the high priest were laid on its head and confession of sins was made over him. He was then led into the wilderness by a man specially selected because he was "timely—ready and fit." This man represented Christ, Who in due time would save us from sin.[5] The "sacrifice" was made for atonement—bringing back together that which had been separated. On this special day, incense created a cloud over the mercy seat as prayers were made, and blood was sprinkled on the east side of the seat, over the bronze altar seven times, and applied to its four horns.

These actions symbolized days to come, when Christ would shed His blood to make an atonement for you.

Day 35

What does it mean to be "holy"?

"So keep My charge: do not practice any of these abominable customs which were practiced before you and defile yourselves by them. I am the Lord your God."
—Leviticus 18:30

Leviticus 18-20

What makes a person holy? Holiness means "to be set apart from what is common."* It is to be distinct from other people. It's to pursue a way of life different from what is practiced by other people in the world. Regarding the Israelites, it was epitomized in Exodus 19:6: "You shall be to Me a kingdom of priests and a holy nation." Holiness had to be realized within the whole Israelite community. They had to act together, and their way to holiness was through emulating My attributes. Only by embracing My values as to what was important and how I intended life to be could they receive My blessing of a long life and have holiness. By dedicating themselves and their actions to Me, they could be consecrated, or made holy. When they were cleansed from sin, they were sanctified, or set apart and unburdened by it.

How could they avoid sinful actions? That is what I communicated to Moses. That is what My laws and instructions to him were all about.

By refraining from certain things, like demeaning their parents, avoiding those who predicted the future using ungodly spirits, not sacrificing their children, not having inappropriate or unnatural sexual relations, and not giving false testimony regarding others to cause scandal, they could avoid much sin. Not doing these things separated them from other nations, who still practiced these things. And, because of these practices, I spewed out the people who inhabited the lands, because they were done in worship of other gods. These were things that grieved Me then and now.

Today, nations and people groups can prosper, and be set apart from others, if they devote their thoughts and actions to Me and not to other gods and ungodly ideologies. When groups of people worship false gods, and sacrifice their own children to them, they do things contrary to how I intended life to be lived. Because of these malpractices, they are, even now, "spewed out" of their own lands, just like the Canaanites.

Today, I still look for those who are willing to be set apart and sanctified in their lifestyle by being devoted to Me in their hearts, minds, and actions.

Day 36

What the priests stood for

*"The priests therefore shall observe My ordinance, lest they bear sin for it
and die thereby if they profane it. I am the Lord, Who sanctifies them."*
—*Leviticus 22:9*

Leviticus 21-23

The priests represented My Son, Who would come later. They had to go a step further in practicing the commandments and laws given to Moses, because it was their job to help preserve and set apart My people so that My Son could come through them as the Messiah one day. They must teach against the practices of foreigners, who shaved their heads and beards and cut themselves to appease their gods when a family member died. I wanted My priests and people to abstain from these practices, and to set themselves apart so that they could be preserved for the day My Son would come.

I did not want My priests, as representatives of Christ, to honor death or practice the worship of it. This was never My purpose. My Son would come to overcome it so people could live forever, which was always My intent. People who do not know or understand Me, who do not know that I am a God of life, often focus on death and try to appease it through death-honoring practices. They allow it to linger in their life, falling into its grip through pain and painful memories. By "cutting their flesh," they become its victim.

The priests stood for life and the celebration of it. They stood for what I had done and would do to save and spare the lives of the Israelites. Sacrificial offerings, which often involved the death of an animal, were meant to remind them of the preciousness of life and the deadly consequences of sin. My instructions on how to celebrate life through annual feasts reminded them of how I delivered them from slavery and gave them a new life and land. The Sabbath was set apart, because they needed a day to remember and be thankful for what I had done for them. It was a day to be free from the burdens of sin and to be mindful of Me. Honoring Me with their first fruits through offerings was a way of acknowledging My presence and the life I would bring to them. Honoring death was never a part of this life I desired for them.

Because the priests stood for My Son, Who is perfect, they could not be "damaged" or "deformed." What was made, in the beginning of the world, was perfect, and only through My Son could I bring people to a new perfection with new bodies one day.

Though some could not act as priests, due to bodily imperfections, all would be made acceptable one day through the perfect love of My Son.

Day 37

How you can help free those in bondage

"You shall not oppress and wrong one another, but you shall [reverently] fear your God. For I am the Lord your God. Therefore you shall do and give effect to My statutes and keep My ordinances and perform them, and you will dwell in the land in safety."
—Leviticus 25: 17-18

Leviticus 24-25

The same laws applied to everyone in the land, whether they are temporary or permanent citizens. If you keep My commandments, never oppressing those who are "down and out," you will dwell in the land safely. My will is never that people be abused or taken advantage of, no matter what their status. Charging ungodly rates of interest to those who are poor and lack resources so you can profit from their neediness was never My will.

I bring people out of bondage so they can freely serve Me and others. Many people come from lands where they were sold into slavery because of sorry, sinful situations and greedy people. Freedom in a land only comes from obedience to Me. When people choose to serve Me, instead of other gods, then I can promise them prosperity and safety in their land. But only if they choose to make Me their God.

The laws of redemption for the Israelites apply even now to you in this way: When a fellow believer is in a hard way, help them! When others are sick, disabled, ailing in old age, or unable to work, offer them some assistance. You will say, "But I can't help everyone!" I don't expect you to. I will place before you those I want you to help. And, you will know in your heart when it's the right time to help them. I will show you how—what to give and what not to offer of yourself and your provisions.

Not every person can be helped. Remember this. Some choose lives of desperation, because they want to remain in bondage, as victims of circumstances. This is really the worship of another god—the god of lack. People who serve this god will excuse their neediness and blame others for it, because they want to serve this idea, instead of serving Me. They may be comfortable in their situation and resistant to change. But, there are many who want to be lifted out of bondage, like the Israelites who prayed to be free. To these I send aid, and you can help Me.

Keep your eyes open for the praying ones, and let Me work in you to will and to do of My good pleasure to bring freedom to those who cry out for a way to "jubilee."

Day 38

My promises to the Israelites and to you

"And I will walk in and with and among you and
will be your God, and you shall be My people."
—Leviticus 26:12

Leviticus 26-27

Here are My promises to the people of Israel. If they walked with Me...
-They would have rain in due season so that their crops would not fail.
-They would have peace from their enemies and overcome any who attacked them.
-They would be protected from wild animals.
-They would be safe, secure, and unafraid.
-They would have My favor and fruitfulness, because I would dwell among them.

But, if they despised and rejected Me...
-They would have terrors and troubles.
-They would suffer from many diseases.
-Their enemies would defeat them, take their land, and eat their crops.
-Their children would be sacrificed.
-They would not receive blessings from heaven and earth.
-They would lack fruitfulness in the land.
-They would experience attacks from wild animals.
-They would see pestilence all around them.
-Their strength would be spent.
-Their food would not satisfy their needs.
-Their cities would be wasted, and their land would become desolate.
-They would be scattered among the nations.

If they wandered from Me, they could humble their hearts and return to Me. Then I could live among them. I would never spurn or cast them away or allow them to be destroyed because of My covenant with Abraham, Isaac, and Jacob. I was the Lord their God.

Even now, I value you as an individual, and I see your heart and "deem you worthy," when you accept what My Son did for you, and allow Him to redeem you, so that you, through Him, can return to Me, and I to you, and be free from sin's resultant burdens.

Then I can be the Lord your God.

Day 39

What was the meaning of the tribal banners?

"The Israelites shall encamp, each by his own [tribal] standard or banner with the ensign of his father's house, opposite the Tent of Meeting and facing it on every side."
—Numbers 2:2

Numbers 1-3

Here is the placement of each tribe of Israel around the tabernacle in the wilderness:

Three tribes camped on each side. On the east side of the tabernacle, farthest north, the tribe of Judah, with 74,600 males, displayed a banner of a crouching lion, because "A lion's cub is Judah... He crouches...like a lion, and like an awesome lion, who dares rouse him?" (Genesis 49:8-12). From Judah, "Shiloh [the Lion of Judah] arrives and his will be an assemblage of nations." South of Judah on the east side, Issachar camped with 54,400 males and a banner of a donkey, because they were "a strong-boned donkey that rests between boundaries" (Genesis 49:14-15). South of Issachar on the east side, Zebulun, with 57,400 men, waved the banner of a sailboat, because "Zebulun shall settle by seashores" (Genesis 49:13) with "interests abroad" (Deuteronomy 33:18). The three tribes south of the tabernacle were: Gad, farthest west with 46,650 men and a three-tented ensign that signified "Gad will recruit a regiment" (Genesis 49:19). East of Gad, Simeon with 59,300 males and a banner of crossed swords, because "Simeon and Levi are comrades, their weaponry is a stolen craft.... Accursed is their rage for it is intense" (Genesis 49:5-6). And, east of Simeon on the south side was Reuben with 46,500 men and a banner of water, because Reuben was "impetuous like water" (Genesis 49:3-4). On the west side of the tabernacle and farthest north lay Benjamin with 35,400 men and the ensign of a howling wolf, because "Benjamin is a predatory wolf" (Genesis 49:27). South of Benjamin on the west side was Manasseh with 32,200 men and a banner with an olive branch, because his land would be blessed "with the chief products of the ancient mountains" (Deuteronomy 33:15). Still on the west side but south of Manasseh was Ephraim with 40,500 men and an emblem of a bull's head, because he was also "like a firstling young bull" (Deuteronomy 33:17). On the north side of the tabernacle and farthest west, Dan, with 62,700 men, was portrayed by a snake, because "Dan will be a serpent...a viper by the path that bites a horse's heels" (Genesis 49:16-18). East of Dan on the north side was Asher with 41,500 men and the sign of bread: "His bread will have richness, and he will provide kingly delicacies" (Genesis 49:20). Naphtali was east of Asher on the north side with 53,400 men and the banner of a hind, because "Naphtali is a hind let loose who delivers beautiful sayings" (Genesis 49:20).

The total number of men was 603,550.

Day 40

What were the Levites' responsibilities?

"This is the way you shall bless the Israelites. Say to them, The Lord bless you and watch, guard, and keep you; The Lord make His face to shine upon and enlighten you and be gracious (kind, merciful, and giving favor) to you; The Lord lift up His [approving] countenance upon you and give you peace (tranquility of heart and life continually). And they shall put My name upon the Israelites, and I will bless them."
—Numbers 6:22-27

Numbers 4-6

The three sons of Levi and their descendants had specific responsibilities regarding the tabernacle. The sons of Kohath, who camped on the south side of the tabernacle, took care of the ark, the table of showbread, the lampstand, both altars, and the utensils, dishes, and showbread in the Tent of Meeting and Holy of Holies. The holiness of each object determined the material in which it was wrapped. The ark was covered first in the tent's veil then the skin of an unclean animal, often a dolphin, and, finally, a blue cloth representing My heavenly grace and healing.* These layers symbolized how uncleanness created the necessity of a shield to separate Me from the people, but My grace and healing could remove this barrier caused by sin. The table, lampstand, utensils, and golden altar were wrapped in the same kind of skin and blue cloth. The table was wrapped in scarlet cloth, symbolizing sacrifice, the shedding of blood, and atonement.* The brazen altar was wrapped in purple cloth. Standing for royalty,* this showed that only My priests could receive offerings from the people, but, one day, My Son would come as a Royal Priest to free them from the necessity of these rituals. Aaron's son, Eleazar, was designated as the overseer of the Kohathites, who packed up the tabernacle to move. The sons of Gershon camped on the west side and were responsible for the curtains, coverings, hangings, cords, and equipment. Aaron's son, Ithamar, oversaw their work and that of the sons of Merari, who camped on the north side and were responsible for the Tent of Meeting's boards, frames, bars, pillars, sockets, bases, and pegs. The number of men between 30 and 50 years old who served, was 8,580. Moses and Aaron camped on the east side of the tabernacle. Every statute of the Law symbolized a time to come. Even the bitter water used for a woman suspected of adultery represented the bitter mix Christ would be offered as He died on the cross. The jealous husband was, like Me, offended when his bride was suspected of wandering in her love and being unfaithful in her heart. The test was to protect her from the husband's wrath if she was innocent. But, if she was guilty, she would be cursed and shamed.

Christ was cursed for you to remove your guilt and the shame of sin.

Day 41

Why were the Levites set apart to serve Me?

"Thus you shall separate the Levites from among the Israelites,
and the Levite shall be Mine [in a very special sense]."
—Numbers 8:14

Numbers 7-8

Each day of the consecration ceremony that lasted 12 days, the prince of a tribe came to present an offering to Me. Judah approached first, then Issachar, Zebulun, Reuben, Simeon, Gad, Ephraim, Manasseh, Benjamin, Dan, Asher, and Naphtali. Each prince brought a silver platter and a basin full of fine flour mixed with oil for a cereal offering. He also brought a golden bowl of incense, a young bull, a ram, and a male lamb as a burnt offering, a male goat for a sin offering, and two oxen, five rams, five male goats, and five lambs as a peace offering. The offerings of each prince were accepted equally by Me.

At the end of the 12 days, I spoke with Moses over the ark's mercy seat and instructed him on how I wanted the Levites to be anointed and consecrated, or set aside for service to Me and the tabernacle. They would replace the firstborn sons of every tribe, who were dedicated to Me. First, Aaron would light the golden lampstand in the Tent of Meeting to signify My presence and participation. He would sprinkle pure water over the Levites, after they had shaved and washed their clothes. Then the Levites would present their offerings before Aaron and his sons, who would lay their hands on the heads of the two bulls offered—one as a sin offering and one as a burnt offering.

The princes of the tribes then laid their hands on the Levites, who were offered by Aaron as a wave offering to Me. They were presented before Me and the whole congregation. This was the final act in the ceremony that consecrated the finished tabernacle and separated the Levites from other tribes as Mine. Every Levite male between the ages of 25 and 50 was set apart to serve and help in the tabernacle.

It was important to celebrate in ceremony what I deemed as significant and important to bring meaning and significance to the symbols that represented the Messiah to come. The Levite men and the priests were a type of Christ, who would come to stand for Me in the presence of all the people.

So they must be set apart as holy.

Day 42

Everything led to Christ

"In the day of rejoicing, and in your set feasts, and at the beginnings of your months, you shall blow the trumpets over your burnt offerings and your peace offerings; thus they may be a remembrance before your God. I am the Lord your God."
—Numbers 10:10

Numbers 9-11

Everything led to Christ. Every inspired symbol, tradition, instruction, and direction. It all meant something important to Me. I wanted the Israelites to celebrate Passover every year at a special time. Why? Not just to remember how I'd delivered them from the Egyptians, but also because, one day, I would bring deliverance through My sacrificial Lamb at this same time of year. Even the cloud that hovered over the tabernacle, which showed My presence and when to move the camp, symbolized future events. One day, My Son would come, ascend from death to life, then appear again in a cloud. The trumpet used to alert the Israelites when they should move represented the trumpet that would be blown when My Son would return for His people. When the trumpet was blown, the tribes set out from their camps. Those on the east side of the tabernacle—the side that represented intervention and salvation—set out first, along with Moses and Aaron. These were the descendants of Judah, Issachar and Zebulun. Next, the Levite descendants of Gershon and Merari set out, bearing the structural tabernacle. Then, those to the south—the side representing truth, Light, and liberation—set out: Reuben, Simeon and Gad. The Levite descendants of Kohath followed, bearing the holy things within the tabernacle. Next came those on the west—the side representing restored unity with Me and divine blessing: Ephraim, Manasseh, and Benjamin. Finally, those to the north, who represented what is permanent and eternal and the place of My celestial dwelling, followed: Dan, Asher, and Naphtali. When My Son returns in the clouds, and His own are gathered to Him, they will come to Him in this way: from the east, south, west and north.

I always disdained complaining. It causes Me grief, because it's a sign of distrust. But even amid murmuring, I brought miracles through Moses, who was faithful to Me. He suffered, as I did, and experienced mental hardships because of the people's moans. The 70 elders formed the Sanhedrin, a select group of leaders chosen to "sit together" with My Spirit to guide them. This ruling group understood My laws and had great wisdom.

One day, they would be instrumental in building and rebuilding My temple in Jerusalem.

Day 43

How I hate complaining!

"But not so with My servant Moses; he is entrusted and faithful in all My house. With him I speak mouth to mouth [directly], clearly and not in dark speeches; and he beholds the form of the Lord. Why then were you not afraid to speak against My servant Moses?"
—Numbers 12:7-8

Numbers 12-14

Do you see the results of complaining about what I've done and who I've selected to lead? Miriam and Aaron did. Even though they were Moses' sister and brother, they still murmured against him and the person he'd married! They questioned his ability to lead, and they set themselves up against him, saying they were just as capable as he was. The reason I'd chosen Moses to lead the Israelites was, not because he was the most capable person, but because of his meekness, his extraordinary ability to trust Me in every situation, and his faithfulness. I spoke to other prophets and messengers through dreams and visions, but, with him, I spoke directly—face to face—because he was willing to hear My words and act on them. When I set a leader up among My people, I will not tolerate evil speaking against them. Even now. Those who speak evil receive evil results, often in the form of physical ailments, because they open a door to evil in their own lives.

When 12 scouts were sent to spy out the land of Canaan, only two returned with a positive report. Joshua and Caleb understood My promises to take the land, and they believed them. They refused to acknowledge doubt in the situation. While others complained bitterly about the number and size of the inhabitants in the land, and resisted My promises, they rested in them, expecting victory despite the circumstances. Instead of looking at the giant size of their enemies, they saw Me as bigger than anything they might face. The ones who grumbled, murmured, and plotted against Moses out of fear and lack of faith, succumbed to disease and died in the wilderness, never attaining the promises. Only two—Caleb and Joshua—reached the promised land.

It is the same today. I promise a life free from fear, but few will choose to believe what I can do for them. I yearn for all people to live in a "promised land," but often those I choose to lead them out of bondage are rejected and despised by the very ones who need deliverance. As a result, many people suffer and die in a wilderness, because they won't trust Me or the person I selected to lead them! All because they don't like the way My message is delivered or what they must do to achieve their freedom.

They can't see past the giants.

Day 44

Why so many drastic outcomes?

"When the congregation was gathered against Moses and Aaron, they looked at the Tent of Meeting, and behold, the cloud covered it and they saw the Lord's glory."
—Numbers 16:42

Numbers 15-17

Why were the measures I used during the Israelites' time in the wilderness so drastic? And why don't you see such extreme outcomes today? Why was the man picking up sticks on the Sabbath stoned to death, yet Jesus' disciples picked grain on the Sabbath? Why were 250 rebellious leaders devoured by the earth and 14,700 Israelites stricken with a plague?

These things, believe it or not, happened to save you. They occurred because I wanted to spare as many people as possible and honor the promise I'd made to Abraham, Isaac, and Jacob. I wanted to bring to pass the hope of a Messiah and open a way of salvation so people could live forever. For these reasons, I had to operate more in the supernatural realm and use extraordinary means. But I could only do these things because of the unusual faith of one man—Moses. I can only perform My works on earth through the complete trust and faith of people. Because of Moses' stance on My promises, and his heart for the Israelites, most were spared, when all might have died, because so many doubted and feared and complained against Me, even after seeing My supernatural power. I couldn't allow even one person to walk away from and deny My commandments without repercussions, because unbelief was contagious. Like leprosy, it spread, if it was not contained. And murmuring and complaining are signs of unbelief. When My Son came, it was different, because He showed the other side of Me that I wanted people to see. He was the perfect combination of human and divine. He displayed My graciousness and forgiving nature. He was powerful, because He had faith and trust in Me, like Moses. And, because of this, I could bring salvation to My people. His life and words brought something bigger and better than the Law. His Law of Love replaced the Law of Moses by bringing that part of Me that could direct and lead those who believed in Him to Me. Because of Him, sin could be reconciled by love.

Supernatural things can still occur when people of faith trust enough to operate them.

Because of what My Son accomplished, it is most important that people believe in Him, so they can see the greatest miracle of all time—the ability to receive My Spirit, hear My voice, and live forever with Me and with Him, as We always intended.

Day 45

Why are My words so exacting?

"Take the rod, and assemble the congregation, you and Aaron your brother, and tell the rock before their eyes to give forth its water, and you shall bring forth to them water out of the rock; so you shall give the congregation and their livestock drink."
—*Numbers 20:8*

Numbers 18-20

My words to Moses were always exacting. Why? Because the Israelites had to see that disobeying them resulted in death. They needed clarity and understanding of how to survive so their descendants could live long enough to produce the Messiah. Only by submitting entirely to My words to Moses could they live and not die in the wilderness. To bring them to the land I'd promised required miraculous intervention on My part and obedience on their part. Why would I replace the Canaanites, who rejected Me, with another group of people who also ran from My words?

The laws about dealing with death were required, because exposure to death could cause disease, which often resulted in more death. A red heifer was chosen as the sacrifice for purification from exposure to the dead. It was sacrificed outside the tabernacle compound, and its blood was sprinkled at the door of the Tent of Meeting seven times. This perfect red heifer symbolized Christ, Who was without blemish and also sacrificed outside the camp.* Unblemished red heifers are rare, just as is the willingness of One Who is perfect to die. The heifer, burned with cedar and hyssop, symbolized cleansing, and scarlet thread symbolized shed blood. People exposed to death were cleansed with water mixed with the heifer's ashes so they could again enter the tabernacle. The priesthood offered to Aaron's sons was My gift to them, and their service to Me in the tabernacle was their gift to Me and to the people. Because their purpose was service, priests owned no land, and the first fruits of sacrifices and the tithes of the people were for them. Their portions were a "covenant of salt" between them and Me. Because they bore and removed the iniquity of the people, their priesthood was an offering to Me.

When Moses struck the rock at Meribah, he rejected My instructions to him. I told him to "tell" the rock to produce water. Instead, he struck it. The rock represented Christ, Who would be stricken to die once to remove your sins. Moses had already struck the rock in Rephidim. That was enough.

I demanded complete obedience from Moses because he stood for Me, and the people must respect My Word through him so they could live.

49

Day 46

The symbolism of the serpent and the well

"God is not a man, that He should tell or act a lie, neither the son of man, that He should feel repentance or compunction [for what He has promised]. Has He said and shall He not do it? Or has He spoken and shall He not make it good?"
—*Numbers 23:19*

Numbers 21-23

The serpent Moses lifted up in the wilderness to heal those bitten by snakes was a symbol. Just as it was raised, so the Son of Man would one day be lifted up so "that everyone who believes in Him may not perish, but have eternal life" (John 3:14-15).[1] Life came through faith in what Moses taught the Israelites. One day, life would come like living water from the well I revealed to sustain them. And Jesus would one day sit and explain to a Samaritan woman at a well that He could give her My living water.

Bronze is made from a combination of tin and copper. Tin symbolizes sin and human nature and the mediation needed for both. Copper represents love, caring, affection, and the divine nature. Because it was as precious as gold, it also symbolized heavenly riches.[2] Christ combined these two natures into one bodily form. So, bronze was used to make the serpent, which represented Him Who would come to heal and mediate for all.

The Israelites offered peace to the inhabitants of the lands on the way to Canaan. They fought with the people of Arad and the Amorites, because they were attacked by them. When Balak, king of Moab, sent for Balaam to curse them, Balaam could not do it, because "the people of Israel shall dwell alone and shall not be reckoned and esteemed among the nations." He saw that I beheld no iniquity in Jacob: "The Lord their God is with Israel, and the shout of praise to their king is among the people." He saw how I had brought them from Egypt and given them the strength of an ox. No one could curse them because of what I had wrought. I made Israel to rise up like a lion that would not lie down until he had devoured the prey.

I cannot lie, because I am not a man with mankind's agendas. All I have foresworn will come to pass. One day, I will reestablish a King in Jerusalem, Who will reign forever as King of Kings. Even now, I am preparing Him a place in Israel, where He will stand and judge. My hand is in everything—every event and every word spoken.

I cannot lie, and all I have spoken will come to pass.

Day 47

How I handle people intent on doing evil

"I see Him, but not now; I behold Him, but He is not near. A star (Star) shall come forth out of Jacob, and a scepter (Scepter) shall rise out of Israel and shall crush all the corners of Moab and break down all the sons of Sheth [Moab's sons of tumult]."
—Numbers 24:17

Numbers 24-26

Balaam was not an Israelite, but I still worked through him. When he asked Me for direction, I showed him, even though I knew he would choose to ignore and misinterpret it. He saw how I blessed My people, because I opened his eyes. He even viewed the future when he envisioned a Star rising out of Jacob. One day a star *would* rise over Bethlehem. Wise men from the east of Israel would recall this prophecy, and a Messiah would rise out of Jacob to later reign and subdue the nations, as Balaam prophesied.

Though King Balak of Moab had called Balaam to curse the nation of Israel, I was able to divert the intended evil into good, bringing seven blessings on My people! Balaam later advised Balak about other ways to bring evil to the Israelites—by enticing them with prostitutes and women who would lead them into idolatry. He died because of his betrayal of Me and his lust for promotion and gain.

Today, I can still work good from evil. The purposes of those who work to bring harm on those I love, with an intent to lead them away from Me, will always be thwarted and averted. I will always turn what is meant for evil into goodness, because I am a good God. What was the matter of Peor? When the Israelites were invited to join in the worship of the Moabite gods, and accepted the invitation, I saw the quick spread of idolatry, even before they had reached the promised land! It had to be stopped. Moses realized this. If the nation turned to other gods and walked away from Me, the world would never be redeemed from Adam and Eve's betrayal. People would never have access to what was intended for them, which required a ransom for what had been betrayed. Access to My Spirit and eternal life was lost and must be regained. Without a Messiah to accomplish this, through Israel's lineage, all would be lost for those on this planet. Permanent death would result, and none would ever be deemed worthy to populate the new heaven and earth I intended for later.

Those brave enough among the Israelites to see what was needed to stop the contagious idolatry, and the resultant doom, were honored for their bold actions to stop the spread of evil among them.

Day 48

What were the Israelites' special feast days?

"The Lord said to Moses, Command the Israelites, saying, My offering,
My food for My offerings made by fire, My sweet and soothing
odor you shall be careful to offer to Me at its proper time."
—Numbers 28:1-2

Numbers 27-30

These are the special feast days described in Numbers and celebrated by the Israelites:[*]

The Sabbath was a weekly convocation day, when the congregation was called together for a formal assembly. No work was done on this seventh day that memorialized Me and the completion of My creation. Celebration of this day began with Adam and Eve, before sin entered the garden, so no sacrifice was required.

The Feast of Passover began on the 14th day of the first month, which was called Abib or Nisan, and was celebrated for eight days. It fell around the first day of spring, in late March or early April of your calendar, and memorialized the Passover in Egypt. The blood of a lamb was smeared on the doorpost, and the Passover meal that was eaten symbolized Christ's coming sacrifice and a new beginning.

The first day of the weeklong **Feast of Unleavened Bread** fell on the 15th day of Abib or Nisan, the day after the Feast of Passover. It was a convocation day when the firstborn were dedicated to Me, and it celebrated the release from bondage in Egypt. Leavened bread, representing corruption, was replaced by unleavened bread during this feast to symbolize how Christ would release people from the bondage and corruption of sin.

The second day of the weeklong Feast of Unleavened Bread was called the **Day of First Fruits** and fell on the 16th day of Abib or Nisan. It was not a convocation day but a day to present the first fruit of the barley harvest to Me. Christ was a "first fruit" to rise from death to life. The seventh and last day of the Feast of Unleavened Bread fell on the 21st day of this first month and was a convocation day that celebrated Red Sea crossing.

The Feast of Pentecost occurred 50 days after the Day of First Fruits, around the sixth day of the third month, which was called Sivan, and coincided with your May or June. It was a convocation day when the first fruits of the wheat harvest were presented to Me. Also called the **Feast of Weeks, the Feast of the Harvest,** and, later, **Pentecost,** it was a shadow of the first fruits of My Son's death and resurrection, when My Spirit would once again become available, and He would be anointed as high priest.

The Day of Trumpets, or **Rosh Hashanah,** which fell on the first day of the seventh month called Tishrei. Falling around mid-September, it was the first day of the Jewish civil year and a convocation day. It announced impending judgment that would occur on the

Day of Atonement nine days later and heralded Jesus's entrance into the world and His later return.

The Day of Atonement, or **Yom Kippur**, was a convocation day and occurred on the 10th day of the seventh month, near the end of September. The holiest day of the year, it signified the cleansing of sin and reconciliation with Me. On this day, the high priest entered the Holy of Holies to atone for the peoples' sins. He stood in place of the coming Messiah, Who would intervene for you on Judgment Day and forgive your faults.

The Feast of Tabernacles was an eight-day feast of ingathering, with the first day falling on the 15th day of the seventh month, in present-day October. A convocation day, the first fruits of the fruit harvest were presented, and for seven days the Israelites lived in temporary shelters called "sukkah," as a reminder of their wandering in the desert for 40 years. Branches from palm and other types of trees were waved in celebration during the first seven days. This final feast of the year was a celebration of ingathering at the end of harvest and a time of rejoicing. It symbolized the gathering together of My people and the marriage supper of the Lamb. It also represented the millennium, when the saints would dwell temporarily on earth until it was made new again.

The Festival of Willows or **Hashanah Rabbah** fell on the seventh day of the Feast of Tabernacles and the 21st day of the seventh month. It represented the final Day of Judgment. It was to be celebrated with the beating of willow branches on the ground to show the casting away of sin.

Shemini Atzeret fell on the eighth day of the Feast of Tabernacles and the 22nd day of the seventh month. It was a convocation day and a celebration of fields being plowed and sown, as the rains fell in late October.

Every special day symbolized an aspect of the Messiah to come and what He would accomplish for the Israelites and all of mankind.

Day 49

Nearing the promised land

"And you shall take possession of the land and dwell in it,
for to you I have given the land to possess it."
—*Numbers 33:53*

Numbers 31-33

The Israelites were finally getting close to the promised land. After 40 years of wandering in the wilderness, they could see it. But, first, they had to fight against the Midianites. This was Moses' last assignment before he died. Why was he told to wipe them out? Remember, his father-in-law and first wife were from Midian. But, more recently, the Midianites had tried to lead Israel astray, into the clutches of idolatry, which included the prostitution of young men and women and the sacrifice of their children to the Midianite gods.

If you had neighbors who were abusing, mistreating, or even killing their own children right next to you, would you dismiss what they are doing, because you thought you should be tolerant of their misdoings? If they tried to lure your children into participating in this abuse, mistreatment, or murder, would you say or do nothing? Or would you speak up, because you knew it was inhumane, terrible, and horrific?

I am a God of love. I will not tolerate the abuse of My people, whom I created and made for good. When groups of people practice this kind of idolatry and kill or abuse their own children for their "gods," which are merely evil spirits, I will not tolerate it. I make sure they are "spewed out" of their land. The nations that Israel was instructed to destroy were those who practiced these abhorrent methods of "worship" and refused to change. If they turned to Me, I allowed them to be brought "into the fold." Foreigners who chose to worship Me and practice My goodness were welcome among the Israelites.

The path to Canaan was long and tedious. An 11-day journey took the Israelites 40 years. They needed this time to become unified as a nation that would follow Me and the leader I chose. Many times, the Israelites tested Me with their complete lack of trust.

But Moses always intervened for My people, as Christ would one day intervene for you.

Day 50

Boundaries and vows

"So shall no inheritance of the Israelites be transferred from tribe to tribe, for every one of the Israelites shall cling to the inheritance of the tribe of his fathers."
—Numbers 36:7

Numbers 34-36

What were the promised and actual boundaries of Israel?

I promised the Israelites a land whose southern border extended from the south end of the Dead Sea, along the Ascent of Akrabbim, then around Kadesh and the Wilderness of Zin. The boundary rounded up to follow the Brook of Egypt to the Mediterranean Sea south of Gaza. The western boundary continued up the coast of the Mediterranean Sea and extended north of Sidon to the coast near northern Mount Hor in modern-day western Syria. The northern boundary went east from the Mediterranean Sea to Zedad (now called Sedad in Syria, north of Damascus), extending as far north as the Euphrates River. The eastern border then went south from Zedad, past Damascus, along the eastern side of the Sea of Galilee, then followed the Jordan River all the way to the Dead Sea.

The actual land inhabited by the 12 tribes of Israel looked more like this: The southern boundary included Kadesh and the Wilderness of Zin, but did not extend as far south to the Brook of Egypt. The western boundary cut up past the eastern boundary of Philistia, north past Ashdod, then west to the Mediterranean Sea south of Joppa. It extended north along the Mediterranean Sea to Sidon at its northernmost point. The northern boundary didn't include Zedad, Mount Hor or the Euphrates River, but sloped from Sidon down to Mount Lebanon and the Jordan River. The western boundary went south along the Jordan River to the Sea of Galilee then jutted out to the west into Bashan and Gilead, now part of Jordan, going down as far as the Arnon River. Boundaries and vows are important to Me. Once the tribal boundaries were established, they must never change through intermarriage among the tribes. The inheritances of families must continue within the tribes. Women with inheritances were instructed to marry men of the same tribe. Cities were set aside for the Levites, who had no inheritance. They were places of refuge for the innocent—any who killed unwittingly and needed a fair trial. No one should be put to death on the testimony of one witness. I wanted people to understand the importance of words and vows too and to know that I always said what I meant—that My words stood forever. Boundaries were promises kept, just as vows should be. My promised land was meant to pass to future generations.

The promised boundaries would be fulfilled at the return of My Son to earth.

Day 51

A new generation that trusted

*"O Lord God, You have only begun to show Your servant Your greatness
and Your mighty hand; for what god is there in heaven or on earth
that can do according to Your works and according to Your might?"*
—*Deuteronomy 3:24*

Deuteronomy 1-3

It was a beautiful land. Moses could see it from a distance, from the top of Mount
Pisgah, near Mount Nebo at the northeastern end of the Dead Sea. All I had promised
I'd delivered. I told the Israelites not to bother the descendants of Esau and Lot in Edom,
Moab, and Ammon, because they were related to Abraham and Isaac, and I had promised
them inheritances and land too. So, the Israelites went around them. But the Amorites of
Heshbon and Bashan attacked them first, and the Israelites retaliated and took their land,
after offering to make peace with them. The land they took—Gilead, on the east side of the
Dead Sea and the Jordan River, became the land of half the tribe of Manasseh and the whole
tribes of Reuben and Gad. Because of the great number of their cattle and herds, this land
was appropriate for them.

The Israelites traveled west of Edom, then east of Moab, until they reached Heshbon
and Mount Pisgah. Instead of being intimidated by the giant-sized people of Bashan, they
heeded My promise and followed Moses. They saw the fortified and walled cities and viewed
the formidable stature of these people, just as the 12 spies had a generation before them,
but, this time, they trusted Me. Even though this new generation had not seen most of the
miracles I'd done, they listened to Moses' words. "You shall not fear them, for the Lord your
God shall fight for you," he said, and they trusted him with all their hearts.

What makes the difference? Why do some generations of people live in fear and distrust
of Me, deny My promises, and reject the leaders I send to them? They do these things even
after seeing My mighty works! Then other generations look up to Me with shining faces
as if they are beholding My face for the first time! This is a mystery. But faith does seem to
follow generations. And, this new generation followed Moses and Joshua with a true heart
of worship, trust, and reliance on Me.

They believed the words of Moses: "The Lord your God has blessed you in all the work of
your hand. He knows your walking through this great wilderness. These 40 years the Lord
your God has been with you; you have lacked nothing."

And so they moved forward.

Day 52

Never forget what I've done for you

"Therefore you shall keep His statutes and His commandments, which I command
you this day, that it may go well with you and your children after you and that you
may prolong your days in the land which the Lord your God gives you forever."
—Deuteronomy 4:40

Deuteronomy 4-6

Oh, that people would always have minds and hearts to hear Me and do My will! If they
would do the few things I instructed for their good: worship and love Me with their whole
being, never disrespect My name, take time for Me and for themselves to rest, honor their
parents, never murder, commit adultery, steal, act slyly, witness falsely, or covet what belongs
to others. If they would simply observe these things with all their minds and hearts, all would
go well with them and with their children. Their days would be prolonged, and My blessings
could extend to their future generations.

When you seek Me with your whole heart and mind and soul and life, you will find Me.

When you turn to Me in your difficult times and give Me your cares, and when you listen
to My words and heed My voice, I can be found by you, no matter where you are.

I would like to lead you to the place where you belong—where you can receive and give
the most blessings. When you worship anything besides Me, including the gods of other
people, or change and manipulate My words, you will wander far from Me to a place where
I cannot reach you, or you Me.

Never forget Who I am or what I have done for you. I am a merciful God, Who will not
fail you or forget My promises to you or to your ancestors or descendants who believe in
Me. If you will walk in My ways, which I have showed you through My Word, you can live,
and it will go well for you. Your life can be long on the earth.

Sharpen My words in your mind so they can cut through the clutter and chaos of the
world. Press them into your heart, then impress them into the minds and hearts of your
children. Talk of them when you sit down and when you rise up. When life treats you well,
and you see how blessed you are, never forget what I've done for you—how I led you to this
place. Tell My story often, and make sure your children understand and hear it too.

And never add to or detract from the words I have given to you.

Day 53

What do I ask of you?

"What does the Lord your God require of you but [reverently] to fear the Lord your God, [that is] to walk in all His ways and to love Him, and to serve the Lord your God with all your [mind and] heart and with your entire being."
—Deuteronomy 10:12

Deuteronomy 7-10

I am the Lord your God—God of gods and Lord of lords. I am a mighty God, Who is not partial and takes no bribes. I execute justice for the fatherless and the widow. I love the strangers and temporary residents, and I provide them with food and clothing when they trust in Me. I am your praise. I am your God. I do wonderful things for you.

What do I ask of you? To have reverent awe of Me. To walk in My ways. To love and serve Me with all your mind and heart and being. To heed My words, which I give you for good to be able to bless and help others. To realize that the heavens and earth are really mine and all that is in them.

My believers may not be great in number, but I choose them above all other people. If you are Mine, circumcise the foreskin of your mind by eliminating the stubbornness and hardness of your heart. Realize that what you have—all of it—came from Me, because I love you and want to give it to you. It was I Who led you out of the imprisoned places into freedom. So, never say in your mind or heart, "My own power and the might of my hands have gotten me this wealth." Remember Who gave you the power to get wealth.

Because I love you, and desire your love, I chose you to be My special one out of all the people on earth. I didn't choose you because you are so great or smart or talented, but because I love you. And, because of that love, I will always keep My promises to you and to your children. I am the Lord your God, the faithful God Who keeps My covenants with steadfast love and mercy toward those who love Me and follow My words to a thousand generations.

What are My promises to you? To bless the fruit of your body, and to bring you increase so that you are never barren. I bless the fruit of your land and hands. I protect you from sickness and disease. But you must trust Me to do this. Never be swayed by the fears of the world.

Submit to Me, instead of the gods of fear and distrust, and claim My promises to you.

Day 54

When two mountains never meet

"Behold, I set before you this day a blessing and a curse."
—Deuteronomy 11:26

Deuteronomy 11-13

When the Israelites reached the land of promise, I told them to pronounce My blessings from Mount Gerizim and the curses resulting from separation from Me from Mount Ebal. What was the significance of this? I wanted them to see before their eyes the results of worshipping Me versus submitting to the schemes of other gods. I wanted them to see how they would prosper and thrive if they stuck with Me as opposed to shriveling and dying at the hands of other gods, who would only deceive them.

Mounts Gerizim and Ebal stand on either side of Shechem, where Abraham, Sarah, Isaac, Jacob, Rachel, Leah, and Joseph were buried. Abraham stopped here when he entered Canaan. It is where I first promised him this land as an inheritance for his descendants.

When you face east from Shechem, toward the sunrise, Mount Gerizim lies to the south, on your right side, and Mount Ebal lies north, on your left side. The right signifies authority and power (Isaiah 41:13, Matthew 26:64, Acts 2:33; 5:31, Colossians 3:1), blessing (Genesis 48:14), strength (Exodus 15:6, Deuteronomy 33:2, Isaiah 41:10 and 62:8, Psalm 20:6; 78:54), sacrifice and cleansing (Exodus 29:20, Leviticus 14:17), sovereignty (Revelation 5:1,7; 10:2), ordination (Leviticus 8:22-24), honor (I Kings 2:19, Psalm 110:1), salvation (Matthew 25:33), and wisdom (Ecclesiastes 10:2).[1] From the foot of Mount Gerazim, springs flow to the inhabitants of Shechem. Its base is lush with green gardens and vineyards.[2] These represent all the blessings that flow from obedience to Me. The left signifies judgment (Matthew 25:33,41), foolishness (Ecclesiastes 10:2), lack of integrity (Matthew 6:2-4), and curses (Deuteronomy 11:29).[1] Without a source of water, Mount Ebal and its base are barren and desolate, representing the effects of curses. The difference between the mountains is a reminder of the results of living with Me or apart from Me.

Blood was never to be eaten with meat by the Israelites. Why did I forbid it? Because I assigned a unique function to blood. It represented life—"the life of the flesh is in the blood"—and could be used as a ransom or payment: life for life. It had expiating power and represented the blood that would be shed by My Son to ransom you one day.

Until that day, animals were sacrificed in place of humans and stood for what the coming Messiah would finally accomplish for you.

Day 55

How to survive and thrive

"If only you carefully listen to the voice of the Lord your God, to do watchfully all these commandments which I command you this day."
—Deuteronomy 15:5

Deuteronomy 14-17

I have always wanted My people to survive and thrive where I have placed them. In My Word, I made it clear how they could do this. Here are the ways....

—Eat "clean" food. You can do this by avoiding the consumption of scavengers, like rabbits, pigs, vultures, eagles, buzzards, raven, ostrich, hawks, owls, pelicans, storks, herons, certain flying insects, and fish without fins and scales. Also avoid anything that dies of itself. If you do this, your blood will be less tainted by disease and impurities.

—Be merciful to the poor among you. If you open your hands to those who lack and give freely, then I can bless all that you do. Remember that your own ancestors were once bondmen and women who served others and did not have the prosperity you enjoy now. Be thankful for all I've given you! And I will make it clear to you with whom to share your abundance.

—Appoint righteous judges in your land, who will never misinterpret or misapply judgment by being partial and taking bribes. These things corrupt the hearts and blind the eyes of the wise. They also pervert the words of the righteous.

—Follow what is just and righteous, so you may live in the land I give you and be blessed and prosper. Follow My words, not the words and actions of those who worship other gods and practice idolatry.

—Never offer Me your second best. Give Me the best of what you have.

—Choose rulers who will follow Me, who will not accumulate for themselves power, wealth, and women, but whose hearts and minds are set on Me and applying My words, not on their own aggrandizement or control over others.

If you do these things, you and your land will be blessed—mentally, spiritually, physically, and financially. Then you will lend to many nations and never need to borrow.

You will rule over many nations and not be ruled by them!

Day 56

The people who spoke for Me

"I will raise up for them a prophet (Prophet) from among their brethren like you, and will put My words in his mouth; and he shall speak to them all that I command him."
—*Deuteronomy 18:18*

Deuteronomy 18-21

Until Christ came, I provided prophets—men and women of God on whom My Spirit lay—who spoke for Me. The Israelites were afraid of My voice and the fire they saw from Me at Mount Sinai. They thought these would kill them, so they asked others to "stand in the gap" by leading them and speaking for Me. So, I raised up men and women and called them from among the people. I put My words in their mouths, until Christ came. He was My final Prophet.

I told the Israelites they would never need soothsayers, diviners, sorcerers, mediums, or wizards to interpret My ways or the future. These imitators actually stood against and apart from Me, never adhering to My words or guidance. And they worked with the help of enemy spirits. I drove these deceivers out of the lands I gave to the Israelites, because their abominable practices led people astray and away from dependence on Me. I wanted My people to come to Me by way of My true prophets, who listened to Me and spoke for Me, until a time when people could come directly to Me for guidance, because of what My Son would bring and make available—My Holy Spirit.

I asked the Israelites to set aside refuge cities in the land, three on the east side of the Jordan River: Golan, Ramoth and Bosor, and three on the west side: Kedesh, Shechem and Hebron. These cities represented Christ as a future refuge and were safe havens for anyone who killed unintentionally. For those who killed purposefully, the elders of their own city could request that they be sent back. Those who were innocent were kept in the refuge cities to be tried fairly and justly. Only the testimony of two or three witnesses could establish guilt. False witnesses were charged with their own accusations.

I fought for the Israelites. Those who lived far off were offered peace, but if they attacked My people, Israel could fight back. The cities of those already in the promised land could not be spared. This was because those who populated the land: the Hittites, Amorites, Canaanites, Perizzites, Hivites, and Jebusites taught and maintained the abominable practices of their gods, including sacrifice of their own children.

They would cause Israel to move far from Me in their hearts into disillusionment.

Day 57

Follow Me honestly

"The vow which has passed your lips you shall be watchful to perform, a voluntary offering which you have made to the Lord your God, which you have promised with your mouth."
—*Deuteronomy 23:23*

Deuteronomy 22-25

I included many details of how to live and be blessed in My communication with Moses. The significance of these instructions is relevant even today. The gist of it all is this: You must trust Me. At the heart of all unrighteousness is a basic distrust of Me as God. Those who want to rebel against Me will find their own unique ways to do this. As a result of distrust, they may disdain or hate how I made them. They might ignore or reject what I intended for them. This might cause them to present themselves as something they aren't or even change their appearance to become quite different from how I made them. You might call this hypocrisy. I call it lying to oneself and denying Me and My intentions for them. These are ways that people look away from their own true nature and step away from Me. It is a form of rebellion.

Some walk away by serving other gods, thinking there is more freedom this way. They offer their minds and hearts and bodies for service to evil spirits, who control them. Some prostitute themselves by giving away what is precious and sacred: their sexuality. Others rebel with their mouths, making promises they will not keep, causing distrust among others, which translates into wariness of Me.

Some "muzzle the oxen" by cutting back on what they owe to those who work for or with them out of greed or fear of lack. This hinders their own ability to accomplish more and is another form of distrust in My ability to provide. This lack of faith may influence a marriage, as when a husband dishonors or betrays his wife out of fear or dishonesty, or a relationship, as when one loans to another who is in need but takes advantage of this neediness by charging high interest.

I gave Moses detailed instructions, because I found in the hearts of people a tendency to move away from Me. They seemed to forget that I am a faithful God, Who will provide in every situation, so they need not take advantage of others' lacks or fall into ludicrous lifestyles. I have always wanted a righteous and good-hearted people, who would follow Me with honesty, and understand that they could live in truth, because what I give them is always good.

And only I can make a person good enough.

Day 58

Why they had to use unhewn stones

"There you shall build an altar to the Lord your God, an altar
of stones; you shall not lift up any iron tool upon them."
—Deuteronomy 26:5

Deuteronomy 26-28

Why did I insist that the altar dedicated to Me on the other side of the Jordan be built with 12 stones never touched by an iron tool? The stones stood for the 12 tribes and signified how I worked among My people. Iron symbolizes what is worldly or man-made.[1] My work could only be done by Me, not by people's hands. The altar I instructed the Israelites to build with unhewn stones was a symbol of what only I could accomplish.[2] Only I could unify a rebellious, stubborn people into one body through My mighty works and bring them into the land I'd promised their fathers on the other side of the Jordan.

One day, I would again bring a people I'd chosen and prepared into a new kingdom "on the other side." It would be one I'd promised to hold for them as an inheritance. These people would be My "living stones of righteousness," because they followed Me to this new place. They would, like the 12 tribes, build the foundation for a new city. And, they themselves would be built upon as a spiritual house for a holy priesthood (I Peter 2:4-5). This kingdom could be set up only by Me.

I made it clear, not just to the Israelites, but to all people, what would happen if they followed Me and heeded My words and what would happen if they didn't. It was all there. And, yet, the people of Israel, My chosen, "peculiar" people, chose to walk away time and time again. What was the result? They suffered immensely. You can see it throughout history. When their kings chose to worship other gods and led them to do so, they dishonored Me and their parents' beliefs. They stole what belonged to others, misled those who were vulnerable, and practiced prohibited sex and sacrifice. They also took bribes and saw the consequences. Though they once were prosperous and feared by other nations, the head and not the tail, when they chose not to serve Me with joy and gratitude, they became slaves again to others. Then, the heavens became as brass, and the earth was as iron. Then, their land was filled with confusion, and their works were destroyed. They grew sick with fevers, and their children were led away to serve others. They were plucked from the land I gave them and scattered from one end of the earth to the other. They were subjected to ungodly practices, which I did not teach them.

And they lived with perpetual anxiety and dread until they returned to Me and realized that only I can build what is great and strong using unhewn stones.

Day 59

You can know My secrets

"The secret things belong unto the Lord our God, but the things which are revealed belong to us and to our children forever, that we may do all of the words of this law."
—Deuteronomy 29:29

Deuteronomy 29-31

The Israelites could not eat the bread or drink the wine that would enable them to recognize Me as the Lord their God. Even after they'd survived for 40 years in a wilderness and had seen how their clothes and shoes never wore out, and how I sustained them, they could not know Me intimately. I could not reveal My whole self to them or give them "eyes to see or ears to hear." I could not show My true relationship to them until One came to earth Who could "open the eyes of the blind." Then they could eat and drink with Him and with Me.

The Israelites who "followed the rules," but lacked My heart, flattered themselves, saying, "I am safe." They walked with stubbornness and rebellion and neglected what was most important to Me—helping the helpless. They were like poisonous roots, and My anger smoked against them. Hypocrites, they were as bad as idol-worshippers who didn't love or acknowledge Me, even after I performed miracles among them. Their names were blotted out. Life was ruined for them.

If your nation becomes a by-word and a wonder among nations, because it has grown desolate, and people ask, "Why has the Lord done this to our land?" here is the answer: Because the inhabitants forsook the Lord, the God of their fathers, and served other gods.

But any who want to know My secrets and understand My ways can know the hidden things that belong only to Me and to those with whom I choose to reveal them. If you heed and follow My words, you will see and understand these secrets, and they will belong to you and your children forever.

If you wander far from Me but return again, like the prodigal son, I will restore to you what you've lost. I will have compassion on you. To Israel: I will gather you again from all the nations where you were scattered. What I ask of you is not difficult, nor is it a secret that I keep well-hidden. My words are nearer than you think, even in your mouth and mind and heart, so you can find and follow them. If you love Me and walk in My ways, then you will live and multiply, and your land will be blessed. I set before you a choice: life or death. If you choose and cling to Me, you will have life and length of days.

And I will go before you and never forsake you.

Day 60

Moses' last song

*"This is the blessing with which Moses the man
of God blessed the Israelites before his death."*
—Deuteronomy 33:1

Deuteronomy 32-34

Moses praised Me in song as he looked out at the promised land. He knew he would never enter the land. He had spent his last 40 years enduring the hardship of leading a group of stubborn and rebellious people, who did not know or understand Me, to this place. Yet I would not allow him to enter it with them.

But he still praised Me! Speaking for Me with an understanding heart, he said: "I (God) encircle you like an iris around the pupil of an eye. You are My pupil. I penetrate you with piercing looks to see your heart. I am like a mother eagle, hovering over you. I spread My wings to protect you. I bear you up to My place in the heights so I can keep a protective eye on you. I alone can lead you out of a wilderness. No other god could do this. I give you food to eat when you are hungry, and water to drink when you are thirsty. I provide the best things just for you. I am the Rock of your salvation."

But sometimes you walk away from Me and think you can live without Me, because you have all you need. You see other gods, the gods of others that seem inviting to you, and you think you should worship them, though they are spirits intent on doing you harm. You forget about Me, the God Who made and protect you. So, My face is hidden from you, and you are left to your own devices. This always brings Me great pain.

But then you see what life is like without Me, how other gods can't do for you what I can. They never intended to. They only wanted your worship. You see how they lead to what is poisonous, bitter, venomous, and pitiless. And when your foot slides into slippery and disastrous places, I relent, because I see how your power is gone—eaten up by others. Then I ask you, "Where are the gods in whom you took refuge? Can't they help you?" You shrug your shoulders and cast your eyes down.

Then you look up and see that there is no god beside Me. Only I can bring you life out of death. None can deliver besides Me. Only I can avenge the evil brought on you by your enemies. So, set your mind and heart on My words, for only I can heal you and give you life. There is none like Me, Who rides through the heavens to help you.

I, the eternal God, am your refuge and dwelling place, the One Who holds you up with My everlasting arms.

Day 61

The secret of success

"Be strong, vigorous, and very courageous. Be not afraid, neither
be dismayed, for the Lord your God is with you wherever you go."
—Joshua 1:9

Joshua 1-4

I revealed the true secret of success to Joshua. I told him to "Be strong and have courage by doing what I have commanded you, never turning from Me or letting My words depart from your mouth. Meditate on them day and night, observing and doing all that is written. Then, you will never be afraid or dismayed. Then, your way will be prosperous, and you will deal wisely and have good success. For I am with you wherever you go, and no one can stand before you all your days. I fight your battles for you. And I will never fail or forsake you."

Rahab understood this secret. She was the least likely person to do what she did. She was a harlot, with little prestige, yet she recognized Me, My power, and what I was doing. She sought Me by sparing the lives of Israelite spies and later received honor. Though she was an outsider, she vowed her support of My people. Though she'd lived beyond the boundaries of My Law, I drew her in because of her great heart for Me.

The scarlet cord she used outside her window to let Israel know her whereabouts was symbolic. Scarlet thread was used in sacrifices with two live birds for the cleansing and purification of any with leprosy (Leviticus 14:4). It was also used with the sacrifice of a red heifer, whose ashes were mixed with pure water to cleanse any exposed to death (Numbers 19:6). Red thread was entwined with other colored threads to make the tabernacle curtains and the ephod (Exodus 26:1 and 28:6). It represented Christ's atoning work on the cross by His shedding of blood.

In Rahab's case, the scarlet cord represented her faith and willingness to leave everything to follow Me, and it signified the salvation her descendant, Christ, would bring. Like the blood of the Passover Lamb spread on the doorposts to spare the lives of the firstborn sons of Israel in Egypt, the scarlet cord spared her life and the lives of her family. It demonstrated the salvation that would be available for people outside of Israel, who would one day be brought to Me by their belief in Him whose blood was shed for them.

"Without shedding of blood, there is no forgiveness" (Hebrews 9:22).

What was My secret of success for Joshua and Rahab?

That they could be strong and courageous if they sought Me with their whole heart.

Day 62

Why was circumcision important to Me?

"At that time the Lord said to Joshua, Make knives of flint and circumcise the [new generation of] Israelites as before."
—Joshua 5:2

Joshua 5-7

Why was circumcision important to Me? Because it represented the contractual agreement I made with Abraham. It was a token of the covenant partnership between Me and My people, and it stood for the promise I would honor because of My relationship with Abraham.

The Moabites and Ammonites (descendants of Lot), and the Edomites (from Esau) also participated in the circumcision rite. It was always performed on the eighth day of life, because eight represents a new beginning for the child, who is set aside as one of Mine and dedicated as a covenant member among My people.

What is the meaning of "circumcision of the heart" (Deuteronomy 10:16)? As the physical aspect of My covenant represented a relationship with Me, it also stood for a commitment of the heart and will to Me. Circumcision meant consecration to Me and the high ideals of My covenant, including holiness, or separation from the world (Leviticus 11:44, Jeremiah 4:4). A true covenant member would be motivated by love for Me (Deuteronomy 6:5) and for his or her neighbor (Leviticus 19:18), or fellow covenant member. Now, "circumcision of the heart" is replaced by My Spirit in you, and this new covenant relationship is made available to anyone who makes Jesus their Lord.

Joshua obeyed My commandment to him that all males must be circumcised before entering the promised land. When their covenant and commitment were renewed with Me, then I could "roll away the reproach of Egypt" by removing the lingering sin of rebellion that had infiltrated their parents' lives and minds in the wilderness. I needed this new generation to be "all in" with Me, willing to follow Me and recognize that I released them from bondage. I even sent My Prince with His sword, representing My Word, to substantiate My presence with them and acknowledge their commitment and covenant with Me. This was necessary before they could inherit the land I'd promised. A covenant with Me required complete obedience, so I could protect them from evil and harm. When Achan decided to do his own thing, apart from the newly formed covenant, all Israel saw the repercussion: death. Disobedience had to be removed to enable Me to help them in their mission so that more lives would not be lost.

Sin never just affects you; it has a contaminating effect on all who surround you.

Day 63

I fought for Israel

"Fear not nor be dismayed; be strong and of good courage."
—*Joshua 10:25*

Joshua 8-10

Do you see how, when you walk alongside Me, and partner with Me, I can do so much for you and for others through you? Then, My will and designs can be accomplished for the good of many. People might say today, "Why did God allow, even support, the Israelites' decisions to kill other people?" The answer is simple. When people worship other gods, or spirits, they bring great evil and resultant death upon themselves and others. When they move far from Me in their thinking, and way of life, their ungodly practices magnify death and result in the sacrifice of their own children.

The Israelites stood for Me and My way—the way to life. Through them, I could bring My message of hope and deliverance to the world, because they worshipped Me. You can see how they were attacked first and how I gave them ways to overcome. The strategy I gave to Joshua at Ai was used later to overcome other enemies. When leaders listen to Me, and do as they are directed, they can defeat any obstacle. The Israelites were beaten in one battle because of one who disobeyed Joshua's instructions. Later, their leaders were misled by the Hivites, and people murmured against them. But no one spoke against the leaders when Joshua led them to victory with an outstretched arm.

When Joshua called all the Israelites, along with their elders, officers, judges, and priests, to stand before Mounts Gerazim and Ebal and recited the Law to them, they listened. They heeded, because they'd seen how, when Joshua moved with Me at his side, they could accomplish miracles. They saw the day-by-day taking over of the land I'd promised to them, often in miraculous ways. And they knew that it wasn't just their doing. It was I who paved a way across the Jordan. It was I who flattened the wall of Jericho, sent the hailstones to halt their attackers, and stopped the sun from setting. They saw how I fought for them.

"Fear not nor be dismayed; be strong and of good courage." This was the promise made to Joshua and the Israelites. Because they believed it, they fought and won and took the land. Then they returned to Gilgal and the altar they'd made to honor Me. Even now, I offer the same promise to those who lean on Me in any battle, whether it's mental, physical, or spiritual: "Fear not nor be dismayed."

With Me, you can be strong to overcome anything.

Day 64

Who were the Canaanite people?

"Not a city made peace with the Israelites except the Hivites,
the people of Gibeon; all the others they took in battle."
—Joshua 11:19

Joshua 11-14

They all came out against Israel. From throughout Canaan, the kings and their followers came to destroy them: Amorites, Hittites, Jebusites—all descendants of Ham through Canaan—and Perizzites, the people who lived in unwalled villages and open country.[1] Only the Hivites from Gibeon made peace with the Israelites. Even the Anakim near Hebron came out. These were the most formidable. Related to the Nephilim giants (Genesis 6:4, Numbers 13:33), they descended from Anak, the son of Arba, a renowned warrior. They were mighty in stature, between seven and 10 feet tall. The bed of King Og of Bashan was 13 feet long. He came from the Rephaim giants, "terrible ones"[2] who were related to the Anakim and inhabited Edom and Moab in Abraham's day. A remnant of them would live on in Gaza, Gath, and Ashdod in Philistia to terrorize the Israelites later, like Goliath, who was destroyed by David. When the Israelite spies first went into the land, they feared these giants, who deterred them from going in. This time, a new generation under Joshua trusted Me enough to approach them fearlessly.

Why did I disdain the religious cults of the Canaanites? Their main god was Baal, and their most popular goddess was Asherah. Baal was represented as a man with the head and horns of a bull. He carried a lightning bolt to symbolize destruction and virility. He was venerated because he'd defeated other gods, according to Canaanite mythology, particularly the gods of the sea and storms. He "overcame" death each year by emerging from the underworld to bring rain to water the earth. Asherah represented fertility as a nude and pregnant woman. She was Baal's mistress, worshipped among trees and poles representing phallic symbols. The worship of both involved the sacrifice of animals and humans—the firstborn of the community's children. Their fertility rites involved worshippers engaging in sexual perversions, including sex with the priests to entice the gods to bring them a good harvest.[3]

"The thief comes to steal, kill and destroy" (John 10:10). What was stolen in this mal-worship? That which is precious and sacred—sexuality as I intended it. What was killed? My children—those I'd blessed with life and the firstborn who should be dedicated to Me. What was destroyed?

The spirits of those meant to live and serve Me forever.

Day 65

Are you a cheerleader or a complainer?

"Joshua asked the Israelites, How long will you be slack to go in and possess the land which the Lord, the God of your fathers, has given you?"
—Joshua 18:3

Joshua 15-18

When the five daughters of Manasseh came forward and asked for an inheritance in the promised land, little did they know the significance of their request. One of their inherited towns was Samaria, and, one day, My Son would sit at a well there and reveal His identity first to a woman. There were five daughters of Manasseh, and the number five represents My divine favor and grace. In eastern culture, a woman would never speak to a man, especially a foreigner, at a well, nor would a man speak to a woman. Yet, Jesus broke cultural norms and spoke to this woman. He did this to show My grace and how I overlooked manmade boundaries and dictates. As you read the Old Testament records, think of what occurred in these places later. What is the hidden meaning in each passage?

The Israelites could not take Jerusalem from the Jebusites during the time of Joshua (Joshua 15:63), but, one day, David would make this city the centerpiece of his kingdom and Mine. Around 1000 BC, about 400 years after Joshua, David's forces defeated the Jebusites and made Jerusalem the Israelite capital. It would remain as the capital until Nebuchadnezzar destroyed the city and temple in 587 BC. In 538 BC, the first group of Israelites returned to Jerusalem from Babylon.

Joshua led the Israelites from victory to victory over the Canaanites, and yet the people continued to complain. Even as the other tribes settled into their promised lands, the tribes of Manasseh and Ephraim came to him with grievances. They felt they deserved more land because of their numbers. "If you are so very great," Joshua responded, "get up and clear more ground for yourselves! Take more from the Canaanites!" Their reply? "But the Canaanites have iron chariots!" Joshua: "You're great and numerous and powerful! You can do this! Even if they are strong, you are stronger!" What did he know that they didn't? That I was always by their side. Joshua was a true cheerleader. Throughout his life, he encouraged trust in Me. He'd watched Moses and how I worked with him. He knew what I could do, because he'd seen My strength in those who turned to Me for help. And he asked, "When will these people ever rise up to believe?" Are you a cheerleader or a complainer? Will you encourage others to trust and rise up to conquer?

Why not become a cheerleader like Joshua!

Day 66

I honor My promises

"There failed no part of any good thing which the Lord had promised to the house of Israel; all came to pass."
—*Joshua 21:45*

Joshua 19-21

Joshua, Eleazar the high priest, and the other leaders of Israel honored My promises to the people of Israel by making sure the promised land was disseminated in a godly way.

The Levites were divided into three groups based on the descendants of Levi's three sons: Gershon, Kohath, and Merari. Only Kohath's descendants, through his grandson Aaron, were priests allowed to minister at the altars. The other descendants of Levi were charged with the care of the tabernacle. Under David's reign, Levites talented in the area or music were assigned to perform instruments and sing praises during ceremonies and feast days.

When the heads of the Levites came to Joshua and Eleazar to remind them that Moses had promised them cities to dwell in and pastureland for their cattle, Joshua and Eleazar made sure that these promises were kept.

The tribes of Judah, Simeon, and Benjamin gave the Kohathites 13 cities: Hebron, Libnah, Jattir, Eshtemoa, Holon, Debir, Ain, Juttah, Beth-shemesh, Gibeon, Geba, Anathoth, and Almon. The tribes of Ephraim, Dan, and Manasseh gave them 10 cities: Shechem, Gezer, Kibzaim, Beth-horon, Eltekeh, Gibbethon, Aijalon, two cities named Gath-rimmon, and Taanach.

The tribes of Issachar, Asher, Naphtali, and Manasseh in Bashan gave the Gershonites 13 cities: Golan, Be-eshterah, Kishion, Daberath, Jarmuth, En-gannim, Mishal, Abdon, Helkath, Rehob, Kedesh, Hammoth-dor, and Kartan. To the Merarites, the tribes of Reuben, Gad, and Zebulun gave 12 cities: Jokneam, Kartah, Dimnah, Nahalal, Bezer, Jahaz, Kedemoth, Mephaath, Ramoth, Mahanaim, Heshbon, and Jazer.

Israel attained the land I'd sworn to their ancestors, and they were able to rest at last. Not one of their enemies withstood them. I delivered them into Israel's hands. Not one good thing I had promised failed to come to pass.

And, just as I honored My promises to Israel, I will also honor My promises to you.

Day 67

Joshua's final words

"If it seems evil to you to serve the Lord, choose for yourselves this day whom you will serve, whether the gods which your fathers served on the other side of the River, or the gods of the Amorites, in whose land you dwell; but as for me and my house, we will serve the Lord."
—Joshua 24:15

Joshua 22-24

Joshua was 110 years old and about to die. Before he passed, he wanted to make sure the Israelites understood what was most important for their survival as a nation. So, he outlined the words they had heard from Moses. And he summarized what was most important. He first reminded them that I had kept My promises to them. He pointed to the land around them, which their parents never imagined they would inhabit. Despite the unbelief, I kept My part of the bargain and fought alongside their children, who trusted and overtook it little by little. Joshua knew what could happen if this new generation, or the next, drifted away from Me. He explained that, to keep this wonderful land, they must be faithful to Me. They could be very courageous, as they had been, if they remained steadfast to keeping and doing what was spoken and written to them by Moses, never turning to the right or to the left from the covenant they had made with Me.

What did this covenant consist of? It stated first that they must put away any other gods from among them. They must refrain from taking up the false worship and practices of the people around them. They must cling to Me as their Lord, being watchful to love Me.

If they would do these things, then I could continue to fulfill My part of the bargain, and I would stand and fight for them against any enemy. Then, they could always eat the precious and plentiful fruit of the land. They could live, survive, and thrive.

I kept my part of the promise. Not one thing was unfulfilled of what I'd spoken through Moses. But they must continue to be faithful to their part of the bargain to maintain their covenant relationship with Me. We would be witnesses to each other's faithfulness.

Joshua understood what I'd done for them. He had lived to see it. "As for me and my house, we will serve the Lord," he said. What about you? Are you still waiting to see a promise fulfilled?

You will, if you stay faithful to Me in your heart, like Joshua.

Day 68

Then they cry out to Me

*"When the Lord raised them up judges, then He was with the judge
and delivered them out of the hands of their enemies all the days
of the judge; for the Lord was moved to relent because of their
groanings by reason of those who oppressed and vexed them."*
—Judges 2:18

Judges 1-3

The Israelites didn't keep their part of our bargain. I promised to be by their side and fight against their enemies if they stuck with Me, but they ignored this covenant and My warnings. They didn't see the importance of pushing out the Canaanites from their land and allowed them to live among them. They went so far as to intermarry with them, so the tentacles of ungodly practices usurped My words. And the terrible customs of Baal and Ashtaroth spread among them and led them away from My spiritual guidance.

What was the result? Other kings took their land and began to control them—even to dictate their ways. First, the king of Mesopotamia rose against them and defeated them. How could this happen? Hadn't I promised I would fight for Israel and that they would live and thrive in this promised land? What happened was that they did not keep their part of the covenant with Me—that they would continue to love and serve Me as their only God. When they turned away from Me to serve others, I could no longer help them to overcome their enemies, as I promised if they stuck with Me. But they didn't.

When the Israelites cried out to Me, I responded, as I always will. I raised up judges—leaders to deliver them from their enemies. First came Othniel, nephew of Caleb, one of the 12 who spied out the land for Moses and returned with a good report. My Spirit rested on Othniel, and he led Israel to victory over Mesopotamia. He overthrew the king and freed the people from tyranny. He judged for 40 years. After him, the Israelites drifted again into idolatry, and Eglon, king of Moab, came with the Ammonites and Amalekites to take control of the land. After Eglon ruled for 18 years, Ehud, a Benjamite judge, devised a plan to kill him and, with My help, led Israel to victory over Moab. The land again had peace under his 80-year rule. Shamgar followed Ehud and delivered the Israelites from the Philistines. But, between each leader, Israel again and again drifted into idolatry. Why? Because people gravitate to whatever seems appealing to their flesh, and they are often deceived. When they do not rely on My Spirit for guidance, they move into unprofitable lifestyles until their circumstances become intolerable.

Then they cry out to Me.

Day 69

A tale of two women

"So let all Your enemies perish, O Lord! But let those who love Him be like the sun when it rises in its might. And the land had peace and rest for forty years."
—*Judges 5:31*

Judges 4-6

One woman prophesied in the hill country of Ephraim under a palm tree that symbolized victory, peace, and eternal life.[1] The other sat in a tent in Naphtali near an oak tree that represented strength, morale, resistance, and knowledge.[2] These two women brought peace to Israel for at least 40 years. Who were they? One was a wise and prophetic judge named Deborah, and she led the way to victory. Israel was oppressed by a Canaanite king named Jabin from Hazor in Naphtali for 20 years. Courageous Deborah rose up to guide Israel to victory against him by encouraging an Israelite man named Barak from Naphtali to go and fight for their land. She even supported him by riding with him into battle. A forerunner of Joan of Arc, Deborah knew that with My leading, they could win over the enemy. But because of Barak's fearfulness, she foretold that his victory would come through another woman's hand. The other woman was Jael. The wife of Heber the Kenite, a descendant of Hobab, or Jethro, Moses' father-in-law, she lived in a tent near Kedesh. Her people were at peace with the Canaanites, so she welcomed Sisera, Jabin's general, to hide in her tent. She gave him salted milk to drink and made a pact of peace with him. When salted food or drink was served in the east, it represented a covenant between people that included a promise for protection. (II Chronicles 13:5.) So, after making such a pact, why did Jael kill Sisera? Because he broke his part of the covenant-agreement by entering "her tent." It was forbidden for a man other than a husband to enter the woman's side of the tent. Sisera, out of fear, hid on her side, thinking the Israelites would never find him there. When he broke his part of the bargain by not trusting in her protection, she was no longer bound to guard him. Lack of trust on the part of men made it necessary for Me to work through these women, who did trust Me. And Deborah sang a song of victory with Israel. Do you trust? Do you have the needed courage to fight for Me?

If you do, you can lead others to great victory, with Me alongside you, whether you are a man or a woman!

$\mathscr{Day}\ 70$

What if I asked you to fight against all odds?

"The Lord said to Gideon, The men are still too many; bring them down to the water, and I will test them for you there. And he of whom I say to you, This man shall go with you, shall go with you; and he of whom I say to you, This man shall not go with you, shall not go."
—*Judges 7:4*

Judges 7-9

What if I asked you to fight a battle that seemed outrageous? What if you made all kinds of excuses, only to realize how I confirmed every requested sign that confirmed I was with you each step of the way? So, you picked participants to help you. But I made you send half of them back, because I wanted you and everyone to know it was Me Who'd deliver you. You were left with only a few but then I told you to separate out even more—those whose hearts weren't fully with Me. So, you were left with only a handful of people to help you win this battle against a formidable enemy. Would you trust Me to win the fight? Gideon did. Out of 32,000 men he ended up with 300. And this handful had to fight against an enemy whose number was like the sand on a seashore! Even the way they'd win seemed crazy! But I knew he could do it. I worked with him just like I did with Moses to overcome his fears. Through a fleece and a dream, I showed him I was beside him. And against an enemy as huge as a swarm of locusts, he would win with trumpets and torches and clay jars. The trumpets were shofars, or ram's horns. These were used by the Israelites to sound the alarm if an enemy was attacking (Numbers 10:9). The ram represented redemption and a substitute sacrificed for sin, as in the case of Isaac.

Later, My Son became sin for you and a sacrifice, like the ram.[1] What is the significance of the torches hidden in clay jars? You "have this treasure in jars of clay to show the all-surpassing power that is from Me, not from you" (II Corinthians 4:7). Clay jars can break and crack easily, as might any who were fearful or prone to kneel before idols. That's why I pruned these fear-prone doubters from the original army. But clay jars can also hold Light, like the jars they used to cover the torches.[2]

I am your refiner, your source of Light and deliverance. The treasure you hold is My Spirit in you. You might be "hard pressed on every side," as Israel was by the Midianites and Amalekites, yet you are never crushed. You might be perplexed by what I ask of you, but you will never be in despair. You might be persecuted, but you will never be abandoned or destroyed (II Corinthians 4:8-12).

Because I am with you always.

Day 71

A leader's vow and a daughter's life

"So I have not sinned against you, but you are doing me wrong to war against me. The Lord, the [righteous] Judge, judge this day between the Israelites and the Ammonites."
—Judges 11:27

Judges 10-12

In Old Testament times, as today, when people were oppressed or taken advantage of by evil leaders, they often sought one to reign over them who had the necessary skills to lead them to freedom, even though that one might be considered an "outsider." Such was Jephthah. Though he was the son of a harlot, and not considered legitimate or "worthy" to lead, like the other sons of Gilead, the people of the land acknowledged his ability as a warrior. He could fight for them. So, they made Jephthah their leader, and he defeated the Ammonites, who sought to take over their land. But first, he made a vow before Me to the elders of Gilead to be their leader if he was victorious over the enemy.

It is not unique for the displaced people of a land to claim ownership of it, even though they have not inhabited that land for many generations. The king of the Ammonites declared his right to take over Israel, because his ancestors had once lived there. But Jephthah reminded him of what had taken place to allow Israel to inhabit the place. The bottom line was this: "You can possess whatever land your god gives you to possess, but all the Lord our God gives us, we will possess."

Then Jephthah made another vow: He would give as a "burnt" offering whatever or whoever came out to meet him when he returned home in peace. This offering was like Isaac's—one of dedication. He knew it might be his child he would see first, and he disdained human sacrifice, as I did. But he also realized that, without My help, he could never win a war with the Ammonites. This vow would not be a sacrifice with fire but an unreserved dedication of something precious to him and to Me. When he won the battle, after I had delivered the enemy into his hand, he returned home to be greeted by his daughter. She accepted his vow and mourned only because she knew she would never marry or be able to provide her father with progeny. This was painful for her and for him, but she honored his promise and left to live a life of consecration as one devoted to serve her whole life at the tabernacle. Before leaving, she bewailed her virginity with her close friends, who still came to visit her yearly in recognition of her great commitment.*

And I honored both her and Jephthah for their devotion.

Day 72

The substance of Samson's strength

"Then Samson called to the Lord and said, O Lord God, [earnestly] remember me,
I pray You, and strengthen me, I pray You, only this once, O God, and let
me have one vengeance upon the Philistines for both my eyes."
—*Judges 16:28*

Judges 13-16

Samson reflected My strength and power to overcome against all odds. His name meant "bright sun,"* because his parents had seen the face of an angel, or messenger, and knew how it reflected My Light. Samson judged Israel for 20 years. Could he have judged longer? Yes, but he submitted to the temptations that arose because of his ability and renown. I warned him many times against being manipulated by godless women, who were directed by fear and greed, but he submitted to his desire for them and didn't heed My warnings. Despite his ability to tap into My supernatural strength to fight and deliver his people from Philistine oppression, his strength was sapped by others' ill intentions.

If Samson had relied on Me more, I could have led him and Israel to greater victory over an enemy who confiscated their crops, goods, and livelihood. These foreigners did not know Me, and they worshipped other gods. They had no scruples and were easily distracted by lust, greed, power, fame, and retaliation. They practiced no real justice, because their eyes were blinded by self-aggrandizement.

Why would I want Samson to kill so many Philistines? Because they stole, killed, and destroyed what belonged to My people. Burning out Samson's eyes and using him for sport and spectacle were examples of their depravity, which resulted from worshipping other gods. It is difficult to live at peace with those who oppress you.

Why don't I appear to more people? I did then, because the times required supernatural intervention for the survival of My people, who lived without access to My Spirit. I needed My Son to be born through and among them one day.

Now, you can live with My Spirit in you to guide and strengthen you.

You don't need My intervention, because you have all the power you need, if you trust Me and believe in My Son.

Day 73

A time of extreme lawlessness

"In those days there was no king in Israel; every man did what was right in his own eyes."
—Judges 17:6

Judges 17-19

It was a "temporary" time. Everyone waited for a king, or, at least, a decent leader. And, while they waited, the Israelites did their own thing—whatever seemed right in their own eyes, whether good or bad. And, often, it was bad. People drifted away from My Law— the instructions I'd given to Moses to guide them. They had always been stubborn and rebellious, but now it showed more than ever. And what happens in lawless times? The inevitable. Things go from bad to worse, until someone realizes how far away everyone has drifted. Then, that person decides a correction is needed—some way to bring people back to the center.

Shiloh was north of Jerusalem in Ephraim's hill country. It was the temporary place of worship, where the tabernacle was set up with its tent and fixtures, until a permanent structure could be built. Here was where My people were to focus on worship of Me. Jacob once explained that the name "Shiloh" meant "the Messiah who would come one day through Judah" (Genesis 49:10). This place, Shiloh, was the focal point of worship for three centuries, until the Philistines destroyed it and stole the ark. Solomon would one day build a more permanent temple in Jerusalem, after David retrieved the ark. But, until then, My people were drifting away from Me. Some were setting up manmade idols in their towns, like the Danites, and designating priests to serve their false gods. This lawlessness and lack of devotion to Me was leading them to outrageous behavior. This included the terrible treatment of those I set aside for honor and respect, like women, who were treated as lesser beings. And sex had become a perverse thing, instead of the sacred gift it was meant to be. Whenever people drift far from Me, they suffer at the hands of cruelty and corruption. It becomes most apparent in the way some handle sex, which I created as sacred between a man and a woman. Because of a lack of devotion to Me, and what I regard as good, people begin to live like those in Sodom and Gomorrah. The result is always abhorrent. In this case, to show how corrupt people had become, one Levite resorted to a drastic and eye-opening move. Sometimes that is what is needed for people to wake up and change their shockingly excessive and atrocious behavior.

Throughout history, it has always taken bold moves to drive people back toward the center—the "bulls-eye" where I live.

Day 74

Israel's civil war

"The Israelites came to the house of God [Bethel] and sat there until evening before God and lifted up their voices and wept bitterly."
—Judges 21:2

Judges 20-21

The Israelites gathered at Mizpah to prepare to fight against their relatives, the Benjamites. The name "Mizpah" referred to the "witness heap" of stones set up by Laban and Jacob to establish a peace pact between them. It was a watchpost pillar, a place set apart for Me to be a witness against any harm done by one against the other. And yet, here the Israelites planned a war against their own people, who had moved far from the covenant made with Moses. All the Israelites were deeply disturbed by the actions of some in the tribe of Benjamin.

In the ensuing war between Benjamin and the other 11 tribes, 40,000 Israelite men were killed. This was out of 400,000 men. Of the Benjamites, with 26,000 originally prepared to fight, only 600 were left standing. During the American Civil War, where brothers also fought against brothers, 620,000 men died. This was two percent of the U.S. population at the time. The number of Israelites killed was less, but a greater percentage of the population was wiped out. The strategy that resulted in victory for the Israelites was the same one Joshua used against Ai: the main army would lead the enemy away from a town, then others would emerge from behind the town to burn it and surround the retreating enemy.

The Israelites wept and consulted with Me at the house of God—the tabernacle in Shiloh. Phinehas, the grandson of Aaron, was high priest then, and he helped them determine how to proceed. My will, My heart, is never that people die in war against each other. But what leads to war? When people drift far from Me into indecency and disrespect for others' rights, chaotic practices of injustice make life unbearable, and many people suffer. When "the law of the land" is "every man do what is right in his own eyes," the eyes of some invariably turn to darkness and shady practices, and their actions inevitably cause great harm to those around them.

But see how a few good, even great, men and women can change a nation. It is so even now.

Some will have the courage to rise up and lead others, who thirst for righteousness, to peace and goodness, often against all odds.

Day 75

What Ruth represented

*"And Ruth said, Urge me not to leave you or to turn back from following
you; for where you go I will go, and where you lodge I will lodge.
Your people shall be my people and your God my God."*
—Ruth 1:16

Ruth

*Naomi's husband and both sons had died, and she wanted to return to her hometown,
Bethlehem, where Another would be born one day.* Only one of her daughters-in-law, Ruth,
had the courage and conviction to go with her from Moab into a strange land with different
customs and beliefs. They arrived in late March, when the barley was first being harvested.
Planted in the fall, barley was always the first grain to ripen in the spring and was called
the "first fruit" during the Festival of Unleavened Bread. The second day of the weeklong
feast, called the Day of First Fruits, was 50 days before Pentecost, and a day to present
the first of the barley harvest. During the harvest, which lasted 60-70 days, Ruth gleaned
what was left in the fields to feed herself and Naomi. One landowner, Boaz, a near kinsman
to Naomi, took Ruth under his wing and offered her protection and sustenance. Naomi
encouraged Ruth to approach Boaz on the threshing floor as he slept. Though women were
forbidden to enter this area where the men worked, one custom permitted a woman to
approach a near-kinsman and remove the mantle that covered his feet to signify that she
desired him to redeem, or marry, her. Symbolically, Ruth lay at Boaz's feet crosswise, which
foretold the cross of Christ, Who would one day descend from her. When he sensed her
presence and awoke, she asked him to "spread his wing of protection" over her. If he chose
to throw his mantle over her, he showed his willingness to redeem her. And Boaz did. But,
though he wanted to marry her, he knew there was another man who was a closer relative,
with this right of redemption. When Ruth left Boaz's side and returned to Naomi, her
mother-in-law's response was to "be at peace." When Boaz approached the nearer kinsman,
the other man had concerns: To redeem the land that had belonged to Naomi's husband,
part of the bargain for a kinsman redeemer, he would have to mortgage his own property
to come up with enough money to buy hers. Plus, taking Ruth as a wife, the other part
of the bargain, could cause problems with his current wife. He pulled off this sandal and
handed it to Boaz, giving him the right of redemption. Boaz and Ruth's son was named
Obed, meaning "servant" or "worshipper." He was Christ's forefather. Ruth represented
the Bride, the Church. And Boaz was like Christ, Who would one day redeem Her.

*And, at a future Pentecost, Christ, the "first fruit" from death to life, would offer His gift
of Holy Spirit to many outside of Israel, like Ruth.*

Day 76

Hannah's heart

"There is none holy like the Lord, there is none besides You; there is no Rock like our God."
—I Samuel 2:2

I Samuel 1-3

Elkanah was a good and godly man, but he could not help his wife, Hannah, who wept because she had no children. He, his wives, and children, lived in Ramah, about 10 miles from Shiloh. They came every year to the tabernacle there, where a stone building housed the Tent of Meeting and Holy of Holies, and they offered their annual sacrifice.

Eli was the high priest in Shiloh, but he did not heed My voice. He ignored My warnings about his sons, who served at the tabernacle as priests. While people grouped around their own pots, eating near the tabernacle, the sons would come and forcefully confiscate the best parts of their meat—the peoples' rightful portions of the sacrifice—leaving the families without much to eat. The sons also insisted on taking the fat from the sacrifices at the altar, which was My rightful portion of every offering. They slept with the women who served at the tabernacle, who had devoted their lives in service to Me. But Eli turned a blind eye to their evil deeds and sat daily on his "throne" at the entry to the temple. He blindly administered justice and transacted business for My people.

When Hannah came to Shiloh with her husband, she stood before the tabernacle and prayed for a child. Eli noticed her but was unable to see her heart, because he did not walk with My Spirit. He accused her of being drunk as she poured out her heart to Me! People without My Spirit can only see the flesh, and they often accuse others of being "out of bounds," when they themselves have no boundaries. With pureness of heart, Hannah accepted Eli's "blessing" and received the answer to her prayer because she trusted in Me. When Samuel was between two and four years old,* she brought him to serve at the tabernacle. How many women would honor a promise in this way? Because of her devotion to Me, I gave her great blessings in return. I blessed her with more children and a son to lead Israel back to Me and anoint a king, who would be a forerunner to the Messiah.

My Spirit rested on Hannah as she prophesied of this coming King, who would bring strength to My people. She told how I guard the feet of those who trust in Me by upholding their steps and keeping them from harm.

My greatest desire is that more women and men would come to Me, as Hannah did, and receive the great blessings I intend for them!

Day 77

I was their Rock

"Then Samuel said to all the house of Israel, If you are returning to the Lord with all your hearts, then put away the foreign gods and the Ashtaroth [female deities] from among you and direct your hearts to the Lord and serve Him only, and He will deliver you out of the hand of the Philistines."
—I Samuel 7:3

I Samuel 4-8

The temple in Shiloh was destroyed by the Philistines, who stole the ark and set it next to their god, Dagon. But when they began to die from a mysterious disease, now called tularemia, that causes skin ulcers and swollen glands from contact with mice, they wanted no part of the ark. They set it on a cart pulled by lowing cows headed back to Israel. It remained in Kiriath-jearim until David brought it to Jerusalem. After this powerful display, why didn't the Philistines believe that My power was greater than their own gods'? They did. But they thought I was God only to Israel.

Samuel judged Israel from Mizpah and Ramah, both southeast of Shiloh. In Ramah, he built an altar of stones. In Beth-shemesh, the ark was set on a great stone, after being returned by the Philistines. Samuel set a stone between Mizpah and Shen and called it "Ebenezer," or "stone of help," because I had been a Rock for Israel by helping them defeat the Philistines. Hannah called me her Rock. David also did later (Psalm 18:2,31). Isaiah called Me the Rock of strength (Isaiah 17:10). These allusions to Me as a Rock also represented My Son, Who would one day be the Rock of salvation to many, and to others a Rock of offense (Romans 9:33). Eli judged Israel for 40 years. During his rule, I became a Rock of offense, because he dishonored Me in so many ways. But Samuel, who followed him as judge, came to Me and said, "If you are returning to the Lord with all your hearts, then put away the foreign gods from among you and direct your hearts to the Lord and serve Him only and he will deliver you...." But they did not see that I could be their stone of help. Samuel came to Me for guidance, and I answered him honestly. When the Israelites asked for a king, this was My answer. "A king will take away your best: children, land, crops, servants, and animals to use for his own purposes. Is this what you want?" But they stubbornly demanded it, because they wanted to be like other people. It is the same today. Instead of leaning on Me for leadership, people demand leaders to rule over them and fight their battles for them. This is because they don't trust Me to fight for them, deliver them, heal their wounds, or guide them to peace and prosperity. They want someone they can look up to or criticize and blame.

It has always been this way.

Day 78

They demanded a king

"If you will revere and fear the Lord and serve Him and hearken to His voice and not rebel against His commandment, and if both you and your king will follow the Lord your God, it will be good!"
—*I Samuel 12:14*

I Samuel 9-12

Samuel judged the kingdom of Israel between the years of 1100 and 1010 BC. * Ramah, six miles north of Jerusalem, was his birthplace, residence, and place of death. Bethel, meaning "house of God," was five miles north of Ramah. Mizpah was three miles west, and Gibeah, Saul's home, was halfway between Ramah and Jerusalem. Bethlehem was 12 miles south of Ramah, and Kiriath-jearim, where the ark was kept, was eight miles southwest of Ramah. I showed Saul to Samuel. "There is the man I told you about." Saul was the best choice available to be king at the time, and Israel demanded to have one, even though Samuel had served them admirably as their most worthy judge. Saul had many faults. He was a worrier. And worriers have a hard time trusting Me. Samuel saw this, but he did as I told him. He always did. I showed Samuel what Saul must do to prove himself to Me, to Samuel, and to himself. Three things were needed to complete his anointing. Each one represented life lived on earth and a new life available later. First, he must go to Bethlehem to Rachel's tomb. This was a place of death and birth. He must recall his ancestors and see the place where One would be born to save mankind later. I wanted him to see that his life stood between death and life for many. He would meet two men in Bethlehem who would speak to him of the donkeys he sought and of his father. The second place he must go was to Bethel, where he would meet three men carrying three loaves of bread, three lambs, and one bottle of wine for an offering. The bread and lambs represented Christ's body broken and His life sacrificed as an offering to Me, when He would lie in a tomb for three days and nights. The wine signified His blood shed once for many. The number three signified a work completed. Saul accepted only two loaves of bread from the men, because My work would not be completed through him. Two denotes difference, and there would be a great difference between Saul and David, who *would* complete the needed work to bring about a Savior. Third, Saul would join a company of prophets near Gibeah. Companies like this were organized by Samuel as schools to teach those willing to learn about and live for Me. This encounter represented My Spirit of life received and manifested by those who trust in Me. Later, Saul must go to Gilgal and wait for Samuel, who sought to teach him patience in waiting for Me—something he would never learn. The Israelites were also impatient. They would not wait until I could bring them a true King. They demanded to have an earthly one now.

Samuel made the most of their ungodly request.

Day 79

All Saul's fears

"And Saul said to Samuel, I have sinned; for I have transgressed the commandment of the Lord and your words, because I feared the people and obeyed their voice."
—I Samuel 15:24

I Samuel 13-15

Saul was more concerned about what people thought of him than what I thought. He was anxious to please people and convince them that he was worthy to be their king. Even though I had set him up in this position, not because of his greatness but by My grace, he never trusted in My ability to keep him there. He fell short, because he believed only in his own power to maintain what he'd been given. He refused My advice time and time again, but I still gave him more chances to prove his loyalty to Me. He failed each time.

Samuel told him to wait seven days at Gilgal, 15 miles from Saul's hometown, Gibeah. He'd meet him there. On the seventh day, Saul impatiently decided to disobey Samuel by offering his own sacrifice. Acting out of fear, he believed he alone must "keep it all together" when his men grew restless. His lack of trust in Me caused his kingship loss.

The Battle of Michmash was won over the Philistines, not because of Saul's great leadership or ability but because of the trust of his son, Jonathan. While Jonathan and his armor-bearer fought the Philistines and created an opportunity for victory for the Israelites, Saul sat under a pomegranate tree, which signified that he sought to be exalted by his own efforts. The Hebrew word for pomegranate comes from a root word, "raman," which means "to exalt, lift up, get oneself up, mount up." He wanted people to recognize him as rightful king, even as he lost their trust by moving away from Me. More than a desire to seek Me as the One who could exalt him, he wanted people to laud him, even when he didn't deserve it.*

He told Ahijah the priest to "withdraw his hand" as he prayed for My guidance in battle. Why? Because Saul wanted everyone to see that he was the one in control. He didn't need prayer to win. He could do this without Me. When the battle was won because of his son's trust in Me, he almost killed Jonathan because of an ungodly and senseless oath he had made, again to show a semblance of spirituality. But his heart was far from Me. Because of other men's righteousness, his son's life was spared. Saul thought he didn't really need My help. He believed His own strength was sufficient. But Israel didn't win battles by of his might or power.

Victory came from others' trust in Me.

Day 80

What formidable giants do you face?

"But the Lord said to Samuel, Look not on his appearance or at the height of his stature, for I have rejected him. For the Lord sees not as man sees; for man looks on the outward appearance, but the Lord looks on the heart."
—I Samuel 16:7

I Samuel 16-18

I always provide a way to do what I ask of you. You may be concerned about the repercussions of your actions or words, but if they are from Me, you'll be covered. I place you under My wings of protection. Samuel was sent to Bethlehem to find a new king. Though he feared what Saul might do to him, he obeyed and trusted in Me.

"Look not on the appearance [of the one I choose], or at his height or stature," I told Samuel. "For I see not as man sees; for man looks on the outward appearance, but I look on the heart." I always have. No one thought to ask David to come and meet the prophet. Why? He was the youngest and least likely to be picked. He was the designated tender of the sheep. Of all the brothers, why would I choose him to be anointed as king? But I did. Why? Because of his heart. As a shepherd, he learned to depend on Me. He sang songs of praise to Me and recognized how I protected him against lions and bears—anything that might attack the sheep. He loved Me with his whole heart. So, I blessed him with My Spirit, and this gave him greater boldness and the ability to see beyond his physical limitations.

The Israelites camped opposite the Philistines, about 13 miles southwest of Jerusalem. Into the Valley of Elah between them stepped a formidable giant, Goliath, whose height reached 10 feet. Descended from the giant Anakims in Philistia, he wore a coat of mail that weighed over 125 pounds. When he spoke threats against My people and Me, the Israelite army backed away in fear. Only David believed he could stand up to this giant. Why wasn't he terrorized like the rest? Because of his trust built over time. Others mocked his faith and tried to burden him with their fears, but he knew I would stand with him in any battle. He'd seen it. I stand by any who stand for Me against the naysayers. There will always be those who doubt My strength and ability. Many, like Saul and David's brother, will fear those with faith and try to belittle them, even extinguish them. But those who stand for Me against all odds, like Jonathan and David, will be supported and spared by Me. What hard choices do you face—what formidable giants?

Will you flee with fear or trust with faith to overcome them?

Day 81

Why Saul sat under a tamarisk tree

"Saul heard that David was discovered, and the men that were with him.
Saul was sitting in Gibeah under the tamarisk tree on the height,
his spear in his hand and all his servants standing about him."
—I Samuel 22:6

I Samuel 19-22

I formed, made, and created all things, but I also gave every human and spiritual being the freedom to choose between right and wrong. When beings put their need for self-esteem, control, and power above an acknowledgement of Me and My will, and are motivated by a fear of losing these, they are usually driven by other forces not from Me. The choice is always between good and evil. You can either trust in Me or trust in My enemy. His aim is to lead any who will follow him far from Me into death and destruction, while My purpose has always been goodness and fullness of life. When any choose his way, they will receive what he has for them: evil-motivating spirits who direct their ways and lead them to death.

Why would a good king try to kill the people who serve him, even his own son? When a king's focus is dictated by rage, jealousy, lack of control, worry, doubt, and fear, he opens his mind to evil. You can see the difference between those who hate and those who love. Saul hated because he was driven by ill motives and spirits. Jonathan loved and saw the good in David, because he recognized his spirit from Me. In your life, you will see both love and hate. If you have My Spirit, the people who also have what you do and seek Me will seek you out and love you, because they recognize the good in you. But those with other spirits, driven by motives apart from Me, will move away from you, even despise and detest you. But never worry or fear them. I will always be there for you and protect you. I will send true friends to walk alongside you and encourage you because of who you are and what you represent to them—Me!

Saul sat under a tamarisk tree in Gibeah, plotting to kill David. The tamarisk tree is known as the "selfish tree," because it depletes all the water from the ground around it, leaving the other plants susceptible to drought and fire.* Though Saul, out of selfishness, sought to destroy David, My purpose would still prevail. I was able to preserve the life of the one I loved, who also loved Me. So, even in the midst of selfishness and evil intent, My loyalty and favor will always benefit those who choose Me.

Like David, you will "go in peace," blessed by faithful friends, free from the bondage of fear, when you seek My ways and will for you, and allow My spirit to direct you.

Day 82

She stood in the gap

*"Forgive, I pray you, the trespass of your handmaid, for the Lord will
certainly make my lord a sure house, because my lord is fighting the
Lord's battles, and evil has not been found in you all your days."*
—I Samuel 25:28

I Samuel 23-25

*Do you see how David, when questioned by his men, inquired of Me instead of succumbing
to their fears?* He came to Me many times with concerns and questions. This is what I loved
about him. Do you see how people, like those in Keilah, may betray you out of fear or spite,
even after you have rescued, helped, delivered them from bondage?

When Jonathan established ties with David and created a bond of friendship, his hand
was strengthened because of the favor I showed David. When he fought alongside his father,
his hand was weakened. He became vulnerable because of the sin of his father, whose heart
wandered far from Me. David never relied on his own abilities or methods to defeat his
enemies. He trusted Me for deliverance and justice, and he respected My authority and
ability to justify. He waited for Me to deal with his enemies.

"Why do you listen to men who say that I wish you harm?" David asked Saul. He
understood that Saul's thoughts were being driven by others, who wanted to manipulate
him for their own purposes. "May the Lord judge between us and be the avenger [if I have
tried to harm you]. That is not my job." He acknowledged Me alone as his deliverer—the
One Who could plead his cause. Even Saul recognized that David deserved to be king,
because he was more righteous and had more integrity than he did.

When Samuel died, David mourned in the wilderness, just as Jesus did after John the
Baptist was beheaded. Both recognized the greatness of godly men who stood for Me. Saul
did not. I give every person opportunities to give, like Nabal, to bless My own out of their
abundance. When people shirk the needs of others, they suffer the consequences.

Sometimes a godly person, like Abigail, will stand in the gap and fill the needs that others
reject and refuse to fill. She prophesied over David, My anointed one, who would "sling out
his enemies from the center of his sling." She released him from the sin of vengeance and was
a pattern for grace and mercy amid chaos and abuse. She exemplified a woman who could
be blessed, even when bound to another who refuted Me.

*Though she was married to a foolish husband, she was filled with the wisdom that comes
from staying close to Me.*

Day 83

What happens when people act out of fear?

"David was greatly distressed, for the men spoke of stoning him because the souls of them all were bitterly grieved, each man for his sons and daughters. But David encouraged and strengthened himself in the Lord his God."
—*I Samuel 30:6*

I Samuel 26-31

David confronted his enemies, instead of fleeing from them in fear. He could do this because he trusted Me. Saul, instead, kowtowed to the people who surrounded him and listened to their words, instead of Mine. He admittedly "played the fool" as a result.

"The Lord rewards every man for his righteousness and his faithfulness," David reminded Saul, "for the Lord delivered you into my hands today, but I would not stretch forth my hand against the Lord's anointed." He knew that only I can reward for good and repay for evil. In the end, I am the true deliverer. Saul acknowledged the truth of David's words and knew that David would prevail because of his righteousness.

When Saul feared the Philistines, who prepared to fight against the Israelites, he inquired of Me. Why did I refuse to answer him? Because of this: Time and again I had tried to teach him to "wait for Me." I had tried to show him that one must be patient for the answer before charging ahead and acting out of one's own volition. But he had never learned this, and he rejected Me by turning to other gods, or spirits, out of impatience.

People who "bring up the dead" deal with My enemy, who deceives them by sending his own evil spirits to impersonate the dead. The adversary deals in death; I deal in life. Saul went to My enemy for guidance, and he was a traitor to Me. As a result, he died.

I worked with David, whom I loved, because of his desire to know and do My will. Even his enemies admired and trusted him. Though at times he wandered from Me, he always came back for guidance and support. He encouraged and strengthened himself in Me. When he inquired of Me, I answered him, because his heart was right and righteous. He loved Me. I overlooked the times he "missed the mark," because he always returned for forgiveness, and he understood My mercy.

He desired to do My will and serve My purposes, not those of the enemy.

Day 84

Decency in the heart of a ruler

"David sent messengers to the men of Jabesh-gilead, saying, May the Lord bless you because you showed kindness and loyalty to Saul your king and buried him. And now may the Lord show loving-kindness and faithfulness to you. I also will do well by you because you have done this."
—II Samuel 2:5-6

II Samuel 1-3

David's heart was good, though he sidestepped My will a few times. People with power often want more. David was different. He was passionate about what was just. He understood that only I can reciprocate with true justice and judgment. That's why he felt the need to strike down the Amalekite, who said he killed Saul. He believed that, because Saul was anointed, it was My job to do with him as I willed. He wept for Jonathan *and* Saul, though he loved Jonathan as a true friend and confidante, because he saw how life is precious and a gift from Me. Though Saul acted as his enemy and tried to kill him, he respected him as his anointed king. David loved life and the One Who gave it.

David began his reign over Judah in Hebron, 20 miles south of Jerusalem. He ruled there for seven years and six months and accumulated six wives and six sons. The number six represents man and man's doings. Though he was anointed, he spent the first few years expanding his own life and family and tribe, while the rest of Israel was ruled by Saul's son, Ishbosheth. This split caused war between the houses of David and Saul.

As David would one day take Bathsheba from her husband Uriah, he claimed Michal as his rightful wife. Saul's daughter was given to him when he was younger; she was his first wife. He felt he deserved her. But she was now married to Paltiel, who loved her. As in the case of Bathsheba, the "precious and only lamb" of Uriah, David decided to reclaim Michal, though he had many wives now, and the other husband mourned for her. Was this right? Maybe not. But it was just, and David stood for justice. Even deserved rulers with hearts toward justice may take matters into their own hands to avenge those who've wronged them. Joab was like this. A fierce warrior, he was prone to give evil for evil instead of trusting Me for rebuttal. He caused David great headaches and heartaches, because, though David craved justice, he also understood forgiveness. Abner, killed by Joab, had repented and had come to him in peace. He did not deserve death.

David realized this, because, even when he did deserve retribution and payment for wrong-doing, I was merciful to him.

Day 85

David's zeal and humility

*"Because of Your promise and as Your own heart dictates, You have done
all these astounding things to make Your servant know and understand."*
—II Samuel 7:21

II Samuel 4-7

David was zealous for Me. I loved this about him. He was humbled by My promise of a
kingdom that would extend forever from him. "Who am I, O Lord God and what is my
house that You have brought me this far?" He acknowledged My mercy and grace.

My instructions in fighting the Philistines were that the Israelites should go around the
enemy and come upon them "opposite the mulberry trees." The mulberry, or sycamine, tree
is the last to bud in spring. It waits to avoid any frost and represents patience in waiting.*
David understood patience. He'd learned to wait for answers from Me. He waited patiently
in the wilderness until it was the right time for him to reign, knowing I had promised him
this.

When David offered a reward to anyone who could take Jerusalem from the Jebusites,
his statement about the blind and lame may seem puzzling. It wasn't that he hated them.
Remember, he gave lame Mephibosheth a special place at his table. The Jebusites had
taunted him, saying that even their disabled men could defeat his strong men. They detested
and mocked David, and he was responding to their rebukes.

When David brought the ark back to Jerusalem, he wore a linen ephod, which was worn
by anyone performing religious service. He donned this instead of royal robes, because he
knew he did not deserve to be king. Titles, position, and power meant nothing to him. He
believed that only I was great and greater than all his household. Why did Uzzah die when
he reached out to steady the ark? Under the Law, no one except the Kohathite priests could
handle the holy things lest they die (Numbers 4:15). The next time they moved the ark,
David made sure it was carried correctly by the right priests.

Whenever anyone does something to glorify Me, someone will belittle the work. David
danced before Me with all his heart, yet Michal despised him. She was Saul's daughter,
raised in royalty and still bitter about being separated from her second husband, Paltiel,
and brought to live with David's other wives in a harem. Her lack of humility caused great
bitterness in her life.

She never had a child.

Day 86

I expect more from those in high places

"And David said to Nathan, I have sinned against the Lord. And Nathan said to David, The Lord also has put away your sin; you shall not die."
—II Samuel 12:13

II Samuel 8-12

David stood for justice. He was a just man, and he was My servant. But in this one thing he did evil by having Uriah, another good and loyal servant, killed to cover up his own misdeeds. This made Me angry. I was displeased, as I always am at this kind of injustice and deception, especially in leaders whom I have designated to rule. Whenever rulers reign by taking advantage of those beneath them and use their power for evil purposes by squelching and obliterating the lives of any who stand in their way, they usurp and overturn their own power and authority.

David's straying from Me in the matter of Bathsheba paved a way for chaos, bitterness, sadness, and discord in his own family. Though I forgave his "missing the mark" when he repented, the consequences of this sin followed him throughout the rest of his life.

Bathsheba's second son, Solomon, was known as Jedidiah, "beloved of the Lord," by Nathan the prophet and others. Though he came after a sinful situation, he was loved by Me, because I loved David. And I chose Solomon to reign after his father. Do you see My great mercy and grace here, as in so many situations, like those with Rahab, Ruth, and Tamar, who were Christ's ancestors?

Though people miss the mark and stray from Me, as in the case of the Apostle Paul, if they come to Me with all their hearts for forgiveness, I will always take them back. And I will always make good from evil. Think of the prodigal son.

I did this for David. Even though he rejected My will this time, he still recognized all I had done for him: I had anointed him as king and delivered him from Saul and given him his master's house and property and wives. He knew he had sinned, and he repented for having taken what was not rightfully his from another. Whenever a leader does evil secretly and tries to hide it deceptively, I will always make it known publicly, because I expect more from those who stand for Me. They are held to a higher standard. I allow rulers to reign if they are just and fair.

If not, they will be dethroned and replaced by those who are.

Day 87

Your bitterest enemies and best allies

"We must all die; we are like water spilled on the ground, which cannot be gathered up again. And God does not take away life, but devises means so that he who is banished may not be an utter outcast from Him."
—*II Samuel 14:14*

II Samuel 13-15

David's sons caused him and Me great consternation. This was because they submitted to others' manipulation and their own deception. Instead of trusting in Me, as David did, for a needful end, Amnon and Absalom gave into their own or others' foolish counsel. When people rely on those who don't follow Me and have their own agendas, they open themselves up to terrible consequences that harm themselves and others and often result in death. I detest falsehood and manipulation of any kind.

One of the wisest people in the affair of Absalom was the woman of Tekoah. She spoke the truth and gave insight into how I work, even in death, to devise ways and means so that the banished are not utter outcasts. During any crisis, the traitors and loyalists are always eventually revealed. David, like Christ later, was betrayed by one close to him—one he had taken into his inner circle of friendship and fellowship. And both David and Jesus prayed for their lives on the Mount of Olives.

Though some conspired against David, some also stuck with him. And the faithful ones included the least likely and most unexpected, like Ittai the Gittite and Hushai the Archite. It is always this way. The ones who come through for you in a crisis will be the people you never imagined to rise up to the occasion.

Because David turned to Me, I gave him a way to overcome an evil situation by sending the ark and the priests back to Jerusalem to "hold down the fort." Hushai would return to counsel Absalom in David's favor, with the purpose being to overturn the words of David's betrayer, Ahithophel, who had once been his "familiar friend in whom I trusted, who ate my bread" (Psalm 41:9). "For it is not an enemy who reproaches and taunts me—then I might bear it," he wrote in Psalm 55:12-14. "But it was you, a man my equal, my companion and familiar friend. We had sweet fellowship together and used to walk to the house of God in company." He had lost his closest friend when Jonathan died, and now he was betrayed by another.

Your bitterest enemies are often those who were your closest friends or family members.

Day 88

When people turn against you

"It may be that the Lord will look on the iniquity done me and
will recompense me with good for his cursing this day."
—II Samuel 16:12

II Samuel 16-18

Some people will lie to attain your favor. This is because they see how blessed you are, and they want your blessing in their lives. Others will falsely accuse you to justify their own lack of favor. Either way, My hand is on your life, and My good will prevail. Some may try to usurp your grace, but remember, My grace can never be taken away by anyone.

Ziba tried to make Mephibosheth look bad and himself the faithful "good guy" to David. It was a ploy that backfired in the end. Shimei accused David of killing Saul and his sons—something that never took place. People will believe what they want to. Others will try to usher in justice by seeking vengeance for you. But this is My job! David understood this and realized that only I can bring good from evil. Ahithophel was a type of Judas and turned against David, who had relied on his counsel and claimed him as a close friend and confidante within his inner circle. When he betrayed David, he paved a path to his own demise. Like Judas, his council came to nothing, and his advice was ignored by others. Both lives ended when they realized they had betrayed themselves. Though David was in a place of great vulnerability, some still had the courage to show up and help him. Shobi, an Ammonite, Machir, from lowly Lo-debar, and Barzillai, the 80-year-old Gileadite, jeopardized their own lives by taking actions that could be interpreted as treasonous if Absalom succeeded as king. They bravely helped David and his followers by bringing them food and supplies. In your own life, when all seems lost, and you end up in a place far from where you intended to be, some will come through for you as arms of My love extended toward you. And these ones will be those whom you least expected to show up.

Absalom's hair represented his glory, and by this he was caught up in an oak or pistacia tree. This tree, with its extensive root system, represents My solitary strength and power.* Absalom was great in his own eyes, but My greatness supplanted his when he was caught up by his "glory" in the tree! When David faced Goliath, it was in the Valley of Elah. Elah is the Hebrew word for the pistacia tree. So, it was in the Valley of the Pistacia that one who trusted Me overcame a giant and accomplished My purposes.

Here again, a tree stood for My greatness and how My good would prevail for My people through those who trusted Me to move them away from the evil intent of others.

Day 89

Honor comes from Me

"And Ziba, the servant of the house of Saul, and his fifteen sons and twenty servants with him, rushed to the Jordan and pressed quickly into the king's presence."
—II Samuel 19:17

II Samuel 19-21

Some will mock you, and some will whisper against you. Those who scream the loudest, because they resent, even hate, your position of honor, will press in with the most fervor to be the first to sing your praises when they fear the consequences of their former behavior toward you. One day, those who manipulate to gain access to your favor, because they seek their own self-preservation, will cower before Me.

People will dispute your right to be honored and cause great disruption by seeking equal honor, thinking they deserve it. I bequeath honor to those I choose to carry out My will. I select those who are open to My voice and have the courage or fearlessness to carry out My wishes. Others will be angry when they aren't chosen. Let them be angry!

The people I seek for My pursuits are those with clean hearts. I look for people who are free from rage and jealousy and more concerned for the welfare of others than attaining what they think they deserve—their own "rights." Those who live to be honored and praised will never be praised and honored by Me or chosen for My special purposes.

David's reign would be controversial today. But he sought Me in his choices and came to Me in matters regarding his kingdom. This is what I loved about him. He sought justice.

Why did he have the seven sons of Saul hung? Because this was the price that had to be paid to spare the lives of many others. A vow had been broken when Saul killed the Gibeonites, with whom Joshua had made a pact. Saul sought to impress the people more than to obey My will. He broke many covenants that had been made with Me. His deflection of My will caused great harm to My people, who served under him. When leaders given great authority and power over others break their vows, or the godly vows of their predecessors, they open doors to droughts, famines, starvation, and heartache.

But when one comes to Me, and seeks to repair what has been broken, I will always carve out a way for that person to lead many far from destruction and hardship.

Day 90

David sang Me a song

"The God of Israel spoke, the Rock of Israel said to me, When one rules over men righteously, ruling in the fear of God, he dawns on them like the morning light when the sun rises on a cloudless morning, when the tender grass springs out of the earth through clear shining after rain."
—II Samuel 23:3-4

II Samuel 22-24

In his last words, the sweet psalmist of Israel described how he saw Me as his Lord:
—He delivers you from all your enemies.
—He is your Rock, Fortress, and Deliverer.
—He is your Shield and Horn of Salvation.
—He is your Stronghold, Refuge, and Savior.
—He is ever worthy of your praise.
—He hears your cries for help.
—He is seen by you on the wings of the wind.
—He makes darkness His canopy over you.
—He hears you, even during chaos and catastrophe.
—He sends forth brightness amid darkness.
—He uncovers the foundations of the world for you to see.
—He draws you out of overwhelming situations.
—He brings you into a large place by enlarging your capabilities.
—He rewards you for your uprightness.
—He shows Himself loving and loyal when you are loving and loyal.
—He shows Himself upright and blameless when you are upright and blameless.
—He shows Himself pure or willful when you are pure or willful.
—He delivers the afflicted.
—He brings down the haughty.
—He helps you run through a troop and leap over a wall.
—He guides the blameless and sets them free.
—He makes your feet like hinds' feet, setting you up securely and confidently.
—He trains you to fight successfully against any enemy.
—He enlarges your steps, so your feet never slip from high places.
—He turns His back on those who hate you.
—He delivers you from strife.
—He executes vengeance and delivers you from violence.
—He shows loving-kindness to His anointed ones.

$\mathcal{D}ay\ 91$

The significance of Gihon Springs

*"The king told them, Take the servants of your lord and cause Solomon my son
to ride on my own mule and bring him down to Gihon [in the Kidron Valley].
And let Zadok the priest and Nathan the prophet anoint him there king
over Israel. Then blow the trumpet and say, Long live King Solomon!"*
—I Kings 1:33-34

I Kings 1-2

Solomon was anointed as King of Israel in Gihon. The springs there were the only source
of water for the City of David. They flowed at the base of the Kidron Valley, which runs
north and south between the eastern wall of the city and the Mount of Olives. David once
crossed this valley weeping and fleeing from his son Absalom. One day, Jesus would cross it
on the way to the Mount of Olives, where he would pray before his own betrayal. Known
later as the Valley of Jehoshaphat, it was the "valley where Yahweh shall judge." Solomon
built My temple over the springs, which served as a "stream of living water" and fed the Pool
of Siloam, where Jesus would one day heal a blind man. The Prince of Peace will return one
day as judge to this valley and reopen the Eastern Gate of Jerusalem. And, later, when the
new city comes to replace the old one on earth, an eternal stream of living water will flow
from His throne and give life to all.[1]

Adonijah called anyone who would follow him to come to the Stone of Zoheleth,
beside the well of En-rogel. The stone was called the "stone of serpents," the root of the
name meaning to "crawl" or "steal on."[2] Adonijah tried to supplant the throne meant
for Solomon. The En-rogel's well, called the "fuller's fountain," was a place where fullers
or washers stamped with their feet on the rock the clothes they washed in the well.[3] It
represented people's attempts to make themselves clean and, in this case, their dishonor of
the true Rock. Well water is limited to the well's container and can leak out if there are cracks
in the sides. A spring, like that in Gihon, can give limitless living water, depending on its
source.

The Cherethites and Pelethites were Philistine clans,[4] who served as David's bodyguards
during his reign. They were loyal to the king, unlike Shimei, who cursed David. When people
turn against My anointed ones, especially in times of their greatest need, it is to their own
detriment.

*David's last words to his son were: "Keep the charge of the Lord your God, walk in His ways,
keep His statutes, His commandments, His precepts, and His testimonies...that you may do
wisely and prosper in all that you do and wherever you turn."*

Day 92

What Solomon asked for

*"So give Your servant an understanding mind and a hearing heart to
judge Your people, that I may discern between good and bad.
For who is able to judge and rule this Your great people?"*
—*I Kings 3:9*

I Kings 3-5

I promised to give him whatever he desired. I do this for all who call on Me. I look to see what your deepest desire is, then I work with you to achieve it, as long as it fits with My will. But to attain what you want takes great trust and persistence on your part, before it can come to pass. Solomon persisted in claiming what I promised him: an understanding mind and a hearing heart to be able to judge My people justly and discern between good and evil. As a result, I gave him a discerning mind, but also riches and honor, because his request pleased Me. If he continued to walk with Me and kept My statutes and commandments, he was also promised a long and fulfilling life.

Because I gave him exceptional wisdom and understanding, and "breadth of mind like the sand on the seashore," his wisdom excelled that of all people, and many came from throughout the world to hear him. He reigned between 1100 and 900 BC, and his kingdom extended from the Euphrates River to Egypt's border. Today, it would include much of Syria, parts of Lebanon and Jordan, and all of Israel and Palestine. It would extend as far south as Aqaba. He secured all this land and had peace with all nations, which was quite a feat in his day and in any time.

Can leaders today lead with this kind of wisdom? Yes. But they must desire and ask for it, as Solomon did. Most rulers gain power through manipulation and deceit. Using their own skills and abilities to win people's hearts with deluding words, they acquire power for themselves and their own purposes. This kind of control can never last and leads to division, destruction, and death.

The only power that can last is God-given. The reigns of those who lead with My help and direction are established, because I know they will serve the people with My purposeful insight. Solomon was "one of a kind," but that doesn't mean that others can't be like him. Those who want a lasting reign must ask for My wisdom.

And I will give it to them freely.

Day 93

Each part of the temple meant something...

"Concerning this house which you are building, if you will walk in My statutes,
execute my precepts, and keep all My commandments to walk in them, then
I will fulfill to you My promises which I made to David your father."
—I Kings 6:12

I Kings 6-7

It had been 480 years since the Israelites came out of Egypt. During all that time, they worshipped in a temporary structure—the tabernacle. Now, finally, Solomon, at David's request, built a more permanent structure for My worship. The temple was 90 feet long, 30 feet wide, and 45 feet high. It was beautifully designed to honor Me. But, I made it clear, I would dwell among the Israelites and never depart from them if they did not forsake Me. They must walk in My statutes, execute My precepts, and keep My commandments. Then I could fulfill My promises to David, their ancestors, and to them.

The cedar used to build the temple represented Me in many ways. The roots of the cedar tree went very deep. Its height reached high to the heavens, and its branches extended to great width. It was the tree of choice because of its strength, beauty, and durability.[1] Its wonderful fragrance signified My desire for those rooted in Me to have a sweet balminess. Inside the temple, the wood was decorated with carvings of gourds and opened flowers. In the "abode of the life-giver," the blooming flowers symbolized fullness of life.[2] The gourd was a sacred symbol for the Hebrews and represented new life and the sun rising in the east.[3] This plant sheltered Jonah at a time of great need in his life, and it showed new life for the people of Nineveh after they repented. The palm trees carved into the walls displayed peace and victory that resulted from justice and uprightness.[4]

The Holy of Holies measured 30 feet long, wide, and high. It was overlaid with pure gold, representing earthly riches and My incorruptibility. Standing for something of great value, it also symbolized the value of worshipping Me.[5] The two cherubim in the Holy of Holies were made of olive wood, which signified My Spirit among the people.[6] Olive oil from this tree was used for anointing. The cherubim stood 15 feet high, and each of their wings measured seven-and-a-half feet long. They were overlaid with pure gold. It took seven years to build the temple; the number seven signifies perfection. Even as near perfect as this magnificent building was meant to be, it could not last.

A permanent house would replace it later through the work of My Son among the people.

Day 94

Why I had to dwell in darkness

"Then Solomon said, The Lord said that He would dwell in the thick darkness."
—I Kings 8:12

I Kings 8-9

Solomon's temple could never contain Me. Even the heavens cannot hold Me. There is no God like Me in the heavens or on earth. Only My Name and the token of My presence were there—in the temple.

But I hearken to the prayers of My people and forgive their trespasses. Even now, I justify the righteous and reward every person according to his or her standing with Me. When you are struck down by your enemies, and you ask for My help, I hear and forgive and bring you back to your rightful place, even after others have stolen what was justly yours.

I can open the heavens and give you needed rain when there is none. I can shut up the heavens to prevent a flood. I can teach you how to walk with Me each and every day. When famine, pestilence, sickness, or death besieges you, and you reach up to Me, I always hear you. I hear in heaven, and I forgive and give to every person according to his or her heart toward Me. And only I know the hearts of all people. My desire is that every person revere and worship only Me all their days. I want all people in every land on earth to know My Name, understand My presence, and look up to Me. I can defend the cause and maintain the rights of those who do.

When you are lured away, or captured by the enemy, and you turn to Me with all your heart and pray to Me, you will be delivered and forgiven. I hear your prayers. I am a compassionate and merciful God. My eyes and ears are always open to you. Like Solomon, reach up your hands to Me and receive My abundance, which I reserve for you. I will maintain and defend your cause and your rights. Only I can do this.

Why does a good God like me, Who lives in light, dwell in darkness or a cloud? Moses and the Israelites discovered the reason: I cannot reveal Myself fully to people, for, if I did, they would die. So, I must remain hidden, obscured. That is why My Son had to come as a human—to reveal My true nature and Who I am.

I promised that My eyes and heart would be at the temple perpetually.

One day, My presence will return to it, when My Son once again reveals himself there.

99

Day 95

Solomon's "Camelot" years

"So King Solomon exceeded all the kings of the earth in riches and in wisdom (skill)."
—I Kings 10:23

I Kings 10-11

Solomon's wisdom was connected to his living alongside Me. Many came to ask him questions about life, because they heard about his sovereign ability to answer them. The Queen of Sheba was one of those who came.

Sheba was a region in Ethiopia, once called Saba. In this land of the Sabeans, the queen's Kingdom of Axum,[1] "Sheba" meant "oath,"[2] and she came to see and prove Solomon's wisdom for herself. What she ended up experiencing left her feeling breathless and overwhelmed. Why? Because she'd never seen a kingdom like this one. No one had. It was, for a time, a place of goodness and plenty, while Solomon reigned with My wisdom. Did I know he would one day betray Me? Yes. But, during the "Camelot" years, he executed justice and righteousness, and I rewarded him for this. Kingdoms like his often do not last. Why? Because leaders, lured by the pleasures of this world, fall far from Me. All people fail at some point in their lives. But I see the goodness in their hearts and reward them accordingly. Though I knew Solomon would fall prey to the deceit of other gods, and even worship them to please his wives, I worked alongside him for many years. Though I knew his son would not heed his ancestors, or the wisdom of his father's counselors, and sacrifice most of the kingdom to pride, I blessed Solomon for the righteous years of his reign. During those blessed years, everyone in his kingdom prospered.

Solomon collected 666 talents of gold in one year. What was the significance of this? The antichrist's identifying number is 666. The strikingness is simple: the antichrist will be a "type" of Solomon, noted worldwide for his "great wisdom." But, in the end, he will use his reign, as Solomon did, for his own aggrandizement and purposes. He will be a global despot, eventually enslaving many people. There were six steps to Solomon's throne. This number connoted man's glory and honor and fame. He brought horses from Egypt, multiplied his wives, and accumulated gold and silver. All these practices were warned against in Deuteronomy 17, because I knew they would turn a person's heart and mind away from Me. As Solomon clung to a greater degree to his earthly props, his reign became more elusive, and My Spirit departed from him.

Rulers who reign apart from Me govern kingdoms that cannot last.

Day 96

When leaders fail to lead as servants

"And the king answered the people roughly and forsook the counsel the old men had given him."
—I Kings 12:13

I Kings 12-14

Jeroboam oversaw all the forced labor of the house of Joseph under Solomon. This "mighty man" saw the abuse of power and empathized with the people, who saw his courage when he stood up to the king for them. But Solomon did not relent of his extreme and harsh demands, and he watched as people began to follow Jeroboam, who "had their back." So, he sought to kill Jeroboam, who fled to Egypt. When Solomon died, Jeroboam returned to Israel and stood with the people, who wanted a king who would not treat them like a taskmaster.

Solomon's son, Rehoboam, inherited the kingdom. But he forsook the advice of his father's older and wiser counselors and favored the counsel of his inexperienced peers. Though Solomon's advisors told him to "be a servant to the people," and they would be loyal and "serve him forever," he chose his friends' advice, which appealed to his pride. "My little finger shall be thicker than My father's loins," he announced. "I will chastise you with scorpions!" He reveled in this tough and manly, but not godly, response to his people's plea.

When leaders forsake their role as servants to the people and are lured in by the worldly "chatter" of their peers, which appeals to their pride, they always end up losing their role as leader. People eventually rebel against despots and tyrants, who try to use them for their own means, with no concern for their welfare.

Rehoboam foolishly lost his kingdom, which had been built and developed through the prayers and efforts of his forefathers—all except for the tribes of Judah and Benjamin. The other Israelites "went to their tents" as nomads who must govern themselves. Their new leader, Jeroboam, quickly forsook his calling by acting out of fear. Afraid of losing his people's loyalty to him as king, he set up false gods on the hills of Israel, so they would not need to return to Jerusalem for worship. Like Saul, he distrusted Me to be able to help him maintain what he had been given.

As a result of fear, he lost his kingship.

Day 97

What makes a blameless heart?

"Asa's heart was blameless with the Lord all his days."
—I Kings 15:14

I Kings 15-17

What does it mean for a heart to be blameless before Me? Does it mean a person must always be perfect? No. David was a good example of one who was without blame, because "he did what was right in My eyes and turned not aside from anything I asked of him all the days of his life." Was he perfect? No. In the matter of Bathsheba's husband, Uriah, he strayed away from Me. But he came back to Me and asked for forgiveness, and I forgave him, though he suffered some consequences later.

Being blameless means following Me and not other gods. In the case of Asa, it meant putting away the gods others had raised up and worshipped, including his own mother's god. He rededicated what was holy to Me, and he restored My temple.

What if people acknowledge Me, even pray to Me, yet they never carry out what I ask them to do? What if they procrastinate and "drag their feet," never actually obeying My call? It's the same as disobedience, or walking away from Me, because they refrain from doing what I called them to do, and distrust becomes their idol. Fear of consequences is their god.

Israel's King Omri bought a hill from Shemer for two talents of silver. He built a city there and called it Samaria. Here, his son Ahab reigned after him for 22 years over Israel. With his wife, Jezebel, he served and worshipped Baal, and he erected an altar and a house for this god. He also made an idolatrous symbol of the goddess Asherah and led all of Israel to worship her in Samaria. He did more to provoke My anger than all the kings before him.

What makes Me mad or sad? The worship of and service to other gods made with human hands, who can never hear or help you. Why do you think the people in lands where they worship other gods suffer so much? It's because they bow down to idols they make and expect an answer, but never do!

I made you! I formed and created you through My Son!

Only I can deliver you or anyone who comes to Me!

Day 98

I am in the stillness

"And He said, Go out and stand on the mount before the Lord. And behold, the Lord passed by, and a great and strong wind rent the mountains and broke in pieces the rocks before the Lord, but the Lord was not in the wind; and after the wind an earthquake, but the Lord was not in the earthquake; and after the earthquake a fire, but the Lord was not in the fire; and after the fire [a sound of gentle stillness and] a still, small voice."
—I Kings 19:11-12

I Kings 18-20

In the days of darkest pain and suffering, one will always emerge to bring light out of the darkness. Elijah was such a one for Israel. He brought back a belief in Me when Israel was being ruled by wicked leaders. Queen Jezebel and the widow of Zarephath were both from Sidon. Jezebel refused to listen to Elijah, but the widow heard and prospered. Why would I allow a severe famine to devastate a land? Do I cause this? Never. It comes because of people turning away from Me to other gods. And the ungodly will always blame those faithful to Me for earthly calamities. What does it mean to "limp?" Why did Elijah use this term to describe the Baal worshippers? It means "to lack firmness, substance, structure, lacking vitality, weary, tired, exhausted."[1] Elijah told the Baal worshippers at Mount Carmel that they "limp between two opinions"—a belief in Me and a devotion to idols. He told their prophets that they "limped about their altar." When people worship anything but Me, they "limp about," because they lack direction, purpose, substance, structure, and a firm belief. They end up exhausted and spent, having no vitality, because their gods can never help them. "Cry louder!" Elijah told the Baal worshippers. "Maybe your god is asleep or on a trip! Maybe that's why he can't hear you!" People harm themselves trying to get the attention of those they worship falsely.

Elijah was a man who had confidence in Me. He had seen My work and heard My voice. He knew I could save and gave Me the glory for it. "He is God! The Lord. He is God!" he shouted. "Wake up, people!" But like any man, Elijah also had feelings. He fled after slaying the false prophets of Baal, who'd brought evil to a whole nation. From fear of Jezebel's threats, he sat under a broom tree. Why? Because the white broom tree has a broad canopy that stands for renewal and restoration. Its flowers emit a honey fragrance, and its branches are perfect for kindling. The embers from it retain heat and provide a warm layer under sand as a mattress on cold desert nights.[2] Elijah knew and heard Me. He also saw that I am not in the storm or the earthquake or the fire or famine.

I am the still, small voice that seeks your heart continually, and Elijah experienced this.

Day 99

When wicked rulers seek power

"For there was no one who sold himself to do evil in the sight
of the Lord as did Ahab, incited by his wife Jezebel."◻
—*I Kings 21:25*

I Kings 21-22

"There was no one *who sold himself to do evil in the sight of the Lord as did Ahab, incited by his wife Jezebel."* Ahab went after idols like those I'd cast out before the Israelites. Do you see how Jezebel, who bowed down to other gods, schemed and incited her husband to commit evil acts as Israel's ruler? You may see the same in your lifetime.

Women were created to help others by inspiring them to righteousness by following Me. They were never meant to lead others to corruption, as Jezebel did. She had many righteous men murdered under her realm to serve her purposes—her own agenda of idolatry. She set up false witnesses to destroy people in her schemes for power. She contrived means to promulgate lies against just and good men to accomplish what she desired. She led a whole nation, including her husband, to worship false gods. The result? A nation in decline, reduced to poverty and lacking resources. Her own husband ended up losing his life and his reign, and a sentence was pronounced against them both.

King Ahab built an ivory palace for himself while he was alive. He also built many cities in Israel. But his reign, and that of his sons, did not last. The rule of ungodly kings and queens never does. When leaders worship something besides Me, they lose whatever power they were once given.

You see corruption around you even now: undeserving people seeking power, control, fame, or riches, which are their gods. As they gain control over people, they cause havoc, corruption, and upheaval. They pit one group against another, like Jezebel, who promoted her gods and killed anyone who opposed her beliefs and desires. So, those who sought Me had to hide, and My prophets lived in caves during Ahab's reign.

But I always release My people from this kind of bondage, and I give just due to evil leaders.

Day 100

I love those who stand for Me

*"When the sons of the prophets who were [watching] at Jericho saw
him, they said, The spirit of Elijah rests on Elisha, And they came
to meet him and bowed themselves to the ground before him."*
—II Kings 2:15

II Kings 1-3

Tishbe lies along the Brook Cherith, where I fed Elijah for many days during a famine. It is east of Jabesh-gilead and the Jordan River, about 22 miles southeast of the Sea of Galilee. It was Elijah's hometown.

I love those, like Elijah, who stand for Me against all odds! I love people who bind themselves hand and foot to My Word and what I represent. Was it easy for Elijah to stand against 50 men, who came to seize and destroy him? No. Of course not. He was afraid. He was a man—a person like you. But he trusted Me for help and guidance. What about you? Are you afraid of people and what they might do to you? Do you fear them more than Me? If you do, then you are bound to them tooth and nail and you must serve them and your fearfulness. But, if you are more in awe of Me, and what I can do, you're free to live and to love on the earth. And you're separated from peoples' phobias. You can exist as I meant you to live—with power and dignity and the rights I've given you. But you must choose.

Elijah was more in awe of Me, as was Elisha, his successor, who requested a double portion of Elisha's spirit. He proved himself to others by listening to My words and speaking them out. And My words always proved to be true. So, people followed him. The proof of any prophet is "Do his or her words prove true?" And what signs and wonders follow him or her for the good of many?

Do you see how godly music can minister to people's souls and open doors to Me and My voice? It worked for Elisha and helped Saul during periods of moroseness, when he called David to play the harp for him. Elijah and Elisha had My heart to help all people live bountifully, free from sickness, lack, even death. This included women and children.

My heart has always been the same, and I love to work through those who trust Me to deliver others from whatever burdens them.

Day 101

It is well

"Run to meet her and say, Is it well with you? Well with your husband? Well with the child? And she answered, It is well."
—II Kings 4:26

II Kings 4-5

Why don't you see the same kind of miracles today that Elisha performed? It's simple. People like Elisha are few and far between. What sort of men were Elisha and Elijah? They were God-fearing, completely trusting individuals, who never wavered from the truth and spoke it boldly. In your lifetime, you may never see such people, because most people have too many doubts and fears and cannot trust Me completely. They have skepticism of one form or another.

When a solid man or woman of God arises and walks the earth, turning his or her face totally to Me, with all his or her heart, mind, and soul, then you will see signs, miracles, and wonders. You'll see people raised from death, the starving fed in famines, and people lacking wholeness healed of death-inflicting diseases.

Another aspect of the availability of miracles is the ability of men and women to receive and believe what seems to be impossible. The Shunammite woman rode over 20 miles nonstop to Mount Carmel to implore Elisha for the life of her son, because she believed he could raise him from death. Why did she think he could do this? Because she saw the fulfillment of his promise in her son's birth. Without her trust, the man of God could not have performed this miracle. She received what she desired, because she refused to acknowledge anything less than her son's resurrection, and she continued to confess that "It is well."

Elisha did as I told him. Complete obedience is necessary for a sign, miracle, or wonder to occur. Did the child rise right away? No. It took several tries before he received the needed breath of life. Elisha had learned from Elijah that he must listen to and obey My voice. And persistence played a part in it. Remember how Elijah prayed seven times for rain? When Elisha fed 100 prophets with very little food, he set a precedent for One later, Who would feed multitudes in the same way. Some, like Naaman, might think that healing must come suddenly with a demonstration of power. But this is not how healing works. It usually comes in the quiet moments with Me, as you bow your head in a prayer closet and ask Me in your own way for My help.

And when I tell you what to do to receive it, you must do as Naaman and obey My voice.

Day 102

I strategically place people to help you

"When the king of Israel saw them, he said to Elisha, My father, shall I slay them? Shall I slay them? [Elisha] answered, You shall not slay them. Would you slay those you have taken captive with your sword and bow? Set bread and water before them, that they may eat and drink and return to their master."
—II Kings 6:21-22

II Kings 6-8
Elisha lived in Dothan, 10 miles north of Samaria. From there, he predicted the king of Syria's every move. Today, I still show the people of a nation, who will listen to Me, how to avoid conflict. When evil befalls a land, people often blame Me and those who serve Me, instead of seeking the truth as to why they are living in despair and disparity. This happens because they've turned away from Me. When they question or doubt the words of those who speak the truth, they always suffer the consequences. Elisha warned people of what would come and how to avoid the outcomes, and his words always came to pass. When he alerted them of impending doom, those who listened were spared. And he was able to lead them to life, as in the case of the king feeding the Syrian soldiers instead of killing them, thus preventing further harm to his own people. The Shunammite woman avoided lack by moving away from her land during a famine, as Elisha suggested.

I will always strategically place people in situations to help them avoid unnecessary pain or lack. See how I placed Gehazi before the King of Israel, just at the time the Shunammite woman returned from Philistia to reclaim her land? Not only was she granted her request, but she was also given provisions to replace what she had lost during her years of separation.

Evil, or good, can pass to future generations. What is taught by parents can become their children's way of life for good or for evil. But I always honor My commitments, even when people turn away from Me. Though the kings of Judah drifted far from Me into the sins of Ahab, I fulfilled My promise to David—that I would give him and his sons a lamp forever. His lineage would continue until the Messiah could come to save His children.

People may not keep their promises, but I always will. When you drift from Me in your thoughts and actions, I am ever ready to bring you back to Me and to fulfill My promise to give you a full and meaningful life of abundance.

Even when you think yourself unworthy, I give My gifts to you freely, because I love you.

Day 103

Reigns of chaos

"Jehu paid no attention to walking in the law of the Lord, the God of Israel, with all his heart. He did not quit the sins with which Jeroboam made Israel to sin."
—II Kings 10:31

II Kings 9-10

This is what the reigns of ungodly men look like! They are filled with chaos, confusion, disloyalty, treachery, and deceit. Even those set up as guardians for the king's sons failed in their responsibility, because they were afraid. These "great men" of Israel were selected for their wisdom, yet they crumbled under pressure. Acting like brute beasts, they beheaded their own charges, because they felt threatened! That is why Jehu felt justified in killing them, but his murdering ways did not stop there. They never do.

I am always pleased when people turn and stand for Me against idols and against all odds. I am the One Who created you and all that you see before you. No other god could do this! I desire your love and loyalty, and I want to have a relationship with you.

That is why I needed to send My Son as My Advocate for you. I wanted the needless killing to stop. I wanted people to see My heart for them, a way to approach Me, and My purpose for them—a life lived in peace. But, even now, leaders bring others to corruption and life lived apart from Me, which always ends in death for many.

Jehu fulfilled My prophecy, and he rid the nation of those who had long led Israel away from Me to idols. But then he himself moved away from what I desired most for him and his descendants. This happens often. A leader to whom I have given the right to lead others from what causes great harm to a nation will grow in self-importance and end up lusting after power, control, or greed. They often replace Me with gods who represent and encourage corruption. They delude themselves, thus ending their right to reign.

Where is your heart today? Do you seek My face and favor? Do you acknowledge Me, the God of Light and Life, in all you do?

Do you act and speak in ways that glorify Me, or another?

Day 104

Why a grandmother killed her descendants

"When Athaliah the mother of [King] Ahaziah [of Judah] saw that her son was dead, she arose and destroyed all the royal descendants."
—II Kings 11:1

II Kings 11-14

What would cause a mother, or a grandmother, to kill off her own descendants? Why would Athaliah do this? Can you imagine? Yet it occurred and has been done before and since. People driven by an insatiable lust for power—to rule and control the lives of others—may be motivated to murder members of their own family, even their own children. They are usually being controlled by demon spirits, whose purpose is to fulfill the command of their leader, the devil, which is to steal, kill and destroy. These spirits lead people to act unnaturally in the face of certain circumstances. They drive people away from a desire to love and nurture others with a lust for power or greed.

Joash was faithful to Me all the days Jehoiada the priest instructed him. He made sure the money offered—all except that meant to support the priests—was used to rebuild My temple. This was his passion. And for this I honored him. Was it right for him to give the king of Syria all the hallowed things in the temple, including the treasury gold, to appease him? No. My desire is always that leaders trust Me to help them, as David did. Joash's fear of reprisal by the Syrian king led him to do this. It also led to his death.

I wanted the kings of Israel and Judah to remove the idols from their lands. This was My deepest desire. But many would not. Why? Because, like Saul, they feared the people more than Me. Whenever a king or a leader is more concerned about what people think of them than what I think, their leadership fails. It takes great courage to lead as I direct, and few people have the fortitude to do it. Men like Elijah and Elisha were rare individuals who did not fear people as much as Me, and they spoke the truth with less concern for reprisal.

Why did Amaziah, who tried to reign righteously, end up lured into a fight against the king of Israel? It was because of his pride. I did not want this for him. I even warned him.

When men or women refuse to listen to or heed My warnings, and they submit to their own pride or lust for power, they always suffer deadly consequences.

Day 105

Some will listen

"When he was 25 years old, he began his reign of 16 years in Jerusalem. His mother was Jerusha daughter of Zadok. He did right in the Lord's sight, according to all his father Uzziah had done."
—*II Kings 15:33-34*

II Kings 15-17

Whenever a king rebuilt or restored parts of My temple, I rejoiced! Jerusalem is the place of My Son's return to earth, when He will stand as King of Kings in the temple. Though many of Judah's kings failed to remove the high places of idol worship, due to resistance from the people, I was pleased to see when some magnified My place of worship. Jotham built the Upper Gate, which symbolized a greater way into My presence.

King Jotham ruled Judah around 742 BC. His name means "God is perfect" or "God is complete," and he followed My ways. He recognized the importance of serving Me by observing his father, Uzziah, also called Azariah. Uzziah had lived an almost perfect life, but, toward the end of his reign, he became proud and decided he had the right to burn incense on the altar. This was to be done only by the priests. When the officiating priest reproved him, Uzziah wouldn't listen and responded with anger. As a result, he became leprous and lived outside of his own kingdom until he died. Because of what happened to his father, Jotham never entered the temple during his time of power.

While his father was alive, Jotham helped him rule the land. As king himself, after Uzziah's death, Jotham lived during the time of the prophets: Isaiah, Hosea, Amos, and Micah. He listened to their messages, and his reign was influenced by them. Though he tried to obey My commands, the people would not heed him or Me, no matter how much he tried to do what was right. I faulted the people and not the king for this. I blessed him with power, because he was personally obedient to Me. I often send a righteous leader to lead people back to My ways, but they may reject his words and his leadership. When this happens, I can bless the leader, but not those who oppose him or her.

Jotham's son Ahaz rejected his father's words and beliefs by going after Syrian gods. He even sacrificed his own son to them! He denigrated My temple by building an altar to another god. He also operated out of fear, instead of trusting in Me. Because he, and Israel, moved away from Me in their hearts to idols brought in from other nations, I removed Israel from My sight. Many were taken captive by Assyria.

This was the first of many diasporas.

Day 106

How I loved Hezekiah!

"Hezekiah trusted in, leaned on, and was confident in the Lord, the God of Israel; so that neither after him nor before him was any one of all the kings of Judah like him."
—*II Kings 18:5*

II Kings 18-19

How I loved Hezekiah! Though his father Ahaz did not serve or worship Me, and Hoshea, king of Israel, never exemplified the kind of leader I wanted for My people, Hezekiah stood alone in his devotion to Me. He looked out to the examples of his forefathers, like David, Asa, Jehoshaphat, and Joash, and he "did right in the sight of the Lord." He began his reign at 25, and he ruled for 29 years in Jerusalem. He removed the high places of idol worship and leaned on Me for guidance all his days.

"Neither after him nor before him was any one of all the kings of Judah like him," because he never ceased to follow Me. And he prospered wherever he went.

When Hezekiah tried to appease the formidable king of Assyria, who had taken much of Israel captive, the evil leader sent representatives to taunt and threaten him, demanding more and more of him. These God-haters belittled My ability to help Hezekiah, even reproaching and defying Me, but Hezekiah responded to each threat by coming to Me. He leaned on Isaiah the prophet's help, and he heeded the advice of true men of God.

I will not stand to be mocked and insulted by people, no matter how much power they appear to have. I will always retaliate through and for those who come and stand for Me.

I love affronts like the one displayed by Sennacherib of Assyria, because then I can show My power and strength to the people. In Hezekiah's day, Sennacherib was viewed as a monstrous threat to the entire region, and few could withstand him. Hadn't he taken captive most of Israel?

Yet, Hezekiah came to Me and spread out the threats before Me. He prayed, "O Lord, the God of Israel, Who is enthroned above the cherubim, You are God, You alone, of all the kingdoms of the earth. You made the heavens and the earth.... Bow down Your ear and hear; Lord, open Your eyes and see...." He implored Me to "save us...that all the kingdoms of the earth may know and understand that You, O Lord, are God alone."

When people come to Me, like Hezekiah, I never refuse their requests. I want to prove Myself strong for them, and so I fight for them!

Day 107

Why do good and godly people suffer?

"Turn back and tell Hezekiah, the leader of My people, Thus says the Lord, the God of David your [forefather]: I have heard your prayer, I have seen your tears; behold, I will heal you. On the third day you shall go up to the house of the Lord."
—II Kings 20:5

II Kings 20-22

Why do I allow godly people like Hezekiah to suffer from deadly diseases? As he reminded Me, "I have walked before You in faithfulness and truth and with a whole heart entirely devoted to You and have done what is good in Your sight." Hezekiah wept bitterly when he understood his condition. And I heard his prayers and saw his tears, and I healed him, so he lived another 15 years—longer than he expected. I also delivered him and Judah out of the hand of enemies like the king of Assyria. Isaiah the prophet acted as an advocate for Hezekiah and pleaded for his life. He stood before Me as a messenger. Today, you have One Who will do this for you! Hezekiah wanted a sign as proof of his healing. What do you require? Hasn't it already been done through the work of My Son?

But why do I still allow good and faithful people to suffer? Because people live in a broken world that has become more and more adulterated by corruption that results from sin and separation from Me. Toxins have been introduced into your environment that never existed generations ago. Whose fault is this? Many make errors in judgment—decisions made in the moment that seem to profit them. Sometimes these choices are made at the direction of My enemy. Contrary to My purposes and desires, toxins negatively affect the lives of everyone, including "good" people, who become ill. But, like Hezekiah, people can come to Me for help. And they have a ready advocate in My Son, Who came to the world to heal them from sickness. But it takes trust and a desire to change for healing to occur. It also requires asking the One Who can give it.

The next two descendants of Hezekiah were evil, but then one arose who was good—Josiah. He walked in David's ways, and, like his forefather Jotham, he rebuilt My house and removed the idols. He received My words through Hilkiah the priest and Shaphan the scribe. His heart was humble, and I blessed him for this. He also heard the words of Huldah the prophetess and repented for the evil works of his ancestors. So I spared him from devastation. Remember that Huldah lived in the Second Quarter of the city.

And often you will find My most committed followers, not in the lavish "first quarters" of society but hidden in the second tiers.

$\mathcal{D}ay\ 108$

The zeal of a leader who lives My Word

"There was no king like him before or after [Josiah] who turned to the Lord with all his heart and all his soul and all his might, according to all the Law of Moses."
—II Kings 23:25

II Kings 23-25

When King Josiah heard the words of My covenant with Israel, he tore his mantle. He called together all the people and wanted them to hear them too. Then, he began his mission—to destroy all the objects used to worship Baal and Asherah. He burned them and spread their ashes over Bethel, where Israel's idolatry began. He broke down the houses of the cult prostitutes, who played a role in the worship of the fertility goddess Ashtoreth and served at the pleasure of the priests.[1] He got rid of the high places and altars devoted to Ashtoreth, Chemosh, and Milcom, and he removed their priests. He defiled Topheth, the "place of burning,"[2] a location in the Valley of Hinnom that surrounded the Old City and included Mount Zion, where worshippers, influenced by the Canaanites, sacrificed their children to the gods Molech and Baal by burning them alive.

After reading the Law, Josiah removed the horses and burned the chariots from Egypt, which were devoted to sun worship. The idolatrous altars on the roof of the king's chambers and in the courts of My temple were broken in pieces and made into dust. He even got rid of all the high places of idol worship in Samaria. In his eighteenth year of reign, Josiah reinstated Passover, which had not been celebrated since Samuel's time.

"There was no king like him before or after who turned to the Lord with all his heart and all his soul and all his might." Sadly, the kings who followed Josiah did not have his same heart or passion, and they ended up submitting to the dominions of other kings, because they did not continue in the ways of Josiah. How could I tolerate the worship of gods and systems that required the sacrifice of Israel's children to demons demanding their blood? I never can.

The Judean kings surrendered all that was devoted to Me to the king of Babylon, who worshipped other gods. They were taken captive, along with all of Jerusalem, except the poorest, to Babylon to serve kings like Nebuchadnezzar. The walls of My beloved Jerusalem, lovingly built by David and Solomon and others, were broken down and the people of the land suffered for many years as slaves to others.

All of this resulted from leaders not returning wholeheartedly to My ways, as Josiah had.

Day 109

What you teach your family matters

"The descendants of Salma: Bethlehem.... And the families of scribes who dwelt at Jabez: the Tirathites, Shimeathites, and Sucathites. These are the Kenites who came from Hammath, the father of the house of Rechab."
—*I Chronicles 2:54-55*

I Chronicles 1-3

Salma was the father and founder of Bethlehem. He was David's great, great grandfather, and the great, great, great grandson of Judah. What is the significance of ancestry? Why did My scribes devote so much space in My Word to it? Why should you pay attention to it? *Because it determines so very much about your life and the lives of others.*

Noah's three sons were Shem, Ham, and Japheth. From each one arose nations in different parts of the world.[1] Japheth's sons: Gomer, Magog, Madai, Javan, Tubal, Meshech and Tiras, were the ancestors of the European nations. From Gomer came the Cimmerians, who settled north of the Black Sea and populated Germany, France, Spain, and Britain. From Magog came the Scythians, who lived north of the Caspian Sea, and the Mongols, who populated east-central Asia. The Medes from Madai settled south of the Caspian Sea, and, from Javan, the Hebrew name for Greece, came the Ionians or Greeks. Tubal gave rise to the Turks, who lived south of the Black Sea. Meshech produced the Slavs, who lived between the Black and Caspian Seas and migrated north to Russia. From Tiras came the Etruscans, who first lived west of the Black Sea and were known as "sea people" by the Greeks, because they lived in lands near the ocean. They worshipped Tiras as their "god of thunder" and called him "Thor." He was associated with many nations, including Thrace, and the countries in today's Balkan Peninsula: Romania, Moldova, Bulgaria, eastern Greece, and western Turkey.

The descendants of Ham, whose name meant "hot" or "black" in Hebrew, migrated to Africa. They were Cush, Mizraim, Put, and Canaan. Cush, also meaning "black," is the ancestor of the dark-skinned Ethiopians. Early in their history, some of Cush's descendants migrated to an area north of the Persian Gulf. From them came Sheba and its queen, and Nimrod, who created a great kingdom that included Babel. A man of great stature, Nimrod's kingdom later extended into Assyria and included Nineveh. From Mizraim came the Egyptians, who settled in northeastern Africa. Put or Phut is the father of the Libyans, who settled in northern Africa and were known as great warriors.

The descendants of Canaan, the Canaanites, settled east of the Mediterranean in the lands of Phoenicia, Philistia, and Israel. They became the Sidonians, Hittites, Jebusites, Amorites, Girgashites, Hivites, Arkites, Sinites, Arvadites, Zemorites, and the Hathites, whom Israel rejected because of their systems of belief and idol worship.

Shem's five descendants were Elam, Asshur, Arphaxad, Lud, and Aram, from whom came five Semitic nations. From Elam came the Persians, who settled northeast of the Persian Gulf. Asshur produced the Assyrians, who lived between the Euphrates and the Tigris Rivers in today's northern Iraq, northeastern Syria, southeastern Turkey, and the northwestern edge of Iran. Arphaxad's people were the Babylonians, who settled in Chaldea, which corresponds to much of Iraq, all of Kuwait, and parts of northern Saudi Arabia, eastern Syria, southeastern Turkey, and regions along the Turkish-Syrian and Iran-Iraq borders. Through Arphaxad would come the Promised Seed. This would be by way of his grandson, Eber, meaning "ever," who was the father of the Hebrew people that included Abraham, Isaac, and Jacob. Lud's descendants were the Lydians, who settled in Asia Minor, now western Turkey. Some of them sailed across the Mediterranean and settled in northern Africa. And from Aram came the Syrians, who located north and east of Israel. Aramaic became the common language of the leading nations of the ancient world and was the language written and spoken by Jesus.

From Abraham and Isaac would come Esau and Jacob. Esau's descendants would include both enemies and friends of Israel, like the Amalekites and the children of Reuel. Known as a "friend of God," Reuel, or Jethro, was Moses' father-in-law and a Kenite from a clan of Midian.[2] Jacob would produce Reuben, Simeon, Levi, Judah, Dan, Naphtali, Gad, Asher, Issachar, Zebulun, Joseph, and Benjamin. Judah was the ancestor to the families of scribes who lived in Jabez, a place that became prominent among the Kenites, who embraced Judaism and became scribes and teachers of the Law. How were the borders of Jabez enlarged? The prayer of Jabez referred to his school there.[3] He desired that I bless him with many more disciples. As a result of his prayer, many Kenites and Rechabites, relatives of the Midianites, went to Jabez to learn the Torah from Jabez and his descendants.

Do you see how important the leanings of a tribe or a clan or a family can be to future generations? It's the same, even today. What you teach, and how you live now, determine how future generations live and if they survive and thrive. Ask yourself, are you leading your own family members to or away from Me?

What you do now matters for generations to come!

Day 110

What genealogy means to you

"All these were enrolled by genealogies in the days of Jotham
king of Judah and in the days of Jeroboam [II] king of Israel."
—*I Chronicles 5:17*

I Chronicles 4-6

"And they had their genealogical record.... All were enrolled by genealogies...." Again, why was genealogy important to Me or to the rulers of Israel? Why should it be important to you? The leaders of Israel recorded it because they knew that family traits and strengths were carried on to future generations. They understood that relatives have similar capabilities.

In these records, it's not hard to see this. Look at the people of Geharashim—a valley of craftsmen. These were families skilled to work with their hands to bring beauty to the tabernacle, the temple, and the kingdom. The linen workers at Beth-ashben were families skilled in weaving beautiful tapestries, again for the service of the temple and tabernacle and for the king and the nation. Who were the potters, and the people of the plantations and hedges, in Netaim and Gedarah? The potters were sons of Shelah, from the tribe of Judah, who carried on this trade for the king. The "dwellers at plantations and hedges" were people skilled in farming and raising plants to use in the kingdom.

There is also mention of "mighty men of strength of mind and spirit." Some were great warriors, who fought for the king, served the nation in battle, and defended the land from invaders.

From the Levites came many who were skilled in music. Most renowned were: Heman, Samuel's grandson, a Kohathite, Asaph, a Gershonite, and Ethan or Jeduthun, a Merarite. From them came whole families of talented musicians, who played instruments and sang before the king and the people on holy days. When you see the Psalms of David, you also see how many were written and performed by these men, who led the nation in praise and worship of Me.

So, you can see why family lineage means so much! What are your strengths? From whom did you get them? What is your family most known for?

What did you inherit from your ancestors that you can use to serve the King?

$\mathcal{D}ay$ 111

Why do people die unjustly?

"And Ephraim their father mourned many days, and his brethren came to comfort him."
—I Chronicles 7:22

I Chronicles 7-9

Amid the lists of genealogical records stands one significant verse: "Ephraim their father mourned many days, and his brethren came to comfort him." What had happened? Two of Ephraim's sons, Ezer and Elead, were "slain by men of Gath...who had come down to steal the cattle."

Why did I want My scribes to include this verse, when the context was the ancestry of My people? I did because it shows My heart. Remember how Job lost all his children in one day and then mourned for many days with his friends, who came to comfort him? Lives mean something to Me, even those that are short-lived. All are precious to Me.

Though it seems unjust, and often people blame Me for the loss of parents or children or friends, it was never My heart or will that people die, especially prematurely. Why then does death, especially unjust death, happen? Because of what it says in the Scripture. It is often because people turn away from Me or fail to heed My warnings. Many times, people's selfish pursuits cause harm to others, including those who are godly. In this case, it was men of ill intent, who forsook Me to gain something illegitimately and unjustly—something that belonged to someone else.

People who steal don't trust Me for their provisions and usually take what they want or lust after from those who are good, who live righteous lives. Remember, in the case of Job, it was the Sabeans and Chaldeans who killed his servants and stole his camels. I did not cause the lightning or the whirlwind that killed his children. I am not a God of dearth, death, or destruction. These are caused by people or circumstances moved by evil forces that are directed by the god of this world, Satan, as Job explained.

Another verse stands out in this section: "Phinehas son of Eleazar was ruler over them [the keepers of the entrance to My house]...and the Lord was with him." Why was I with Phinehas? Because of his zeal for Me. When some Israelites defied Moses by initiating idolatrous practices in the camp, Phinehas stood for My honor, and that of Moses, and made atonement for the people, thereby saving many more from destruction.

As a result, I made an everlasting covenant with him, as I do with you when you take a stand for Me.

Day 112

What David required from his followers

*"All these, being men of war arrayed in battle order, came with a perfect
and sincere heart to Hebron to make David king over all Israel; and
all the rest also of Israel were of one mind to make David king."*
—I Chronicles 12:38

I Chronicles 10-12

What did David look for in his warriors? When men came to him in Hebron, before and after Saul was killed, he met them with this request: "If you have come peaceably to me to help me, my heart shall be knit to you; but if you have come to betray me to my adversaries, although there is no violence or wrong in my hands, may the God of our fathers look upon and rebuke you." Each person must make a pledge of peace and loyalty to him.

Today, leaders still look for this in their followers: Who will be loyal and trustworthy, and who will not? David's strength was his extraordinary ability to see into men's hearts. I saw his heart and chose him because of this. It was I Who taught him how to read others'. True leaders can do this.

Looking at David's list of warriors, it's easy to gloss over these "mighty men." But if you look closely, you'll see some patterns. Many were brothers, like Eleazar and Elhanan, Abishai and Asahel, Shama and Jeiel, Jediael and Joha, and Jeribai and Joshaviah. Other warriors came from the same city, as did Helez and Ahijah, Ilai, Eleazar and Elhanan, Maharia and Heled, Jonathan and Ahiam, and Ira and Gareb.

Interestingly, David included men from enemy tribes, like Zelek the Ammonite, Uriah the Hittite, Ithmah the Moabite, and Abiel the Arbathite. Why would he allow them to infiltrate his ranks? Because he could see their hearts and commitment. It didn't matter to David from where people came, as long as their hearts were pure and sincere.

Many came, even from Saul's tribe, to fight with David, and each tribe brought special talents. The Benjamites were great bowmen; the Gadites made great officers; those of Manasseh were courageous; Judah's men were skilled with spears and shields; Simeon's were brave warriors; and Issachar's had great understanding. Zebulun's men had experience as trustworthy troops; Naphtali's made good captains; Dan's were organized; and Asher's were able fighters.

All together, they brought peace and joy to Israel with their combined abilities.

Day 113

I loved David's zeal!

"Seek the Lord and His strength; yearn for and seek
His face and to be in His presence continually!"
—I Chronicles 16:11

I Chronicles 13-16

When David became king in Jerusalem, the first thing he wanted to do was to bring the ark to him. Why was this so important? Because he knew the ark of the covenant represented My presence among the people. And this is what David desired the most. Saul never sought this during his reign, because he didn't want to include Me in his daily affairs. The ark resided in Shiloh, within the sacred tent of the tabernacle, for about 400 years. After it was captured by the Philistines, while Eli was still high priest, it was returned to Kiriath-jearim in Israel after seven months. Then it remained there for almost 100 years, through the judgeship of Samuel and the reign of Saul. But David, with his heart leaning toward Me, wanted it in Jerusalem, at the center of his life and those in Israel. He wanted it as a focal point for the people so they would always know that I was there with them and that he was king only because of Me.

On the day David gathered all the people to bring the ark to his city, there was great joy among them, because they saw the heart of their king—to please Me. So why did one man, Uzza, die while trying to steady the ark on the cart? He died because most people were forbidden to touch the holy things of the tabernacle. (See Numbers 4:15.) If they did, they would die. Only specifically-anointed and appointed priests could carry the items from the Holy of Holies, like the ark, according to My Law.

David was offended by Uzza's death, because he thought his zeal was enough. He thought his eagerness to please Me would cover any discrepancies in how the Law was carried out. He didn't understand the importance of obeying every jot and tittle of it, and that, until the Messiah came, all had to abide completely by it. Only the blood of this One could cover and fulfill it so that all could access the holy things and My presence without the result being death. When Christ died, the veil of the temple that separated the Holy of Holies, including the ark, from the people was ripped from top to bottom. This showed that now anyone could come into My presence, not just those ordained as priests.

I loved David's zeal, and I exalted his kingdom and made him a forerunner to My Son, because he was willing to come and inquire of Me, seek My presence, and praise Me continually.

Day 114

What was this promised house?

"For You, O my God, have told Your servant that You will build for him a house (a blessed posterity); therefore Your servant has found courage and confidence to pray before You."
—I Chronicles 17:25

I Chronicles 17-20

What was this house I promised to build for David that would last forever? And what was this hoped-for kingdom? What did I offer him that gave him the confidence and courage to pray to Me?

David asked, "Who am I, O Lord God, and what is my house and family that You have brought me up to this?.... You are God and have promised this good thing to Your servant."

Why did I give victory to him wherever he went? David was special to Me because he didn't seek or follow evil, as other kings did. His heart was pure before Me, and he executed judgment and justice among his people. Though he had to fight for peace in his land, I gave him victory after victory in subduing those who rose up against Israel.

David would never see the completion of an earthly house for Me—My temple. Nor did he get to see the spiritual house of My dreams or the forever kingdom I promised while he lived on earth. But, because of his great dedication to Me—he dedicated all he acquired to My Name—I told him about the house and kingdom that would come later and last forever. I told him how these would come one day through his own progeny and be completed by way of the Messiah.

My Son would help Me complete this treasured house, a spiritual one, one day. It would be greater than any temple on earth, and it would "house" My saints, My believers—those who'd receive My Son as their Lord. And He would bring a new kingdom to earth, where He'd reign forever from this new house as its Head.

Of this, David could only see a glimpse. Even now, though you have a larger view of what I am building and how, the completion is still hidden from you. But, because of what My Son accomplished, you can have David's confidence and courage to pray before Me, and, one day, with David, you'll rejoice to see the final result.

And you will shout for joy!

Day 115

Why would a census make Me angry?

"Only may the Lord give you wisdom and understanding as you are put in charge of Israel, that you may keep the law of the Lord your God. Then you will prosper if you are careful to keep and fulfill the statutes and ordinances with which the Lord charged Moses concerning Israel. Be strong and of good courage. Dread not and fear not; be not dismayed."
—*I Chronicles 22: 12-13*

I Chronicles 21-25

Why would I be angry at David for taking a census? Because he knew better! People only had the right to count or number what belonged to them. Israel did not belong to David. It belonged to Me! In Exodus 30:12, I told Moses, "When you take a census of the Israelites...each one must pay the Lord a ransom for his life at the time he is counted. Then no plague will come on them when you number them." Only I could command a census, and it must be done by receiving a ransom to "atone for," or make amends for, the counting. David insisted on doing it his way. Later, he begged Me to take away his sin-guilt, and he asked that the people be spared. When leaders go against My words, it's not just they who suffer the consequences. The people under them are affected too. David repented, saying, "Great and many are your mercies." He recognized My greatness, but also My grace. How thankful you should be for the One I sent, Who stands before Me, continuously interceding for you, making amends for your sins and the shortcomings of others, so that you don't have to suffer like the Israelites for wrongful acts of disobedience.

David built an altar on Ornan's threshing floor atop Mount Moriah. His prayers there staved off a pestilence, and this site later became the location of Solomon's temple. When David crowned Solomon as king, his message was this: "You will prosper if you are careful to keep and fulfill the statutes and ordinances with which the Lord charged Moses concerning Israel. Be strong and of good courage. Dread not and fear not; be not dismayed." David knew the truth of this message, because he'd lived it. He had learned the hard way that one must do things My way, not one's own way, for endeavors to work out well. This was life under the Law of Moses. David set My house in a permanent place, no longer to be carried as a tabernacle from one place to another. He said, "The God of Israel has given rest to His people, and He dwells in Jerusalem forever."

Here, My house would abide and, one day, My Son would reign in a new Jerusalem, and many would stand and thank and praise Me for all I'd done, especially for My great mercy in providing a way to live no longer subject to the Law.

Day 116

Why did David pick Solomon to reign?

*"Give to Solomon my son a blameless heart to keep Your commandments,
testimonies, and statutes, and to do all that is necessary to build
the palace [for You] for which I have made provision."*
—*I Chronicles 29:19*

I Chronicles 26-29

Why did David pick Solomon to reign after him, out of all his sons? After all, he was not the eldest. Would David have been disappointed to know that Solomon would one day allow idol worship in the kingdom he'd fought so hard to preserve for Me? Actually, it was I Who chose Solomon to sit on the throne. Of all David's sons, I knew he would build My house, using the instructions I gave to David, and see its completion in his lifetime. Though he turned away from Me later, during most of his days he served Me well with wisdom—better than others would have.

I search the hearts and minds of people, and I understand the wanderings of their thoughts. Though Solomon's mind would deviate, he had more "staying power" than the others, who immediately sought their own aims and ambitions. Do I pick perfect people to rule over others? Never! Because there are none. Only One would ever live up to all My expectations, and He would live on the earth for a short time. Others may serve Me, and even live and breathe for Me for a while, but all will fall short in some way. This is because of human nature and the lures of this world.

I loved how David tried to follow My lead in most matters. But he failed in some situations. He learned that one must "know the God of your father (have personal knowledge of Him, be acquainted with, and understand Him; appreciate, heed, and cherish Him) and serve Him with a blameless heart and a willing mind.... If you seek Him, you will find Him; but if you forsake Him, He will cast you off forever.... Fear not, be not dismayed, for the Lord God, my God, is with you. He will not fail or forsake you."

I gave David the plans for My temple and instructions for its service. He selected from among the Levites those who could care for the instruments, objects, treasuries, and storehouses, and those who would man the gates. He chose from among many families those who would provide the service and the songs for worship. He knew that "our days on the earth are like a shadow," and though riches, honor, power, and might come from Me, all lives are short-lived.

He wanted a house that would stand forever, and this was his passion and Mine.

Day 117

The difference between David and Solomon

"Solomon said to God, You have shown great mercy and loving-kindness
to David my father and have made me king in his place."
—II Chronicles 1:8

II Chronicles 1-5

Solomon did everything right when it came to building My temple in Jerusalem. He hired the right person, Huram-abi, a trusted counselor of Hiram king of Tyre, who was very skilled in carrying out the design. Solomon collected gold, silver, precious stones, and special kinds of wood for its structure and overlay. Unlike other kings, he did not confiscate what David had set aside for building the temple to use for his own purposes. When I asked what he desired most, he asked for greater wisdom to lead My people. And I was happy to give this to him, along with riches and honor. Other than bringing chariots and horses from Egypt, which was forbidden under the Law (Deuteronomy 17:16, 17) because they were dedicated to sun worship, he carried out what his father expected and hoped for by building and beautifying My house.

The decorations were grand! The molten sea of metal, used by the priests for washing, was much more magnificent than its portable predecessor. Measuring 15 feet across and seven and a half feet high, its bronze bowl had a brim like a lily and represented the miracle of the Israelites' crossing the Red Sea. The bowl was supported by 12 oxen, which stood for the 12 tribes and My strength to uphold them. The ability to wash from it represented the cleansing quality of My Spirit in people and a clean heart that comes from exposure to My Word.[1] The pomegranates on the pillars stood for righteousness, because they have 613 seeds, corresponding to the 613 commandments found in My Law. They also represent fruitfulness, knowledge, and wisdom. When Solomon designed his crown, it was based on the "crown" at the top of the pomegranate.[2]

Solomon appeared to do everything right. He even made sure the musicians played in unison, producing one harmonious sound of praise. But doing everything right does not make for a pure heart, and, unlike David, he lacked passion for Me. When he brought the ark from Gibeon to rest in My temple, he didn't dance with joy before Me as David had done when he brought the ark from Kiriath-jearim. He lacked his father's godly exuberance and zeal.

And this was his ultimate downfall.

Day 118

Solomon's prayer

"For I have chosen and sanctified (set apart for holy use) this house, that My Name may be here forever, and My eyes and My heart will be here perpetually."
—II Chronicles 7:16

II Chronicles 6-8

When Solomon prayed over the temple he built for Me, he knelt down, spread his hands to heaven, and he said, "There is no God like You in heaven or in the earth."

He acknowledged Me in all My ways and how:
-I show mercy, loving kindness, and honor those who walk before Me with all their hearts.
-I keep My promises and confirm My words spoken.
-I hear and heed your requests from My dwelling place.
-I justify the righteous and reward all according to their right standing with Me.
-I forgive those who return to Me with their whole heart.
-I teach the best way to walk and show people how to overcome adversity.
-I return to people what they deserve and acknowledge their ways.
-I know peoples' hearts and endeavor to bring them into My fold.
-I welcome strangers and open My doors to anyone who comes to pray in My house.
-I rejoice over My zealous ones and celebrate with those who love Me.
-I heal lands and offer health and wholeness to those who turn to Me and seek My face.
-I establish My throne and honor My promise to David for a descendant to reign one day.

I acknowledged Solomon's prayer. I appeared to him and said, "I have heard your prayer and have chosen this place."
One day you will see My true house and My throne in all its splendor.
And you will cry when you behold Me and realize Who I am and how many ways I have loved you.

Day 119

When a king's focus moves away from Me

"Your father [King Solomon] made our yoke grievous. So now make lighter the grievous service of your father and his heavy yoke that he put upon us, and we will serve you."
—II Chronicles 10:4

II Chronicles 9-12

There were many positive things about Solomon's reign. Under him, Israel was united and had peace from all its enemies. The Israelites experienced prosperity, the likes of which they'd never known. He brought unusual and exotic things to the kingdom from far-off lands, such as precious algum wood from Ophir in India. Standing 33 to 65 feet tall, the algum tree provided a heavy, fine-grained wood that was impervious to most insects.[1] Prized for its color, fragrance, durability, and texture,[2] its bark and stems were used to make red dye, and its wood was used to make the instruments of worship. That is why the tree stood for "praise."[1]

Solomon finished the temple that his father David longed to see. It became the center of worship for all of Israel. It took seven years to complete, and he made sure the Levites were organized to care for it and bring music into it. He spent 13 years building his own grand house, then he built a house for Pharaoh's daughter. He also constructed the House of the Forest of Lebanon, which stood 45 feet tall and was 150 feet long and 75 feet wide. Also called "the armory of the house of the forest" (Isaiah 22:8), it was built for the storage and display of things like gold shields and drinking vessels.[3] But then he moved on to build places of worship for his wives' foreign gods.

Often people, especially rulers, start out well, with good intentions and purposes centered on Me, but then they begin to wander into self-promotion, and they begin to lean on their own strength, instead of Mine. Their focus moves from Me to their own accomplishments. This happened to Solomon. By the time his son Rehoboam came to rule, the Israelites had grown discontent and weary with the burdens put on them by a despot who ruled for his own self-aggrandizement. Rehoboam was crowned in Shechem because the people were fed up with all the building and elaboration in Jerusalem, and they demanded it. When David was made king, he made a league with the elders of Israel (II Samuel 5:3). Rehoboam did not. He listened only to his cohorts, who proved to be unwise. By not listening to or heeding the people he represented, he lost most of his kingdom. Then his years were spent defending the little bit he had left. Peace and prosperity eluded him.

This is always the result when reigns focus on self-promotion.

Day 120

Can anyone fight against Me and win?

*"For the eyes of the Lord run to and for throughout the whole earth to show
Himself strong in behalf of those whose hearts are blameless toward Him."*
—*II Chronicles 16:9*

II Chronicles 13-16

How can you fight against Me and ever win? You can't. As King Abijah of Judah pro-claimed, you can try, but "you cannot prosper." When leaders stand tall for Me, allowing Me to lead them, inviting Me to be their head, I won't fail to fight for them. I'll deliver them from their enemies, as I did Abijah, even when the odds seem stacked against them. I'll give them victory when they rely on Me.

I give peace to a land. Judah's King Asa sought Me and taught his people to inquire of and for Me, even to crave Me as their vital necessity. And he saw how I gave them peace. He said, "The land is still ours, because we sought the Lord our God; we have sought Him...and He has given us rest and peace on every side."

Asa cried to Me, "O Lord, there is none besides You to help, and it makes no difference to You whether the one You help is mighty or powerless. Help us, O Lord our God! For we rely on You, and we go against this multitude in Your name. O Lord, You are our God; let no man prevail against You!"

I will never falter from defending a person who calls on My Name. Azariah the prophet told Asa, "The Lord is with you while you are with Him. If you seek Him...He will be found by you; but if you...forsake Him, he will forsake you.... Be strong...and let not your hands be weak and slack, for your work shall be rewarded." He told him that, in the years Israel was without Me, there was no peace in the land, and that "vexing afflictions and disturbances were upon all the inhabitants."

When Asa led his people to make a covenant to seek Me with all their heart, I gave the land rest and peace round about. Later, he chose to ally himself with the king of Syria against Israel's king, instead of depending on Me for help.

I sent Hanani the prophet to remind him that "the eyes of the Lord run to and fro throughout the whole earth to show Himself strong in behalf of those whose hearts are blameless toward Him."

Day 121

When leaders seek Me

"And Jehoshaphat stood...and said, O Lord, God of our fathers, are You not God in heaven? And do You not rule over all the kingdoms of the nations? In Your hand are power and might, so that none is able to withstand You."
—*II Chronicles 20:5-6*

II Chronicles 17-20

When you seek and yearn with all your heart for Me, then you are encouraged in all My ways. King Jehoshaphat of Judah sent princes, Levites, and priests throughout the land to teach from My Book. As a result, his name became great so that even former enemies—Philistines and Arabs—brought him gifts and tribute.

He also understood justice because he knew My heart in all things. When he sent judges throughout the land, he told them, "Be careful what you do, for you judge not for man, but for the Lord, and He is with you in the matter of judgment.... There is no injustice with the Lord our God, or partiality or taking of bribes." Judge in "the fear of the Lord, faithfully, with integrity and a blameless heart," he said.

Dealing "courageously" was important to him. Why? Because he'd seen the miserable leadership of a corrupt king. He also saw the peoples' lack of courage to stand up to the king's evil ways. He saw how King Ahab of Israel encouraged lying from his own prophets by rewarding them for their deception. And he saw how this corruption led to Ahab's death in battle. He knew that, when a leader leads for his own honor and gain, not to glorify Me or to walk in My ways, his or her selfishness trickles down to all the people. And all who serve the ruler become corrupt, with hearts bent on self-aggrandizement and not on integrity or righteousness in judgment and justice, which come from Me. All the people suffer as a result.

When the Moabites, Ammonites, and Meunites came against Jehoshaphat, he first turned to Me for help. Then he asked his people to come to his aid. Out of all the cities of Judah, they gathered to him. He never used fear to motivate or stir them up for battle. He encouraged them to seek Me. Praying before them, he said to Me, "In Your hand are power and might, so that none is able to withstand You." And I answered him through his prophet, who said, "Be not afraid or dismayed...for the battle is not yours, but God's."

Jehoshaphat, unlike Ahab, learned that leaning on Me and My words through righteous prophets always brings the best results for oneself and one's people.

Day 122

Why do people rebel against Me?

"Yet [God] sent prophets to them to bring them again to the Lord;
these testified against them, but they would not listen."
—II Chronicles 24:19

II Chronicles 21-24

After a godly person reigns and brings peace and prosperity to a nation, why would the next generation rebel against Me and bring great sorrow to the people? Jehoshaphat's son, Jehoram, gained the throne, killed his siblings, and "walked in the ways of the kings of Israel." He "did what was evil in the eyes of the Lord." I would never destroy David's lineage because of My promise "to give a light to him and to his sons forever." So, I allowed Jehoram's destructive reign, even when he "debauched spiritually the inhabitants" of the land. The result? Those who had reconciled with his father, Jehoshaphat—the Philistines, Arabs, and Edomites—turned against him. His children and wives were carried away with his possessions. He lost everything, including his own life. He had an incurable bowel disease and died a painful death, "and his people made no funeral fire to honor him, like the fires for his fathers." His reign ended after eight painful years.

With record after record showing the results of evil reigns, why do leaders insist on pursuing their own ways, apart from Me, which always lead to destruction? It is often because they follow the lead of people close to them, ignoring the examples of those who've gone before them. They kowtow to a desire to please those whose acceptance and praise they desire. They also act out of pride.

Jehoram married Ahab's daughter, Athaliah, and she pursued the ways of her parents, who worshipped other gods and lusted after power. She brought corruption to her husband's and son's reigns, and she extended evil to future generations. Rulers always have a choice. Jehoram and Ahaziah could have followed Me. But they chose to heed ungodly words. The gods of power and control corrupt absolutely, and the love of these gods leads to even more corruption. But, even amid wickedness, you will find some who stand for righteousness, like Jehosheba and her husband, Jehoiada.

I will always work on behalf of those who are good, who want to serve Me to overcome evil, so that the people of a land can rejoice in Me once again.

Day 123

The more pride, the less power

"But when [King Uzziah] was strong, he became proud to his destruction; and he trespassed against
the Lord his God, for he went into the temple of the Lord to burn incense on the altar of incense."
—*II Chronicles 26:16*

II Chronicles 25-28

I have the power to help or to cast down. When leaders hear and heed My words, they are victorious in all things, and their people prosper. But when they act out of pride or self-importance and turn to other gods, their ability to succeed evaporates. The more pride a person has, the less power he or she has to move ahead and prosper.

As long as Judah's king Amaziah and his son Uzziah followed and sought Me, inquiring of Me, they were strong, and their leadership never flagged. But when pride set in, this led to their destruction. Amaziah decided, after succeeding in battle against Edom, that the Edomite gods were better than Me, so he set them up as idols, bowed down to them, and encouraged others to follow his lead.

Uzziah was so sure of himself that he decided to act as one of My anointed priests and burn incense on the altar in My temple, which was forbidden. This was after I'd supported and encouraged him in his passions. I'd given him great ideas for farming, winemaking, and machines for defense. Because of his inventiveness, his fame spread, and he became known for his knowledge. But, like Solomon, it all went to his head, and he began to think he was as good as Me. This was his downfall. Unlike Uzziah, Jotham "grew mighty" because "he ordered his ways in the sight of the Lord his God." Despite his righteous leaning, people continued to be corrupt. Often, I will set up a good person in a land to speak for Me and bring the people back to a life centered in Me, but the land will remain in distress if the people refuse to listen and change.

In the next generation of Judean kings, Ahaz turned and destroyed what Jotham had built. Besides burning incense to other gods, he "burned his sons as an offering, after the abominable customs of the nations" that I had driven out. So, the Syrians defeated him. Even the people of the northern kingdom of Israel overcame him and the Judean people "because they had forsaken the Lord, the God of their fathers." Why is a nation brought low? It is always due to faithlessness on the part of its leaders or its people.

Pride and the worship of other gods brings inevitable ruin.

Day 124

Revival!

"Hezekiah did...what was good, right, and faithful before the Lord his God."
—*II Chronicles 31:20*

II Chronicles 29-31

What brings a revival or the returning of My people to Me? It starts with a leader who is passionate, like King Hezekiah. The first thing he did when his reign began was to clean My house. Why was it dirty or defiled? Because it was filled with the paraphernalia of idol worship. He realized that his ancestors had forsaken Me. They'd turned their faces from Me and their backs to Me by closing the doors to the temple, extinguishing the lamps that symbolized My presence, and burning incense to other gods. Hezekiah saw the results of this: My turning away from Judah. And he wanted Me back!

To accomplish this, he first designated certain Levites to oversee the praise and worship that David had once ordained. And he set up ones to serve My house. Next, he reestablished the celebration of feasts, starting with the Passover, which hadn't been observed since King Jehoshaphat's reign. He sent word throughout the kingdom and encouraged everyone to come to Jerusalem to celebrate. Though some laughed and mocked his request, "the hand of God came upon Judah to give them one heart to do the commandment of the king and of the princes." And many came so that there was "a very great assembly." And when they arrived, they experienced great joy! They ended up celebrating longer than expected. Instead of staying one week, they extended their stay by two weeks.

Although some hadn't prepared themselves for the Passover, in accordance with the Law, Hezekiah understood My great grace. He knew that I'd pardon those who earnestly sought and yearned for Me, and that I'd hearken to him and heal the people anyway. Even after they all returned to their homes, Hezekiah's work did not stop. He appointed priests and Levites to continue to praise in the gates of My camp. And he announced that all the feasts ordained by Moses would be celebrated throughout the year. He made sure the priests were taken care of, and he prepared special storage chambers to keep extra supplies for them. He did "what was good, right, and faithful" before Me with all his heart. And he prospered along with the people.

What causes revival?

A passionate pursuit of Me by a leader and the followers to celebrate My goodness and mercy in a land.

Day 125

The right combination to overcome

"Be strong and courageous. Be not afraid or dismayed before the king of Assyria and all the horde that is with him, for there is Another with us greater than [all those] with him."
—II Chronicles 32:7

II Chronicles 32-33

It always takes a combination of things to win a battle. It first takes a confident attitude in individuals and leaders. Assurance comes by speaking and believing the positive encouragement of My Word, including My promises. In a nation, or an individual, it then takes trust, persistence, and consistency to act on the words and assurances.

Hezekiah exuded My strength as his enemy approached Jerusalem. He said, "Be strong and courageous...for there is Another with us greater than all those with him. With him is an arm of flesh, but with us is the Lord our God to help us and to fight our battles." The people listened and relied on his words. They also followed My instructions. Believing My words is a good start, but those who follow Me must also do as I tell them. Hezekiah and his people built a tunnel, still in existence today, that diverted the springs in the land to the city, so that, when the king of Assyria attacked, the people of the city would always have a source of water.

When the enemy forces came and tried to create fear among the Jews and distrust of their king and of Me, Hezekiah came to Me for help. And I sent an angel to "cut off all the mighty warriors and commanders and officers in the camp of the king of Assyria." Later, the enemy king's own offspring killed him in his god's house.

Because of his confidence in Me, King Hezekiah "was magnified in the sight of all nations." But as often happens to leaders who experience victory, he became proud. Later, he "humbled himself for the pride of his heart, both he and the inhabitants of Jerusalem," and I was able to continue to help them.

I will always try the hearts of men and women so I can know all that is in them. Hezekiah almost died, but I extended his life, because he turned to Me. I can do this for you and for others who turn to Me with all their hearts, because I want to show My favor and grace to all the people on the earth.

Though I knew Hezekiah's son would turn against Me, I allowed him and his descendants to reign, knowing that one day Another would come through them to trust Me completely.

Day 126

Those who speak for Me

"And Hilkiah and they whom the king had appointed went to Huldah the prophetess, the wife of Shallum son of Tokhath, the son of Hasrah, keeper of the wardrobe. She dwelt in Jerusalem, in the Second Quarter."
—II Chronicles 34:22

II Chronicles 34-36

As long as this earth remains, there will always be people who bring My messages of hope and certainty to others. They are often hidden from view in society, beneath the surface of nations that reject Me. They are set aside, and at least a few people are aware of their presence. But, often, they live apart from the rulers, in the "second tiers" of society to protect them from those who want to destroy them.

Huldah was a prophetess during the reigns of two Judean kings. She dwelt in Jerusalem in the times of Manasseh and Josiah. She and her husband lived "under the radar" in the Second Quarter of the city. Most people knew of her and understood that she spoke words from Me. But many leaders had not wanted to hear her words until Josiah came along.

As king of Judah, Josiah had a heart for Me. He turned the nation back to following Me when he heard the words of My Law. Hilkiah the priest found Moses's scrolls buried in the ruined temple and handed them to Shaphan the scribe, who read the words to Josiah. What was the king's response to hearing the words that were hidden beneath the rubble? He tore his clothes, because he realized how his people had drifted far away from My intentions for them and had suffered the consequences. Hilkiah went straight to Huldah. He knew that she would tell them how to make amends for the great separation from Me that had resulted. And she would disclose My true thoughts about Judah's future. She did not disappoint him, and Hilkiah brought back her words to the king, who listened and acted. Josiah wanted the land to return to the way I had meant things to be.

I will always introduce people who will speak for Me to those who seek My will. Because they are often disdained, even threatened, by those who do not want to hear them, I often keep them hidden until the time when people rise up who want to know Me. If you truly seek My words and My will, I can show you those who will speak for Me. People who want to know what I think often summon anointed ones to relay My words if they themselves are unable to communicate directly with Me.

The words of those who are spiritually anointed will always bring benefits and blessings to those who listen and act.

Day 127

No one can stop My work

"Thus says Cyrus king of Persia: The Lord, the God of heaven, has given me all the kingdoms of the earth, and He has charged me to build Him a house at Jerusalem in Judah."
—Ezra 1:2

Ezra 1-4

Whenever a great work is started by Me, many will oppose it. The people of Judah, after 70 years in captivity, were surprised to find themselves being encouraged by an unlikely person. The king of Persia wanted them to return to Jerusalem and rebuild their temple. King Cyrus's heart was stirred up. And he decided to support the Jews. How did this happen through a Gentile king who ruled over an idolatrous empire? I can stir up the hearts of even the most unexpected people. Remember this as you pray for those who seem to be far away from Me and My calling. If I put a person in your mind and on your heart, know that I am working in you to pray for that person. Sometimes I may give you specific directions on how to reach out and help them.

I often use leaders to serve My purposes. And I can work through those who don't do or say things the "right" way and are rejected by the more acceptable people in society.

The Jews were excited and joyful. They were seeing the fulfillment of prophecy—to be allowed to return to their own land out of captivity. They thanked Me for inciting favor in the king of Persia, who recognized that I had given him the kingdoms of the earth and wanted My people to be able to return to their land and worship in their temple. Cyrus even gave the Levites and temple servants the vessels and dedicated items which King Nebuchadnezzar had stolen from them. He blessed the Judeans and wanted them to prosper in their endeavor. He realized that My people needed a place where they could go to worship Me. Later, My Son would come to make worship available at any time and place through a spiritual temple He would build. But then, the Jews needed a physical place that represented what would come later.

As the Judeans prepared to lay a new foundation for My physical temple, they gave thanks, sang, shouted, and cried so loud that the sound was heard miles away! But the Persian governor and his associates in Samaria wanted to maintain control of the land of Israel, and they wrote to the king to complain about the Jews' efforts to resurrect the temple. They falsely accused them in a letter to the king, who decided to stop the building out of fear. And so, the great effort and joy was detained.

But remember that, if I am behind a work, no man or woman can stop it.

Day 128

A timeline for reigns and events

"Blessed be the Lord, the God of our fathers [said Ezra], Who put such a thing as this into the king's heart, to beautify the house of the Lord in Jerusalem, and Who has extended His mercy and steadfast love to me before the king, his counselors, and all the king's mighty officers. I was strengthened and encouraged, for the hand of the Lord my God was upon me, and I gathered together outstanding men of Israel to go with me to Jerusalem."
—Ezra 7:27-28

Ezra 5-7
This BC timeline outlines events in the books of Ezra, Nehemiah, Esther, and Daniel:

607...Judah was led captive under Judah's King Jehoiakim.
597...Many more Judeans were deported under Judah's King Jehoiachin.
586...Babylon invaded Jerusalem and destroyed the temple.
559-530...The Persian King Cyrus II reigned and decreed that the temple be rebuilt.
538...King Cyrus II took over Babylon.
537...Daniel prospered under King Cyrus II.
535...Zerubbabel oversaw the rebuilding of the altar and the foundation of the temple.
530-522...The Persian King Cambyses reigned.
522-486...The Persian King Darius I reigned.
522...Construction of the temple was stopped by opposition.
520...The words of the prophets, Zechariah and Haggai, were recorded.
520...Rebuilding of the temple was resumed.
516...The temple was finished and dedicated.
486-465...The Persian King Xerxes I, or Ahasuerus, reigned.
473...The Persian Queen Esther was recorded as reigning.
465-425...The Persian King Artaxerxes reigned.
458...The second exiled group returned to Jerusalem, 90 years after the first group.
458...Ezra set up the service to the temple with the priests, Levites, and scribes.
445...The third exiled group returned, and Nehemiah rebuilt Jerusalem's walls.
440...The book of Ezra was written.
433...Nehemiah returned to Jerusalem and instituted reforms.
430...The books of Nehemiah and Malachi were written.

During the reigns of Cyrus, Darius, Xerxes, and Artaxerxes, Persian-appointed governors opposed the rebuilding of the temple and Jerusalem.
The plans I appoint will always come to pass, even when some oppose them.

Day 129

Ezra's dilemma

"Arise, for it is your duty, and we are with you. Be strong and brave and do it."
—Ezra 10:4

Ezra 8-10

Ezra was joyful, strengthened, and encouraged to see how I had worked to bring him and his people home again to their promised land after so many years in exile. He saw how, if they trusted in Me, I'd protect them. But his joy turned to grief when he reached the land and realized, as he gathered the people together, how many had broken My Law. What had they done that was so bad? Some had married foreign wives. Today, that wouldn't seem so terrible, because foreigners can believe in Me through Christ, but then this was considered abhorrent, because it was contrary to My Law. So, Ezra demanded that the men separate themselves from their wives. Why such an extreme request? Comments on the book of Ezra from *The Amplified Bible,* explain:

"The apparently great severity which characterized Ezra's divorce policy, as shown in chapters 9 and 10, becomes thoroughly justified when Israel's tragic experiences because of marriages with heathen women are considered. The consequent idolatry, first of King Solomon, for example, and then of the whole nation, was fatal. God's wrath had been so great that He not only took the kingship from Solomon, but eventually turned the Israelites over to their enemies and left the promised land desolate, while the people bewailed their fate as captives in a heathen country. Ezra, to whom the keeping of God's law was of constant concern, had been born in captivity among exiles who hung their harps on the willow trees and grieved for the country, for the peace and prosperity which their now justly offended God had once given them. Nothing could have been more abhorrent to Ezra than that the Jews should again fall into the snare of idolatry. His action in leading the exiles to give up their foreign wives and their children was the only way out if God's consuming wrath was not again to be incurred. That those still living of the 42,360 men who over 80 years before had made up the congregation also saw complete separation from the foreign women as the unavoidable solution is obvious from the fact that only four spoke against it. However, those who were now actually married to native heathen women were only 17 priests, 10 Levites, and 86 laymen—113 in all, according to the records, though the list may be incomplete."

Ezra understood the need for complete obedience to every word of My commandments and laws so that My people could survive and thrive in a cruel and exacting world.

Day 130

I will fight for you!

"I answered them, The God of heaven will prosper us; therefore we His servants will arise and build, but you have no portion or right or memorial in Jerusalem."
—Nehemiah 2:20

Nehemiah 1-4

Unless My hand is on a person, to steer his or her way, the projects or endeavors pursued will not endure. When My hand is on you, and you follow My lead, your efforts will last and accomplish My purposes for them. I was with Nehemiah, and he knew it. I led him to hear the words of his kinsmen, who came from Judah and reported the state of the temple and Jerusalem.

I was with Nehemiah when he stood before King Artaxerxes in Persia, holding his cup. And I worked in the king's heart to allow Nehemiah to begin his efforts to rebuild the walls surrounding the city and the temple. I heard his heartfelt prayers to Me, and I always hear yours.

Nehemiah's project started and ended with the Sheep Gate. This is meaningful because it represents the sacrifice of a Lamb, Who would come later. Why was it important that he record the names of the people who worked on the gates? Because these same people would be instrumental in manning the gates of the new city on a new earth later.

Whenever you attempt to do something I've led you to do, like repairing a breach between Me and people, and you try to put back together what's been torn apart, there will always be scoffers like the men Nehemiah faced in Jerusalem. But never give up, because I am with you!

As the taunts increased against Nehemiah's efforts to rebuild My city, his first response was not to give up but to "give them to Me." He prayed that I would deal with those who resisted My work. He knew that those who opposed him also opposed Me, and they brought their own vexation upon themselves, because they turned their backs on Me. They were trying to inhibit My ability to bless and to help My people.

If you have a heart and mind to work for Me, and you come to Me in prayer, I will always be with you to accomplish what you set out to do, despite any opposition.

And I will always fight for you!

Day 131

Differences between good and bad leaders

"But the former governors lived at the expense of the people and took from them food and wine, besides forty shekels of silver. [a large monthly official salary]; yes, even their servants assumed authority over the people. But I did not so because of my [reverent] fear of God."
—Nehemiah 5:15

Nehemiah 5-7

Do you see the difference between a self-serving leader and one who serves Me and the people? Nehemiah set the standard as a good leader. He never demanded his due rights, but he made sure his people had what they needed. He said, "Former governors lived at the expense of the people and took from them food and wine, besides 40 shekels of silver [a large monthly official salary]; yes, even their servants assumed authority over the people. But I did not so because of my [reverent] fear of God." Nehemiah went a step further than the rest. He demanded that any who had taken advantage of others' poverty by charging high interest on loans must stop immediately. He also required that those with more than enough must return to the disadvantaged their "fields, vineyards, olive groves, and houses, and also a hundredth of all the money, grain, new wine, and oil that you have exacted from them."

People who were taking advantage of others' neediness saw Nehemiah's justice and their own selfishness. They agreed to his demands and realized their error.

These are examples of a true leader, who sets a standard of justice which people are willing to follow. When a good leader leads by acknowledging My will and desires for My people, he or she never takes advantage of his or her position or power to the detriment of others.

Whenever a great work from Me begins, the enemy will stir up a few people to hinder it. The people he uses are those who are bound to their own or others' schemes, with the result being greater power and control and money for themselves.

Some may try to frighten you from your purposes by threatening you with losses. They may try to lead you into doing something wrong, or contrary to My will, by inciting your fears so that you attempt to protect yourself. But, like Nehemiah, turn your thoughts to Me for affirmation and strength. And I will always be there to protect and help you!

I am your true defense.

Day 132

How a land can prosper

"[And Ezra said], You are the Lord, You alone; You have made heaven, the heaven of heavens, with all their host, the earth, and all that is on it, the seas and all that is in them; and you preserve them all, and the hosts of heaven worship You."
—Nehemiah 9:6

Nehemiah 8-10

Ezra's prayer opened the doors to prosperity for his nation:

—He acknowledged My many blessings and promises.
—He encouraged praise to Me for all I'd done for Judah and Israel.
—He exalted My name and lordship over heaven and earth and all they encompass.
—He explained the many miracles I performed in fulfilling My promises.
—He reminded them of ancestors who turned their backs on Me and the repercussions.
—He renewed His people's confidence in Me.
—He elaborated My greatness, mercy, might, faithfulness, graciousness, and love.
—He talked about how I never forsook them, even when they walked away from Me!
—He asked Me to help them in their hardship, despite their faithlessness to Me.
—He encouraged the people to create a new covenant to serve Me with all their hearts.

When Ezra blessed Me as the great God, all the people answered, "Amen! Amen!" and lifted up their hands in prayer. They bowed their heads and worshipped me with their faces to the ground.

The Levites helped the people understand the Law by reading it and helping them to decipher it. When they wept, Nehemiah, Ezra, and the Levites told them, "Don't be grieved and depressed, for the joy of the Lord is your strength!" Ezra reminded them that I am a gracious and merciful God and that I would hear and deliver them from their enemies.

After his prayer, he set a seal on a new covenant with the leaders and priests and people. They were bound to never forsake Me again, knowing that the richness of their land could only be enjoyed through a partnership with Me.

I desire partnerships like this today.

When people of any land come to Me and make a pact to serve and honor Me in all they do, My great bounty will always abound in that land.

Day 133

I remember what you've done for Me

"O my God, [earnestly] remember me for good and imprint me [on Your heart]!"
—Nehemiah 13:31

Nehemiah 11-13

Nehemiah's heart was to do good for Me. He wanted Me to remember him for what he'd done. He'd assigned faithful priests to protect the people's tithes and gifts that were to be distributed to the temple servants. He'd set up singers, as David did, to play before Me, offer their praise, and bring joy to those who came to hear them. He'd set guards at the gates of the city to protect what was built.

You can learn so much from Nehemiah, who brought a beaten-down people once again to a moment of victory. Below are the ways he accomplished what I called him to do.

—He prayed to Me before he spoke to the king of Persia about My purpose for him, which was to go to Jerusalem from Babylon and coordinate the rebuilding of My temple. Remember, he was the king's cupbearer, his "right-hand man."
—He reiterated My promise of prosperity and success when others scoffed and ridiculed My intent for him.
—He prayed for Me to be the judge of those who taunted and made fun of him.
—He successfully set up people in family groups to rebuild the walls of the city.
—He set a watch along the wall to protect the people and the city from enemy attacks.
—He encouraged My people not to fear their enemies, to remember that I am great, and that I would give them needed courage and fight for them.
—He watched as I frustrated the evil plots and plans of their enemies.
—He reminded people of My goodness and My intent to bring them prosperity.

When people turn to Me, ask for guidance, and come to know My purpose for them, I can raise them up to be leaders of efforts that glorify Me and help others through the ages.

Day 134

How offense creates havoc and hatred

*"And the king loved Esther more than all the women, and she obtained grace
and favor in his sight more than all the maidens, so that he set the
royal crown on her head and made her queen instead of Vashti."*
—Esther 2:17

Esther 1-4

*King Ahasuerus, also known as Xerxes, ruled Persia, and his reign extended from India
to Ethiopia during the 5th century BC.* He was a good ruler, because he was just, and he
encouraged freedom throughout his kingdom. Unlike Manasseh, Solomon's son who lost
most of his kingdom, he consulted with truly wise men and relied on their judgment in
many matters.

Ahasuerus's wife, Queen Vashti, refused to come to him at a significant time because of
her pride and lack of respect for her husband. She was offended by his request to show off
her beauty, and she chose to openly dishonor him. As a result, King Ahasuerus turned to his
counselors. What was their advice? To find another queen. Esther was chosen for this role
when many, including the king, recognized her grace and favor. Above all the women in the
kingdom, she stood out in every respect. Where did this favor come from? Me, of course.
Was it a coincidence that she was chosen? Absolutely not. I wanted her in the palace for a
reason. I knew she would heed Me and Mordecai, who had raised her.

People who worship other gods are often deterred by offense. Something said or done
easily affronts their pride and threatens to weaken their self-importance. They often resort
to spreading lies and innuendo about those they consider their enemy to maintain their
position or power. People without a foundational understanding of Who I am are often
shaken and vexed by small things that are said or done.

It was an offense that caused Haman to whisper lies about the Jews in the king's ear to
try to motivate him to assassinate them. He had decided that striking out against Mordecai
wasn't enough. His anger against this man for not bowing before him was stirred up, and
it caused him to entice the king to sign a decree against the Jews. Misplaced anger stems
from offense and often creates havoc and hatred toward groups of people. Even today. Our
enemy, Satan, still uses indignation to stir up resentment toward ones I've chosen through
lies, innuendo, and propaganda by emphasizing differences. But always look to see what I
can do to use this for the good of My people!

See how I can deliver and bless My people using those I've strategically placed, even today!

Day 135

Choices that save lives and bring honor

"Then Queen Esther said, If I have found favor in your sight, O king and if it pleases the king, let my life be given me at my petition and my people at my request."
—Esther 7:3

Esther 5-10

How did Queen Esther save her people, the Jews? She relied on Me for courage. She trusted in Me to help her. What do you think she was doing for three days, while fasting, before she approached the king? She was praying. She was asking for My guidance. She knew that no one was allowed in the presence of the king unless he requested it. She had not been called by him for over a month. But she couldn't wait. Her plea for her people was urgent. If she didn't try, they'd be destroyed because of the king's decree. Even in her urgency, she waited on Me.

She was wise and patient. When she did approach the king, she relied on My direction and did not blurt out her petition. Even when the king held out his scepter for her to come to him and asked her what he could do for her, she waited to reveal her request. She invited him and Haman, who had devised the evil decree to destroy the Jews, to a special dinner. Even then she waited.

It was at a second dinner that she finally revealed what she wanted. With great humility and respect for the king, she unveiled the outcome of the evil decree: her own destruction and that of her people. She also explained to the king that his decree against the Jews would cause him ultimate damage, because his hand would be against Mine. It was her great wisdom, patience, and reliance on Me that saved her and her people, My people.

Mordecai refused to bow to any besides Me, and his choice seemed to cause him and many others great consternation and possible destruction. Your choice to worship and serve Me in this world will always come at a cost. Those who move against Me will attempt to obstruct you and your efforts. But do you see how I worked on Mordecai's behalf and lifted him above all the people because of his choice to stand for Me?

I can work in you, even in the toughest of situations, when you are faced with the greatest adversity and fear! I can work to will and to do of My good pleasure, and I can spare many lives when you ask and act with reliance on Me.

And My good pleasure is always to promote health, life, and all that life can offer.

Day 136

When you think you have it all together

"For the thing which I greatly fear comes upon me, and that of which I am afraid befalls me."
—Job 3:25

Job 1-5

Job had pride, and he was afraid. His life *seemed* to be blameless, even perfect, before Me. He had done all the right things. He'd abstained from evil, and he worshipped Me through all his actions. But he had one fear—that his children might have sinned. He tried to make them "clean" by covering their shortcomings. He offered sacrifices in case they might have cursed or disowned Me in their hearts. He was frightened for them, and, in this one thing, he didn't trust Me. Though he worshipped Me in all he did, he lacked ultimate trust in Me and My purposes for him and his family.

Pride also directed his choices. He thought he could control his life and his children's, and how I viewed them, through his religious acts. He believed that his own righteousness could create a hedge around them. His trust and hope lay in his own uprightness and integrity.

Often, when people think they can control all their outcomes, it's this distrust of Me and My ability to direct their ways that opens a door to disruption. When you think you're in total control of your life, and you "have it all together," this is when I may allow an interruption, so you can see that, actually, you aren't in charge of everything. My strength supersedes any weakness and powerlessness. When Jesus asked his disciples to go out in a boat without him, did He know a storm was coming? It was during the storm that He walked out to them and showed them Who He was.

Though Satan may work against you and cause havoc in your life, as he did in Job's, and cause the closest ones to you to reject you and try to denigrate your trust in Me, I am always with you for good! My purposes are just, and I look for those on earth whose aims align with Mine.

Why is life and its continuance offered to the miserable and bitter ones, who long for death, while those who desire life die young? It's the way of the world as long as Satan rules it, because his desire is to steal, kill, and destroy all that is good. My way is life lived abundantly (John 10:10). And, one day, you will see a world where I am the King.

And I will rule it, as I always intended, with My pleasure to bless all who live.

Day 137

Do you think the world is unjust?

*"For [God] is not a mere man, as I am, that I should answer Him, that
we should come together in court. There is no umpire between us,
who might lay his hand upon us both, [would that there were!]"*
—Job 10:32-33

Job 6-11

Have you ever been in so much despair that you begged Me to die? Have the circumstances around you oppressed and belittled you to the point that you wished you were never born? Have you felt, in your condition, that even your closest friends could not comfort you and that their words made you feel like you were in a desert? You felt that nothing had meaning anymore, and I was too far from you.

Do you think that the world is an unjust place and that what's happened to you is the result of My not caring for you? Do you suffer and feel like that suffering will go on forever, even as long as you live, and that life is too hard to bear? Do you live without hope of things ever changing or getting better? Is every night sleepless with only tossing and turning and fretting? Do you despise your life?

Job felt all these things. And he realized that his days on earth were short, even swifter than a weaver's shuttle. Life was like a puff of wind. And he thought that, in his remaining days, he would never see anything good again, because he'd lost everything that meant something to him. He loathed his current existence and asked Me to look away from him, because he thought I'd brought these calamities on him.

Even his friends blamed him for his dilemma. They accused his children of getting what they deserved. "The hope of the godless shall perish," Bildad told him, "and God will never uphold wrongdoers." Everyone gets what they deserve, he implied. "But how can mortal man ever be right with God, Who is not a man and may not understand our weaknesses?" Job responded. "No one can ever be good enough to deserve His approval! So how can we mere mortals presume to ask what He is doing or why He allows such injustice in the world? Or why innocent people suffer and wicked ones rule!"

"How can I ever be cheerful or happy?" Job asked dolefully. "When I am afraid, I will suffer even more. I desperately need an 'umpire,' a mediator between me and God, someone to stand up for me to Him and speak against my accusers!"

And that is why I sent My Son.

Day 138

Do you want someone to stand up for you?

"Oh, that there were one who might plead for a man with God and that he might maintain his right with Him, as a son of man pleads with or for his neighbor!"
—Job 16:21

Job 12-16

Do you wish someone would stand up for you? Do you feel like you always must stand up for yourself when people accuse or attack you unjustly? Do you feel like people look down on you, because your life hasn't turned out the way you wished it would? Do you see contempt in their eyes when they've never experienced what you have? Do you wonder why the ones who act immorally, whose god is themselves, seem to have it all, while others do everything the right way, yet they suffer for it?

Life seems indiscriminate. And no one is safe. Even having a good character doesn't count for anything. It's often the good and kind people who die first. And it seems like I, with all My wisdom and might, can't do a darn thing about it! Wise people's efforts are corrupted, and even great nations come to naught. How can anyone justify the conflict between what should be and what is really happening? You see supposedly righteous people defaming others to gain their own fame and favor. What is that all about? And why don't I do anything about all of this? Why does it seem that I am so far away and uninvolved? Why do I allow such bad things to happen in the first place?

It seems like I turn away at the most crucial times and ignore your cries for help. You sometimes see Me as a judge sitting high up on My throne in heaven, looking down on you critically with no mercy. Many people do. They see Me as One Who could help them but won't, as One Who has the power over life and death but won't use it wisely. And they see their own life waning and feel powerless to control the outcome. They feel hopeless and helpless, even when they think there might be life after death. The reassuring, or disparaging, words of others don't help them, and many times they feel like it's fruitless to voice their complaints.

Job knew who had torn up his life. He acknowledged it wasn't Me Who had brought this ruin upon him. And he recognized that he needed someone to vouch for him, someone who could stand up for him to this enemy-accuser.

He longed for "one who might plead for a man with God."

He saw how he and all mankind needed a mediator, a savior.

Day 139

Job's real Vindicator

*"For I know that my Redeemer and Vindicator lives, and
at last He [the Last One] will stand upon the earth."
—Job 19:25*

Job 17-21

Do you feel like people make fun of your weaknesses and whisper about your faults? Do people stand against you and disdain and mock you? Do your own friends turn against you? Do they try to please those who reject you to gain acceptance and recognition? Do these things cause you grief, because you once admired and loved them? Do you wonder where are the wise people who can come to your side and defend you?

Are all your purposes and hopes frustrated? Do you feel like your heart is broken, and everything that was once important and of value to you has been stolen? Do you dwell in this hopeless state to the point of welcoming death? Do you think that, even your closest friends and relatives have forsaken you and given up on you? They talk about you behind your back and criticize everything you do. They say you're a loser.

You cry for help, but no one can hear you. Even I don't seem to have a clue. You feel like I surround you with darkness and force you into a place where you are trapped. You think I have broken and stripped you of everything important to you. I pull up all your hope like a tree. I treat you like an adversary and send troops to besiege you. I move all your family and friends far away from you, and no one remembers you anymore. Your most loved ones turn against you. You ask them to show you some pity, but you receive no response from them.

Do you wonder, like Job, why ungodly people seem untouched by hardship? "They spend their days in prosperity" and peacefully go about their business until they die, even though they have no desire to know Me.

But Job realized something after all his commiserations. "Who can teach God knowledge, seeing that He judges those who are on high?" He finally woke up. People may seem to prosper during their lifetime, but one day they will answer for their choices. He began to see that, though all might turn against him, I would not. He saw Me as his Redeemer and Vindicator. And He believed that, one day, his Redeemer would stand on the earth and judge all people fairly.

For this day, he pined.

Day 140

What is true wisdom?

*"But to man He said, Behold, the reverential and worshipful fear of
the Lord—that is Wisdom; and to depart from evil is understanding."*
—Job 28:28

Job 22-28

"What is wisdom?" Job asked. And where does it come from? It seems to elude you at times. It is often hidden, like Me, from the ways of mankind. Only I seem to know where to find it. And, though I understand the way to it, and possess great knowledge—enough to "hang the earth over nothing," give pressure to the wind, measure the waters on earth, and make rain with thunder and lightning, I seem to keep it hidden in a dark place.

Why do I allow wicked people to continue to prosper and even give them strength to use and misuse the earth's great resources—silver, gold, iron, and copper—for their own purposes? I seem to let them go so far as to upend the mountains I made and disrupt streams meant to provide pure water for all. Why would I allow the disruption and corruption of the very assets I made?

This earth, though grand with all its wonder, is a temporary place. The creations made to exist on it are but "mere fringes of My force, the faintest whisper of My voice." And though the wicked "lie down rich" now and misuse what I made for their benefit by taking advantage of others' weakness, one day "terrors will overtake" them. One day, the days of earth will end.

And then, all will be judged by their actions. Those judged as righteous, who knew Me, will live in a better place.

This earth is but a symbol of My power and wisdom. It is an example of what I can do. I alone possess true wisdom. Job understood that "the reverential and worshipful fear of the Lord—that is wisdom; and to depart from evil is understanding."

Those who partake in this worship, understand My wisdom, and depart from evil will be among those who inhabit a new place, where every resource stems from My love and is used in thankful praise and worship of Me and what My Son accomplished.

Day 141

Do you long for the "good old days?"

"Oh, that I were as in the months of old, as in the days when God watched over me."
—Job 29:2

Job 29-33

Do you commiserate over your life and wish you lived once again in the "good old days," when life was really great? Do you think about the time when your parents were still alive or when you laughed and frolicked with your children or friends and enjoyed times together? Do you long for the days when you were younger, when people adored or looked up to you and sought you out, because they saw how wonderful your life was and how wise you were, and they wanted the same things for themselves? Then you were a leader and a helper of others. And you thought your life would always be this way.

You envisioned your children surrounding you in your old age. Along with their own children, they would relish your presence and seek out your wisdom. They would gaze at you with admiration, because they thought so much of you!

But life hasn't turned out this way. Not at all. Now you are mostly by yourself. You're alone, and your loved ones are far away from you. Many friends have passed on before you. The ones who are left have nothing to do with you. They have their own lives to live. They don't have time for you. They see you as a pariah, a needy one, now. And they can't spare the time or effort to come and visit you. They seem to wish for your early demise, so they won't have to be burdened with your care.

Alone, you suffer physically and mentally. You cry out to Me, but I seem to avoid you. You ask Me, "Why am I still alive?" "Why won't You stretch out Your hand to help me?" When you expected My goodness, you got only bad things. You ask, "Don't all the great things I've done count for anything?"

Those close to you even tell you that you must "get your act together." They say you think too highly of yourself, and of Me, and that they are the truly wise ones. They have the real insight as to how things work, and you should listen to them.

But what about Me? Can't I help you?

Day 142

Why should you believe in Me?

"Where were you when I laid the foundation of the earth? Declare to Me, if you have and know understanding. Who determined the measures of the earth if you know? Or who stretched the measuring line upon it? Upon what were the foundations of it fastened, or who laid its cornerstone, when the morning stars sang together and all the sons of God shouted for joy?"
—Job 38:4-7

Job 34-38

Do you wonder why you should believe in Me, when you see so much suffering and the fates of those who are loyal to Me? Have you drawn the conclusion that those who turn to Me have no more advantage than those who live life for their own ambitions? Do you question why you should attempt to live for My glory and a life beyond this one and not just for your own benefit? What difference does it make anyway? Will your life be better if you trust Me? Will you see different results if you lean on Me? Can I protect you from the outrageous actions of others or from weather that turns unpredictable and uncontrollable? Do I have this kind of power? Who am I really?

I answered these questions for Job "out of the whirlwind." What does this mean? It means that, when you feel most desperate, like life is whirling around you, and things are happening randomly to you, and you question where I am in all of this, then I will come and show you how I am present with you, even amid your storm.

Like Job, I will, if you look to Me, show you my deepest secrets, and I will reveal to you the whys and wherefores of life on earth and beyond. Your eyes will be opened, and you will behold a spectrum outside of yourself and your misfortunes. You will see My glory in all its phases and the wonder of a world beyond what you can imagine.

I do this for those who love Me, who stick with Me through the hardships of life on earth. When you are beset by worries and fears, and wonder where I am, just wait. I will show up, and you will see Me.

Though you can't see My face yet, you will recognize Me in a dream or a vision or a person or a thing that comes to you. I will be there, and you will see Me in that place.

But you must persist and wait for that moment of recognition.

Day 143

I will replace more than what you've lost

"And the Lord turned the captivity of Job and restored his fortunes, when he prayed for this friends; also the Lord gave Job twice as much as he had before."
—Job 42:10

Job 39-42

There are some who want to be Me. They try to annul My judgment and belittle My work to appear more righteous, justified, and even better than Me! They deck themselves with majesty and dignity, and they represent themselves as more knowledgeable than I am to rule the world. You may try to debase these proud ones, to take them down a notch, but you can't. Only My right hand can save you from them.

There are some things too great for you. People may try to recreate what I've done and make things "better," but they only succeed in corrupting what I created. And some creations can never be "tamed," as much as some may try to do it. Everything under the heavens is Mine. I made it all! So why continue to try to outdo Me? You never can. You will only frustrate yourself and others. Many things are beyond your comprehension, or power, to outdo.

Yet you try, without My help, and without coming to Me for help!

"Everything under the heavens is Mine; therefore, who can have a claim against God?" Yet people continue to try to master what can't be mastered by them, resist what I've set in motion, and unravel what I've designed and woven. The same people who try to desecrate My works would never dare to come and speak to Me face to face! They're too afraid. They weave their evil deeds behind closed doors.

But if you will wait for Me to come to you, I will. And I'll show you Who I Am and reveal Myself to you. Though you have only heard of Me, you'll see Me and begin to understand.

And, if you will humble yourself before Me, and ask for My forgiveness, as Job did, and pray for those who've done you wrong, then I can abound toward you. I can restore what you've lost in life, and give you more, even more than your dreams!

But you must first pray for those who've offended or wronged you, and forgive them.

Day 144

How to be happy

*"Let all those who take refuge and put their trust in You rejoice; let them ever sing
and shout for joy, because You make a covering over them and defend them;
let those also who love Your name be joyful in You and be in high spirits."*
—*Psalm 5:11*

Psalm 1-8

Why did David and his worship leaders compose the Psalms? Because they wanted a way
to praise Me through music. These songs written by David, Asaph, the sons of Korah,
Moses, Heman, Ethan, and Solomon were arranged by Ezra. They show how to be happy
by meditating on and delighting in My words. This is also the secret to prosperity and being
able to stand on solid ground in this life and the next. Knowing My thoughts and intentions
for you releases you from fears. If you're concerned because some are conspiring against you,
or scheming to do you harm, you need never be afraid. David understood this. He knew
how I laugh at those who try to deride Me or My people. I mock their efforts. Why? Because,
ultimately, My ways will prevail.

One day, My decrees will be carried out completely by the Son I've begotten. When He
reigns on earth, the nations will be His inheritance. Then, the uttermost parts of the earth
will be His possession. So, the leaders who choose to act unwisely against Me now should
beware! Those who pay homage to Me will have lasting reigns, and those who serve Me now
will rejoice and be blessed. Those who seek refuge in Me will be envied. Though many rise
up against you and try to cause you harm, or mock your belief in Me, I will always be your
shield. I will lift you high above them. You never need to fear people, even when thousands
of them surround you! Salvation belongs to Me. I bless and protect My people.

When you cry out to Me, I hear you. I free you from your distress when you feel hemmed
in. I listen to you when you sigh and groan. I release you from your fears. I set you apart
when you turn and stand for Me. And I make you dwell in safety and give you the ability to
lie down in peace.

I hate lies, and I reject deceitfulness and bloodthirstiness. The people who propound
these things will not win out in the end. Those who worship Me are always welcome in My
house, where love and mercy and truth abide.

And those who enter it will sing for joy, knowing I defend them.

Day 145

Wait for Me

"As for me, I will continue beholding Your face in righteousness (rightness, justice, and right standing with You); I shall be fully satisfied, when I awake [to find myself] beholding Your form [and having sweet communion with You]."
—Psalm 17:15

Psalm 9-17

I have made Myself known. I the Lord Who maintains your right when you stand for Me. I am your refuge and high tower of defense when you feel oppressed. I am your stronghold in times of trouble. Those who know My Name and understand My mercy lean on Me. They seek Me, because they know I hear their cries.

Nations will rise against Me. They'll sneer at My power and judgments, because they seem distant. But they'll sink into the pits they create from their unbelief and lack of trust in Me. They may boast against Me and arise with pride and arrogance to devise schemes against My people. They may think that no one can come against them, because they are too powerful. They may slay the innocent and lurk in secret places, believing I will never see their evil deeds since I am quite forgotten. But remember this: I see the things they do, and I take notes. And, one day, I will make things right as a helper of the fatherless, the needy, and the innocent. I will break the arms of the wicked, because I am the Lord Who is King over all forever.

I prepare and strengthen and direct the hearts of the humble. I hear the cries of the oppressed. You can take refuge in Me. My throne is in heaven now, but, one day, it will reside on a new earth. My eyes behold, and I test and prove the righteous. I abhor and judge the wicked, who love violence. One day, you will behold My face. And, though it seems like godly people are vanishing more and more each day and being replaced by deceitful ones, who boast that "There is no God," I will set those in safety who turn to Me. My words are as pure as silver refined seven times. I keep My promises.

Though it seems like I hide My face from you, and your fears are multiplying, I will lighten your eyes so you can see My face in the darkness. You can be happy, knowing I deal bountifully with you and work on your behalf. I value those who live for Me and speak My truth, who uphold what is right and just. I save those who trust Me and hide them in the shadow of My wings.

In My presence, you can find great joy and sweet communion with Me.

Day 146

I am your Rock

*"The Lord is my Rock, my Fortress, and my Deliverer; my God, my
keen and firm Strength in Whom I will trust and take refuge,
my Shield, and the Horn of my salvation, my High Tower."*
—*Psalm 18:2*

Psalm 18-22

I am your Rock. I am your Fortress and Deliverer. I am your Strength and Shield. I am the Horn of your salvation, your High Tower. Though I seem hidden from you, I reach from on high and draw you out of many waters. I deliver you from those who hate you. I am your Stay and your Support. I delight in you.

I reward your righteousness. I show Myself kind and merciful to you when you are kind and merciful. I cause your lamp to be lit and illumine your way through darkness. I help you run through a troop and leap over high walls. When you take refuge and trust in Me, I make your feet like hinds' feet, so you can stand firmly and securely in dangerous places. I hold you up and make you great. With Me, your feet will never slip. I gird you with strength and subdue your enemies. I deliver you from peoples' strivings.

Exalt Me, because I am the God of your salvation. Sing praises to Me, because I show you and your offspring great mercy and steadfast love.

The heavens declare My glory. The firmament proclaims My handiwork. My laws are perfect. My testimony makes you wise. My words make your heart sing and your eyes brighten! They endure forever, because they are true and right. I see your lapses and faults and make them as nothing when you bring them to Me. I make you acceptable. I refresh and defend you. I grant you your heart's desire and fulfill your plans and petitions. I answer you with the saving strength of My right hand. I make you rise up and stand when you trust in Me. I send blessings of good things and give you life. I make you overwhelmingly glad with the joy of My presence. I show you ceaseless mercy and love.

Will I ever forsake you? No. Though you can't see Me in dire situations, when you are faced with death, I am always right next to you, just as I was beside David and My Son.

Praise Me for My power! I use it to help you. When you cry out to Me, I deliver you. You need never wonder if I will show up for you. I will never disappoint you. People may laugh at your trust in Me, but I have always been your God in Whom you can trust.

I called you from your birth, and I am always very near you.

I hear you.

Day 147

I turn your mourning into dancing!

*"You have turned my mourning into dancing for me; You
have put off my sackcloth and girded me with gladness."*
—Psalm 30:11

Psalm 23-31

I am your Shepherd. What does this mean? It means that I feed and protect you from harm. I take you to plentiful places, where you can be satisfied and fulfilled. I restore life to you and refresh you physically, mentally, and spiritually. When death threatens you, I give you courage so you're not afraid. I remind you of My presence.

As your shepherd, I comfort you. The soothing oil I anoint you with is My Holy Spirit, which flows through you and brings you into an abounding place of goodness, mercy, and unfailing love. With it, you enter My courts and My house. Your hands and heart become clean, because I wash them with the truth of My presence.

I made the earth, filled the seas, and established the rivers and currents. With Me, there is no falsehood. I bring you to My mountain of truth, where you can stand in My presence. With Me, you gain access to My gates. I am your King of glory. When you lean on Me, you're never ashamed or disappointed. You begin to see things through My eyes. I guide you. I'm the God of your salvation. When you wait for Me, I am merciful to you. I do not look upon your lapses or youthful transgressions. I pardon them, because I love you. When you're humble, you begin to experience My path of mercy and love.

Companionship with Me is sweet. When you seek it, I reveal to you My innermost secrets. I unravel mysteries and disclose deep meanings to you.

When you're lonely or distressed, I am gracious toward you. As your refuge, I deliver you from oppressions and troubles. When you seek Me, I vindicate you. When you rely on Me, I make you steady as you walk on the right paths. You can lean on Me for support. Though false people surround you, I can wash your hands of them and bring you to My altar of truth, where I show you what is sweet and right. I give you integrity. I'm your Light. With Me, you need never dread or fear what's around you.

In any day of trouble, I hide you in My Shelter. I set you high on My Rock. Seek My face, for I'm your Help. I heal you. Wait for Me, for I give you courage. I bring you life. Sing praises to Me, for I'm the Shepherd and Stronghold of your soul.

I turn your mourning into dancing.

153

Day 148

I'm your hiding place

"You are a hiding place for me; You, Lord, preserve me from trouble, You surround me with songs and shouts of deliverance. Selah [pause, and calmly think of that]!"
—Psalm 32:7

Psalm 32-37

I am your hiding place. I preserve you. I surround you with songs and shouts of deliverance. I instruct and teach you in the way you should go. As you lean on Me, I encompass you with My mercy and love. I forgive you. Rejoice in Me. Give thanks to Me. Sing to Me a new and joyful song. For My Word is right. My work is faithful. I love justice. And I see you.

The earth is an example of My loving-kindness. I made the heavens by My Word and all their host by My breath. I keep the deep places in store for a later time. I speak, and it happens. I bring the plans of some nations to naught. I make people's schemes of no effect. My counsel stands forever, and My thoughts last for all generations. I bless nations who worship Me. I choose My own heritage. My eye is on those who revere Me. I deliver from death and famine those who wait and hope for My mercy and love. I am your Help and Shield. You can rejoice in Me!

I hear and deliver you from all your fears. When you look to Me, your face radiates My Light and My love. My angel encamps around you to protect you. Through Me, you'll never lack any beneficial thing. I help you refrain from speaking anything that is not right. Crave Me, and you will have peace. My ears hear your cries, and I deliver you from all your distresses. Take refuge in Me, for I redeem you.

Though others pursue you and try to catch you in their nets to destroy you, My angel will obstruct them. Though some conspire against you, I will vindicate you with My just hand. I am pleased when you prosper. I stand up for you. My mercy and love extend to the skies and My faithfulness to the clouds. You can find refuge under the shadow of My wings. You can feast on My abundance and drink from the stream of My pleasure. I am the Fountain of Life. In Me, you see Light.

Never fret because of people bent on doing evil. Their actions will come to nothing. Delight in Me, and I will give you the secret requests of your heart. Roll every care onto Me, and I will take care of them and you.

Rest in Me, and together we will inhabit a new world.

Day 149

What makes you sad?

"Why are you cast down, O my inner self? And why should you moan over me and be disquieted within me? Hope in God and wait expectantly for Him, for I shall yet praise Him, Who is the help of my [sad] countenance, and my God."
—Psalm 43:5

Psalm 38-45

Do you feel so sad that you wish you would die? David did. I made him king and brought him through terrible times in the wilderness, where he fought for his life. But now he groaned and moaned. Why? Because he knew he had neglected Me in his heart. He'd turned away from Me in the matter of Bathsheba and Uriah. He had a good man killed to cover up his own failing. Now he saw the consequences. He'd asked for forgiveness, and I'd given him that. But I could not prevent the outcomes. A child died. And his other children turned against him.

He knew he could fight any battle and win. He could overcome Goliath with a slingshot by trusting in Me. But he could not control his own progeny, who worked and schemed against him with his closest friends. Because of this, he grew depressed, as you would be if your own family members betrayed you. And he mourned the loss of Absalom. But he learned something as he lay on his bed. He saw how life is transient. And only I can control the results for good. He realized what life was like without Me. So he cried. And I saw his tears. I restored his strength, and I helped him to feel gladness once again. I put a new song in his mouth—a song of praise. And he realized how walking and talking with Me was more desirable than anything else in this world. Even life itself!

When he saw My faithfulness during brokenness, despite his failings, and when he understood how I'd always stood up for him, even when others didn't, then he magnified My Name. When he knew that I saw the secrets of his heart, and still loved him, he rejoiced in Me.

When you lie on a bed of suffering, as David did, I can transform your weakness into strength. I can sustain and refresh you. I am merciful and gracious. Though some conspire against you, I can raise you up and requite you. I set you on a cushion in My presence. Though tears have been your food day and night, you can gaze up and see My face and hear My song sung to you in the night. Like David, you can say, "Why should I be sad?"

"Why should I moan, when I know You are with Me?"

Day 150

I will always be there for you!

*"God is our Refuge and Strength [mighty and impenetrable to temptation], a very present
and well-proved help in trouble, therefore we will not fear, though the earth should
change and though the mountains be shaken into the midst of the seas."*
—Psalm 46:1-2

Psalm 46-54

What would you do if things on the earth suddenly changed? What if volcanoes started
exploding lava all over the place? What if the seas roared, and the land trembled from
earthquakes? What if nations began to rage against each other and kingdoms were toppled,
causing havoc in the world? Would you panic? Would you be afraid for your life or others'?
No! Why not? Because I will always be your Refuge and your Strength. I am ever present
and a proven help to you in times of trouble. I am amid it all. I can make wars cease, even to
the ends of the earth. I can dissolve the things meant for destruction. So, be still and know
that I am God, the Lord of Hosts, Who is with you.

Exalt Me above the lies and innuendo you hear, because I am your High Tower and
Stronghold amid the propaganda. Shout out to Me, and clap your hands. Sing to Me out
of joy and triumph, for I, the Lord Most High, am a great King over all the earth. I own
the cattle on a thousand hills, and I can subdue people, even nations, under My feet. I reign
overall.

I choose your inheritance for you, and, one day, you will sit alongside a river whose
streams will make you glad within My city. You'll praise Me on My holy mountain, where
I will sit with My Son, as princes gather around us. Mount Zion will be a fair and beautiful
place—a city of the great King! And on it, I will rule with My right hand of righteousness
and justice. And all will rejoice to see it. Remember that I am your guide unto death and life
afterward. I am your God forever.

Those who boast now of their riches cannot ever redeem themselves with their wealth,
because the cost of their ransom is too great! They, like everyone, will perish one day, and
they will leave their wealth to others, who will realize that the belongings and deeds of those
who live apart from Me cannot last. I will gather My saints to Me one day. And those who
found grace in My sight will declare My righteousness as I rule as Judge over all. I am God,
your God.

And I will always be there for you.

156

Day 151

Are you terrified of death?

"Be merciful and gracious to me, O God, be merciful and gracious to me, for my soul takes refuge and finds shelter and confidence in You; yes, in the shadow of Your wings will I take refuge and be confident until calamities and destructive storms are passed."
—*Psalm 57:1*

Psalm 55-62

Are you terrified of death? Do horrors overwhelm you? Do you wish you had wings like a dove so you could fly away and be at rest from your worries and the problems you face? Would you like to wander far away from it all and take up lodging in the middle of a wilderness, where no one can find you? Are you trying to find some shelter from a tempest? Do you feel like your family and friends desert you and don't understand you? Some even turn against you. David felt all these things too. But he realized something. He saw how he could call on Me, and I would come to him. I was there with him in his distress. I heard him. And I helped him. I gave him peace when people came against him. He learned to trust Me, and, because of this, I could help him overcome his fears of what people could do to him. He no longer feared, because he saw how I kept his feet from stumbling into their pits. I delivered him, even from death.

You can find the shelter you seek in the shadow of My wings. There you can take refuge until the storms of life have passed. As you wait there, I can work on your behalf and reward your trust in Me by bringing to pass My purposes for you and completing them. I can even save and spare you from slander and the reproach of those who try to swallow you up and trample you down. Your life may be among lions with teeth like arrows and tongues like swords, but they lay their own traps and dig their own pits.

Fix your heart on Me confidently and steadfastly. Awaken to My glory and sing to Me, because My mercy is great. It reaches up to the heavens, as do My truth and My faithfulness. I can break the teeth of lions. I can divert the arrows aimed at you by breaking them apart. I can make the righteous rejoice by bringing them a resounding reward, because I am God, Who judges the earth. Though your enemies may belch out insults, swing swords of sarcasm, ride you with ridicule, and try to slay you with slander, I will laugh them to scorn. For I am your Shield against any onslaught!

Through Me, you will always do valiantly, for I am the Rock that is greater than anyone or anything—the Rock that cannot be moved.

Day 152

You can swear by Me!

"Blessed be the Lord, Who bears our burdens and carries us day by day, even the God Who is our salvation! Selah [pause, and calmly think of that]!"
—*Psalm 68:19*

Psalm 63-68

You can swear by Me. You can bind yourself to My authority and acknowledge My supremacy. You can devote yourself to My service and declare My works to others. Why? Because I defend you against those who seek your harm. As you rest beneath My wings and take refuge in Me, you can see My glory and power, and you can praise Me.

To Me belongs silence. Where? In My place of rest and peace! It is where you can abide in reverent wonder. It is where your heart bursts with praise, because you see Who I am and what I've done for you. It's a place I want you to come as often as possible, because here you can be delivered from all physical, mental, and spiritual burdens. Here, you can receive healing as needed. Here, I can forgive and free you from all your failings. Here, you can hear My voice and enter the courts of My holy temple.

By accomplishing amazing things for you, I answer you with My righteousness. I am your confidence and your hope. I founded the mountains with My power. I still the roaring seas and the tumults of the people. I make the place where morning and evening are birthed shout for joy. I enrich the earth with My bounty, and I send rain as needed, so that even the hills, meadows, and valleys sing together!

Make a joyful noise to Me and sing of My honor and glory. Praise Me, because My works are awesome and glorious. See how I fight for you and rule with My might forever. It is I Who watch over the nations and judge people fairly. By My saving power I guide, lead, and steer them so that the righteous remain. All can rejoice in Me, because I am a Father to the fatherless and a Protector of widows and orphans. I place the solitary ones in families. I also lead prisoners to prosperity.

I bear your burdens for you. I carry you day by day, and I crown your years with wonderful goodness.

I am your deliverer.

Day 153

Are you a stranger in your own home?

"I have become a stranger to my brethren, and an alien to my mother's children."
—*Psalm 69:8*

Psalm 69-73

Do you feel like a stranger in your own home among your own family members, who disagree with and deride you? Are you dealt with unjustly? Are you persecuted, insulted, or reproached for what you stand for? Are you jeered at and humiliated? Do you blame Me for this? David did. Because he felt all these things.

I hear your complaints. And I rescue you from your sinking fears. I deliver you from the drowning concerns you feel. I never hide My face from you or reproach you, because I love you. My mercy is tender and plenteous. My love is a sweet and comforting thing. By these, I can set you free. Some may try to break you and cause you to fall, even seek your destruction. Though none come to comfort you, I am always at your side.

One day, you'll dwell with Me forever. I am your hope. I am the source of your confidence. I have been your benefactor from the time you were conceived. I am your refuge. In Me, you will always find trust, because I will never forsake you. Even when you are old and frail, and your strength is spent, and your abilities have deteriorated, I am never far from you. I stand up for you to your enemies, whether they are people or circumstances. And those who dishonor you will themselves be defamed.

You can praise Me, because the number of My righteous deeds can't be counted. My mighty acts bring you strength, even in your weakness. I never forsake My own, especially when they're old and gray. I give them breath to declare My strength to the next generation. There is none like Me, for My righteousness reaches to the heavens. I give new life to the down-hearted, and I encourage those who turn to Me with their troubles. I alone can do wondrous things. I judge and defend the poor, deliver the needy, and crush their oppressors.

One day, My Son will have dominion over the earth. Then the righteous will flourish, and peace will abound. Those who dwell in the wilderness will bow down before Him, and all nations will serve Him. He will redeem His own from oppression, fraud, and violence. The least fruitful places will flourish.

And all people, including kings, will bless and praise Him, because His name will endure forever!

Day 154

Only I can set things straight

"We give praise and thanks to You, O God, we praise and give thanks;
Your wondrous works declare that Your Name is near and
they who invoke Your Name rehearse Your wonders."
—Psalm 75:1

Psalm 74-78

I own the day. I also own the night. I established light. I fixed the borders of the earth and the seas. I made summer and winter. My wondrous works declare that My Name is near, and those who invoke My Name will rehearse My wonders. I never forget My adversaries—those who revolt against Me, whose voices ascend continually from the dark places of violence. When the right time comes, I will judge all uprightly. Though the earth teeters, along with its inhabitants, I will set it right again and steady its pillars.

Some may boast now of their great ability to make things right. They proclaim that they truly understand how things work, but they really seek their own personal aggrandizement. Only I can promote and elevate in the long run. I am the true judge. I put down one and lift up another. Only I can set things straight.

Sometimes you will wonder where I am. You have heard of My works and what I've done, yet you can't see them now. I seem to have deserted the earth and those on it. You wonder if I'm hiding. But I'm not. I am close to you always. Though you hear of My marvelous acts of old—how I saved Israel from the Egyptians and parted the Red Sea and sent the Israelites manna and meat in the wilderness, you wonder where I am now. Where are My mighty works? You look around at the chaos and confusion in the world and wonder why My right hand does not prevail. You see the evil that prevails and question when I will ever show up and correct things.

My time is in My hands. The sanctuary I built reaches to the heavens. Though you can't see it now, it is established forever. And, one day, it will reside on a newly-made earth, where the righteous abide with Me. Though you can't see it now, it exists and will be seen by all one day. And the spirits of those who were steadfast and faithful to Me will live in it.

Recount My blessings and works to the children today so that they may know of My love and have hope for a new day, when this world ends and a new one begins.

I want them to abide with Me there, just as I want you to.

Day 155

I answer you in a secret place

*"You called in distress and I delivered you; I answered you in the secret place of thunder;
I tested you at the waters of Meribah, Selah [pause, and calmly think of that]!"*
—*Psalm 81:7*

Psalm 79-86

My hand is on the people of My right hand—those I've planted in the land. I groom, prune, and make them strong for Myself. I revive and restore them, and My face shines on them like the sun, giving them nourishment and light. They are saved for My purposes, and their lives will continue, even into a new age and time. For My purposes never cease. What I call you to do now, and how you respond to My calling, will affect your assignment in the next life. I answer you in a secret place. Though it seems like a place of thunder at times, it is actually a place of silence and peace. You may think My requests are questionable, even glaringly outrageous, but when you listen to Me and walk out My wishes, then I can subdue your enemies—the people or things that torture and threaten you and others. Then I can administer true justice on the earth.

When judges and magistrates judge unjustly by showing partiality to the wicked, they walk in the darkness of complacent satisfaction. And the fundamental principles upon which the administration of justice rest are shaken. Those who hate Me raise their heads and lay crafty schemes against My people. They consult together against My "set-aside" ones. They seek to wipe them out. But they will be put to shame. They will perish. And all will know that I am Most High over all the earth.

Blessed are those whose strength lies in Me, whose hearts and lives pave highways to Zion. They go from strength to strength, and they will appear before Me one day in My new city. I see their faces, because they're anointed. They understand that one day in My courts is better than a thousand anywhere else. For I am their Sun and Shield. I bestow grace and favor and honor, even heavenly bliss, to them. I withhold no good thing from them, because they walk by My side. And, as they look confidently toward Me, they are blessed above all. I speak peace to them, and My salvation is near them, because they desire My presence. With Me, mercy and love and truth converge, and righteousness and peace kiss each other. Follow My footsteps. Unite your heart with Mine. Then you will find righteousness. Then you will see mercy and graciousness. For I am good. I am ready to forgive. I am abundant in mercy and love to all who call on Me. There is none like Me. I alone am God.

I alone can comfort you.

Day 156

Even if you drift far from Me

"For a thousand years in Your sight are but as yesterday
when it is past, or as a watch in the night."
—*Psalm 90:4*

Psalm 87-91

Rivers will run from My city one day—precious springs of life and joy. And those who live there will drink from them and be revived daily.

Your morning prayers come to meet Me, and your songs of praise are ever before Me. Blessed are those who know the joyful sound of My voice. They walk in My Light, and the favor of My countenance brightens their way. They rejoice in Me, because I give them strength and visions, and I anoint them with My holy oil. They cry out to Me, "You are my Father, my God, and the Rock of my salvation!" And the throne of My Offspring will endure forever as the days of heaven.

Even if you drift far from Me, My loving-kindness and faithfulness will never fail you. Though it seems like I've cast your crown to the ground and made you a reproach to others, and even shortened your days, I remain in My dwelling place and offer you refuge always.

Remember that 1,000 years to Me is like a single night watch. I see everything in you through the revealing Light of My countenance. Whether you live to age 40 or 80, life flies away, and a heart filled with wisdom can only come from Me.

Life lived with Me is full of rejoicing and gladness, and, when you dwell in My secret place, you remain secure under My shadow. I am your Refuge and Fortress in any storm. I cover you with My pinions and shield you with My wings. You may see destruction and sudden death all around you, but you will not be touched by them, because you make Me your dwelling place. There, you need never fear terror or evil or death. For I give My angels special charge over you to defend and preserve you in all your ways. And they will bear you up.

When you set your love on Me, I deliver you. Though a thousand fall beside you, death will not touch you. Because you know My Name, I set you on high. I am with you in any trouble.

I will never forsake you.

Day 157

Sing a new song!

"O sing to the Lord a new song; sing to the Lord, all the earth!"
—Psalm 96: 1

Psalm 92-101

Some are gifted with the ability to praise Me with instruments of song. These are like the birds who bring pleasure merely with their singing. They remind you of My presence and, through them, you can hear My voice singing love songs to you.

Even trees can remind you of Me. Those who are righteous, because they trust in Me, are like palm trees. They are stately, upright, and fruitful. They bend in the storms of life and never break, because they depend on Me. Like great cedars, they are majestic and durable. They grow in grace and bring forth fruit, even in old age. They are full of vitality and rich in the verdure of trust, love, and contentment. They are robed with majesty, strength, and power.

I am mighty—even more amazing than the seas' waves and breakers. I teach knowledge and reveal the futility of peoples' thoughts, which are only a breath. I instruct, give power, and bring calmness amid adversity. When you feel anxious, I can comfort, cheer, and even delight you! I hold you up so your feet won't slip, because in My hands are in the deep places of the earth. I am the Rock of your refuge. Even the heights of the hills are Mine! Strength and beauty are in My sanctuary.

Sing to Me a new song! Declare My glory among the people. Marvel at My works, for I am worthy of praise. I made the heavens. Through Me, the world is established. Let the heavens be glad. Let the earth rejoice. Let the seas roar and the fields exult! For, one day, I will come with My Son to judge and govern the world from My throne of truth. Then, the earth and the heavens will declare My righteousness, and all will behold My glory. Even the rivers will clap their hands, and the hills and trees will sing for joy! For I am good. My mercy and love last forever. My faithfulness endures through all generations.

So, make a joyful noise to Me! With your voice or instrument break forth and sing!

For, in this way, you will enter My gates and My courts by your praise!

Day 158

Why don't I respond more quickly?

*"Hide not Your face from me in the day when I am in distress! Incline
Your ear to me; in the day when I call, answer me speedily."*
—Psalm 102:2

Psalm 102-105

Why don't I act more quickly to answer your prayers? I have ultimate control over heaven and earth. Why does it take Me so long to change things for the better? You know that one day I'll appear with My Son in glory. You know that nations will worship and revere My Name then, and all the kings of the earth will be awed by My power. People yet to come will praise Me. But where am I now?

I seem to look down from the height of My sanctuary in heaven to view the earth. I seem to ignore the sighing and groaning of people in prisons, who are trapped and appointed for death. I seem to allow affliction and weakness and do nothing about them. I even seem to bring people low with sorrow and shorten their days. It seems like I was involved at the beginning, when I created what you see now, but where am I now?

I have always been the same. I am ageless and only through Me do you dwell safely. Remember what I've already done for you and do even now! I continuously forgive your faults and failings—the times you walked away from Me. I heal your sicknesses. I pull you out of many pits and bring the fulfillment of your dreams. I bring you satisfaction. I help you overcome situations by renewing your strength when you feel weak. I make things right when you are mistreated and oppressed.

I never hold a grudge against you, even when you turn your back on Me. I never repay you for the wrongs you commit against Me. And yet you ask, "Where are you now?" I crown you with My love, and I make you beautiful.

My mercy toward you reaches to the heavens. I place your shortcomings as far from Me as the east is from the west. I know how you are made, and I remember that your days disappear like the wind. But My mercy and love last forever, even to your children's children. Look around and see what I've done. Through My wisdom, I made the earth to be full of My riches. How long did it take Me? Remember, time is in My hands.

Do I hide My face from you now? How can you think that? I always work on your behalf. My covenants are imprinted on My heart. I also remember My promises to you.

And I will fulfill them at the right time and place.

Day 159

When your courage melts away

"For Your mercy and loving-kindness are great and high as the heavens!
Your truth and faithfulness reach to the skies!"
—Psalm 108:4

Psalm 106-109

I promised David that one day I would gather My people from the nations to a place where they could give thanks and praise My Holy Name. One day, many will gather in My holy city, where they will acknowledge and bow down before the King—the One Who will return with you. And you, along with the chosen ones, will praise My Name and see the face of My Son. Then, you will see My ultimate consolation and deliverance for you and for all My people.

But now, you cry to Me. And I promise I'll deliver you in your present need. I can satisfy your longings and fill your hunger. Though you sit in darkness, in the shadow of death, bound up in your afflictions, and you continue to cry out to Me, I will save you from your distresses. I can break apart the bonds that hold you back. I sent forth My Word to heal and rescue you from the pit and destruction, because I wanted to hear your shouts of joy and your songs of praise!

As storms gather, and winds of torment increase around you, and you reel and stagger from them like a drunken person, your courage may melt away, and you may feel yourself at wits' end. But cry out to Me, and I will hush the storm to a calm and gentle whisper. I will still the waves that beat against you. I will bring you to your desired haven like Jesus did with His disciples in the boat.

I can turn a wilderness into a pool of water and dry land into water springs for you. I prepare a place for you even now. I pour contempt on those who try to cause you to wander in waste places, where there seems to be no way out, because I want to hear your songs of praise to Me!

My mercy and loving-kindness are as high as the heavens. My truth and righteousness reach to the skies! When deceitful ones speak against you, and loved ones surround you with words of hate, and even betray you, you may feel like you are a reproach among many, who shake their heads at you.

But I will always stand at your right hand and fight for you to save you from any who condemn you!

Day 160

Out of the womb of the morning

"Your people will offer themselves willingly in the day of Your power, in the beauty of holiness and in holy array out of the womb of the morning; to You [will spring forth] Your young men, who are as the dew."
—Psalm 110:3

Psalm 110-118

Out of the womb of the morning, My Son will appear in His glory. In the beauty of holiness and in holy array, He will return for you. Then My young men and women will spring forth like the dew and help Me execute judgment in the land, and we will raise our heads together triumphantly. Give thanks with your whole heart, because My upright council will be made known. Delight in My works. They are honorable and gracious, and My righteousness endures forever. My works are always merciful, loving, and compassionate, and they are revealed to those who seek Me. My works are established. They represent My truth and uprightness. Those who seek My will and worship Me will have access to My wisdom. They will also attain good understanding and know their own skills and abilities, which will be used for Me so that they have meaning in life.

One day, My offspring will be mighty on the earth. Now, they can be blessed, knowing that prosperity and safety exist in My house. Light arises from darkness in My presence. When you stand with Me, you are never afraid of bad news, because your heart is firmly fixed by trusting in Me. Your life is steady and established, and you are never afraid, because you know your desires are fulfilled in Me. And My desire is that you have reason to praise Me from the rising of the sun to its going down and from the far corners of the east and west! I am higher than any person, nation, god, or political scheme! There is no one like Me! My seat is on high, and I can raise the poor out of dust and lift the needy from ash heaps and dung hills and seat them with princes. I can make the barren fruitful and joyful. The earth trembles at My presence, because I can turn rocks into pools of water. I do what I please.

Others may ask where I am, but you know I abide in the heavens. Unlike manmade gods, who resemble the people who made them, I am your Help and Shield. You can take refuge in Me, knowing I bless those who worship Me, whether they be great or small, and I set them in large places, where they need never fear what anyone can do to them. I am your Strength and Song and Salvation.

Rejoice in this day I have made, knowing Who is the Cornerstone of My temple, which is reserved for you and for the day of His coming!

Day 161

What My Word can do for you

"Great peace have they who love Your law; nothing
shall offend them or make them stumble."
—Psalm 119:165

Psalm 119

David sought My Word with his whole heart. He inquired of Me. He yearned and longed to hear what I had to say. He stored My words in his heart, so he would not sin against Me. With his lips, he recounted what he'd learned of Me. He meditated on My precepts and respected My ways—the paths of life I had marked out for him. He delighted in My statutes and refused to forget Me. He observed My words diligently and walked in My ways. He opened his heart, even his griefs, to Me. Why did he think it so important to do this? Because he knew that, by this, he would be blessed—happy and fortunate. Then, he'd never be put to shame. Then he'd inherit My promises to him. And I would never forsake him. Then I could teach and instruct him in the ways of life. And I could deal bountifully with him as I can with you.

I could open his eyes to behold wondrous things. I could revive and stimulate him, show him favor, and establish his steps. I could raise him up and strengthen him. I could remove falsehood and unfaithfulness from him. I could give him a willing heart to serve Me. I could give him great peace so that nothing would offend him or make him stumble.

My Word is a lamp to light your way. Through it, I can teach you and give you understanding. I can show you the meaning of life through truth, wisdom, discernment, and knowledge. I can even lead you to right paths, where you will not go astray. I can give you the answers you need for those who taunt and reproach you. I can give you courage to speak My words, even to leaders and kings. I can restore you to vigorous life and health. I can confirm My promises to you and offer you mercy and loving-kindness. I can cause your heart to rejoice, as I did David's, and give you hope, liberty, and ease. I can give you a new life.

I hold you up and provide comfort and consolation to you. I even cause you to sing. Through My words, you can recognize Me, know My Name and what it represents to you, and how I am your portion. I can help you to be a companion to those who also desire to hear My words. I can make you glad, heartened, and happy. I can deal bountifully with you. For I am good and kind, as are My words to you.

And I will always be more to you than any amount of gold or silver.

Day 162

Only in Me is peace

*"The Lord will keep your going out and your coming
in from this time forth and forevermore."*
—Psalm 121:8

Psalm 120-134

"I am for peace," David wrote, *"but when I speak, they are for war,"* and, *"my life has too
long had its dwelling with him who hates peace."*

Where does peace come from? It can only come from Me. I am your help in times of
discord, when those around you seem to be in an uproar, shouting against each other. I
made the heavens and the earth. I understand the ins and outs of all people. And peace can
only come when they turn to Me for help. I can bring them to a sure place, where their feet
will not slip or be moved. I am the keeper of safety. I shade you from harm and keep you
from evil. I direct your going out and coming in.

But you must pray for peace, especially the peace of Jerusalem, for this is My "resting
place." For the sake of My house, you must seek, inquire for, and require its good. Then, I
will have mercy on you. Then, the waters that would have overwhelmed you will themselves
be swept away, and the torrents against you will be removed. And you will be like a bird
escaped from the fowler's snare. The trap will be broken, and you will escape. When you
realize that your only help comes from Me, the One Who made heaven and earth, you begin
to understand that I surround you with good. When your heart is right, you have peace. I
turn captivity into liberty and restore lost fortunes. I cause those who sow in tears to reap
in joy and singing.

When you turn to Me for help, the house you build will last, and your efforts will never
be in vain. Only I can keep you safe. Only I can make your life fruitful and blessed. You
can surround yourself with the things you think will protect you, such as alarms, warnings,
and barriers, but only I can create a hedge around you and make your way prosperous. I can
maintain your peace, because I can "cut asunder the thick cords by which the wicked bind
you." Only I can free you from the fears that enslave you.

With Me, there is always forgiveness. I do not keep accountings or treat you according to
your shortcomings. With Me, there is mercy, loving-kindness, and plenteous redemption. I
can calm and quiet your soul. I can give you hope for a future. In Me, you will find the rest
and peace you seek. My desire is that all people dwell together in unity.

But this can only be done in and through Me.

Day 163

I knew you before you were born

"Your eyes saw my unformed substance, and in Your book all the days [of my life] were written before ever they took shape, when as yet there was none of them."
—*Psalm 139:16*

Psalm 135-141

I know you. Because I designed you. I saw you before you were born, even before you were conceived! And then, I knew everything about you and what you would and could do. I understand you and why you are the way you are. Nothing is a secret to Me. I see your inner thoughts, and I know your struggles. I see when you get up and when you lie down. I even search out the steps you will take each day. Not a word you utter is hidden from Me!

I surround your every move with My presence. If you could see Me, you would realize that My hand is on your life for good. But you must trust Me. What I know is far beyond your comprehension. I will reveal what I know and Who and What I am to you little by little, if you ask. I am in everything and around everything. You cannot escape from Me. But why would you want to? My hand can lead you and hold you up. My Spirit can guide you, whether you are in heavenly places or places of death.

Darkness hides nothing from Me. Because I am Light. I knew you when you were but a speck in someone's imagination. I knit you together in your mother's womb. She loved you, but I loved you even more. I look on you longingly, desiring your love in return. I made you beautiful by combining the best parts of your parents. Through Me, you were embroidered and knit together using the most wonderful colors and concepts to dazzle and delight the most profound thinkers, philosophers, or mathematicians on earth!

My eyes saw you before you were formed, and I began to write your story in My book. I included all the days of your life before they took shape. I saw your life as very precious to Me. My thoughts of you were many and wonderful and more numerous than all the sands on earth!

Awaken to My love for you! Realize how wonderful you are to Me and why I designed you to be so beautiful and amazing. I see and delight in you. You are to Me more precious than anything else I've made—any of My creations.

See your beauty today through My eyes, and know that I designed you as you are for a purpose—My own.

Day 164

Lean on My shoulder

"Cause me to hear Your loving-kindness in the morning, for on You do I lean and in You do I trust. Cause me to know the way wherein I should walk, for I lift up my inner self to You."
—*Psalm 141:8*

Psalm 142-150

I am your refuge. When you feel overwhelmed by circumstances—when people turn against you or can't help you, I am there. When no one cares for you, and you have no place to run, cry to Me, and I will deliver you. I will bring you out of your prison and deal bountifully with you, so I can hear your voice rising in thankful praise to Me.

When you lean your head on My shoulder, you'll hear My voice of loving-kindness, even in the mornings as you sit with Me. When you walk with Me in the evenings, I'll show you the way to walk. When you come to Me during the day, and lift your inner thoughts to Me, I'll show you what to do. Even when you're fleeing from enemies who try to hurt you, I'll hide you in the shadow of My wings. I'll bring your life out of trouble and free you from distress. I'll subdue those who come against you.

Your life may seem like a passing shadow, but, each day, I give you a new song to sing for Me. I fill your garners and bring you to a place of peace and happiness, for you are blessed when I am your Lord. Every day has its reason, and, in each day, I want to hear your voice raised to Me in gratefulness, even amid chaos and confusion. Even when you're overwhelmed with sadness. I long to hear your songs of praise. For I am gracious and just, full of compassion, slow to anger, and abounding in mercy and love toward you.

Though life seems hard now, you will see My glorious kingdom and be amazed at its fulfillment one day. It's an everlasting kingdom, where we'll reign together forever. Even now, I uphold those who fall and raise up those weighted down when they look to Me. My desire is to open My hand and satisfy every living thing with favor. For I am near to all who call on Me. I hear their cries and preserve those who love Me.

The purposes, plans, and thoughts of princes, or leaders, will one day perish. So don't put your trust in them. When your hope is in Me, the One Who made all you see, including the stars, the One Who is faithful, then you can have hope for a future life. Then you are happy, knowing My reign will last forever.

And, each day, I give you a new song of praise—a reason to sing to Me!

Day 165

Where does wisdom come from?

*"For the Lord gives skillful and godly Wisdom; from
His mouth come knowledge and understanding."*
—*Proverbs 2:6*

Proverbs 1-4

What is wisdom? And where do discernment and understanding come from? How does one receive instruction and discretion or thoughtfulness and integrity? How is the knowledge of these divulged?

Sound counsel comes first from one's parents or guardians. Wisdom starts with those who know and teach My ways to their children. From Me, children can learn restraint, what is right and good, and how to avoid evil. Temptation starts when one is young and inclined to do the opposite of what one is told to see what will happen. Some will take advantage of youthful questioning and uncertainty. They'll lead the naivest ones to take advantage of the weak and, eventually, into theft and even death. Those without direction are lured by those with more power and authority. People who draw others to do evil set up their own traps. They are ambushed by their own evil.

Sound counsel is acquired by wise people who hear and abide by My words. Wisdom comes through My Spirit and its leading. It calls to you constantly and is never hidden. Scoffers will laugh at it and deny its evidence. They will delight in self-confident fools, who hate understanding and propound what is false. But My wisdom always stares them in the face and cries out to them at every noisy intersection between good and evil. It is only through an acceptance of My Spirit, and the truth it brings, that anyone can understand My words of wisdom, which are made known through Me.

Those who refuse to accept My counsel eventually come to a place of terror and panic. They are overtaken by a whirlwind of desolation and calamity, and they are overcome by storms of distress and anguish. They call for Me then, but can't find Me, because they refused what I had offered them all along. But those who hearken to Me will always dwell securely with confidence and peace, not having any fear or dread of evil, because they treasure My words and hear My wisdom and direct their hearts to them. They are led to paths of justice, and they attain great discretion and deliverance from the lies of evil people.

For My words give length of days and years of life, and they bring health and healing to those who heed them.

Day 166

Those who seek My words find Me

"I love those who love me, and those who seek me early and diligently shall find me."
—*Proverbs 8:17*

Proverbs 5-8

The whole purpose of My written and spoken Word is to protect you from evil and danger. My words bring life to those who find them. They bring healing and health. But you must guard your heart with all diligence, for out of it flow the springs of life. How do you protect it? By heeding what's written for you and listening for My voice. I provide the guardrails necessary to avoid any pitfalls. I can warn you against those who might lead you away from Me and the purpose I have for you. I have your best interest at heart.

Some will try to take your focus from what is good and right—loyalty and truth—and try to lead you to a place of dishonesty, corruption, and pain. Through accusations, they will try to steal away your soul and infect it with lies. The result is always loss and entrapment that lead to death "for lack of discipline and instruction."

Out of your own goodness, you may want to help others, who seem to have fallen into a pit. It may be a hole they've dug for themselves. You may think about loaning them money, which you've worked hard to attain. But never sign your name to a document that requires you to pay off their debts. If they can't repay them, you put your own life and accomplishments at risk. It's easy to be "hoodwinked" by those who "wink with their eyes," but have contrary hearts and a lack of integrity. Ask Me for guidance. I will always warn you against slippery people and situations. Not every act of kindness is advisable or good.

Here are the things I despise: a spirit of pride that causes people to think more highly of themselves than of Me, lies and innuendo, the shedding of innocent blood, evil thoughts and plans, false witnesses, and the sowing of discord among people. My words can guard you from these. They can lighten your way. They can protect you from evil and the consequences of it, which may result in destruction and death. The words of My mouth are righteous. In them, there is nothing contrary to truth. They are plain to those who want to understand them. When you receive and heed My instructions, it's better for you than any amount of silver, gold, or precious gems. My words give right counsel and sound knowledge. They never lead you astray. "I love those who love Me and those who seek Me early and diligently shall find Me."

And blessed are those who endeavor to find Me.

Day 167

When people overreact to you

"Hatred stirs up contentions, but love covers all transgressions."
—Proverbs 10:12

Proverbs 9-12

Have you ever noticed how, when you try to correct or bring My Light to some people, they become very angry? Their reactions are inappropriate and out of proportion to your comments. They may even attack you and accuse you of what you brought to their attention. They may try to "turn the table" on you by pointing out your "ignorance" of the matter. These are the "simple ones" discussed in Proverbs. They are easily led astray by false reports and waiver in their understanding. They have no real insight or standards, and they try to abuse you for your firm belief that is based on the solid principles of My Word. Scorners are those who have great contempt and disdain for those whose views disagree with theirs. They think anyone who doesn't see eye to eye with them is despicable and unworthy of voicing their views. You see these scoffers among those with strong opinions or views based on innuendo and propaganda. Because the shaking of broken platforms based on lies makes them feel insecure, trying to instruct or enlighten them is a waste of time. Ignore their insults. Remember, the tongue of the wise brings healing, and wisdom comes only from Me and My Word.

Through Me, your days are multiplied, and the years of your life are increased. "If you are wise, you are wise for yourself; if you scorn, you alone will bear and pay the penalty." Self-confident fools, who reject Me, are noisy. They voice their opinions loudly so everyone can hear. Simple ones, who don't know Me, waiver and are easily led astray.

Those who spew and devise evil are deceived, but counselors of peace bring joy to all. The treasures of wickedness profit nothing, and the mouths of the godless destroy others. But righteousness delivers you from death. "The hand of the diligent makes rich" and "The mouth of the righteous man is a well of life." Encouraging words lessen anxiety and make others glad by guiding them to goodness. "Hatred stirs up contentions, but love covers all transgressions."

When people heed My instructions, their efforts and earnings profit them and others—they lead to life. When people neglect or refuse My correction, they go astray and cause ruin to themselves and others. When the storms come, the righteous are left standing, and only they will later inhabit the earth.

Those who allow themselves to be chiseled and pruned by trial, and come to Me for guidance, will grow and reign in godly wisdom.

Day 168

Words can heal

"A soft answer turns away wrath, but grievous words stir up anger."
—*Proverbs 15:1*

Proverbs 13-16

Words are important. They mean something. When they're spoken at the right moment in the right way, they are like honey to the soul—sweet to the mind and healing to the body. Do you know people who don't understand this? They blab on and on with meaningless chatter and don't pay attention to the impact of their words. These are "fools" who invite shame to themselves and contempt from others. Their multitude of words expose their folly. Trying to impress others, they breathe falsehoods and spread pollution. Idol talk leads to poverty—mentally, spiritually, and physically. And those who despise My counsel bring destruction on themselves and endanger others' lives. Their lips produce a scorching fire, and their whispers divide close friends. When their own satisfaction is more important to them than life lived with Me, self-confident fools consider it hateful and offensive to give up the evil upon which they have set their hearts. Their way is paved with rocky obstacles and impassable swamps. Scoffers never find wisdom; they are blind and deaf to it, because it doesn't fit in with their agenda. They never seek wise counsel. They sneer at sin and become its victim. They lack self-control and "foam up quickly and fly into a passion" when anyone obstructs their plans. They are "hasty of spirit" and expose their own folly. Hot-tempered, they stir up strife and anger. Their envy, jealousy, and wrath are rottenness to their bones.

But "he who is slow to anger has great understanding." When you guard your mouth, you keep your life. Words used rightly are beacons that grow brighter and bring rejoicing. They are a fountain of life to others. They pave your way with good understanding, favor, and abundant satisfaction so that even your children can walk more easily in your path.

"A calm and undisturbed mind and heart are the life and health of the body." "A soft answer turns away wrath," and those slow to anger appease contention. The words of the pure please Me, because, when you are wise, your tongue has healing power, like a tree of life. Your lips disperse knowledge as you inquire after and find My understanding. When you heed wise counsel and study how to best answer others, leaning on Me for understanding, you rejoice the hearts of those around you, because from Me comes the wise answer of the tongue.

When you roll your words and your works onto Me, I cause your thoughts to agree with Mine, and I establish your plans as successful.

Day 169

Are you a wise person or a fool?

"Many plans are in a man's mind, but it is the Lord's purpose for him that will stand."
—Proverbs 19:21

Proverbs 17-20

What do you listen to? Do you admire people who harp on insignificant matters? Are you deceived by people who seem intelligent but are just rebellious, have their own agenda, and love to stir up strife? Do you enjoy hearing pithy criticisms of others, because this makes you feel better about yourself? Do you especially like to hear digs about people who've made it big, though the digs are unsubstantiated and probably untrue.

Remember that "whoever rewards evil for good, evil shall not depart from his [or her] house" and "the beginning of strife is as when water first trickles from a crack in a dam." "He who justifies the wicked and...condemns the righteous [is] ...[exceedingly disgusting and hateful] to the Lord." "Those who are glad at calamity [and others' suffering] shall not be held innocent or go unpunished." "But those who cover and forgive offenses seek love."

Spared words and cool spirits are signs of understanding. Even fools who hold their peace are thought to be wise. Self-confident people who like to display their own personal opinions are fools. And fools' lips bring contention, a snare, and ruin. Their haughtiness comes before disaster. When they answer a matter before hearing the facts, they are filled with shame. But the words of the discreet and wise are like gushing streams of sparkling, fresh, pure, and life-giving water. Those who restrain their anger and overlook offenses have good sense, while every fool loves to quarrel. Humble people seek understanding and are honored for this. They know that death and life are in the power of the tongue, and they will draw out wisdom from others like water from a deep well. It is better to be poor, but walk in integrity, than to be rich and speak perversely. Foolish people cause ruin to themselves and resent Me for the consequences. But those who gain My wisdom love life, prosper, and find good.

The reverent worship of Me leads to satisfaction in life, because, though people have their own plans, My purposes will stand.

Day 170

Do I (God) have power over evil leaders?

"The king's heart is in the hand of the Lord, as are the watercourses; He turns it whichever way He wills."
—Proverbs 21:1

Proverbs 21-24

You may think I have no power over leaders. You may imagine that they do whatever they want to oppress people. What about Hitler? Why did I allow him to harm so many people? I give all people freedom to choose what words they hear and heed. Whether or not they listen to Me is always their choice. Sadly, many who gain power are attracted by voices of evil that lure them with promises of power and control over others. But, ultimately, their hearts and lives are in My hands, and I turn them whichever way I will. Though their ways may seem right in their own eyes, I weigh and try their hearts. Things like haughtiness, overbearing pride, misuse of people, lying, deception, violence, and the refusal to act justly are all things I hate. I work in every situation to straighten the crooked paths. I render to every person according to his or her own works. And the lamp of the wicked will eventually be put out. Remember, it's not your job to repay evil. It's Mine.

Though many suffer from a leaders' actions, they will be repaid for their suffering later, if they turn to Me. When people trust Me, they can be redeemed, justified, and restored to their rightful place of honor and respect. This may happen in the next life. I, your Redeemer, am mighty to save, and My Son will always plead your cause. When justice is done, it will be a joy to the righteous, but to evildoers it will mean dismay, calamity, and ruin. The wicked will become a ransom for the righteous, and their false accusations will perish along with them. The words of those who listen to Me will endure. No human wisdom or understanding or counsel can prevail against Me. When scoffers are driven out, contention goes with them, and strife and abuse cease. I keep guard over wisdom and allow those who have it to overthrow the treacherous. I love those with pure hearts, and people who use gracious speech and are diligent will stand before kings. But those who oppress others for gain will come to want. I reveal the certainty of true words so you can give right answers. My heart rejoices when I hear you speak the truth!

Give me your heart, and let your eyes observe and delight in My ways.

Day 171

The words of the wise are precious gifts

"By long forbearance and calmness of spirit a judge or ruler is persuaded,
and soft speech breaks down the most bonelike resistance."
—Proverbs 25:15

Proverbs 25-28

Your words are life-changing! Wicked words can dethrone the righteous, and boastful words can remove you from high places. Words that disclose secrets bring shame, while words spoken at the right moments are precious gifts. The words of the wise are like beautiful ornaments to those who need them, and the words of faithful messengers bring refreshment. False boasters are like clouds and wind without rain, but gentle speech breaks down the most bonelike resistance. False witnesses are like pounding sledgehammers, and songs sung to heavy hearts are like taking away their blankets in cold weather. Backbiting tongues cause anger, and quarrelsome scolding drives away even close family members. But good news from home is like cold water to a thirsty soul. When people can't rule over their own spirits, their words are like broken down cities without walls. If you try to reason with fools, you become like them, and you make them seem wiser in their own eyes. If you give honor to them, it's like placing stones in a slingshot. The unreasoning wrath of fools is heavier than weighty sand. You can pound them like a pestle in a mortar, but their foolishness will not cease. And they still think they are wise.

When you try to meddle with strife that is not yours, you are like someone who pulls a dog up by its ears. Where there are no whisperers, contention ceases. Quarrelsome words inflame strife, and hateful people store up deceitfulness. Lying tongues hate those they wound and crush, and sweet-talking words work ruin. Loud flattery is like cursing, and contentious words are like continuous dripping. But the sweetness of a friend's heartfelt counsel brings great joy. When people forsake My laws, they praise the wicked, and when a land transgresses, it has many rulers. Evil people don't understand justice, but those who seek Me understand it fully. When the wicked rise to power, people hide, but when they perish, the righteous increase.

When a ruler has discernment, understanding, and knowledge, the land has stability.

Day 172

What makes a person virtuous?

*"The fear of man brings a snare, but whoever leans on, trusts in,
and puts his confidence in the Lord is safe and set on high."*
—Proverbs 29:25

Proverbs 29-31

"Where there is no vision [no redemptive revelation of God], the people perish." But those who keep My laws, and the laws of the land, are truly blessed. A virtuous person, whether a woman or a man, is capable, intelligent, and blessed.

A virtuous person shows...
—The ability to put Me first, even during trouble, privation, or sorrow.
—The ability to trust Me, never falling into fear, doubt, or distrust.
—The ability to speak godly wisdom, verbalizing only what is kind and good.
—The ability to avoid idleness and its fruit: gossip, discontent, and self-pity.
—The ability to focus on what is most important first.
—The ability to take care of oneself physically, mentally, and spiritually.
—The ability to be strong and ready to do every God-given task.
—The ability to rejoice in the future.
—The ability to build trust and inspire confidence.
—The ability to comfort and encourage through words and deeds.
—The ability to work creatively to bring abundance.
—The ability to use time wisely.
—The ability to provide so their family never lacks what is needed.
—The ability to have foresight and diligence that enable abundance in dire times.
—The ability to encourage one's spouse to be their very best.
—The ability to adorn oneself and one's family with My strength and dignity.
—The ability to look beyond one's self to help others.

And, finally, those with these characteristics can accept the praise of others for who and what they are, because they exemplify virtuosity.

Day 173

What do you seek above all?

"For to the person who pleases Him God gives wisdom and knowledge and joy; but to the sinner He gives the work of gathering and heaping up, that he may give to one who pleases God. This also is vanity and a striving after the wind and a feeding on it."
—*Ecclesiastes 2:26*

Ecclesiastes 1-2

What do you pursue and seek above all? Is it fame? Or fortune? Love or pleasure? Is it power and wealth? Control? Or is it merely to be satisfied and happy?

Some people work hard to build a good life for themselves and their families. They may build a house or acquire land. They may plant a garden or an orchard or a vineyard. They may raise livestock or create a pool for watering or swimming. They may hire servants to do the dirty work while they gather treasures. Whatever they desire, they work to acquire. They seem happy with their acquisitions, and they surround themselves with enjoyable things.

But life moves on. And, when they are older, they look at life and realize how quickly it has passed them by. They see that an end comes to their pursuits, whether they are strong or weak, rich or poor. In the end, everyone ends up the same, and the wonderful things done are forgotten by the next generation. All their possessions pass on to others, often to people they never knew, who cannot appreciate the time, effort, or toil that went into gaining them. In the end, whether they are wise or not, all people die and leave behind what they've acquired. Isn't this like striving after the wind, which circles around, but goes nowhere? Isn't this pure vanity and of no profit in the end? Solomon thought so. What must you conclude from it all? Maybe you should just eat and drink and enjoy your life and not be grieved or burdened by striving to accomplish and attain so much?

Who can really enjoy life apart from Me?

"For to the person who pleases Him God gives wisdom and knowledge and joy; but to the sinner [apart from Him] He gives the work of gathering and heaping up, that He may give to one who pleases God."

Day 174

The many seasons of your life

"To everything there is a season, and a time for every matter or purpose under heaven."
—*Ecclesiastes 3:1*

Ecclesiastes 3-4

In your life, you'll experience many seasons. Each season will be unique. During some seasons, you'll experience hardship and suffering and pain as you flounder around, trying to find your purpose. You'll wonder why you struggle so much as you try to place each "stone" just right, so you can build a beautiful structure. But, after a while, you look at what you've made and realize it wasn't what you wanted. So, you throw your hands up in the air, tear it all down, sigh as you look at the crumbled-up mess, and decide to start all over again. You do this several times with little success and greater frustration.

Eventually, as you gaze at the heaped-up hash you've created, you wonder what it would look like if you included Me in the process. "What do I have to lose?' you ask yourself. So, you decide to follow My lead and work hand in hand with Me. With Me as your Partner, you begin to see something lovely emerging. You are thrilled, and you embrace this new season, because you see how I make everything beautiful when you stick with Me. And you have a much greater sense of how all the pieces now fit together like a perfect puzzle that displays a masterful design.

I planted eternity in your heart. This divinely implanted sense of purpose can only be satisfied by Me. And My gift to you is that you can live and enjoy the good of your labor. But you must receive My gift. What I do endures forever. Nothing can be added or subtracted from it. Not so with peoples' works. Their lives last only for a short time. I sift and separate out plans and efforts, and I choose those that accomplish My purposes. Those apart from Mine will eventually die out.

You may cry now because you see only loss and oppression around you. But, one day, this will all change, and you will shout for joy, because a new season has come to the earth.

And it will be a time of great rejoicing.

Day 175

How to accomplish your dreams

*"For a dream comes with much business and painful
effort, and a fool's voice with many words."*
—Ecclesiastes 5:3

Ecclesiastes 5-8

What is most important to you? Remember that, to accomplish your dream, you must focus on your goal, and apply yourself diligently to it. Meaningless words and vacant promises will not help you accomplish what you strive to achieve. And a multitude of ambitions will cause you to fail at them all because of a lack of focus.

The prolific abundance produced by the earth can benefit everyone, but, if you love having more than enough above all, you will never be satisfied or happy with what you have. Those who work for what they have, and expend effort to attain it, sleep better than those who are rich and never satisfied. Those who gamble with their gains may lose all they've worked so hard to achieve. Remember, it's My gift to those who work to be able to enjoy the fruit of their labor and benefit from it. It's fruitless and of no avail to bemoan the "days of old," when you can live now and enjoy life and the fruit of it.

Those who are truly wise understand that life must be lived to the fullest every moment. "For wisdom is a defense even as money is a defense, but the excellency of knowledge is that wisdom shields and preserves the life of him who has it." And who can make straight what I have made crooked? No one knows the future but Me or if one will face days of prosperity or adversity. In all times, I am present to help and provide.

It is never good to be "over-religious," striving to make oneself appear more righteous, for even good people sin. It's also unwise to be wicked or foolish. The result of these is always premature death. It's never My will that people die before their time, but some avoid future evil days through death. Don't take to heart words spoken against you, for you yourself have spoken against others.

And no one has ultimate power over life except Me.

181

Day 176

Live life with all your might!

"Whatever your hand finds to do, do it with all your might, for there is no work or device or knowledge or wisdom in Sheol (the place of the dead), where you are going."
—*Ecclesiastes 9:10*

Ecclesiastes 9-12

Don't believe everything you read and hear. Trying to find answers through many sources will frustrate you and make you bitter and resentful. The simple words of a Shepherd can bring you understanding and precious peace. Treasure the time you have, and remember Who gave you vitality while you have it. Walk in the ways of your heart, and let joy cheer you. But remember that following worldly lusts brings sorrow and wastes what could have been good. Expending effort on worthless pursuits brings emptiness in the end and a life worth little. And being over-afraid and hesitant to do what's needed now, because you're waiting for the perfect time to expend the effort, will also bring emptiness and poverty in the end.

The words of wise people are gracious, forgiving, and bring favor. They understand that wisdom is better than might and, though spoken quietly, their words are mightier than the shouts of the foolish. Wisdom is better than weapons, but one unwise comment can destroy much good. A gentle and calm person can put a stop to great offenses, while those who dig pits for others themselves fall into them. Whatever your hand finds to do, do it with all your might, for there is no work or knowledge or wisdom in death.

When you're old, and your sight is darkened, and your hands tremble, and your knees buckle, and your ears cannot hear, and you have no appetite, and your hair turns white, and your desire fails you, and your blood becomes trapped in your veins, remember Who made you and where you are going. The whole duty of mankind is summed up in this: Revere and worship and know Me, and try to understand the original purpose of My creation, which includes you, the object of My goodness. Understand the roots of all character, the foundation of all happiness, and how I help you adjust to all circumstances and conditions in life.

For I see every work done under the sun, whether it is for good or for evil, and I am the ultimate judge of it all.

Day 177

How I view you

"[He exclaimed] O my love, how beautiful you are! There is no flaw in you!"
—*Song of Solomon 4:7*

Song of Solomon 1-4

Notice the difference between how you view yourself and how I view you! You see yourself as flawed and full of imperfections. You think you are too fat or too thin. Your skin is imperfect; your eyes are too close together or too far apart. Your body and your personality are too flawed for Me, or anyone, to love you. You've made mistakes. Your own family and friends remind you of them. How could I accept you as you are?

And yet I do. I see you as beautiful, lovely, perfect. You are My bride, and I adore you. I long to spend time with you and feel your eyes upon Me. Your love is better to Me than any fine wine. The fragrance of your prayers rising up to Me is precious and pleasing. I see you as ravishing. You're a jewel, a gem. Your love ravishes My heart, and one look from you gives Me the incentive to fight for you. I see no flaw in you. I desire you to come away with Me to a secret place. Abide with Me in the seclusion of a hidden cleft in a solid Rock, where I can see your lovely face and hear your sweet voice. There, I can hide you from all the storms that threaten you. Let Me take away the "foxes"—the little things that spoil the vineyards of our love. Let Me remove these far from you, so we can enjoy our time together and look upon each other's beauty, uninterrupted by disruptive things and people who mean to do you harm. Come to Me, even if you've been far from Me, and life has imprisoned you because of its demands on you. Come back and spend lovely time with Me.

Come away from the lion's den, My fair one, and see how much I adore you. Come to Me to the mountain of myrrh and the hill of frankincense. Gaze upon Me—your King. See the crown on My head and know I come for you to save you from hardship. I am designing a beautiful palanquin to carry you away one day and spend eternity with Me.

Dream of Me, My promised bride, for one day we will be together always.

Day 178

How I adorned you with My beauty

"[Joyfully the radiant bride turned to him, the one altogether lovely, the chief among 10,000 to her soul, and with unconcealed eagerness to begin her life of sweet companionship with him, she answered] Make haste, my beloved, and come quickly, like a gazelle or a young hart [and take me to our waiting home] upon the mountains of spices!"
—Song of Solomon 8:14

Song of Solomon 5-8

When I put My hand "by the hole in the door," I am seeking that one place in your life where I can reach your heart. There, I pursue you through that one area where you need Me the most. And that is where you'll find Me. As your Shepherd-Lover, I reach you through small openings in your life. I often knock and knock. I even leave My "calling card." When you finally open the door to let Me in, you can't see Me, but you know I've been there. Then you seek Me. And, as you look, you experience sadness, sometimes persecution and opposition, because others don't understand your desperate pursuit. Your heart and soul are often wounded. But though others try to demean your search by trying to steal what is most important to you, you eventually find Me, because I also continue to pursue you and your love. You encounter Me in a beautiful place, far away from the humiliation of those who've rejected you and Me. Where I live is in a garden of love, and there you will find Me. There, My voice is sweet, and you discover that I am lovely. I delight in you and share My love with you. Life becomes precious. You find that I am your best friend. And you are beautiful to Me and always have been. In My eyes, you are perfect. You stand alone, and I am held captive by you. Let Me be to you as the Chief among 10,000 to your soul! Because I have always longed for your love. Seek Me with your whole heart, and know that one day I will come for you and take you with Me to My mountain of love. What I long to hear most from you is "Come quickly!" Because I desire, more than anything, to gaze upon the face of the one I've adored and adorned with My beauty. My Spirit makes you lovely. Our spiritual companionship makes you radiate and brings out the sweetness in you.

And one day, we'll go to our waiting home upon the mountain of fragrant spices!

Day 179

When children oppress you

*"The people shall be oppressed, each one by another, and each one by his neighbor;
the child shall behave himself proudly and with insolence against the
old man, and the lowborn against the honorable [person of rank]."*
—Isaiah 3:5

Isaiah 1-3

"As for My people, children are their oppressors, and women rule over them." "Your leaders cause you to err, and they confuse (destroy and swallow up) the course of your paths." By their exactions and oppressions, they rob the people and ruin the country. They encourage children to behave proudly and insult their elders. The lowborn stand against those who are honorable. People are crushed by each other. But, one day, these lofty tormentors will bow down, and their haughtiness will be brought low. Proud looks will be humbled. And the work of peoples' hands that once was worshipped will be revealed for what it is. Then, I will be exalted. I will stand to judge and to show what people are made of. I will contend against those who intimidate.

Then, I will take away their finery and reveal what was beneath their veils. As for the wicked, what their hands have done will be done to them. One day, I will avenge Myself on My enemies—the rebels who loved bribes and manmade customs more than Me, who turned a deaf ear to the fatherless and widows. They will be purged away like dross, because their hands were full of blood.

Those who are willing and obedient will eat the good of the land one day, because they know and believe what is right. They seek justice. They relieve the oppressed and correct the tormentor. Though their sins are red as crimson, I will make them white as snow, because I will forgive them. In the latter days, when My Son comes to reign on earth, the mountain of My house will be established. It will be the highest point on earth, and all nations will flow to it. They will seek His teachings and want to walk in His ways. He will judge the nations and decide disputes. Then, there will be no more war. Pacts with the ungodly will not exist.

Because all will walk in the light of My Son.

185

Day 180

Once I planted a lovely vineyard

*"Let me [as God's representative] sing of and for my greatly Beloved...
a tender song of my Beloved concerning His vineyard [His chosen
people]. My greatly Beloved had a vineyard on a very fruitful hill."*
—Isaiah 5:1

Isaiah 4-7

Once I planted a lovely vineyard that produced luscious fruit. I poured My love over it, and it made My heart glad to see it. I spent years preparing the ground to create an ideal environment in which to plant My seeds—the choicest I could find. Nothing was too good for My vineyard. I worked through My leaders to cultivate its fruit—My people in their new land. We formed laws to support and help them to survive and thrive, free from harm and destruction. I instructed them through the prophets I sent. Everything was prepared to bring them the best in the land and to bless their future generations.

But the people turned against Me. And I could see little that was just or good in them anymore. Instead, bloodshed and oppression prevailed. I looked for uprightness, but I heard only cries of distress at the hands of their leaders. Scoffers challenged any belief or hope in Me. Some laughed and ridiculed, saying, "Let Him hurry and send His Son so we can see Him!" They called evil good and goodness evil. They were wise in their own eyes and shrewd in their own sight. They loved to mix drinks and justify the guilty while removing the rights of the innocent. Their roots became rotten, because they rejected and cast away My teachings—the just laws I had given them. They treated Me, and those I sent, scornfully, and they despised My words. For this reason, I was angry. I saw how children treated their parents and despised the teachings that brought them life. This pained Me. I knew that this rejection was by the "wild grapes" on the vines I'd prepared for good. And I knew they would bring corruption to the plants I'd lovingly groomed. The hills I cultivated to birth a beautiful, fruitful vineyard would produce briars and thorns. Enemies would abound and take away what was meant to be a blessing. And so, I made another way. One day, My Son would come to gather My precious grapes—the true fruit of all My efforts.

And all would see what I'd prepared for that day, and the wine from My vines would be unlike anything the world had ever seen.

Day 181

When will there be peace on earth?

"The people who walked in darkness have seen a great Light; those who dwelt in the land of intense darkness and the shadow of death, upon them has the Light shined."
—Isaiah 9:2

Isaiah 8-10

How can I save you, or anyone, when there is so much darkness around? So many turn away from Me to consult with evil! You look around and see so much distress and depravity! Just remember, these are widespread among those who don't trust Me. Though I give many signs and wonders, some will never see or believe what I've done. Many wondrous things have taken place in Israel. Didn't I, through Isaiah, predict that a virgin would conceive a Son? Didn't I explain, through My prophets, that He would minister "by the way of the Sea of Galilee?" From Him would come a great Light to those who walked in darkness. "For to us a Child is born, to us a Son is given...." He would be the Prince of Peace. So, where is this peace now? Many of My prophecies have been fulfilled. The Messiah came to earth. He was born and lived and died. He even rose from death. So, when will justice and righteousness prevail on earth? When will the throne and kingdom of David be established? Many have asked and wonder now, "Why is it taking so long for all the prophecies to be fulfilled, especially the ones about peace?" They disclaim My promises, because they don't see them fulfilled fast enough. Impatiently, they teach lies. They lead others to error. They speak folly and profanity. Wickedness burns in them like fire, and many sacrifice their own family members. They destroy their own flesh. Judges issue unrighteous decrees, and magistrates are unjust and oppressive. But enemies will devour them, because they are hypocritical and godless and make their nations the same way. One day, they'll discover that their idols can't defend them. Though they think they have power, they'll see that they have none. But you need not fear. Even amid evil, you need not fall into their terror or believe that all is doomed. Why? Because I am your Hope. You trust and honor Me above all else. You know that I am your Sanctuary—a sacred place of rest. To others, I am a Stone of stumbling, a Rock of offense. But you wait for My Son, and you look and hope for Him Who will be a sign of My power. You show My might and Light during darkness.

"For to us a Child is born" and *"the government shall be upon His shoulder."*

Day 182

How to see inside people

"The Spirit of the Lord shall rest upon Him—the Spirit of wisdom and understanding, the Spirit of counsel and might, the Spirit of knowledge and of the reverential and obedient fear of the Lord—and shall make Him of quick understanding, and His delight shall be in the reverential and obedient fear of the Lord. And He shall not judge by the sight of His eyes, neither decide by the hearing of His ears."
—Isaiah 11:2-3

Isaiah 11-14

I want you to be able to see inside people. I want you, like My Son, to be able to read thoughts and discern hearts. Not to judge them by sight, or by what others say about them, but to understand what they are made of—what motivates them. Because My Spirit rested on My Son, He had infinite wisdom and understanding. He had superseding counsel, because He had My Spirit of knowledge. It is My Spirit that gives you the ability to judge righteously, decide fairly, and be able to overcome possible oppressors. When My Spirit prevails in people on the earth, then all can be at peace. Even animals and nature respond to My Spirit. One day, when My Son returns, the earth will be full of a knowledge of Me. Nations and leaders will seek an understanding of Me. Then, My Son will send a signal to assemble Israel's outcasts from among the nations, and they will reclaim what was once theirs. And the surrounding nations will comply with their requests as many return to their land by walking across part of the Red Sea that has dried up and along a highway from Iraq. Then, My people will shout as they return, "The Lord God is my strength and song! He is my salvation! For He has done excellent things! Let the whole earth know this!" And the earth will be at rest.

Like Lucifer, some want to reign over Me. They set themselves up as gods by exalting themselves. They shake up nations and overthrow cities. They destroy the land I set aside, and they slay My people. Though they make the world a wilderness of hate now, one day they'll be thrown down. Then, My purpose for the earth will be made known as I stretch out My hand over all nations. And the poorest of the poor will feed freely and the needy will lie down in safety.

For I founded Zion for a purpose; in her the poor and afflicted of My people will find refuge.

Day 183

All will be changed

"In that day will men look to their Maker, and their
eyes shall regard the Holy One of Israel."
—Isaiah 17:7

Isaiah 15-19

The most unlikely things will happen one day. Nations that once roared and raged against My people, stripping them of what belonged to them, will themselves be rejected. A signal will be raised on the mountains. A trumpet will be blown. My Son will ride on a swift cloud to earth. "In that day men will look to their Maker, and their eyes shall regard the Holy One of Israel."

Then, those who rushed against Me and My people will be removed. Then, a throne will be established in mercy and lovingkindness. And One shall sit on that throne in truth and faithfulness in the tent of David, judging and seeking justice and being swift to do righteousness. Though gladness was taken away, and joy from the once-plentiful fields where singing was once heard, all will be changed.

People who were oppressed under the fierceness of their leaders will cry out to Him, and He will deliver them. They will know Me in that day and gladly vow a vow to Me. There will be a highway from Egypt to Assyria (now Iraq), and the Egyptians will worship Me with the Assyrians. Israel will form a pact with Egypt and Assyria, and it will bring great blessings to the earth.

I will say, "Blessed be Egypt My people and Assyria the work of My hands and Israel My heritage." And ambassadors from Ethiopia will bring a present to My Son.

A people tall and polished from a nation strong and victorious will bring this gift to the place of worship of the name of the Lord of Hosts to Mount Zion in Jerusalem.

Day 184

About when does Isaiah speak?

"The key of the house of David I will lay upon his shoulder; he shall open and no one shall shut, he shall shut and no one shall open. And I will fasten him like a peg or nail in a firm place; and he will become a throne of honor and glory to his father's house."
—Isaiah 22:22-23

Isaiah 20-23

Are the prophecies of Isaiah meant for his time or for a time to come? The answer is both! Many of Isaiah's prophetic predictions have happened. They were meant for the Jews of his day. But they also foretell a future time. Isaiah told of a time when Israel would be besieged by hostile armies from a terrible land "from the desert." The Desert of the Sea referred to Babylon,[1] now in Iraq. He also predicted that Babylon's king would be slain, and his kingdom would fall. These prophecies were fulfilled. But they would happen again. Often the predictions meant for a prophet's day also indicated events in the future.

What was the Valley of Vision? It was the name for Jerusalem, from which many prophetic visions arose.[2] It is the place of many significant events in the past, present, and future. It is the place where My Son will rule one day for 1,000 years.

Isaiah encouraged those besieged by enemies to return to Me, repent of arrogance and idolatry, and humbly come to My side. Instead, he saw people making their own "reservoirs" to save themselves, then eating and drinking more than before. Their view was, "Let us eat and drink, for tomorrow we die!" You will see this in your own lifetime. When Isaiah spoke of Eliakim, the governor of the palace, as "father to the inhabitants of Jerusalem and the house of Judah" and one having "the key of the house of David," who would be "a throne of honor and glory to his father's house," he also spoke of My Son, Who would come later. The peg fastened to a sure place, but later removed, referred to the Jews, who were given the promises, yet rejected Me. Cities like Tyre, "the merchandise of the nations...bestower of crowns, whose merchants were princes and whose traders were honored on the earth" were places then and later that would be brought to ruin because of their idolatry and horrendous practices against My people.

The gain of those who rejected Me would benefit those who dwelt in My presence.

Day 185

How to have peace amid turmoil

*"You will guard him and keep him in perfect and constant peace whose
mind [both its inclination and its character] is stayed on You, because he
commits himself to You, leans on You, and hopes confidently in You."*
—*Isaiah 26:3*

Isaiah 24-27

How can you have peace when there is so much turmoil around you? And if things get worse, as Isaiah predicted they will, how can you possibly remain joyful during so many mental and physical disturbances? It is simple, but not easy. I can keep you in perfect, constant peace if you focus on Me. How can you do this? What does it involve? It means that you must commit your thoughts to Me. It means you lean on Me and trust in Me in every situation. It means you have confident hope in Me that, even when you see bad things happening around you, hear extremely disturbing words, or experience life-changing events, you will trust Me to take care of you. When people come against you, turn to Me, and ask Me for help you give the right response. Remember the source of hatred. It never comes from Me! You may be battling against spiritual forces of evil. Let Me arm you against them. Let Me fight for you. Only with Me can you win.

I am your Rock. My way is one of peacefulness, and only those who walk with Me walk a level or straight path. Those who deal unjustly, and encourage hatred, cater to the wind. Their ways are always unstable. Now, your soul yearns for Me, and your spirit seeks Me earnestly. You know that only when My righteous judgments prevail on the earth will its inhabitants know peace. Though I ordained peace for you, and desire it for you, you see how people who once received My favor turn against Me and My people. You see the wonderful things I've done, and the continual revelation of My purposes, and you wonder why others can't see them too. You also realize that some mistakenly believe that only they can deliver the earth from evil. One day, all will see what I've always wanted them to see. Even after so much destruction, a day will come when My Son returns to the earth. He will swallow up death and abolish it. He will wipe away every tear.

A trumpet will blow, and He will gather together those who understand, and they will rejoice with Him and worship together on the holy mountain of Jerusalem.

Day 186

I will show you how to proceed

"For thus said the Lord God, the Holy One of Israel: In returning [to Me] and resting [in Me] you shall be saved; in quietness and in [trusting] confidence shall be your strength."
—Isaiah 30:15

Isaiah 28-30

In the trials of life, I will instruct you how to proceed. For I can show you precisely when to sow, winnow, and reap. Right instruction can only come from Me, for I am wonderful in counsel and excellent in wisdom, and I can bring you the most effective results. I work through My Spirit in you, which you receive when you believe in My Son. He's the precious Cornerstone. Isaiah looked forward to His coming—the revelation of the sure Stone—Who would come and lay the foundation for a new temple to be built. Now, whoever believes in, trusts in, relies on, and adheres to Him will never be ashamed. When He comes again to execute justice and righteousness, those who believe need never be afraid. Only those who made lies their refuge and took shelter in falsehoods will be swept away with their death covenants. All their sources of confidence will fail as the multitudes of nations who fought against Jerusalem will become a dream—a vision in the night. Consider what I tell you. You can choose to understand or not. You can close your eyes and deny that it will happen. You can say that My words emanate from a sealed-up book. You can repeat meaningless prayers to other gods and pretend to be religious and righteous. But none of these things will cut mustard. I beg you, heed what I say! Those who presented themselves as wise, but did evil behind closed doors, will perish. The ones who turned things upside down to accomplish their own evil ends and questioned the One Who made them, saying, "He has no understanding," will cease. Those who watched for an occasion to accuse My people shall be cut off. Even now, they lay traps for those who uphold justice, and they thrust aside the innocent with false pleas. They accuse others of being offensive so they can condemn them. But they will see the Holy One of Jacob when He returns. And those who erred in spirit will understand as they are judged, while those who rested in Me will be saved. Now, let quietness and confidence be your strength. Know that you are blessed as you look and long for My Son.

Listen for His voice! He will say to you, "This is the way. Walk in it."

Day 187

The thousand-year reign

"Behold, a King will reign in righteousness, and princes will rule with justice. And each one of them shall be like a hiding place from the wind and a shelter from the storm, like streams of water in a dry place, like the shade of a great rock in a weary land [to those who turn to them]."
—Isaiah 32:1-2

Isaiah 31-35

The thousand-year reign of My Son, when He returns to this earth, is a fulfillment of My promises to Israel. Isaiah describes that time, when "the Lord of Hosts will come down to fight upon Mount Zion and upon its hills," and He will "defend Jerusalem; He will protect and deliver it." He will prevail over Israel's enemies. And those who dealt treacherously with My chosen ones will be confronted and destroyed. My Son will be exalted, and He will fill Zion with justice and righteousness and remove the oppressors. Then, there will be stability, salvation, wisdom, and knowledge. Worship of Me will be the treasure it was meant to be. Though many bitterly weep now and are afraid, then they will have no fear. They will have plenty as their eyes behold the King, and they see a peaceful land that stretches before them. Instead of insolence and fierceness from those who despise them and Me, My people will see Jerusalem as a quiet habitation—"a tent that shall not be taken down." And My people will say, "the Lord will be for us in majesty and splendor a place of broad rivers and streams.... For the Lord is our Judge, the Lord is our Lawgiver, the Lord is our King. He will save us."

As I promised Israel, My Son will come to give recompense and fight against evil. The blind will see, the deaf will hear, the lame will leap, and the dumb will sing for joy. The weak will have strength. All the Lord's ransomed ones will come singing with joy to their homeland along a highway called the High Way to Zion. Sorrow, sighing, and sickness will flee away. Even the wildernesses will be glad, and the deserts will bloom in that day. When will the heavens dissolve? When will the skies roll up like a scroll? When will the stars and planets drop like figs from a tree? These things will occur when the thousand-year reign ends. Then, this earth will be replaced with a new one.

And Our reign will commence with a new heaven and earth, which will last forever.

Day 188

Because he prayed

"And Hezekiah prayed to the Lord."
—Isaiah 37:15

Isaiah 36-38

Deceivers will try to convince you that they are in the right and you are in the wrong. They will try to convince you that, if I do exist, I'm on their side. The king of Assyria's military official claimed that I had told him to go up against Hezekiah and his people. But I hadn't sent them. He tried to instill fear in the Judeans by saying that I would not and could not deliver them. When people come against you, claim power over you, and say that I can't deliver you, how should you respond? How did Hezekiah's leaders respond? They didn't offer an answer. Instead, they went to the king, who came to My prophet and asked for prayer.

People will mock you for your belief. They will reproach and insult you. They will defy Me. But I will always stand up for you. I will rebuke those who castigate you. And My message to you is the same as it was to Hezekiah: "Do not be afraid because of the words you have heard." Those who try to deceive you will themselves be deluded.

What was Hezekiah's response to the threats against him and his kingdom? He prayed. In his prayer he acknowledged Who I am and what I had done. He laid bare his fears before Me, and he asked for My help in overcoming them. He recognized My power and ability to help him and to make others see that only I am the true Lord of all. And I came through for him, because he prayed.

I come against arrogance from anyone who defies Me and My ability to save. I always do. And I will defend you, take your side, and be your security, just as I did for Hezekiah. Because he continued to ask for My help, when he became ill, I added years to his life. I gave him a sign to reassure him of My ability to help him. But you don't need a sign. Why? Because you already have one.

The true sign for you is the spirit that resides in you, which you received when you prayed and believed in My Son.

Day 189

Only I can tell you the things to come

"Who has directed the Spirit of the Lord, or as His counselor has taught Him? With whom did He take counsel that instruction might be given Him? Who taught Him the path of justice and taught Him knowledge and showed Him the way of understanding?"
—Isaiah 40:13-14

Isaiah 39-41

Who can know the future or tell you what will happen next? Only I can see what lies ahead. Only I know My plans and what I have prepared for the people on the earth. Have all people seen My revealed glory, as I promised? No. Not yet. But I keep My promises. And a way has been prepared for that day. Then, the crooked places will be made straight, and the rough places will be made smooth. My majesty and splendor will be revealed. Now, all flesh is as frail as grass. It eventually withers away and fades like flowers. But, one day, you will behold My Son. And He will rule with My strong arm and bring rewards and recompense to the earth. He will be like a Shepherd to My people. He will gather them like lambs in His arms and lead them to a beautiful and fruitful land.

I have guided the destinies of generations and nations from the beginning. I sit above the circle of the earth, and I bring dignitaries who oppose Me to nothing. I make unjust judges and rulers as chaos. They are scarcely planted when I blow on them so that a tempest takes them away, and their deeds are scattered. Who is like Me? Do you still not understand Who I am and what I can do? How can you think your life is hidden from Me, and I do not regard you? I never grow weary. I give power to the faint. Those who wait for Me are renewed in strength. They run without being weary. They walk and don't faint. For I can subdue nations and make rulers over kings. You need never fear, because I saw you from the ends of the earth and chose you. So, why would I cast you off now? I am your God. I can strengthen and harden you to difficulties. I can hold you up with My right hand of justice. Those who are angry with you will be put to shame and come to nothing. I say to you, "Fear not; I will help you." And, one day, you will see the Holy One of Israel. Then, people will understand how My hand was in it all.

No one else can offer you right counsel or protect you the way I can when you ask for help.

Day 190

Who can do what I can?

"Fear not, nor be afraid [in the coming violent upheavals]; have I not told it to you from of old and declared it? And you are My witnesses! Is there a God besides Me? There is no [other] Rock; I know not any."
—Isaiah 44:8

Isaiah 42-44

See how I feel about the gods people make with their own hands! And what do I think of the people who worship them? I am a jealous God. I find the actions of those who worship other gods detestable and shameful. They do not know or understand, for their eyes are clouded with delusions and lies. Their lives are filled with confusion, chaos, and worthlessness. And they bring their evil upon the people of a whole land or nation! Who is like Me? No other Rock exists. None. Only I can declare the future. And, because I am your Rock, you need never fear violent upheavals. I am your Lord, your Holy One, Creator, and King! Besides Me, there is no Savior. And no one can take you from My hand. When I work, no one can reverse what I've done. I formed you from your mother's womb. I made you as you are. I made all things. I stretched out the heavens and spread out the earth. I frustrate the signs and confound the omens of false prophets, whose forecasts are based on lies.

Why were the Jews persecuted by the people of other nations? Because they understood that I am the true God, and they refused to worship false gods. And the "god of this world" doesn't like that! You know Who I am. Though others persecute you for not accepting their false teachings, you know that I am He Who blots out and cancels your transgressions. I do not recall your sins. I converse with you, one on one. Only I hear your pleas. False gods can't do this. Will you be defamed by others for your belief in Me? Yes. But you can sing a new song along with Me later. You can praise Me from the ends of the earth. Why? Because I will again bring Light to the nations through One Who can open blind eyes and bring prisoners out of darkness. Former things will pass away. My Son, though not recognized by many the first time He came, will return and go forth like a Warrior. He will shout My words to all the nations.

I have held My peace and restrained Myself for too long, but then I will make darkness into Light.

Day 191

I did these things for you!

*"I will give you the treasures of darkness and hidden riches of secret places, that
you may know that it is I, the Lord, the God of Israel, Who calls you by your name."*
—Isaiah 45:3

Isaiah 45-48

I called you by name. I even chose a new name for you. And I'll reveal your secretly-bestowed name one day, when you stand before My Son. I chose your name before you knew Me. You see, I made the earth for you. I formed light and darkness for you. I make crooked paths straight for you. For you, I can make peace out of calamity. I can bring showers and rain down righteousness for you. All pure, spiritual, heaven-born possibilities are found in My Holy Being. I give you the treasures of darkness and hidden riches in secret places. I declare things openly that are right, though I seem concealed. I speak, and it comes to pass. I purpose things, and they happen. I bring near My righteousness when it seems far off. Though it feels like you are tried in a furnace of affliction, I never forsake you. I never allow those who do not worship Me to triumph over you. And, even in your old age when your hair is white, I will carry and bear you.

My hand laid the foundation of the earth. I spread out the heavens, and, whenever I call to them, all the elements which I created work together to execute My decrees. I declared from the beginning what would happen on earth. I spoke things and made them known. They were never done in secret. Many proclamations came to pass so you would know Who I am.

Who am I? I am the Lord, the Holy One of Israel, your Maker. There is no God besides Me. Only through Me can you say, "I have righteousness, salvation, and victory, and the strength to achieve." Through Me, your offspring are justified and can also see My glory. I am the First. I am the Last. I am the One Who teaches you how to be prosperous. I lead you in the way you should go. I am uncompromisingly just and righteous. Look to Me to be saved, for only I can do this for you. I am God, and there is no other like Me.

One day, every knee will bow before Me, and all will swear allegiance to Me.

Day 192

I keep you close to Me

"Listen to me, O isles and coastlands, and hearken, you peoples from afar. The Lord has called me from the womb; from the body of my mother He has named my name. And He has made my mouth like a sharp sword; in the shadow of His hand has He hid me and made me a polished arrow; in His quiver has He kept me close and concealed me."
—Isaiah 49:1-2

Isaiah 49-51

I chose you. And I will never forget or forsake you. I am always by your side to help and strengthen you, to work with you and lead you to My glory. You see, I tattooed a picture of you on the palms of My hands so you are ever before Me! That is how much I love you. I keep you close to Me, and I conceal you until the time I need you to act for Me. You may think your efforts are in vain and ask, "How does what I do benefit anyone?" I will reward you for every action meant for Me. In My eyes, the things you do for Me are honorable, and I give you the strength to accomplish even more. You see, I set you, YOU, as a Light to the nations. My desire is that My salvation will extend to the ends of the earth! And I need your help to do this. Though great nations of people reject and despise Me, one day rulers will see My Son, and they will bow down before Him.

In your day of salvation, I heard and helped you. I answered your prayer. Now I preserve you as a covenant-keeper to My people, to help them attain what I want to give them: salvation and a great inheritance that they will see one day. I want you to speak to those who are bound in shackles and to say, "Come forth!" To those in spiritual darkness, "Come see the Light of the Sun of righteousness!" Lead them in all the ways they should go so their pastures are not deserts. Guide them from the mirages of this world to a place where they won't hunger or thirst, for "He Who has mercy will lead them, and by springs of water He will guide them." Many will come. They'll come from far away, even from as far away as China! And you can help make a way for them. Together, we can comfort them and have compassion on them. Look and see all the ones I bring to you! Though you feel alone, and your efforts seem fruitless, many will come.

For I am the Lord, and any who wait for, look for, hope for, and expect Me will never be ashamed, because I plead the cause of My own.

Day 193

One day you will fully understand

"Therefore My people shall know what My name is and what it means; therefore they shall know in that day that I am He who speaks; behold, I AM!"
—Isaiah 52:6

Isaiah 52-55

One day, you will know My name and what it means to you. You will recognize My voice and know it is Me Who speaks to you. When My Son rose from death and ascended to Me, He made My Spirit available through a belief in Him and what He accomplished. Now you can discern My voice by listening through My Spirit in you. You can know it is Me Who speaks to you. And when He returns, you will see and know even more.

One day, watchmen will lift their voices and sing for joy when they see the return of the Lord to Zion. Then, all the earth will witness My salvation through Him. For, though He was once an object of horror and astonishment, then He will startle the nations and shut the mouths of the doubters. Though He was despised, rejected, and forsaken by those who did not appreciate His worth, they could not stop the outcome of what He accomplished. He bore your grief, sickness, weakness, and distress. He carried away your sorrow and pain. He was wounded and bruised for you. He endured many lashes to remove your shame and shortcomings. For you, He suffered so you could have healing and wholeness.

When He was oppressed, He did not speak. He was buried with the wicked, even judged guilty, to take away your blame. He offered His life for yours. And when He died, I raised Him up so you could be one of My offspring. Because He bore your sins, you can stand with Him. Now, you have no reason to fear or have shame or depression. Your reproach has been removed because of what He did. He is your Vindicator. When you feel lacking, forsaken, or grieved, remember that He redeemed you. He paid a great price for you. And even when it seems like the world is crumbling around you, remember My covenant of peace and completeness through Him. When people strike out against you, I will vindicate you. For My ways are higher than your ways, and My words never return void.

They always accomplish what I choose, and I have chosen you.

Day 194

A house of prayer for all people

"All these I will bring to My holy mountain and make them joyful in My house of prayer. Their burnt offerings and their sacrifices will be accepted on My altar; for My house will be called a house of prayer for all peoples."
—Isaiah 56:7

Isaiah 56-59

Can people be saved who never knew My Son? Can those who never believed in or received Him find salvation? Yes. By acting justly and righteously and coming to Me humbly. By living rightly with Me and obeying My will. But how can a person know My will? By My words. But what if a person never hears or reads My words? They have been written in peoples' hearts. Therefore, all are without excuse when they act unjustly and do evil. But though they know it instinctively, many still choose evil. They turn away when they are led astray. And their choices create a separation between them and Me so that My face is hidden from them, and they cannot hear Me. They can't recognize truth, and justice is perverted. Those who depart from evil sometimes become prey to others. Because of this, I saw that all needed an Intercessor—One Who could live among them and intervene between them and Me. My house is a house of prayer for all people. Anyone can come, regardless of race, culture, color, or creed. I called others to join with Israel. Today, I call all to My Son.

The wicked, who choose evil over good, are like the troubled sea that never rests. They have no peace. They promote disunity and discord. Those who take refuge in Me have peace. And they have healing. One day, they will inherit My holy mountain. Humble ones who are penitent, and righteous ones who died before their time and avoided the evil to come, will be revived to inhabit eternity. What pleases Me? Not religious acts done to make one look good, but righteous acts, like helping Me to break off the things that enslave others physically, mentally, and spiritually. You can help Me remove these yokes of oppression. How?

By choosing to satisfy the needs of those afflicted, with the help of My Son; then your Light will rise out of darkness, and your gloom will become like the noonday.

Day 195

Why did Jesus stop reading?

"The Spirit of the Lord God is upon me, because the Lord has anointed and qualified me to preach the Gospel of good tidings to the meek, the poor, and afflicted; He has sent me to bind up and heal the brokenhearted, to proclaim liberty to the [physical and spiritual] captives and the opening of the prison and of the eyes to those who are bound. To proclaim the acceptable year of the Lord [the year of His favor]...."
—Isaiah 61:1-2a

Isaiah 60-63

When Jesus read from the book of Isaiah in Luke 4:18, why did He stop reading in the middle of verse two of chapter 61? Because He was proclaiming that My Spirit was on Him. He was saying that He was anointed and qualified to preach the good news of what I'd foretold. He was letting the world know that I'd work through Him to lift the lowly, release the afflicted, bind their wounds, heal the brokenhearted, and free those who were captive physically and spiritually. He'd do these things while He lived. But He stopped there. Why?

Because what followed in Isaiah would come later—when He returned to earth. The rest of this verse, and the verses that follow, describe something very different: "A day of vengeance." What does this mean? It means that a day will come when He'll return as a warrior-leader to redeem My people. He'll set things straight, and He'll reign in Jerusalem. He'll fight against the wickedness of the Antichrist. He'll rectify those who were wronged, because He loves justice and hates violence and oppression. He'll establish the everlasting covenant I made with My people. He'll cause justice to spring forth through the power of My Word. And "for Zion's sake," He'll not rest until My city is vindicated and her salvation "radiates as a burning torch." As all nations and leaders behold My glory, I'll give My city a new name. All who gather to her will drink My new wine and praise Me, because the land will prosper through peace, and all who come to her will honor her beauty. Behold, I proclaim it to the ends of the earth! All will acknowledge Me and recognize My Heritage—the Holy People, the Redeemed of the Lord.

These are those who desired Me and were pursued by Me, who were never forsaken, because I am mighty to save!

Day 196

Israel's new name

"He will call His servants by another name [as much greater than the
former name as the name Israel was greater than the name Jacob]."
—*Isaiah 65:15b*

Isaiah 64-66

One day, My people Israel will be known by a new name. Just as I renamed Jacob, Abraham, and Sarah, I will give them a new name that represents who they are. Then, their former troubles will be forgotten. They will be glad and rejoice to see how I make Jerusalem a place of rejoicing. The sound of weeping will cease, and cries of distress will end. Israel's houses and vineyards will be their own; no one will occupy them or use them for their own purposes. They'll enjoy the work of their own hands, and their offspring will be blessed. They'll call, and I'll answer them directly. I won't be hidden from them. The wolf and the lamb will eat together. The lion will be as tame as an ox, because My peace will flow from My holy mount.

Heaven is My throne, and earth is My footstool. No one can design a proper resting place for Me. For I made everything. Those who are humble or broken, who tremble at My Word, and revere My commands—these are the ones I look upon with compassion. I disdain hypocrites—people who feign worship but have distant hearts. They choose their own ways and delight in their own misdeeds. They bring fears upon themselves and others. I try to call out to them, but they won't answer. I speak to them, but they don't listen. They choose evil over justice. They hate you for what you believe and cast you out for My name's sake.

One day, I'll make things right. I'll extend peace to Jerusalem like a river. She'll be the glory of the nations, and you'll be comforted by her. You'll rejoice to see My powerful hand revealed, for I'll gather all nations and tongues. They'll come to see My glory. "They will declare and proclaim My glory among the nations." All flesh will worship Me. These things will occur during the thousand-year reign of My Son. After this, I'll rend the heavens. Then mountains will quake and flow down at My presence. I'll create a new heaven and earth the likes of which you have never seen. And it will abide forever, with a new Jerusalem.

Former things will pass away and be remembered no more.

Day 197

What will happen to Israel?

"Before I formed you in the womb I knew and approved of you [as My chosen instrument], and before you were born I separated and set you apart, consecrating you; [and] I appointed you as a prophet to the nations."
—Jeremiah 1:5

Jeremiah 1-3

I knew you before you were born. I set you apart before you were formed. In the same way, I chose the people of Israel. Though they may seem unworthy of Me, I picked them out—designated them for My purposes. My desire was that they speak for Me. I appointed them as My special ones to root out, pull down, and destroy what was wrong in the world and plant what is right. I am still active in the lives of My people, both those of Israel and those who come to know My Son. I watch over these. With your help, we can prepare them for things to come.

What is to come? Jerusalem, My city, will be attacked by forces from the north that will surround her to take control of her. Israel was set apart by Me. She was the first fruit of My harvest. Those who seek to destroy her will be overtaken by evil, because they come against Me and My purposes for her. Though she has offended Me at times by turning away from Me, she is still Mine. Though she may forsake Me, the Fountain of Living Waters, and hew out her own broken cisterns, or ways of worship, I will never forsake her. I won't allow others to feed on her crown, which I gave her. I will break Israel's yoke of bondage. I will burst her bonds, not so she can live freely without Me, but so she can be bound by My love'. Even when she has turned against Me, I have pursued her.

In Israel I planted a choice Vine, My Son. And, one day, she will be Mine again. She will return to Me as her True Love. She'll recognize Me through the Son she bore for Me. But, until that time, she'll suffer when others attack and demean her. Though she may forget Me, she'll come to Me again, and I will become her closest Companion. One day, I'll bring her back to her land, not as a group, but individually—from cities, tribes, and peoples—back to Zion. Then I'll give her spiritual shepherds to feed her with knowledge, understanding, and judgment.

I will be present with her, and Jerusalem will be known as the Throne of the Lord.

Day 198

My children are stupid

"My people are stupid, says the Lord...; they do not know and understand Me. They are thickheaded children, and they have no understanding. They are wise to do evil, but to do good they have no knowledge [and know not how]."
—*Jeremiah 4:22*

Jeremiah 4-5

My children are stupid. They don't know or understand Me. They're thickheaded. They have no understanding. They're wise to do evil but ignorant of what is good. They don't realize that when they turn from Me, their land becomes wasted. Mountains tremble, and birds flee away. Fruitful places become deserts, and cities are wasted. Their land becomes desolate. Every city is emptied as people flee.

Please don't wait for this to happen. See if you can get others to listen. Look for those who seek justice and truth. These may be hard to find, but, for one uncompromisingly righteous person, I can spare your land from desolation. I seek and pardon truth-tellers. I recognize their hearts. I honor them, even when they don't fully know the way to Me. I can work with them to teach them. But I can't abide those who harden their hearts against Me and refuse to repent of evil.

You may be frustrated, because you see great men and women and expect good judgment from them. You think they'll make decisions based on what is just, but find the reverse to be true. I see this too. And it angers Me. How can I ignore it? These are people I've fed, clothed, and allowed to receive honor. Though they're surrounded with good things, they forsake Me for other gods, who can't help them. They ignore My warnings from the people I send to them. I must recompense their evil and make it right again for your sake. If they don't turn to Me, mighty nations will come against yours with quivers filled with deadly missiles. These enemies will consume your food and cruelly use your sons and daughters. They'll impoverish your cities and destroy them. If you serve other gods, I can't help or protect you. You'll end up serving the strange idols of other lands. Don't be foolish. Don't ignore My warnings and accept what is appalling and horrible. Only I can place a barrier around you to protect you and your land.

So speak up!

Day 199

Where was I?

"Thus says the Lord: Stand by the roads and look; and ask for the eternal paths, where the good, old way is; then walk in it, and you will find rest for your souls. But they said, We will not walk in it!"
—Jeremiah 6:16

Jeremiah 6-7

Why did I allow My people, the Jews, to suffer so much throughout the years? Why didn't I try to help or protect them from abuse and spare them from the cruel and oppressive dictates of foreign rulers? Where was I in all of that?

Of course, I was with them as I am with you. Why did it all happen? Read and see with eyes wide open. I warned them this would happen through many years and many voices. Jeremiah was one among those I sent to warn them. What did I say through these prophets? I told them that they must return to Me. "Listen and obey My voice," I said, "and I will be your God and you will be My people; and walk in the whole way I command you, that it may be well with you." But they would not listen. They "followed the counsels and stubborn promptings of their own evil hearts and minds, and they turned their backs and went in reverse instead of forward," so I could not help them. Sure, they came to worship in My house, as some do today, but this was a mere formality. It was a religious act to show they were "doing the right thing." But were they?

My house became for them a "retreat between acts of violence." What were these acts? They oppressed the helpless. They shed innocent blood through judicial means. They ran to other gods and made offerings to them. They stole, murdered, committed adultery, and swore falsely. Truth and faithfulness vanished from their mouths. They sacrificed their own children to other gods. "They were the worst kind of rebels," publishing slander against Me and My people. I rejected them, because they rejected Me. Did I warn them against their behavior and its consequences? Yes. I sent countless prophets to them. Jeremiah warned and encouraged them with many words to amend their ways, so they could continue to live in the land I gave them. But they wouldn't listen. So, they were dispersed among foreigners, who didn't understand or acknowledge their ways of worship.

This is why they suffered.

Day 200

Even birds know My laws

[Even the migratory birds are punctual to their seasons.] Yes, the stork [excelling in the great height of her flight] in the heavens knows her appointed times [of migration], and the turtledove, the swallow, and the crane observe the time of their return. But My people do not know the law of the Lord [which the lower animals instinctively recognize in so far as it applies to them]."
—Jeremiah 8:7

Jeremiah 8-10

Even birds instinctively know My laws—the things I prepared for them. They observe their appointed times of migration and don't argue that there might be a better way! Yet, My people don't follow My laws, which I set up as the best ways for them to live and prosper. Everyone turns to his or her own individual path, and many don't recognize that I created everything for them. They say they're wise and learned and know what they need to do, and yet they make My laws a falsehood—codes of ceremonial observances. They don't seek Me in anything. They proclaim peace when there is no peace. As a result, the fruitfulness I meant for them vanishes. Though I meant health and healing for them, I can't restore them when they don't desire My presence as the Great Physician. Leaders bend their tongues as bows to shoot out lies like arrows that pierce and kill. They gain strength and rule from evil. They don't know, understand, or acknowledge Me.

Even animals and birds flee from land that becomes a wilderness. This happens when wise, skillful people glory in their own wisdom and skill, and mighty, powerful people boast about their strength. They refuse to listen to Me or walk in My ways. Why do the rich brag about their wealth? Don't they understand where it all came from? Let them glory in this: the ability to know Me, the One Who practices loving-kindness and righteousness. Many can't trust their neighbors or family! Because they speak slander, dwell in deceit, and refuse to know Me. Though they speak peaceably, in their hearts they lay snares. Don't listen to those who come against you for what you know is right. Their beliefs are empty and futile. Their gods can't help them. I established the world by My wisdom. No one can direct their own steps. Only I can spare them from the terror that threatens.

There is none like Me.

Day 201

I hear your complaints

"Uncompromisingly righteous and just are You, O Lord, when I complain against and contend with You. Yet let me plead and reason the case with You: Why does the way of the wicked prosper? Why are all they at ease and thriving who deal very treacherously and deceitfully?"
—Jeremiah 12:1

Jeremiah 11-13

Even when you complain against Me and argue with Me, I treat you fairly and justly. Even when you try to reason with Me, as if you understand more than Me, I am patient with you. You've asked, and you continue to ask, "Why do wicked people prosper? Why do You allow this? Why do the treacherous and deceitful thrive and live with ease, while good and honest people suffer? You act like you know me, but You try my heart and put me to the test. Why don't You do something to stop all the evil around me? How long must I mourn and wither because of wicked leaders? Even wildlife suffers because of people's evil ways."

What is My answer to all of this? If it seems hard to handle the way things are now, while there is some peace to be found, then who will survive when things really get bad? I understand how you feel and why you complain. You're sad to see even your own family members turn against you. I am sad too.

"My heritage became...like a lion in the forest." She uttered her voice against Me. Then other nations destroyed her vineyards and trampled on her, making her into a desolate wilderness. But if nations would learn My ways, then they could be built up amid My people. Those who glorify Me will see Light and be spared a lifetime of darkness. Their feet will be placed on right paths where they won't stumble in the dark. Israel asked, "Why did these things come upon us?" and "Why were we scattered like chaff and subjected to tyrannical foreign nations?" "Why were we treated like slaves, suffering violence?" It is simple.

Because you wouldn't heed My warnings. But though you mourn now, and look for Me, one day it will all change. My Son will return and have compassion on you, and He will bring all My people back to their own heritage and land.

And those who learn My ways and heed My call will see My great Light.

Day 202

Never fear those who disagree with you

"Your words were found, and I ate them; and Your words were to me a joy and the rejoicing of my heart, for I am called by Your name, O Lord God of hosts."
—Jeremiah 15:16

Jeremiah 14-16

People listen to those who agree with their own views. And what you hear some saying may not be true, even though many people agree with them. Only I know the truth and can reveal it to you. People sometimes set up false gods—beliefs in people or things that seem solid, even predictable, but aren't. They do this because they want security, peace, and promises from those above them, whom they hope will maintain these for them. But they cannot see what lies beneath their beliefs, which are based on false premises.

How can you tell if a belief is true or false? Simply by looking at what lies at its base. Does it substantiate the truth I've taught you? Or does it denigrate Me and My words? False assertions are easy to spot. Just keep listening. If they put down others who don't agree with them, have no proof of what is stated and represented, and are devoid of facts, they are not real. Watch what those who propound them do and how they act. From this, you'll get your evidence, not from what they say.

They can't change the weather, though they promise as much. Though they curse the leaders I send through the airwaves and make them out to be contentious, because they don't agree with their views, one day they'll seek their help.

Those I've sent as spokesmen have always born reproach, but if they continue to speak My words, they'll see why I chose them. Though they sit alone now in their views and experience uncertainty, I'll bring them to a settled place of safety.

Many may fight against and argue with you for what you believe. Remember, I am with you, and others will not prevail against you. I'll deliver you from the hands of the ruthless.

I promise.

Day 203

I search the mind and try the heart

*"I the Lord search the mind. I try the heart, even to give to every
man according to his ways, according to the fruit of his doings."*
—*Jeremiah 17:10*

Jeremiah 17-20

Do you see the difference in your life between when you trust Me and when you don't? When
you trust in people or your own ability more than in Me, you're always disappointed. You
become like a naked person wandering in the desert. You dwell in parched places with little
prospects for good. But, if you rely on Me, and have hope and confidence in Me, you're
like a tree planted by fresh, pure water. You can spread out your roots and absorb all that
is good. You're never afflicted by dry heat—the pressure of evil around you. You don't have
the anxieties of others, and your life bears good fruit.

It's hard to understand your own mind sometimes. Where do thoughts come from? I
search all hearts and give everyone what they deserve, depending on what they do with their
thoughts. Those who deal unjustly to get gain end up losing it all in the end. Those who
depart from Me and My words will disappear one day.

Only I can lead you in the right way. Only I can heal you. When others question My
predictions and the words of those I send, remember that I'm a refuge to those who trust
Me, even in evil days. Listen to Me! Do what I tell you! Turn away from those who speak evil
and criticize anyone who speaks the truth. I can preserve you and your land. Though others
plot against you and My leaders, I'll intercede. Though they try to dig pits for My children,
I'll intercede. Though they shed innocent blood and sacrifice children to their gods, I will
put them to shame. Their schemes will not succeed or prosper. Some denounce those I send
with warnings. They want to watch them fall. They want to prevail against them. They want
revenge. But everyone will see one day that I am the Lord of Hosts, "Who tries the righteous,
Who sees the hearts and minds of all people."

You will see My response when you commit your causes to Me. You may ask at times,
"Why was I ever born? What is my life worth?" I will show you.

One day, you will see My rewards for all you've done for Me, in My Name.

Day 204

Every day you have choices

"Thus says the Lord: Behold, I set before you the way of life and the way of death."
—Jeremiah 21:8

Jeremiah 21-23

Every day you have choices. You can either choose ways that lead to life or ways that lead to death. Just remember, the more paths you take with Me at your helm, the more I can do for you, both now and later. My greatest desire is that you turn to Me and not to other gods—the things or people others worship—and that you help to defend the oppressed—those who suffer mentally or physically or spiritually. When you build your own house through righteousness and justice, and pay others justly for their service, then it will be well for you. But if your eyes and heart are drawn to dishonesty, oppression, or violence, I cannot help you.

I am disappointed by leaders when they turn against Me and end up destroying and scattering My sheep. My greatest hope is that you'll help Me by visiting and attending to those who are Mine. Then, I'll visit and attend to you. Remember, one day I'll gather the remnant of My flock out of all the countries, where they've been driven, and I'll bring them again to their folds and pastures. Then, they'll see fruitfulness. And I'll set up shepherds over them who will feed them. And they'll fear no more. Then, My Righteous Branch will reign over them as their King. He'll wisely execute justice and righteousness in their land. And all will call Him by His Name: The Lord Our Righteousness. Then, false prophets, priests, and leaders, who've chosen courses that lead to evil, whose ways are ungodly, will be driven out to fall on slippery, dark paths. There, they will no longer lead My people astray or encourage evildoers to speak lies.

Don't be suckered now by the words of those who seem to know it all, people who "have all the answers," yet don't acknowledge Me. They're full of emptiness, falsity, and futility. They fill others with false hopes, speak visions from their own minds, and propound stubbornness against Me. They're not from Me. I will still accomplish My purposes. You'll understand one day. It'll all make sense.

Remember, no one can hide from Me, for I fill heaven and earth.

Day 205

One day all will recognize Me

"I will give them a heart to know (recognize, understand, and be acquainted with) Me, that I am the Lord; and they will be My people, and I will be their God, for they will return to Me with their whole heart."
—Jeremiah 24:7

Jeremiah 24-26

One day, My people will recognize Me. They will see that I am their Lord. With their whole heart, they'll return to Me. Many were scattered throughout the earth because of the curse brought on them when they turned away from Me. They suffered from famine, pestilence, persecution, and early death, because they failed to heed or listen to Me. They willfully chose other gods and opened a door to an evil I never intended for them. They turned away from devotion to Me, the One Who called and chose them. They lost the voice of mirth and gladness and became blind to the Light that could show their way home to Me. They were enslaved to the kings of other lands. Though I'd given them many and great privileges, and expected some response from them, they forsook Me.

The nations will one day fight against each other and against Me, and they will ruin all that is good. Their fearful noise will come to the ends of the earth. Evil will go from land to land, and a great whirling tempest will rise up. Many places will be wasted, because they turned away from Me. I sent prophets and visionaries over many centuries to warn the people on earth of impending doom. I keep trying to bring them back to Me, to avoid this evil. I even sent My own Son to lead them to a way of peace, but many still reject Him and Me. They kill those who speak for Me, because they don't want to hear My urgent warnings.

It's not too late for you. Listen to My voice, and stand in the gap between Me and those who choose to hear. You can bring many back to Me and protect them from the harm others wish to impose on them.

One day, My Son will return to earth and restore peace to My people. Prepare for this day. *Then, you'll see the fruit of your actions and the rewards for faithfulness.*

Day 206

I know the plans I have for you

"For I know the thoughts and plans that I have for you, says the Lord, thoughts and plans for welfare and peace and not for evil, to give you hope in your final outcome."
—Jeremiah 29:11

Jeremiah 27-29

I know the thoughts and plans I have for you. They are for your welfare and peace, and not for evil. They are to give you hope for a future life. But what about now? What about the times you must live under the leadership of ungodly people, who don't know or trust Me? Leaders will not always see things as you do. It was like this for Jeremiah. The Judeans were carried away captive by the king of Babylon and forced to live in a foreign land. Why? Because their leader refused to listen to Me or the man I sent to warn him. I continuously called out to him. I promised him and his people freedom if he would just heed My words. But would he listen to Me or to Jeremiah? No. When you are faced with a dilemma like this, call on Me for help. Come and pray, and I will hear and help you. Seek Me. Inquire of and require Me. You'll find Me when you search for Me with all your heart. I can release you from whatever captivity you find yourself bound by. Though you might be enslaved by fear or anxiety, you can be freed from it all!

Only I can release you from captivity. I determine where power lies. I made the earth, its people, and all the creatures on its face by My powerful, outstretched arm. And I give power to whomever seems right and suitable. Even the final outcome of things on earth is determined by Me. Know that My way is always to bring goodness and peace. When people speak falsely about Me and misrepresent what I've said, don't pay any attention. They may make false promises, but they can't fulfill them. Don't listen to their attempts to persuade you to doubt My intentions or My existence. Bend your ear to Me, and find out what I intend for you. Hear the truth when it's spoken by people who know Me. Don't be afraid when you're surrounded by uncertainty and the anxious fears of people who spread lies. I have your best interest at heart and can direct you to My goodness.

Remember, only I truly know the thoughts and plans I have for you, and I can reveal them to you if you come to Me and ask.

Day 207

What is the significance of Zion?

"They shall come and sing aloud on the height of Zion and shall flow together and be radiant with joy over the goodness of the Lord.... And their life shall be like a watered garden, and they shall not sorrow or languish any more at all."
—Jeremiah 31:12

Jeremiah 30-31

Throughout history, few nations or groups have cared about the welfare of Zion. Many have said, "This is Zion, whom no one seeks after and for whom no one cares!" This is because they've not understood her significance. They couldn't see her purpose or Who chose her and why. They tried to destroy her because they were jealous of her beauty and did not recognize who she was. But, one day, "I will release from captivity the tents of Jacob and have mercy on his dwelling places; the city will be rebuilt...and the palace will be dwelt in after its former fashion." Then, My people will be multiplied, and their congregation will be established. Their oppressors will be squelched. A Prince will reign, Who will boldly approach Me. The thoughts and intents of My mind and heart will be accomplished through Him in the latter days of earth. I look forward to that day, when I can be a Husband to My people, their Good Shepherd Who leads them to a watered garden. This will be a place where their mourning turns to joy, where I can comfort them and make them rejoice. Then, they'll be My people, and I will be their God. Out of the new city will come thank-filled songs and merry voices. My people will come from the uttermost parts of the earth to celebrate with Me.

I promised a new thing in the land: I would rejoice beside My Bride, who'd woo and seek Me. I'd remember My first love, Israel. Even as I bore the disgrace of her youth, she was My darling child. My affection was stirred again and again, and My heart yearned for her. I'll always have mercy, pity, and loving-kindness for her. Even though she slid backward, I'll help her retrace her steps to find Me in My habitation of justice and righteousness on My holy mountain, where My city will be rebuilt. There is hope for your future, whether you are Jew or Gentile. I promised a new thing to all: a new covenant, where My Law would be written in the hearts of My people.

Then I would be their God and they would be My people.

Day 208

Call to Me and I will answer you

"Call to Me and I will answer you and show you great and mighty things, fenced in and hidden, which you do not know (do not distinguish and recognize, have knowledge of and understand)."
—Jeremiah 33:3

Jeremiah 32-33

Who was the Righteous Branch I promised to come from David? Who was this Person Who would come one day and deliver the Judeans and Israelites from captivity? Who'd execute justice and righteousness in the land? And make things as they once were and bring prosperity out of desolation?

Under Him, My city would be restored as a place of health and healing, peace and truth. Joy and gladness would be celebrated, as the voices of My Bride and My Bridegroom brought sacrifices of thanksgiving to My house. My people would come here and dwell safely. I'd be their God, and they'd be My people. I'd give them one heart, and they would worship Me forever for the good of themselves and their children.

I made the heavens and earth by My great power. I'm the Lord of all flesh. There is nothing too hard for Me! I show loving-kindness to thousands, and I am great in counsel and mighty in deeds. My eyes are open to all your ways, and I reward you for what you do. I made a covenant with My people, Abraham's descendants, and I'll not turn away from accomplishing what I promised. I established My promise in their hearts and will rejoice with them in the land I give them.

I've honored the promise I made to them long ago. I brought My Righteous Branch, My Son, to them. And He'll return again to fulfill and complete the promises of My covenant with them by ruling in the land I gave them and making it prosper once again. And they'll call Him "The Lord is Our Righteousness."

Call to Me and I will answer you, as I did Jeremiah, and I will show you great and mighty things that once were hidden.

And I'll always honor My promises to you, as I do with Israel.

214

Day 209

I hate slavery and love commitment

"Every man should let his Hebrew slaves, male and female, go free,
so that no one should make a slave of a Jew, his brother."
—Jeremiah 34:9

Jeremiah 34-36

I hate slavery. I've always made it clear how I feel about it. I never intended or desired that any of My people should be subjected to it. Slavery means "submission to a dominating influence."* Through it, a person is subjected to the whims, cares, and will of another. Life is controlled by the dictates of the owner, and the one enslaved cannot freely follow My direction or embrace My desire for him or her. I have a unique calling for each person, and everyone can embrace this mission by freely coming to Me then making choices to walk before Me to attain the best portions of life. Future rewards are based on the fruitfulness of every person's walk on earth. When one is enslaved by another, it is harder for that person to freely follow My direction, though I can work things out for good, if that person fully trusts in Me.

In the New Testament, you can see an example of My heart in the Apostle Paul when he wrote to Philemon and encouraged him to set free his slave, Onesimus. I want all people to live in My grace, freely following Me. Slavery is bondage, and it was never My desire or My will for My people.

I love commitment. You see a great example of this in the lives of the Rechabites, whom Jeremiah used as an example to the Judeans. These were a group of people who followed the words of their ancestor, Jonadab, who told them to drink no wine and dwell in tents. Through loyalty, they followed and obeyed his instruction for over 200 years! Though the reason for his dictate might no longer exist, they remained committed to it. I don't ask you to blindly follow the wishes of your ancestors, but I do appreciate loyalty and obedience to what I ask of you. And what I request will never be foolish or vain or purposeless.

If you are in bondage to anyone or anything, My desire is that you be set free.

I can do this for you, if you ask.

215

Day 210

How will you react to a crisis?

"I will surely deliver you; and you will not fall by the sword, but your life will be [as your only booty and] as a reward of battle to you, because you have put your trust in Me, says the Lord."
—Jeremiah 39:18

Jeremiah 37-39

It is not the people you expected to be there for you who usually show up when you need help. It may not be close family or friends who come through in a crisis. When fear strikes peoples' hearts, they flee from their duties and fail the ones who need them most. Because they're afraid, they depose their duties and desert the posts I intended for them to occupy. Though they may have the capability to help, they hide out with trepidation. It takes unusual people to overcome their fears in life-threatening situations. These are people who can stand under pressure. In emergencies, often it's not the ones you thought would rise to the occasion. As an example, the one who pleaded for Jeremiah's life was a foreigner, a eunuch, and a servant. Ebed-melech may have been the last person on earth Jeremiah imagined would come to save his life. He was a Cushite from Ethiopia. But he was in the right place at the right time. Courageously, he went to the king to plead for the prophet's life. Others whom Jeremiah had spent great amounts of time and effort trying to encourage through prophecies, warnings, and visions, deserted and left him for dead. They were afraid of the truth he spoke, because it threatened their hopes, plans, and beliefs. It contradicted what others were saying would happen. Ebed-melech was the only one who fearlessly begged for the life of the prophet as he stood dying in the mire of a cistern. As a result, Ebed-melech's own life was spared, because he trusted Me over the will of others.

What will you do when an emergency arises, and others need your help? How will you act, or react, when you're called to save the life of someone whom others despise? Will you act fearlessly and trust Me to back you up? Or will you cave under the negative pressure of nay-sayers, who refuse to heed My advice? You always have a choice, but I encourage you to do what I put in your heart. Do the right thing so you can receive the rewards I want to give you.

Though you may not see the fulfillment of My blessings now, be assured that you will.

Day 211

How do rulers gain control over people?

"Be not afraid of the king of Babylon, of whom you are fearful...; be not afraid of him, says the Lord, for [he is a mere man, while I am the all-wise, all-powerful, and ever-present God] I [the Lord] am with you to save you and to deliver you from his hand."
—Jeremiah 42:11

Jeremiah 40-43

When those with a desire for power over others decide to dominate a land, they do exactly what the king of Babylon did to Judah. They remove those who are powerful, educated, and wealthy from the land—those with the most influence over others. Anyone with the ability to fight back, manipulate, or lead are removed. Often, they are killed. Then it's easy to control the rest of the people, who are powerless. Sometimes those who want control replace those "better off" with the poor and uneducated of the land, because they have little means to rebel. This is an ancient strategy. It's how the king of Babylon sought control.

But the Judeans were warned before this happened. Jeremiah told them many times to submit to King Nebuchadrezzar, then all would be well with them. The king would allow them greater freedom to stay and work in their own land. But they wouldn't listen. Because they rebelled against Jeremiah, many were removed, leaving the land desolate. To those who remained, Jeremiah gave another warning: "Stay put. Don't try to escape to Egypt." The sword would follow them there, he advised. They could not escape from it, or from Me. If they heeded his words, I could save them.

But they thought they knew better. People often do. They question My warnings and proceed down their own paths. They think they are wiser. But they can't discern the future.

When you lean on Me for understanding, I can give you the surety you require. I offer it freely to anyone who will listen. When you're confused about which way is the right way, come to Me. I will always guide and lead you down the best path for you.

Because I always have your best interest at heart.

Day 212

What was the Healing Balm of Gilead?

"Go up into Gilead and take [healing] balm, O Virgin Daughter of Egypt!
In vain do you use many medicines; for you there is no healing or remedy."
—Jeremiah 46:11

Jeremiah 44-46

People are stubborn. Though I keep warning them, they persist in following their own worthless pursuits. I may tell them to worship only Me, the One true God. But they continue to manufacture their own manmade idols. In Jeremiah's time, many worshipped the "queen of heaven." Entire families were devoted to her. Children gathered wood for sacrifices to her, men made her altars, and women kneaded dough for cakes to honor her. Who was she? She was the Assyrian and Babylonian goddess. They called her Ishtar, Ashtoreth, and Astarte. She was the wife of Baal, also known as Molech, and she was a fertility goddess. Some Judean women worshipped her, because they saw their land subjugated under the Babylonian Empire and thought she must have great power. They thought she could help them bear children. In those days, it was very important to create progeny. Barren women were considered a disgrace to their husbands. Children brought family lineage and support, especially as their parents aged.*

I made people. I made heaven and earth. Only I have the power to bring health, prosperity, and fruitfulness. No queen of heaven, then or now, can do this for you. Worship of idols or people, even dead ones, can never save or help you. That is why I pleaded with the Judeans to return to Me. "Go up to Gilead and take healing balm, O Virgin Daughter of Egypt. In vain do you use many medicines, for you there is no healing or remedy." What was this healing balm? It was a rare medicinal perfume. From the terebinth or balsam trees in Gilead, it was used to make an aromatic salve or ointment. Gilead was a mountainous area north of the Dead Sea. When Jesus died, his body was anointed with this balm. That is why some called Him the Healing Balm of Gilead.

What I desired for Judah and Israel, I also desire for you. That you come away from those who cannot help or heal you. Come to My Son Who died for you.

Only through Him can you receive what you need—the healing balm of salvation.

Day 213

Why have lands and people been destroyed?

"But it shall be in the latter days (the end of days) that I will reverse the captivity and restore the fortunes of Elam, says the Lord."
—Jeremiah 49:39

Jeremiah 47-49　　　　　　　　　　　　　　　　　　♦

Moab was destroyed. Why? For two reasons. First, because these descendants of Lot turned against Me to worship other gods. The national deity of the Moabites was Chemosh, whose name meant "destroyer" or "subduer." He was seen as a "fish god."* Related to Abraham, the Moabites knew of Me, but still decided to worship this god, who could do nothing for them.

Secondly, the Moabites derided and deposed Israel from the land I'd given her, and they stood against Me and My plans for Israel. Through arrogance, Moab fought against the Israelite tribes who occupied the land east of the Jordan River. As a result, "joy and gladness are taken away from the fruitful orchards and fields and from the land of Moab."

Throughout history, when nations, leaders, and people lifted themselves up against Me and My people, they've experienced ruin. The same result came to the people of Ammon, Edom, Damascus, Hazor, and Elam. Why? Because they turned to other gods against Me and My people, who will always be My crown. The Israelites were chosen because of My promises to Abraham, Isaac, Jacob, David, and others who knew and worshipped Me over other gods and helped to make a way for My Son to come to earth.

Some nations, once destroyed, will be restored in the latter days. These include Moab and Ammon, now the lands of Jordan and the modern-day provinces of Ilam and Khuzestan in southern Iran and Iraq.

The latter days are part of the thousand-year reign of My Son, Who will come to rule in Jerusalem as King of Kings and bring justice and judgment to the earth after a period of great destruction under the evil rule of those who reject Me and all I have done.

Day 214

Who is like Me?

"For who is like Me? And who will challenge Me and prosecute Me for this proceeding? And what [earthly, national] shepherd can stand before Me and defy Me?"
—Jeremiah 50:44

Jeremiah 50

The people of Israel have been "hunted and scattered sheep—driven hither and thither and preyed upon by savage beasts." Like lost sheep, whose shepherds deserted them, they've gone from one sin to another, forgetting their own resting place. And all who found them devoured them, saying, "We are not guilty, because they sinned against the Lord and are no longer holy to Him, the One Who was their true habitation of righteousness and justice, the Lord Who was the Hope of their fathers." Why did they place such blame on the Jews? "Because," they said, "they weren't faithful to their God. They killed the prophets and even the Son He sent to them." But they themselves would not have recognized Him.

I will fight for Israel. Why? Because she was My first love. One day I will destroy her enemies. And I will bring her home again to her fold. She'll feed again in fertile places, and her soul will be satisfied upon the fragrant hills of Ephraim and Gilead. In those days, the iniquity of Israel will be sought, but there will be none. They'll look for the sins of Judah but won't find any. For I will pardon a remnant—those preserved after a long tribulation. Though they were blamed for the death of My Son, He will welcome them and become their Shepherd. And those who lived righteously in My truth will be raised to live in the paradise I create for them.

Israel's Redeemer is strong. "The Lord of Hosts" is His Name. He will surely and thoroughly plead their case and defend their cause. He'll give rest to the land of Israel and the enslaved nations on the earth. He'll recompense My people according to their deeds and fight against those who defiantly revolt against them and the Holy One of Israel. Who is like Me? Who can challenge or prosecute Me? What earthly shepherd can stand before Me and defy Me or My Son?

None!

Day 215

I am a God of recompense

"He made the earth by His power; He established the world by His wisdom and stretched out the heavens by His understanding."
—Jeremiah 51:15

Jeremiah 51

I plead your cause and take vengeance for you. And you need never fear rumors and reports of violence between nations. Because I fight for you. I made the earth by My power. I established the world by My wisdom and stretched out the heavens by My understanding. When I utter My voice, there is a tumult of waters in the heavens. I cause vapors to ascend from the ends of the earth. I make lightning for rain and bring wind from My treasuries.

When people turn from Me, they become stupid and brutish. The works of their hands become worthless—full of delusion and worthy of derision. And they perish.

He Who is the Portion of Jacob is the One Who formed all things, and Israel is the tribe of His inheritance. "For Israel has not been widowed and forsaken, nor has Judah, by his God, the Lord of hosts, though their land is full of guilt against the Holy One of Israel."

What do I think of nations who try to take down Israel's inheritance? How do I react when people enter My city's most sacred places, plunder her treasuries, destroy My temple, then serve the fruit of My vineyards to others, making nations drunk on My wine? What happens when leaders devour and crush My people then fill their own bellies with My delicacies?

I plead My case—My people's cause. I take vengeance for them. My sea comes upon the perpetrators and covers them with the multitude of My waves. I execute judgment for My people.

One day, you will behold the justification of the righteous.

In that day you will rejoice with Me and the true Portion of Jacob, My Son.

Day 216

What causes good or bad outcomes?

*"Jehoiachin put off his prison garments, and dined
regularly at the king's table all the days of his life."*
—Jeremiah 52:33

Jeremiah 52

You can see two different outcomes for two kings. The life of King Jehoiachin, Josiah's grandson, ended well. The king of Babylon showed him favor by bringing him out of prison, speaking kindly to him, and giving him a seat above the other captive kings in Babylon. Jehoiachin put off his prison garments and dined at the king's table all the days of his life. Because he heeded My words.

King Zedekiah, Josiah's son, faced a very different outcome. After he was captured outside Jerusalem, the Babylonian king slew his sons before his eyes, along with all his princes. Then his eyes were put out and he was bound with shackles and put in prison. He pushed a grinding stone, like Samson when he was captured, for the rest of his life. Because he renounced the warnings of Jeremiah.

What made the difference? Remember Jeremiah's prophecies? In one, I gave him a vision of two baskets filled with figs that were set before the temple. One held good, healthy figs; the other held bad, inedible figs. I told Jeremiah that the good figs were the captives of Judah, who left their land at My instruction to serve the Chaldeans. These I could protect and help because they obeyed My warnings. In Babylonia, I could set My eyes on them for good and give them an understanding heart. And, I promised, one day I would bring them home again.

The bad figs were those who, against My warnings, remained in Judah and went to Egypt. These I had to give up as a dismay and a horror to be tossed among the kingdoms of the earth for evil, to be a curse in all the places they would go.

The difference in outcomes was determined by whether or not one had a listening and obedient heart.

Day 217

I sent a Comforter to help you

"For these things I weep; my eyes overflow with tears, because a comforter, one who could refresh and restore my soul, is far from me. My children are desolate and perishing, for the enemy has prevailed."
—Lamentations 1:16

Lamentations 1-2

You've seen the pictures of children and old people slain and men and women dying in their prime. It's shocking and distressing to see. Then it was by the sword. Now they are gassed, maimed, hung, or shot to death. Why would I, a good and just God, allow this? Couldn't I step in to stop such horrendous acts? Don't I care about the people I created? Why do I allow this to happen? Jeremiah also asked these questions. He pleaded with Me to stop the violence against My people. He begged for mercy, justice, and revenge against their enemies. He saw the destruction of holy places and was upset to see the defilement of the Holy of Holies. How could this happen? He saw children sacrificed by their starving parents. He blamed Me for it all. He begged the inhabitants of Jerusalem to set up a Wailing Wall, where their "tears would run down like a river day and night." Today it still stands in Jerusalem, as people beg for a comforter to relieve their suffering. They want someone to come and heal the "Virgin Daughter of Zion."

I did send Someone. Through His violent death and rise from death, My Son came to bring healing and reconciliation to Israel and beyond. His life on earth was the culmination of all the Israelites sought, begged for, and longed for. And the Comforter He made available after His death is My Holy Spirit, which now abides in those who believe in what He accomplished. But why is this world still a dark place? Because of the refusal of many to accept My healing through this Comforter. I didn't create the world to be a place of darkness. I am Light and Life. But I give people choices. And some choose the darkness and disbelief over Light and Life. Those who surround themselves with gloom bring it to others. Many blame Me for this plight and the resulting fear and desolation. Even Jeremiah did. But this was never My will. And I show, even now, a way to goodness and comfort, peace and prosperity. But often people choose to turn away from Me and My Son and inhabit a darkness they can't overcome on their own.

But if they would only receive My Comforter....

223

Day 218

Have I turned away from you?

"This I recall and therefore have I hope and expectation: It is because of the Lord's mercy and loving-kindness that we are not consumed, because His [tender] compassions fail not. They are new every morning; great and abundant is Your stability and faithfulness."
—Lamentations 3:21-23

Lamentations 3-5

Do you feel like I've turned away from you? Do you think My hand is against you or that I lead you into darkness? Do I surround you with bitterness and anguish? Have I walled you in and weighed you down with unbearable chains? Do I close My ears to your cries and shut out your prayers? Do I only confuse you by making things seem crooked and out of place? Do I pull you in pieces and lie in wait to destroy you? Do I cause arrows to pierce your heart, so you are filled with bitterness and then cause others to think less of you because of your suffering? Do I take away your peace and make you miserable so that you forget what goodness and happiness feel like? Have you lost all hope or expectation of anything good ever happening to you? Jeremiah felt all these things. But then, he realized something. He recalled the times when I was merciful, loving, and kind. He remembered how I was compassionate and how I'm stable and faithful, even when the world is not. I was always there for him. And so, he said, "The Lord is good to those who wait hopefully and expectantly for Him." He had hope again.

I allow people to go through hardship by giving them the freedom to make their own choices, so they can learn and grow in wisdom. I don't grieve or afflict them. I never deprive people of their rights or subvert their causes. Evil does not come from Me! I am the One Who pleads your case. That's why I sent My Son—to show you this. I rescue and redeem you. I hear your voice and send relief. I see your tears and feel your fears. I help you overcome them. I render recompense when others try to harm you. I support your cause. Those who set themselves up as My representatives, yet stalk and lurk and take advantage of others' fears and needs, are not Mine. Those who speak and act falsely, without integrity or honesty, who shed innocent blood to accomplish their wicked goals, will be dealt with. Turn to Me now, because only through Me can goodness be restored to you.

Because I am only good.

Day 219

Are you an "adamant?"

"Like an adamant harder than flint or a diamond point have I made your forehead; fear them not, neither be dismayed at their looks, for they are a rebellious house."
—Ezekiel 3:9

Ezekiel 1-3

Ezekiel's vision was a reminder. I wanted him to make sure the children of Israel knew that, even during devastation, hardship, and exile, I was still the holy and powerful Lord of all creation. I wanted them to see My majesty and glory. I want you also to know that I am still on the throne, and I can handle every situation and bring good out of it. I move powerfully in and through the affairs of every nation to work out My own unseen plan. Even when events seem unredeemable, I am at work. I am never wrong and never late.

The four creatures Ezekiel envisioned appeared to others. They are a special, exalted order of angelic beings, and their purpose is to declare My holiness. They lead others in worship and adoration of Me. They represent justice. There are four of them, because the number four represents My creative works on earth. Their wheels are a display of My Spirit, and their ability to turn them quickly as needed shows My omnipresence. Their eyes show My omniscience, and their elevated position represents My omnipotence. The entire vision, including the view of My Son on the throne, gives a view of My glory, which is supreme, imminent, and extends into and throughout the whole universe. Why did I give this vision to Ezekiel? Because he was called to do mighty things and speak in courageous ways. He needed My supernatural encouragement to be able to do what I asked of him. I needed him to be like an "adamant." What does this mean? An adamant is a stone like a diamond that is so hard that it cannot be broken. Now, I ask the same of you. Can you stand strong and firm like an adamant? Why do I ask? Because, like Ezekiel, you will face stubborn, opinionated, and hard-hearted people. Some will rise against you and resist the truth. But you must be like an adamant, never bent or broken. Never be discouraged or dismayed by their words or looks, knowing that they reject Me, not you. Continue to speak what I tell you, because I'll guide and give you the right words to speak.

And those who choose to listen will hear you!

Day 220

Why are the Jews persecuted?

"Then shall you know, understand, and realize that I am the Lord...."
—Ezekiel 6:13

Ezekiel 4-7

You have seen the historical devastation of the Jews. You have heard how they were persecuted, taunted, reproached, and killed, and how they became a horror and an astonishment among the nations. Their hands became feeble, and their knees grew weak as water. They watched their own children as they were sacrificed. They suffered by fire, and many were burned up. Evil landed on them as a destructive force, and no amount of silver or gold could save them.

Why did I allow this? Why did I sit by and watch as My people suffered under this torment? I tried to prevent it. I gave them many warnings over many centuries. I predicted that this would happen. It would be a result of their wealth becoming a stumbling block to them and their turning in pride to make their own images to worship.

They "changed and rebelled against My ordinances more wickedly than the other nations, and against My statutes more than the countries round about." They became "turbulent and raged against Me." As a result, the things I warned would happen did, and the Jews became a disgrace among the nations.

Can this happen again? Yes. It has been predicted. Can anything save My people from impending evil determined against them? Yes, if they come to Me and begin to understand all that I have done for them, and acknowledge that I am Lord of Lords, and My Son is King of Kings. But they must turn from evil and refrain from making idols of gold and silver, and worship Me only. They must live lives of goodness and mercy, blessing others by their very existence, instead of using others for their own selfish gain. And, they must realize that only I can give them what they need and want, including fulfillment.

My greatest desire is that all people, including the Jews, "know, recognize, and realize that I am the Lord."

Day 221

What are cherubim and what is their purpose?

"Every one had four faces: the first face was the face of the cherub, the second the face of a man, the third the face of a lion, and the fourth the face of an eagle."
—*Ezekiel 10:14*

Ezekiel 8-11

Cherubim are a reminder of My majesty, glory, and abiding presence. They sing praises to Me continuously and stand for My goodness and authority. They guard My spirituality and magnify My holiness and power.[1]

What are the four faces of the cherubim? They are portraits of My Son as signified in the four gospels. The face of a lion shows Him as King, as described in the book of Matthew. The face of an ox (or cherub) portrays Him as a Servant, as represented in Mark. The face of a man shows His humanity, as Luke does. And the face of an eagle proclaims Him as My Son, the Son of the Most High, as John does.[2] The hidden hands under the creatures' wings represent the hands of people through whom I can work on earth.[1]

Why was I so upset with Israel? Because her people worshipped other gods in secret. Some of these gods represented nature, including earth's creatures and weather, or climate. They believed that worshipping these gods gave them some control over the earth and their surroundings. It might even enable them to have power over the effects of the sun—its temperature and how it affected their lives. The Babylonian god, Tammuz, represented all these things to them, as well as greater fertility, health, and the ability to remain young and avoid death.[3] Why did the Israelites "put a branch to their nose" in worship? The custom was to hold out the branch of a tree, dedicate it to their god, touch the idol with it, then place it to their nose or mouth as a token of worship or adoration. This was a direct affront to Me. It was like they were thumbing their noses at Me.[4] It is those who refuse to worship the gods of other nations and people who will be "marked out" by Me. To these I will give a new heart and a new spirit with which to worship Me in a greater way. I love and appreciate them, because of their devotion to Me.

To these I send My Spirit of Life to be able to live forever.

Day 222

Two idols

"Therefore speak to them and say to them, Thus says the Lord God: Every man
of the house of Israel who takes his idols [of self-will and unsubmissiveness]
into his heart and puts the stumbling block of his iniquity [idols of silver and
gold] before his face, and yet comes to the prophet [to inquire of him], I the
Lord will answer him, answer him according to the multitude of his idols."
—Ezekiel 14:4

Ezekiel 12-15

People allow their hearts to turn away from Me by worshipping two idols: self-will or unsub-
missiveness and silver and gold or material possessions. When people enable these priorities to
take precedence in their lives, their choices are determined by them. They become enslaved
to idols and estranged from Me. When people grow apart from Me through these stumbling
blocks, they begin to believe lies. They turn for advice to those who agree with them and can
prop them up by making them feel good about themselves and the falsehoods they embrace.
Instead of helping them prepare for hardships, or teaching them how to recognize truth so
they can endure and survive later, these "advisors" become a party to their future suffering.

It's hard to speak the truth, especially to those who want to believe what is false. It's
hard to stand in the face of hatred that's propelled against you by those who follow idols.
You may have to endure threats from those who hate Me, because they're taught lies. But
your assignment is this: to "stand in the gap" for a few—those I'm calling back to Me.
Remind them of My vision for a peaceful planet, where My Son will reign one day as King
of Kings. Some will rebuke you and spew out words like, "This will never happen! None of
the promises He made will come to pass. The world gets worse, and nothing changes! It's
up to us to change and remake the planet!" You can reply: "The days are at hand for the
fulfillment of His vision." It's imperative that you prepare those I'm calling. Lead them to
seek Me and the truth I've given. People can never make new what's been corrupted in the
earth. A new heaven and earth can only come from Me.

I want more people to come and hear and follow Me, so they can survive and thrive now and
be a part of the new world I have in store for them later.

Day 223

You are beautiful to Me

"I clothed you also with embroidered cloth and shod you with...leather; and I girded you about with fine linen and covered you with silk. I decked you also with ornaments and I put bracelets on your wrists and a chain on your neck."
—Ezekiel 16:10-11

Ezekiel 16-17

I made you as you are, and you are lovely and acceptable to Me. My work in and through you make you beautiful. When others disdain or mock or think less of you, or you yourself wonder who you are, I come and make you worthy. I give you a wonderful purpose. When you were born, I saw and chose you. I gave you life, because I wanted you to know that I was there. I wanted you to realize one day how much I love you. I wanted you to recognize Me. I was there continuously throughout your life, protecting you from harm and making sure you had clothes to wear and food to eat. I took care of you, even during dire circumstances when others thought you good for dead. I was a Father to you. I made sure you had more than you needed. I looked over you, and I smiled at your beauty. I laughed and cried with you because, to Me, you are precious and beautiful.

See Me as your Father, your Lover, your Friend, your Brother. I am all these things to you. I always have been. I give all I have to you, because I adore you. Anything you ask of Me I will do My best to give to you. I even work through others to help you. But there are limits to what I can do, since every person has freedom of will. I can't reform peoples' lifestyles or choices, even when they need to adjust to be able to live. I can prompt them toward needed change, but they must heed Me. I can help you with these things if you come to Me.

Please don't turn away from Me. Don't get tricked, thinking that people, money, contradictory belief systems, even you yourself, can do a better job. It's not possible. And the beautiful body, soul, and spirit I gave you to use for My glory—please don't misuse them by giving them freely to others who will use and abuse them. And please don't offer your own children as sacrifices for something that seems good, like your time or freedom.

These children are My children too, and I love them, just as I love you.

Day 224

I want you to live!

"Have I any pleasure in the death of the wicked? says the Lord,
and not rather that he should turn from his evil way
and return [to his God] and live?"
--Ezekiel 18:23

Ezekiel 18-20

I have no pleasure in death. My will has always been that people prosper, have health, and be able to survive and thrive! This was always My desire. Yet, some say I cause death. They accuse Me of being unfair and unjust. Isn't it people who are unfair and unjust, who also cause death?

I judge people righteously. I look at what they do--their thoughts and actions--and let them decide whether or not to walk in My ways. What are My ways? What do I like? I like people to act lovingly, with kindness, to treat others as they themselves want to be treated. I want them to have compassion on others, including Me! I desire their worship, since I am the One Who made and love them. I see people for who they are and don't judge them by the actions of those who lead or parent them.

My desire is that you live! I also want you to have a new mind and heart and spirit, which only I can give you. I want you to understand that I am your Lord, Who sanctifies you by setting you apart from others. I made you to be an ornament and a glory among others, just like I did Israel. I want you to see Me for Who I am. I want you to know, understand, and realize that I am the Lord your God, and that I accept you graciously as a pleasant odor. I lead you out from among others. One day I will gather My people from the countries to which they are scattered and manifest My holiness to them in the sight of all nations. When My Son returns to reign on the earth, all will seek Me because of My power displayed in them.

Even though you have at times turned away from Me, because you did not know Me, I continuously draw you back to Me. You are My child, and I love you. Like a true parent, I forgive your lacks--the times you "miss the mark." My desire is that you be fired up with the fire only I can give you.

I want everyone to see the light in you that I have kindled--a fire that can't be quenched even by death!

Day 225

Will you accept the challenge?

"I sought a man among them who should build up the wall and stand in the gap before Me for the land, that I should not destroy it, but I found none."
—*Ezekiel 22:30*

Ezekiel 21-22

Throughout history, many have used the prophecies of Ezekiel as an excuse to torment the children of Israel. Israel's behavior did grow more disgusting when they dishonored their parents, had incestuous relations, neglected their widows and orphans, accepted bribes, wrongfully treated the needy, and took forbidden interest and dishonest gain. I considered these acts of oppression and extortion outrageous. They showed how far the Israelites had moved away from My desires for them. When people act in these ways, they incur harm to themselves and others. And I'd called Israel to a higher purpose. As a result of these behaviors, they were scattered and dispersed among the nations and tormented by foreigners, in fulfillment of prophecies. Some say the Jews deserved this, because they'd turned away from Me—the One Who did so much for them. After all, I'd saved them from the Egyptians, fed them in the wilderness, appeared to them through visions and angelic messengers, and even sent them My Son. But they killed Him.

But those who use the Jews' backsliding behavior as an excuse to mistreat, persecute, or oppress My people will live out a worse nightmare. Why did I, a God of mercy, allow bad things to happen to the Israelites? Remember, they had voluntarily made a covenant with Me. And they knew the consequences of disobedience. They were well-informed. Yet, they agreed to the outcomes. They chose other ways, knowing what would happen. They had plenty of warning. Isn't it the same today? I don't like disobedience, because I know the end results of it: heartache, suffering, sickness, sadness, and death. Yet I put up with sin patiently, because I know the end of it all. There will be no more disobedience when "He comes Whose right is to reign in judgment and righteousness." Then, all that is evil will be overcome, and people will live in peace and joy through My love. Until then, this world is filled with corruption. A few will stand against it. And I'm looking for those who are willing to stand in the gap for Me.

Will you accept the challenge?

Day 226

Death was never My desire

*"You shall be a sign to them and they shall know,
understand, and realize that I am the Lord."*
—*Ezekiel 24:27*

Ezekiel 23-24

Why would I kill Ezekiel's wife, the desire of his eyes? People may think that I took away his wife, and they will use this as proof that I am a cruel and merciless God, Who gives life then takes it away in one fell swoop! Why would I kill her? I didn't. But I knew that she would die. My desire from the beginning was to create life and a place of prevailing goodness, where it could thrive. I desired a pleasurable and delightful place, where sadness was nonexistent, and death could not destroy. But people have chosen to listen to adversarial voices that never intended good for them. The goal of these forces was always to steal, kill, and destroy them, along with the world I created for their benefit. One way these enemies inspire death and destruction is by causing people to sacrifice their own precious children to other gods. Even now, people are encouraged to perform devastating and outrageous acts that surrender their progeny to other gods.

In Ezekiel, when I told the prophet that his wife would die, I did this to prepare him. I knew that, if his wife lived, she would suffer. So, I allowed her to die, because I am merciful. I want people to live long lives. My original intent was that they live eternally with Me. And I have made a way for this through My Son. When I allow people to die, it's not because I desire it. I always warn them how to avoid death, but when detrimental choices are made over time, it sometimes can't be avoided, and I permit it so people will not suffer more than necessary.

In Ezekiel's case, I used his wife's death as an example to the Judeans. I told him how to react—he was not to mourn. This would show the Judeans that, when they were exiled to another land and lost what was precious to them—birthed in Jerusalem, they would have no time to mourn the loss of their beloved city and land. I prepared them for what lay ahead.

One day, I promised, they would recoup all that was lost, and this is My promise to you.

Day 227

Why cities are destroyed

*"And you shall know (understand and realize) that I am the Lord [the
Sovereign Ruler, Who calls forth loyalty and obedient service]."*
—Ezekiel 25:5

Ezekiel 25-27

Some great cities have stood through time. Think of Athens or Rome. And then there was
Tyre. She was once a great city, known throughout the world. But she began to think too
highly of herself. She said, "I am perfect in beauty." Businessmen came from many lands to
trade with her, because she was so prosperous—laden with goods and precious things. They
praised her for her workmanship, and she gushed. Their words became more important to
her than the One Who made her possible. Because of her self-importance, she decided to
traffic in goods and people and beliefs apart from Me that brought even more wealth and
praise and aggrandizement from others. She began to exchange the lives of people for goods,
a practice I detest, because she treasured the gifts she received from those who lauded her.
She grew to love how people and lands looked up to her great wealth and abundance. This
became her god—the worship and acclaim of others. But this was also her ruin.

When a city turns from Me and makes profit more important than life itself, this makes
Me sad. People who make idols of the things I gave them exclude Me from life, and they
can't enjoy or appreciate it as I intended. It becomes corrupted. My Spirit gives life, and the
attempts to exclude it from life bring only death and destruction. That's what happened to
Tyre. And this is the fate of all cities and nations and people who push Me away from their
daily affairs.

Cities and lands that turn against Me and My people become hateful and destructive, and
are bound to be ruined. Such was the fate of not only Tyre, but also the cities of Ammon,
Moab, Edom, and Philistia.

*When you come to Me, and include My Spirit in your thoughts and prayers and daily
doings, you'll see My hand of blessing on your life and on the lives of those who deal with you.*

Day 228

When is pride a bad thing?

"Thus says the Lord God: Because your heart is lifted up and you have said and thought, I am a god. I sit in the seat of the gods, in the heart of the seas; yet you are only man [weak, feeble, made of earth] and not God, though you imagine yourself to be almost more than mortal with your mind as the mind of God..."
—Ezekiel 28:2

Ezekiel 28-30

What is wrong with pride? Why do I dislike it? Isn't pride in oneself and one's accomplishments a good thing? Is pride ever good?

I gave you all that you have. Through Me, you can accomplish big or little things. Because of Me, you can breathe, move, and live. Every good thing that comes to you is from Me. Your ability to accomplish things by thinking things through and working with others for a purpose are gifts from Me! I formed, made, and created you and all that surrounds you. I did these things so you could succeed. I want you to be happy, even proud of your accomplishments. But, because I've given you all these things, don't I deserve your acknowledgement and praise?

If you begin to think too highly of yourself, like the king of Tyre, and you begin to imagine that through your own efforts and abilities you've accomplished great things and don't need My help, then you set yourself up for a fall. Like Lucifer. He was once My bright Morning Star, My "right-hand man." I set him up on My Holy Mountain, where he led My worship with praise and music. I made him beautiful with My gems. But his heart became lifted up, and he began to think he could do a more superior job of directing things than Me. This was his downfall. And this is when pride becomes sin. When people think they're better than I am, refuse to thank Me for what I've done, and set themselves above Me, then pride becomes a destructive fire that consumes them. This often happens with those who have greater responsibility. They think that they're wiser than the wise, that their ability supersedes others, and that their own greater understanding of things brought them riches and power.

When people begin to imagine their mind is better than Mine, they set in motion their own destruction, because I'm the only Lord God, Who made everything.

Day 229

What should be the pride of nations?

*"All this is so that none of the trees by the waters may exalt themselves
because of their height or shoot up their top among the thick boughs
and the clouds, and that none of their mighty ones should stand upon
[their own estimate of] themselves for their height, all that drink water."*
—Ezekiel 31:14

Ezekiel 31-32

Many leaders have assumed superiority over others. They've thought themselves more capable and worthy of controlling others' lands. They've believed that their ways were superior to others'. Examples are the Egyptians, the Assyrians, the Babylonians, the Persians, the Romans, the Greeks, and more recently, Great Britain, Japan, Russia, Germany, North Korea, China, and the United States. This happens when the leaders and their people move away from Me and refuse to come to Me for guidance. Pride can bring lawlessness and set in motion degradation in trade and in life. Fire comes out from the midst of those who live by self-assuming pride, and it causes destruction. When leaders become like Lucifer—full of pride and the assumption of superiority—their downfall becomes certain. Remember the forbidden tree in the garden? What did eating its fruit represent? Ezekiel uses a mighty tree to symbolize Egypt. By it, he confronts Pharoah and his nation by showing how they'd become so magnificent that other trees, or nations, were coming to rest under their branches and worship their grandeur. He wanted the people of Egypt, and Israel, to see that this tree represented people's temptation to lift themselves up in pride and begin to think that they were able to do mighty things without My help. But, when people fall into this thinking, the result is always disastrous. Remember, I am the Lord, the Sovereign Ruler, Who calls forth loyalty and obedience. The leaders of a land may choose to overpower or demolish a group of people by stealing their wealth, but I will not tolerate this kind of oppression. Eventually, they themselves will be demolished. My desire has always been that people come and ask for guidance and depend on Me for support and sustenance. Then, all can be blessed. After all, I created everything to be a blessing, not to be used to oppress others. One day, a Horn will spring forth from Israel. Then people will understand that I am the Lord. This Horn of glory will save My people and lead them to their own rightful land.

He himself will be the great Pride of Nations.

Day 230

Feed My sheep

"I will raise up over them one Shepherd and He shall feed them, even My Servant David; He shall feed them and He shall be their Shepherd."
—*Ezekiel 34:23*

Ezekiel 33-34

Do you remember when My Son told Peter to "feed My sheep?" Three times He encouraged Peter and the other disciples. He was referencing My promise here from Ezekiel that one day He would feed My sheep and cause them to lie down and rest in peace, though others had needlessly neglected them. Until He returned, it would be His followers' responsibility to "feed" them. My sheep had wandered aimlessly in wilderness places for years, searching for Me and not finding Me, but My Son (and His helpers) would seek them out and find them. They were scattered over all the earth, and no one cared to look for them. This was because of the hardhearted harshness of rulers who, instead of feeding and caring for them, neglected them for their own gain. My sheep were misled by "shepherds"—leaders who acted for their own benefit.

But, one day, as I promised, I'd raise up a Shepherd, Who would care for them. Unlike the opportunists, who took advantage of the sheep by eating their fat and stealing their wool, this Shepherd would be their servant. He'd bring a new covenant of peace to make them and their land a blessing. Then, My people would be secure and know that I am the Lord. They'd no longer be a prey to the nations. And My Son would be their Prince and their Lord of Lords.

Until that day, My Son and I ask you to "feed My sheep" by caring for and tending to them. You are a "watchman on the wall." This means you can warn others of impending danger. You can let them know when an enemy is getting ready to strike them, they are about to "miss the mark," or they make a mistake that would cause them to stumble and fall. If I show you something amiss in yourself or another, and I tell you to say something, it's your responsibility to speak. If you do, but they will not listen, then their blood is on their own head. But, If you don't say anything when you know you should, their blood is on your head. Each person is accountable for his or her own actions and obedience.

Let others know that I am a Good Shepherd, and I care for My sheep.

Day 231

Why do I allow such desolation?

"A new heart will I give you and a new spirit will I put within you, and I will take away the stony heart out of your flesh and give you a heart of flesh. And I will put my Spirit within you and cause you to walk in My statutes.... And you shall dwell in the land that I gave to your fathers; and you shall be My people, and I will be your God."
—Ezekiel 36:27-28

Ezekiel 35-36

Why did I allow so much destruction and desolation to Edom and other nations? Why did Ezekiel prophesy this, and why would I allow this to happen to the descendants of Esau? Aren't I a God of compassion?

Yes, but I am also a God of justice. And I can only tolerate what is just on the earth. When people boast and magnify themselves above Me, when they multiply their words against Me, or treacherously lay waste to cities and land, which I gave to My people, I must bring justice and what is due to them. My desire is that My people dwell securely in their land, being confident that I am their Lord. I cry when I see anyone treated as prey among the nations or devoured for devotion to Me. I don't want people to be afraid. I want them to trust Me as their Sovereign Ruler. Even now, many want to possess what I gave those who are Mine. They speak evil of My people and crush them from every side. They make them a derision and a prey. It makes Me angry to see them treated so shamefully. Because I am just, I allow those who cause this kind of reproach to suffer the same.

One day, I will cause Israel to return to her former estate. I will do better for her than at the beginning. She will prosper and be like the Garden of Eden. Her children will never again be sacrificed to idols. And she will be honored among the nations, because I will vindicate her suffering. I will do this to reestablish the holiness of My Name, to separate it for its holy purpose from all that defiles it. My Name, now profaned among the nations, will be known and understood by all, who will realize that I am the Lord.

Through the work of My Son, I offer you now a way to a new heart and spirit, so you can walk and talk with Me in this life and be able to enjoy life in the next, alongside those I've called.

Day 232

From dry bones

*"I shall put My Spirit in you and you shall live, and I shall place you in
your own land. Then you shall know, understand, and realize that
I the Lord have spoken it and performed it, says the Lord."*
—*Ezekiel 37:14*

Ezekiel 37-39

Can I bring life out of death? Can I raise up dry bones and make them live again? Can I spare My people from devastation?

In the "latter" days, the people of the earth will see. My people will gather from the four corners of the earth to regroup in Israel under the leadership of a King—My Servant, Shepherd, and Prince. And many who were dead will be resurrected to live among them. Then, I will show the world how I set apart and consecrate Israel for My holy use. And My sanctuary will stand amid it.

But nations, driven forward by the enemy, will gather against My land and My called-out ones to demonstrate their strength and hatred for Me. They will be mustered for service upon the mountains of Israel to descend like a storm. The land will be covered with people and weapons.

Then, the nations will see My supernatural strength, especially when all seems lost. In that day, many will see a great shaking—a cosmic catastrophe such as has never been seen before. Every living creature on earth will be shaken by My presence! Mountains will be thrown down. Walls will fall in place. Torrents of rain, hailstones, fire, and brimstone will fall from the sky and cover the enemies as they swarm like locusts against My people.

The devastation will be so immense that weapons will be used as fuel for seven years afterward. And it will take seven months for the house of Israel to bury those who rose up against them.

I will demonstrate My greatness and be recognized, understood, and known in the eyes of many nations, who will finally realize that I am the Lord.

Day 233

I care about every little thing

"The man said to me, Son of man, look with your eyes and hear with your ears and set your heart and mind on all that I will show you, for you are brought here that I may show them to you. Declare all that you see to the house of Israel."
—Ezekiel 40:4

Ezekiel 40-41

Ezekiel received a detailed description of My temple. I wanted him to see what it would look like one day, when My Son returned to reign in Jerusalem and lead Israel as a nation. Why did I show him so much detail, even describing the décor and patterns on the walls of the sanctuary? Because I wanted to encourage him and others by allowing them to see how I would rebuild the ruined temple. My desire was for them to realize that the Messiah would reign in a beautiful place designed just for them, where they could worship Me and be inspired with awe.

I am a God of detail. I care about everything. That is why I describe even the measurements of My special place of worship. When one is passionate about a project, he or she likes to describe it, down to the last detail. I am passionate about My temple and My city. I am excited for My people to behold it with their own eyes and be astonished at the glory that only My Son can bring to it. The number of steps from the outer court, the length of the gateway, the number of tables, and the use of palm trees and cherubim as decoration were all symbolic. Why did I choose to show only two faces of the cherubim—that of a man and a lion? Because, here, they represent My Son. The man's face shows His human side, the part of Him that came to earth and lived among you, the side with which you can identify. The lion-face displays His victorious side—the side that overcame death for you and reigns now with Me on high. This One will return to earth one day as King of Kings and stand with you. The palm tree represents the upright, victorious, and triumphal entry of the Messiah.* When Jesus rode into Jerusalem on a donkey, the palm branches spread before Him represented the spirit's victory over the flesh and the end of conflict. Every detail had a meaning, just as every detail in life means something in the scheme of My plan. That's why details are important. Every piece of life, every moment of each day, fits into a larger picture.

And, one day, you will behold the completed masterpiece with your own eyes.

Day 234

Like the sound of many waters

"Behold, the glory of the God of Israel came from the east and His voice
was like the sound of many waters, and the earth shone with His glory."□
—*Ezekiel 43:2*

Ezekiel 42-44

He will come from the east. Like the Morning Star rising, He'll lighten the earth, and it will shine with His glory. His voice will call like the sound of many waters, "Come and behold!" He'll reopen the east gate, known as the Golden Gate or Gate of Mercy, and He'll enter the reconstructed temple to welcome those whose hearts are purified into His courts. His new dwelling place among the children of Israel for 1,000 years will be larger than any temple that preceded it. Instead of eight, it will have 12 tribe-inspired gates.

Will foreigners be allowed to enter into His courts? Once, only Jews could come here to present their sacrificial offerings. These blood sacrifices allowed Me to look the other way from their sins. But, when My Son returns, I can receive anyone who believes in Him and receives the anointing spirit He bequeaths on them because of His own sacrifice. All will be made clean who come to Him with a trusting heart; He will purify them. I will still require My priests, the "sons of Zadok," descendants of Levi who did not stray from Me, to minister in the temple and perform sacrifices. But foreigners, even non-Jews, will be allowed to come into the courts to worship. Will there be sacrifices then? Yes. Priests will act as My representatives to execute the judgments I give them. They'll perform sacrifices on the new altar as a memorial to Me. Though My Son was the ultimate sacrifice, and hearts are purified only by Him, they'll offer sacrifices again on the altar as a reminder of what was needed to cleanse them from sin. Though righteousness and holiness will prevail in His presence, those with bodies of flesh will still have a sin nature and will need to be reminded how offensive sin, or separation from Me, has always been.* I am a holy and righteous God.

But when the new heaven and earth arrive, after this thousand-year reign, then there will be no need for sacrifices, because all will live with spiritual bodies that cannot sin.

Day 235

Your promised inheritance

"None of My people shall be separated from his [inherited] possession."
—Ezekiel 46:18

Ezekiel 45-46

The prince in Ezekiel is not the Messiah. He is described as making a sin offering for himself as well as the people. So, you know he is a man with a sin nature that must be atoned for. He is able to have children to whom he can give an inheritance. Jesus will not have children, even while He lives on earth. The prince is an overseer of Jerusalem, who serves under the Messiah's authority. He enters and exits the temple through the portico of the gateway and joins the people who gather at the temple for the appointed feast. When he brings a freewill offering, the gate facing east is opened for him.* Only the King, the Messiah, can keep this gate unlocked permanently.

Why is it so important that leaders not take away their people's inheritance by oppression or other means? Why do I emphasize to the Israelites the importance of never separating any from what they inherited? My point is this: each person's endowment from Me is his or hers alone. What a person attains from Me is a gift freely given to that person. To the Israelites, it was the promised land. The families of each tribe had an allotment that remained within those families. Your legacy comes from promises I made to you long ago, which were fulfilled through My Son. It is a spiritual endowment.

The promise of land to the Israelites pertains to the future—a future place on earth. The promise of a future life for you was made real by My Son when He became the sacrificial lamb, thus removing the sin-stained barrier between Me and mankind. With that hindrance removed, people can now freely come to Me and accept their true inheritance. And that heritage includes life through eternity and a special place in My kingdom on a new earth. I will never allow anyone to steal this from you. You can tell people about My promises to them and what is available, but your birthright will always remain with you.

That is what Ezekiel spoke of, emphasizing that no one can take from you what I have promised—your true inheritance.

Day 236

What the new city will be like

*"Wherever the double river shall go, every living creature which swarms
shall live. And there shall be a very great number of fish, because these
waters go there that [the waters of the sea] may be healed and
made fresh; and everything shall live wherever the river goes."*
—*Ezekiel 47:9*

Ezekiel 47-48

What will I call My new city? I will name it "The Lord is There," because I will reside
among My people through My Son, Who will be present among them. It will be like the
old Jerusalem in some ways—it will stand where it's always been. But it will be perfect,
with new walls, borders, and gates. And it will be beautiful. The temple in its midst will
be much larger, more imposing, and more magnificent than any that stood before it. From
the threshold of My sanctuary, a spring will emerge. And its water will flow from the right
side of the temple, growing deeper and wider as it ripples down, eventually becoming a river
that reaches the Dead Sea. Everything its water touches will be purified. Even the Dead Sea
will be filled with edible fish. Along its banks, many trees for food and healing will flourish.
Every month the trees will produce new fruit.

The land will be a land of health and prosperity, a place of peace and healing. My people
will reside under the perfect reign of the King. All who live under Him will glory in His
presence, praise His coming, and realize My fulfilled promise of goodness for the Jews. Even
foreigners will be given an inheritance among them, because they came to believe in Me. The
land bequeathed to the priests, the sons of Zadok assigned to the temple, will surround the
city, and the first fruits will be devoted to Me. Twelve entry gates will embrace the city walls.
On the north side, three gates will represent the tribes of Reuben, Judah, and Levi. The
east side gates will stand for Joseph, Benjamin, and Dan. The south side gates will be named
for Simeon, Issachar, and Zebulun. And the west side gates will hearken Gad, Asher, and
Naphtali. Instead of two gates for Joseph's sons, one gate will be dedicated to Reuben, even
though he once forfeited his share among the tribes. Then, all will see My face of forgiveness
reflected by the visage of My Son.

He will establish a kingdom on earth for My people unlike any seen before.

Day 237

The revealer of secrets

"The king answered Daniel, Of a truth your God is the God of gods and the Lord of kings and a Revealer of secret mysteries, seeing that you could reveal this secret mystery!"
—Daniel 2:47

Daniel 1-2

Do you see how, even in an unrighteous kingdom, I can work through godly men and women? And do you see how wise men and women can save many lives when they seek My wisdom in dire circumstances? This is the point of the book of Daniel. I want all people to know that, even under the reigns of God-rejecting rulers, when all hope of freedom seems lost, I can work miracles through those who trust Me! Daniel could live a life devoted to Me, because he trusted Me for answers to the sticky situations in which he found himself. When he was told to eat certain foods, and knew they were unhealthy because of what I'd taught the Israelites through Moses, he stood up for what he perceived as right. He asked for other food, even though the consequences to him might have proved fatal. He depended on Me for wisdom. And, of course, I backed him up.

When the king had a dream, but couldn't remember it and knew it was significant, he demanded that the "wise" men in the kingdom tell him the dream and interpret it for him. No one stepped forward, and he threatened to kill them all. It was Daniel who came to the rescue and offered to tell the king his dream and the interpretation. The first thing he did was to pray with his friends. He asked for My help. When I answered him through a vision, his first response was praise and thankfulness to Me! He acknowledged to all that only I can reveal secrets, change seasons and rulers, and give wisdom to the wise. This is what I loved about Daniel.

I gave a vision through a dream to the king, not just to show him the future, but to reveal to you what is to come. Some of the kingdoms in the vision have come and gone, but, of those yet to come, one is most important—that of the Stone.

This is the Stone "set at nought by the builders"—My Son, Who will come one day to reign as King of Kings and Lord of Lords.

Day 238

When should you say something?

"Then Daniel, whose name was Belteshazzar, was astonished and dismayed and stricken dumb for a while [concerned about the king's destiny], and his thoughts troubled, agitated, and alarmed him."
—Daniel 4:19

Daniel 3-4

Whenever people attempt to rise above Me through pride and arrogance, they will always be brought low! People remember how Shadrach, Meshach, and Abednego were thrown into a furnace of fire. They will recall how One stood with them in the furnace, and not a hair on their heads was singed! But they often don't remember the point of the story. Wasn't it that these believers stood up for Me, even when their lives were threatened with death? They declared to King Nebuchadnezzar that, even if I couldn't save them from being burned to a crisp, they would never bow down to the image he'd made! They said this because they understood that I am the Most High God, who rules over kingdoms and gives them to whomever I will and sets over them the humblest and lowliest of people.

When Daniel interpreted a dream for the king, wasn't it to warn him that, if he continued to vault himself up with pride, he'd be relieved of his kingdom? Yet the king ignored this warning and magnified his own works. And the dream was fulfilled. After years of living "out of his mind," Nebuchadnezzar finally acknowledged and honored Me, and he realized that I was above all things, even him! He regained his right mind when he lifted his eyes up to Me, instead of focusing on himself. This truth still applies today. Was it difficult for Daniel to confront the king with this message? Yes. Remember, he "was astonished and dismayed and stricken dumb for a while," when he heard the dream, "and his thoughts troubled, agitated, and alarmed him." But the king assured Daniel to "let not the dream or its interpretation trouble or alarm you." By this, and by checking in with Me, Daniel was assured that he could tell the king the interpretation without being concerned for his life. When push comes to shove, and you are not sure if you should tell someone a truth that could save his or her life, come to Me for reassurance. I will make it clear.

I can give you certainty in the midst of uncertainty and reveal to you what you should say.

Day 239

I can shut the lions' mouths

"He is a Savior and Deliverer, and He works signs and wonders in the heavens and on the earth—He Who has delivered Daniel from the power of the lions."
—Daniel 6:27

Daniel 5-6

I rule kingdoms and give them to whomever I will. Belshazzar, Nebuchadnezzar's son, didn't acknowledge this truth, and his reign ended abruptly. He'd heard of My power and might from his father. And, though I warned him with words written by My own hand, his heart remained defiant, and he was slain by Darius, the king of the Medes and Persians.

Belshazzar reigned over present-day Iraq. Darius reigned over what's now Iran, and I allowed him to have greater power and dominion. But, even an all-encompassing ruler can be deceived. Darius was tricked by his courtiers, who did not like the favor and blessing bestowed on Daniel. They saw him as a threat to their own power and plans, so they conspired against him. As a group, they decided to present a decree to the king that would appeal to his pride. The new law proclaimed that if anyone petitioned any god or man besides the king, that person would be thrown into a lions' den. They knew this was the only way they could remove a man of integrity like Daniel. And their plan worked! The leaders convinced the king of the need for such a decree, which forced all people to come only to him for any request. It wasn't until these kingpins brought their accusations against Daniel, who never stopped praying because of their plot, that Darius realized the true intent of the decree he had signed. And he was very disappointed in himself for falling for such a sadistic scheme. He was also sad, because he respected and liked Daniel. He spent a night fasting while Daniel sat among the lions in the den. In the morning, first thing, he went to see if Daniel's God was powerful enough to save him. He was not disappointed then.

When others accuse you because of your faith, remember that I can shut the mouths of lions. As Darius declared in a decree to all in his kingdom:

"He is the living God, enduring and steadfast forever. His kingdom shall not be destroyed and His dominion shall be to the end of the world."

Day 240

Why don't I show you all that lies ahead?

*"But the saints of the Most High [God] shall receive the kingdom
and possess the kingdom forever, even forever and ever."*
—Daniel 7:18

Daniel 7-8

A few people throughout history have been able to see into the future through visions and dreams. Their ability comes from seeking Me with their whole hearts and spending countless hours asking and searching My Spirit for answers. But even those who pursue Me so diligently cannot see everything.

Why don't I show you all that lies ahead? Because you couldn't handle it if I did! Many visions are masked with mystery and cannot be easily discerned. This is because they are not meant to be understood by everyone. They're given to those, like Daniel, who desire to understand Me and My will for themselves and others, can handle the truth, and will reveal it to those I choose. These prophets are willing to spend countless hours trying to discover the sense I can bring to this chaotic world. They realize that My prophecies are often meant to warn people of things to come. When they finally do come to pass, then those who paid attention will understand the deeper meaning of what was once prophesied.

For now, My greatest desire is that you live life day by day and moment by moment. That is all I ask of you. It is all that anyone can do. Anything beyond that is too overwhelming. Even Daniel, who asked for My visions and the meaning of what I showed him, felt overwhelmed after seeing what I revealed. What lies ahead will not involve everyone. I had to explain to Daniel that the things he saw were in the distant future, so he would not worry or be afraid for his life. Part of what I showed him lies even beyond you. And if you do your best to live for Me each day by walking in My Spirit, you will be prepared when the time comes. You'll be like the maidens who came to attend the wedding described by Jesus, who were prepared, because they brought enough oil to keep their lamps lit while they waited. My Son will appear one day. He will come through the clouds from heaven. And no one knows when this will happen.

He will arrive suddenly to take dominion over all the earth, and the greatness of His kingdom will be given to the believers for a possession forever.

Day 241

When you set your heart to understand

*"He said, O man greatly beloved, fear not! Peace be to you! Be strong,
yes, be strong. And when he had spoken to me, I was strengthened
and said, Let my lord speak, for you have strengthened me."*
—Daniel 10:19

Daniel 9-10

Why don't My Son or My angels appear to more people? Think about the times when they did show up. Wasn't it always to people in situations where they needed supernatural support and encouragement? They required extra help to be able to overcome obstacles and do something extraordinary for Me. These people were called out to bring a specific message or accomplish an almost impossible feat to bring My people closer to salvation and readiness for the next life. When My Son or one of My angels appeared to these people, their first words were often "Fear not!" That's because their appearance was always shocking to those whom they confronted.

Daniel described My Son's appearance as "a Man clothed in linen, whose loins were girded with pure gold.... His body was a golden luster like beryl, His face had the appearance of lightning, His eyes were like flaming torches, His arms and His feet like glowing burnished bronze, and the sound of His words was like the noise of a multitude of people or the roaring of the sea."

On seeing Him, Daniel grew weak and faint. And only he could see Him! That's because he alone among men had set his mind and heart to understand and humble himself before Me. His great humility and integrity opened the door for Me to send My Son to help him.

My Son's appearance was delayed by His enemies, who linger in the air, trying to prevent My answers from reaching those with prayer requests on earth. But My power is greater than any other force in the universe, and no one can keep Me from accomplishing what I have determined to do.

And I will be there for you when you, like Daniel, set your heart to understand Me, ask for My guidance, and humble yourself before Me.

Day 242

A time of shattering and crushing

"The teachers and those who are wise shall shine like the brightness
of the firmament, and those who turn many to righteousness
[shall give forth light] like the stars forever and ever."
—Daniel 12:3

Daniel 11-12

Here is what I wanted Daniel and others to see regarding future events and their affect on
people in the end times....

The last earthly ruler will achieve his ends through flattery and cunningly hypocritical conduct. Coming from the "north," he will promise peace and unity to those he intends to destroy. Many who are allied with him will be broken and swept away. His power will rise unexpectedly, and he will use a small group to overcome others. From the beginning of his rise to power, he'll work deceitfully and devise plans against strongholds. He'll disguise his purpose—to crush My people. He'll form agreements with those who once worshipped Me and were considered wise and prudent. He'll make common cause with Jews who've abandoned My covenant. The insincere ones among My people will lose courage and desert to him, and he will seduce them. But the people who know Me will prove themselves strong and stand firm. Truly wise ones, who understand My Word and My ways, will help many to understand the truth of what is happening.

He will exalt himself above all gods and speak astonishing things against Me. He will prosper until what has been determined is done. His idol is a god of fortresses—strong towers that glorify him. Those who acknowledge him will be honored—they will be given rulership over many. But they will pay a price. He'll enter Palestine and pitch tents between the Mediterranean Sea and Mount Zion. He'll overthrow many in the Middle East, but the people of present-day Jordan will be spared. He'll stretch out his hand against countries, including Egypt. But he'll eventually come to his end with none to help him. A time of shattering and crushing will last three and a half years. It will be a time of testing and refining. Though wicked and deceitful people will outdo themselves, many will end up blessed, because they waited expectantly and endured to the end.

Those who know and believe in Me will do exploits.

Day 243

When people think they don't need Me

"But I will have love, pity, and mercy on the house of Judah and will deliver
them by the Lord their God and will not save them by bow, nor by
sword, nor by equipment of war, nor by horses, nor by horsemen."
—Hosea 1:7

Hosea 1-5

My desire has always been that people respond to My love and recognize all that I've given them. And that they acknowledge from where their abundance comes. But generation after generation of people reject Me and My promises time and time again. They turn to false gods, who can't give them anything of lasting value. And their children suffer for it. When people prosper, and have all they need, they often turn away from Me. "We don't need God," they say. "We can take care of ourselves! And the gods we've made—they'll help us when we need it!" Because they live without any knowledge of Me, their lives are filled with negativity: fear, killing, stealing, abuse, and infidelity. In the end, they experience violence and bloodshed. Then their land mourns and produces little. And the people languish and die, including their children and the animals, birds, and fish—all because they lack an understanding of Who I Am.

But when the going gets tough, and life becomes unbearable, suddenly they need Me! And they realize that the idols they've made can't help them. When the sources they depended on dry up, they beg for My help. Powerless, they seek Me.

Even when people wander far from Me, I will always call out to them. And, one day, they'll recognize Me through the work of My Son, even if it's in the years of the millennial kingdom, when He returns to earth. Then people will realize that it was I Who gave them everything and lavished blessings on them. Then, My people will hear Me speak tenderly to them. They'll recognize and cherish Me as their provider. I will be a husband to My beloved offspring. They will flourish under My leadership and sing as when they were young. I'll remove all idols and make a covenant with all living creatures to live in peace. And the heavens and earth will respond to My requests. The sword will be broken. Justice and love and mercy will reign. And I will say, "You are My people."

And they will say, "You are My God!"

Day 244

My desire and delight

"Sow for yourselves according to righteousness; reap according to mercy and loving-kindness. Break up your uncultivated ground, for it is time to seek the Lord, to inquire for and of Him, and to require His favor, till He comes and teaches you righteousness and rains His righteous gift of salvation upon you."
—Hosea 10:12

Hosea 6-10

I especially wanted My people to "sow in righteousness." What does this mean? I wanted them to acknowledge Me through every word and action. I desired that they allow Me to work through them via My Spirit. Then they could "reap in mercy and loving-kindness." But often My people waver in their love. They "are like the night mist or...the dew that goes away early." They think the occasional mealtime prayer or attendance at a religious gathering will make them righteous and holy. Actions and gifts without heart don't impress Me. "For I desire and delight in dutiful steadfast love and goodness, not sacrifice, and the knowledge of the acquaintance of Me more than burnt offerings." I am sad when there is hostility and persecution in My house. Many practice falsehood. They revolt against Me and worship idols. They plot wickedness and reap injustice and oppression. They eat the fruit of lies and trust their own strength. They persecute those who speak for Me to try to warn them of the consequences of their actions. They even call My chosen people crazed fools and fanatics. Many make excuses for corruption to justify their enormous enmity. They pick leaders who lead with their bellies, lie, and devise evil against Me and My people. Like vultures, they set up leaders I've not chosen and remove leaders without consulting Me. They "stretch out their hands with scoffers and lawless men." They're driven by idols of silver and gold. They sow the wind and reap the whirlwind. They invite thieves into the land to devour others' livelihood. Their ungodly alliances consume their strength. If you will seek Me and require My favor more that people's approval, then I will teach you righteousness and rain My gift of salvation on you. My deepest desire and delight come from those who sow and reap My steadfast love.

One day, you will rejoice to see the face of Him Who can bind you up with His healing goodness.

Day 245

Who can understand these things?

"Who is wise, that he may understand these things? Prudent, that he may know
them? For the ways of the Lord are right and the just shall walk in them,
but transgressors shall stumble and fall in them."
—Hosea 14:9

Hosea 11-14

I am the Holy One among you. What does that mean? It means that I will not come in
fierce anger to destroy backsliders or enter the new city with wrath and retribution, even
though My people have at times turned against Me. Jacob once contended with One I sent
to confront him. In the strength of his manhood, he had power with Me. But it was because
he wept and sought My favor that I spoke to him as a man, and, through him, to the children
of Israel. But though he and others spoke for Me, their children still turned away from Me.
When Israel was small and insignificant, I loved and called her My child. I took her by her
arms and taught her how to walk. I set her free from Egypt's bondage, and I healed her.
When she was fatherless, I gave her love, pity, and mercy. I overlooked her faithlessness. But
she ignored those I sent to her. She pushed Me away and refused to return My love. I begged
her to come back to Me. When she grew rich, I implored her not to let her abundance cause
her to sin through self-importance and the worship of other gods. I asked her to hold fast
to love and mercy, righteousness and justice. "Wait expectantly for Me!" I pleaded. For My
Son will come one day, and He will reward those who are faithful. He'll enter the gates of
Jerusalem and lead with a lion's roar. And My sons and daughters will hurry to meet Him,
trembling with awe and eagerness out of other lands. When He returns, His beauty will be
like the olive tree and His fragrance like the cedars of Lebanon. Those who dwell under His
shade will be revived, and, through Him, all will find love, pity, and mercy. I will heal all
faithlessness. I will love Israel, and My anger will be turned away from her. My people will
blossom like the lily. They'll know that there is no God but Me and no Savior besides Me.
Through My Son, I'll ransom My own from the power of relentless and uncompromising
death, because He'll offer a new way through rebirth. Who is wise to understand these
things? My ways are right, and the just will walk in them.

But transgressors will stumble and fall because of them.

Day 246

I will be your refuge

"For the day of [the judgment of] the Lord is coming; it is close at hand."
—Joel 2:1

Joel

The day of the Lord will come. It will start as a day of darkness with clouds and thick mists. People who are hostile to Israel will invade the land. As dawn spreads upon the mountains, they will arrive and spread fires. Flames will burn behind them, leaving the lands scorched like a desolate wilderness. Moving as a never-before-seen multitude, they'll cause anguish and harm to Israel. Not changing their course, they'll move forward over barriers. The earth will quake before them. The heavens will tremble. The sun and moon will be darkened, and the stars will stop shining. This day will be terrible beyond words. Who can endure it?

But then, My Son will come unexpectedly. He'll utter His voice before His army. His host will be great and powerful, following Him as He executes My Word. And those who follow Him, and come to Me with all their heart, will be able to withstand the evil hordes. I'll remove the northern destroyer's army and drive it into a desolate land, where its stench will fill the air. I'll do great things to save My people, because I'm merciful, slow to anger, and abounding in loving-kindness. I am jealous for the land of My people, and I have pity for them. I will restore what has been stolen from them. I will revoke any sentence pronounced against them. And they will be satisfied and never again be put to shame. They'll rejoice and have no fear. Then shall Jerusalem be holy.

In that day, I'll pour out My Spirit upon those who are Mine. Their sons and daughters will prophesy, their old men will dream dreams, and their young men will see visions. I'll show signs and wonders in heaven and earth. All will know that I am with Israel. With the help of My Son, I'll gather together all nations to the Valley of Jehoshaphat and execute judgment on them for their treatment of My heritage, which they scattered abroad. As multitudes gather in this valley of decision, My Son will thunder and roar from Zion, uttering His voice from Jerusalem. He will make the heavens and earth shake.

And whoever calls on My name shall be delivered and saved, for I will be a refuge and a stronghold for My people.

Day 247

I will always warn you

"Surely the Lord God will do nothing without revealing
His secret to His servants the prophets."
—Amos 3:7

Amos 1-4

No one can ignore My voice for an entire lifetime. For I have roared out of Zion. In what way have I shouted? My outcry came in the form of a Son, and no one can ignore His life, His death, and what He accomplished! For His fame has spread throughout the whole earth. And I showed My power, might, and My heart through Him. Didn't I show much of My strength even before He came to earth? How can you deny seeing the works of My hands? Don't I stop or start the rain in answer to your prayers?

I do nothing without revealing My secrets first to My people. No catastrophe occurs without My warning. But most people refuse to listen. They reject what I say, even the words of those I send to warn them of disasters.

Some are willing to sell the just for a piece of silver and the needy for a pair of shoes! They provoke Me by creating misery and misusing even those in their own care. Do you think slavery first started with the people in Africa being so mistreated? Look again at history. Slavery is no new thing. Even the Israelites, after living as slaves in Egypt for many years, were sold as slaves by slave-traders from Gaza, who carried away and sold many of them to their neighbors in Edom.

Of all the people on earth, I chose Israel and delivered the Israelites from bondage in Egypt because of Abraham's steadfast belief in Me. Now I choose you. But like the Israelites, you must follow Me. Then, you'll be free from any harm that is purposed against you.

You will avoid pending doom and disaster when you turn to Me and listen to those I send to you. Remember that I formed the mountains and created the wind, and I can reveal My thoughts to you. I make the morning, and I tread on the heights of the earth.

I am the Lord, the God of hosts; that is My Name.

Day 248

I still see you

"Seek Me [inquire for and of Me and require Me as you require food] and you shall live!"
—Amos 5:4

Amos 5-9

I see you. I know who you are and what you think and what is important to you. And I long to be an integral part of your life. Though you may try to hide your brokenness from Me, not mentioning My name or acknowledging Me for fear of reprisal, I still see you. Though you sing idle songs and drink lots of wine and are not grieved by the state of affairs around you, you can't hide from Me. You may try to silence those who warn you, who try to save you from destruction. You may reject their messages. You may incite others to hate My messengers to protect your own angry and guilty thoughts, which you know are wrong and undeserved. I still see you.

Though you think all will be well in the end, because you make your own world, one day you'll have a rude awakening—in the day of the Lord, when My Son returns to the earth. Before His return, all Light will be removed from the earth, and those who remain will see only darkness. Those who did not heed the warnings will be overwhelmed. Those who are wise will keep silent, because it is an evil time when people will be afraid to utter My Name. Those who thought they could control what happens on the earth by ushering in systems and government leaders to manage life and create safety will be surprised.

I can touch the earth so it melts. I make rivers rise and pour sea water over the earth. The Lord is My Name. I sift people like grain, not allowing one kernel to fall and be lost. Evil ones shall die by the sword, but those who are blessed will be planted in their own land of plenty. A remnant of Israel will return to theirs. Those who seek Me and require Me like food shall live in it. A day is coming when the mountains will drop down sweet wine, and the hills will overflow with blessings. I formed the constellations and turn deep darkness into morning. I can save you from destruction if you ask and come to Me out of hiding, because...

I still see you.

Day 249

What is the day of the Lord?

"For the day of the Lord is near upon all the nations. As you have done, it shall be done to you, your dealings will return upon your own head."
—Obadiah 1:15

Obadiah

Each book of the Old Testament offers insight into what happened in the past. You can also discover what will happen in the future and in the last days on earth. Obadiah's book describes how the land of Edom, now Jordan, will be involved in the final days, and how it will be a scene of the destruction of world power. What does he mean by the Day of the Lord? It's the time around My Son's return when He will rule the earth for 1,000 years. Before He comes, an antichrist will reign. When all Light is gone, because My children are removed and little knowledge of Me can be found, many who still believe in Me will be killed. This servant of Satan will control the world and all world power. Great darkness will cover the earth, and many will die in cataclysmic events and wars.

But My Son will return in that darkest hour like a fiery light, bursting through the clouds. And many will be astounded at His coming with My saints. Many on earth will fall to their knees and weep. Then a battle will be fought. Nations will come to combat My Son and My saints. Led by a Satanic leader, their desire will be to destroy all those who represent Me.

My Son will overcome these evil ones. As the Great Deliverer, He will go up to Mount Zion, joined by the exiles of the children of Israel and their deliverers, to reign and judge the earth. Then those who initiated violence against My people, including those who were compliant with their destruction, will be judged.

Obadiah speaks against Edom, who mounted up like a prideful and arrogant eagle to gloat over Israel's ruin. Other people and nations have risen to launch attacks against the Jews throughout history. The Nazi symbol of pride was an eagle.

In the day of the Lord, those who desecrated the mountain of My holiness by taking advantage of My people, confiscating their possessions, and never repenting of their evil, will themselves be cut off forever.

Day 250

What if I asked you...?

"I cried out of my distress to the Lord, and He heard me;
out of the belly of Sheol cried I, and You heard my voice."
—Jonah 2:2

Jonah

What if I asked you to speak mercy and forgiveness to someone who caused you great harm? What if I asked you to help a person or group of people who caused death to your family or spoke and planned evil against you?

That was Jonah's dilemma. I asked him to be a spokesman for Me and warn the Ninevites against impending doom and disaster. He was the one I chose to do this for two reasons: one, because I knew he could, and two, because he needed to learn firsthand just Who I really am.

But Jonah was angry. He didn't want to complete My mission and go to Nineveh. The Ninevites were Israel's enemies. They'd caused great harm to his people. So why would he want to save these god-forsaken Gentiles? Why wouldn't I, instead, judge and punish them for what they'd done? He didn't share My love for them. He wanted them to suffer in the same way he'd seen his own people endure agony at their hands. Though he thought I might be a gracious and merciful God, maybe even kind and good, it wasn't until this experience that he saw just Who I really am. He saw how I give many chances to those who continue to "miss the mark." He saw how, when sinners turn to Me, I can revoke any sentence of evil against them and stop any momentum of harm moving toward them.

When he experienced My hand of miraculous deliverance in his own life, after he'd deserted Me, and saw what I would do to spare his life and protect him, his heart changed, and he followed My lead.

One day, I'll ask you to help someone or ones who have hurt you. One day, you will be called to offer a delivering hand to some who've harmed you or those you love. What will you do? How will you react?

Then, like Jonah, you must go so others can live, survive, and thrive in My grace, mercy, and peace.

Day 251

The Breaker will break forth

*"The Breaker [the Messiah] will go up before them. They will break
through, pass in through the gate and go out through it, and
their King will pass on before them, the Lord at their head."*
—Micah 2:13

Micah 1-4

Now, many speak against My people. But then, when He returns, My Son will emerge and tread on the high places of the earth. And His followers will press through the gate into Zion with their King, the Breaker, going before them—the Lord at their head.

Over many years, rulers have hated and detested My people. They've resented My hand on those who are Mine, and they've even stripped the flesh off their bones and broken and chopped them in pieces like meat for the kettle. They've declared "holy" war against them. But, one day, I will collect the remnant of Israel and bring them together like sheep into a fold, like a flock into their pasture. And they will hum with praise.

Hear this, you rulers—you who reject justice and pervert what is right, who cover Zion with blood and Jerusalem with falsehoods! One day, nations will say, "Let us go to the mountain of the Lord, that He may teach us His ways, and we may walk in His paths." For the law will go out from Zion, and My words from Jerusalem!

One day, the Breaker will judge between peoples and make decisions for all nations. And swords will never be lifted against each other ever again.

People walk now by the name of their own gods. Then, people will walk by My Name forever. Nations once assembled against My people, not knowing or understanding My plan, will watch as I gather them together like sheaves to the threshing floor. And their treasure and their gain will be devoted to the Lord of all the earth!

Then, My mountain will be established as the highest among the hills, and people will flow to it!

Day 252

What I desire most

*"But as for me, I will look to the Lord and confident in Him I will keep watch; I will
wait with hope and expectancy for the God of my salvation; my God will hear me."*
—Micah 7:7

Micah 5-7

What do I desire of you? Do I want you to work to try to please Me? Do I crave sacrifices
that include the lives of your own children? Do I want to see how rich you've become and
all that you've accomplished without My help? My true desire is to see your love and mercy
and to see you walk humbly before Me. I've tried so many times to tell you that My wish for
you to treat others justly and fairly with honesty and kindness, including your own family
members.

Now, you shut your mouth for fear of reprisal from those closest to you, who choose to
believe lies. Now, you work yourself into a frenzy, trying to be acceptable to the gods others
have created. You neglect those who need you.

Godly men and women have perished from the face of the earth. There is none upright to
show others My way. Many scheme and perform evil. They follow leaders who take bribes
and are twisted between evil and justice. Like overgrown briers, they meander and live in
confusion. But I still plead your cause and execute judgment for you. I fight for you against
evil, even when you keep asking, "Where are you?" and you can't seem to find Me. One day,
you'll behold Me through Him who will come to reign from sea to sea. And many will see
the light He will bring and My righteous deliverance.

Once born in Bethlehem, He will return to stand and feed His flock with strength and
majesty. And those who follow Him will dwell in peace under Him Who is great to the ends
of the earth.

Who is like Me Who forgives? I Am He Who passes over your transgressions so that I can
fulfill the promises I made to Abraham and to you.

I am the One Who delights most of all in showing you My mercy and loving-kindness.

Day 253

I have My way in the storm

"The Lord is good, a Strength and Stronghold in the day of trouble; He knows (recognizes, has knowledge of, and understands) those who take refuge and trust in Him."
—Nahum 1:7

Nahum
Nahum describes what will happen to nations that come against Me. He gives details of how those who cause harm to My people will suffer. And he asks why any nation would be crazy enough to plot evil against Me! And yet they do. Leaders turn to treacherous counselors who incite them to violence, wickedness, and worthlessness. They think themselves strong in their own strength, but they fight against the One Who can make the mountains tremble and quake so that the earth heaves at My presence.

I am slow to anger and great in power, but I will by no means clear the guilty. Those who come against Me and My people cannot stand before My indignation. Think of the oppressive nations in your recent past. Those who crushed their own people by carving up land for their own pleasure and repressing them for their own gain. They've always ended abruptly. For I have My way in the whirlwind and the storm, and the clouds are the dust of My feet. I can dry up rivers and seas or cause floods. I can make hills melt away.

I am your only Strength and Stronghold in the day of trouble, when you choose to take refuge and trust in Me. I pursue your enemies and make an end of them. One day, you'll behold My Son, Who will publish peace to the nations. And you will celebrate His arrival, because He will bring an end to the evil in the lands. And He will bring healing.

Only those who have not wanted to know Him will faint. Their knees will smite together, and they will have anguish. Because they'll see smoke, fire, and the desolation of those who plotted evil against Me and endeavored to destroy the earth by betraying nations for the benefit of their own idols.

But My own people, those who have loved Me, will clap their hands as they gather together on My holy mountain, where they will celebrate My feasts forever.

Day 254

The just shall live by faith

"The Lord God is my Strength, my personal bravery, and my invincible army; He makes my feet like hinds' feet and will make me to walk [not stand still in terror, but to walk] and make [spiritual] progress upon my high places [of trouble, suffering, or responsibility]!
—Habakkuk 3:19

Habakkuk

People have asked Me many questions throughout the ages. "Why are You silent while wicked people destroy the good ones?" "Why is there so much trouble in the world, with the rise of strife and contention, destruction and violence, yet You sit there and do nothing?" "Why do You allow justice to be so perverted?"

My answer to these questions has never changed. "I am putting into effect a work the likes of which you would not believe if I told you!" If you are watching, you will see the results in the lives of those whose god is their own power. They are loaded with guilt! Their pride never allows their souls to be straight or right. They are always restless, because their desire for more can never be satisfied. They grow weary with emptiness, falsity, and futility. Wine and wealth have become treacherous for them, because they misuse both to take advantage of others. And those who obtain gain by treacherous means, and set their dwellings up high to avoid calamity, forfeit their own lives, because they don't trust Me.

One day the earth will be filled with the knowledge of Me, as the waters cover the sea. My glory will cover the heavens, and the earth will be full of My praise, as people behold My brightness and realize that My power lies hidden in rays that stream from My own hands. My ways are everlasting. My goings are of old. I can shake nations, scatter mountains, push back surging waters, and control the sun and the moon. No person on earth can do what I can. I go and return for the salvation of My people and the deliverance of My anointed ones. That is My purpose. And the just shall live by faith in Me and have confidence that I am doing what is right. They'll know that My righteousness and justice will ultimately prevail, because I am their Strength.

I make their feet like hinds' feet to be able to stand and make spiritual progress on the high places of trouble and suffering.

Day 255

He will come singing!

"Seek the Lord [inquire for Him, inquire of Him, and require Him as the foremost necessity of your life], all you humble of the land who have acted in compliance with His revealed will and have kept His commandments; seek righteousness, seek humility [inquire for them, require them as vital]. It may be you will be hidden in the day of the Lord's anger."
—Zephaniah 2:3

Zephaniah

He will come singing. A Mighty One. He'll rejoice over you with joy and bring you rest and peace. With love, He'll never mention your past mistakes or recall your faults. After this King comes, you'll never again experience evil or fear.

Then, all My people will utter only clear speech from pure lips. They'll call on My name and serve Me with one unanimous consent. They'll lean on one shoulder—Mine. Those once dispersed and despised will come back to Me, bringing their offerings. Before this, nations will gather to proclaim war against Me. For I mean to bring them all together to deal with them, because they afflicted you. I'll pour out My indignation on the earth and consume it with the fire of My zeal. Why? So that those who exulted in their own majesty and worked through pride to consume you will be removed.

But I will leave a remnant of people who trust Me. They will seek refuge in and be confident in My name. I will gather these outcasts together and make them a praise and a name in every land, where they were once taunted and tortured.

Those who once sat and said, "The Lord will not do good or evil because He can't" and "He doesn't exist or have any ability to work" will be shocked in that day to see their own great losses. They'll walk around like blind men with no place to go, because they walked away from Me. Their silver and gold, which they relied on, will not be able to deliver or save them. Their surroundings will be consumed.

But I prepared a special sacrifice—that of My Son—and He will set apart and spare those who accept His invitation to bring them to salvation against that day.

Day 256

Why do you always feel like a failure?

"You have sown much, but you have reaped little; you eat, but you do not have enough; you drink, but you do not have your fill; you clothe yourselves, but no one is warm; and he who earns wages has earned them to put them in a bag with holes in it."
—Haggai 1:6

Haggai

Why do you work so hard, yet never have enough? Why do you spend countless hours trying to succeed in life, but you still feel like a failure?

Hear My words through the prophet Haggai: "Consider your ways and set your mind on what is happening! You sow much, but reap little. You eat, but are never satisfied. You cover yourself with clothes, but are always cold. Your earnings go into a bag full of holes!"

Why? Because you ignore what I need your help to build—My house on the earth. You run and run, like a mouse on a wheel that never stops spinning, to adorn your own place and make it beautiful. But you leave Me out of the picture.

Everything you have is Mine! All you have I gave to you! Look around and see how I have blessed you, and how I've given you what you need to succeed. And I was always there to make you prosper in ways beyond your means. But you ignored Me. So, you never gained anything. You never could get ahead.

One day, it will be different. You'll see Me shake the earth when the Desire of all the nations arrives. Then, even the starry heavens will quiver in His presence. And then, My house will shine with splendor, the likes of which you've never seen. And then, there will be peace and prosperity.

You can be strong, alert, and courageous if you just follow Me and My purpose for you. If you just listen for My calling to you. I am with you, and I can fill you to overflowing every day if you come to Me with open arms and hands to help.

There is much you can do now—ways you can serve Me in this life so you can receive greater rewards later—in that day.

Day 257

You can help build My temple

"Thus says the Lord of hosts: If you will walk in My ways and keep My charge, then also you shall rule My house and have charge of My courts, and I will give you access [to My presence] and places to walk among these who stand here."
—Zechariah 3:7

Zechariah 1-6

You can have a part in building My temple. How? By "walking in My ways and keeping My charge." Long ago, a remnant of Israelites returned to their land from exile to rebuild the temple that was destroyed in Jerusalem. The temple I need your help in building now is not a physical one. It's made up of people who are called to help with its construction, not with physical stones, but spiritual ones created from the hearts and minds of those who diligently seek Me and anticipate My Son's return to earth. My eyes "run to and fro throughout the whole earth" looking for these precious "stones."

My Son will return one day as My Branch. He is called the Branch, because He was the offspring of David and came from the "tree" whose roots were from David's and Abraham's stock. This title emphasizes His humanness—the fact that He must come from Adam to redeem, or purchase back, mankind by what He would accomplish. One day, He'll rise up in His place on earth to build another physical temple by working with His followers. He'll "bear the honor and glory of My only Begotten." He'll sit and rule on His throne, and He'll reign in the counsel of peace with the authority of two offices: Priest and King. I will be a wall of fire around His new city. Those who've walked in My ways and kept My charge will also rule alongside Me. They'll oversee My courts, access My presence, and be given special places to stand and minister. Then, the earth's curse, caused by those who stole from My people what is rightfully theirs, will be lifted. The nations who plundered My people and touched the apple of My eye will be crushed. But many will join Me and be My people. They will come from far off to help build the new temple. And the weight of many obstacles—mountains made from mole-hills—will be removed, as the true Finishing Stone of the temple, the Cornerstone Who is My Son, will obliterate all that is false.

And the believers will shout, "Grace, grace!"

Day 258

Learn how to listen to Me

"These are the things that you shall do: speak every man the truth with
his neighbor; render the truth and pronounce the judgment or
verdict that makes for peace in [the courts at] your gates."
—Zechariah 8:16

Zechariah 7-10

I want your hands, not your hearts, to be hardened like adamant stones, prepared for the battle. And, unlike hearts that devise and imagine evil, I want your hands and mind to be intent on executing true judgment, showing mercy, kindness, and tender compassion. This I need you to do to prepare for evil days.

You must learn how to listen to Me. It never helps to rebel against Me or ignore My warnings. Only I can prepare you for days to come. I alone can bring you the truth you need to thrive and survive. Right now, here are things I want you to know that can bring you goodness and peace both now and later: *always speak the truth, render righteous justice, never devise evil or injury to others, and refrain from false promises.* Then you will have needed peace!

One day, many will come to My city to seek My Son and ask for His favor, because they'll see that I am with Him. Many will shout, "Rejoice, Daughter of Zion! Behold your King comes!" The first time, He arrived in lowliness, riding on a donkey through the city's gates. Then, He established a covenant with His people by His blood. And His life bought salvation. He made a way for the release of the imprisoned from pits of destruction. But the next time....

He will be triumphant over all on the earth. And His dominion will be from sea to sea. And He will restore double your former prosperity—all that was lost or stolen from you. He will defend and protect you from your enemies. And you will become like a precious jewel in His crown. You will be lifted high and shining over the land. And all will see how great He makes My people's goodness and beauty, because He is My Cornerstone, and you are His gems. And I will strengthen Israel, and they will glory in My Name.

These things will happen because I am good, and I bring what is beautiful to My people.

Day 259

The wealth of the nations

*"I will bring the third part through the fire, and will refine them as silver is refined and
will test them as gold is tested. They will call on My name, and I will hear and
answer them. I will say, It is My people; and they will say, The Lord is my God."*
—Zechariah 13:9

Zechariah 11-14

What is the difference between good and bad shepherds? Good shepherds lead My flock
back to Me. Evil shepherds take advantage of My flock by trafficking or selling them for a
profit. They refuse to protect them from "wolves." One day, the evil shepherds will be cut
off, because they do not work for Me! A day will come when one especially false "shepherd"
will deceive many and lead them astray. He'll neglect those who were scattered from the
flock: young people who turned away from Me and those who are weak, wounded, or
broken. In his eyes, these "sheep" are already lost. He'll focus on those who are "fat and
full," who willingly follow him to gain wealth and power. He'll manipulate and eventually
break them. But he himself will be injured in his arm and right eye. And the nations who
follow him and destroy Jerusalem will suffer from a great plague that causes their flesh to
rot, their eyes to corrode, and their tongues to decay. When these enemies of Israel gather
to destroy Jerusalem, they'll create great havoc, and half the city will go into exile. Only one
third of the citizens will survive—those who are tried by fire. But My Son will return to fight
alongside these survivors. Many will mourn when they see Him, because they'll realize how
they blindly rejected Him and didn't recognize Him as the Messiah when He came the first
time. He Who was sold like a beggar for 30 pieces of silver and pierced through will stand
and fight for them on the Mount of Olives, surrounded by the saints who return with Him.
Then there will be continuous evening light, as the nations gather against Jerusalem and the
land around it becomes like a plain, so only the city is lifted up. Amid great confusion and
panic, My Son will rise up as King and unite those who remain. The wealth of all the nations
will be combined as those who are left go up to worship Him in Jerusalem. Those who serve
Him in other lands will have rain when needed, and many will call on My Name.

*I will hear and answer them and say, "It is My people," and they will say, "The Lord is my
God!"*

Day 260

Give Me your best

"Unto you who revere and worshipfully fear My name shall the Sun of Righteousness arise with healing in His wings and His beams, and you shall go forth and gambol like calves [released] from the stall and leap for joy."
—Malachi 4:2

Malachi

Now, the loud, proud, and arrogant receive special praise and recognition. When they speak against Me, they go unpunished. And so, you may say, "How does it profit me to serve or believe in God? No matter how much I try to follow His ways, evil people still prosper the most." You may stop trying so hard and begin to think, "What difference does it make if I make a half-hearted effort? It all turns out the same anyway! I never get any reward." You begin to think you're doing Me a favor by offering Me what's left of your best—just enough to get by and still look good. And what you offer Me you wouldn't give to your worst enemy! You look around at others, and you think they're better off than you are. You think the grass is greener elsewhere, and you decide to leave your spouse and children—the offspring I gave you to raise—for others more in line with your desires or lusts. You corrupt your covenant with Me and forsake those who depend on you. Your marriage was meant to bring you peace. Instead, your life is filled with chaos. And I hear you say things like, "Everyone who is evil is really good," and, "God still likes me, even when I walk away from Him and give Him my second best." One day, My Swift Witness will come. As the Messenger of My covenant, He will make sure all offerings are given with the right heart. He'll judge against evil and those who oppress others. He'll discern between the righteous and the wicked—those who serve Me and those who don't. And He'll acknowledge those who talked often of Me and thought on My Name—those whose names are written in My book of remembrance. He'll publicly recognize them as My precious jewels, My unique possession, My special treasure. To those who revered and worshipped Me, the Sun of Righteousness will arise with healing in His wings and reconcile them with those who were separated from them. Return to Me, and I will return to you. Give your best to Me.

Then I will open the windows of heaven and pour out a blessing that you will not have room enough to receive!

Day 261

He was a man

"The people who sat (dwelt enveloped) in darkness have seen a great Light,
and for those who sat in the land and shadow of death Light has dawned."
—*Matthew 4:16*

Matthew 1-4

Why was the kingdom of heaven at hand? Wasn't it because the King was present? Why did a few fishermen drop their nets and follow Jesus directly? Wasn't it because they'd already heard so much about Him from the whispers of others? The people were hungry—not for food, but for a savior! They wanted a leader to direct them out of captivity. They were tired of the Roman oppression. They wanted freedom to live what they'd been taught—that they were the chosen people. They'd read that one day a Messiah would lead them out of captivity, like Moses did out of Egypt. This person would obliterate godless rule so they could savor life to the fullest in their own land. Then, there would be great peace and abundance. Because of these things, they longed for a savior. Desiring freedom, some were willing to set aside their daily routines and sit at the feet of One Who reminded them of their hidden hope. Excitement and expectation surrounded this man. Like any doting dad, I watched His birth, cried when He cried, shouted when He took His first steps, and clapped My hands when He spoke His first words. I wanted to work within Him as His Father and Guide but couldn't until later. As He grew, I watched His every move, and I encouraged Him. He sensed My presence. Others saw how I was with Him. But it wasn't until He received My Spirit, at John's baptism, that He could easily talk with Me. Then, I could be the Father to Him that I had wanted to be all along. Many people in Israel at this time didn't understand the promises from the Old Testament. They couldn't see that My Son must come first as a man to live among them and show them My true heart. They didn't know that, this time, He must come to suffer and die among them. He must become a sacrifice to end their separation from Me and allow My Spirit to come and live in them when they believed in what He did. They saw only His humanness and how He was born of broken men and women, like them. They didn't fathom that He would return later as King of Kings and Lord of Lords to reign and bring peace and prosperity to the earth.

But not yet.

Day 262

Why are you so anxious?

"But seek (aim at and strive after) first of all His kingdom and His righteousness (His way of doing and being right), and then all these things taken together will be given you besides."
—Matthew 6:33

Matthew 5-6

Why are you so anxious about your life? Why do you keep asking, "How will I pay for this?" or "How can I make ends meet?" You can walk through life filled with fear and always distraught about things you can't control. Or, you can trust Me and know that if you focus on Me and seek My Son's kingdom, I will take care of all your needs! Only I can fully provide for you. Only I am constantly with you. Only I can help you each moment of every day. And I always will, if you trust Me. So why be anxious about today or tomorrow and what they might bring?

What I desire most is to fulfill My promises to and through you. And, to do that, I need you to open your heart to Me! I want you to willingly follow My lead! Because I'll always direct you to what's best for you. You'll never be disappointed! When you hunger and thirst, I'll be there to provide provisions for you. When you seek My peace, I'll fill you with its goodness. When others mock you for your faith, I'll back you up and reward you for your faithfulness.

Those who do things for rewards now will get what they desire: recognition by a few. But those who seek My approval will get a greater reward from Me later. Be a Light in this world! Be the salt that adds savor and flavor to others' existence on earth. You can do this by forgiving quickly, not harboring malice, making peace with others, and offering more than others expected. If you forgive people for their mistreatment of you, I can forgive you for your own shortcomings—for falling short at times.

Your eye is the lamp for your soul. How you view things and other people determines how much Light and goodness fills your own life.

And where your treasure is, there will your heart be also.

Day 263

Seek and you will find

*"Whatever you desire that others would do to and for you, even so do
also to and for them, for this is (sums up) the Law and the Prophets."*
—Matthew 7:12

Matthew 7-9

As you judge, you yourself will be judged—by others and by Me. It is easy to point out peoples' faults and failings. But what about your own? Are you aware of the things that prevent you from freely approaching Me? I've given you special talents and abilities that glorify Me and bring others closer to Me. Don't waste them by offering them to "hogs"—those who will never appreciate who you are or what you can do with Me.

Seek and keep on seeking Me. Knock and keep on knocking. Then, you can gain access to My presence. If you continue coming to Me for help, advice, and direction, I will continuously guide you. But you must persist despite the naysayers. There will always be those who doubt My ability and accuse Me of being disinterested. They're the ones with their own evil intent. I am always good.

The way to Me is narrow, because there is great pressure against those who try to come. And false teachers are always looking for prey—those they can deceive and lead astray. Disguised as sheep, they are really wolves. Remember, healthy trees bear good fruit. Worthless trees bear bad fruit. And not everyone will enter My presence. Some feign to be followers, but they build their houses on sand. Build your house on the true Rock—My Son.

My Son cured many people while He walked on the earth, because He had My power. But His main aim was to teach. When people asked for His help, He freely gave it, because, like Me, He is love. He sought the fellowship of those who would follow Him.

He was criticized by the religious leaders, because He hung out with people considered to be "broken." But He knew peoples' hearts and who would believe in Him. It is the same today.

Often it is the irreligious, broken ones who really want to hear the truth.

Day 264

What I want for you

"Come to Me, all you who labor and are heavy-laden and overburdened, and I will cause you to rest. [I will ease and relieve and refresh your souls.]"
—*Matthew 11:28*

Matthew 10-11

Many people live for what they can get now. They seek earthly rewards and recognition. And this is all they will ever receive. But that is not what I want for you.

For you, I desire a life of peace free from the distresses of an earthly existence and the anxieties of peoples' approval. When you "sell your soul" to gain acceptance by others, including your own family members, you lose yourself and what I intended for you. It may be difficult to follow Me or acknowledge your belief in Me when others around you deny My presence. But if you will acknowledge your faith in Me, even under this pressure, I will also acknowledge you when you stand before Me one day. But you must persevere to the end.

Be on guard against those who oppose Me. When people reject your message, shake the dust from your feet and move on. Don't let them judge you for your faith. When you acknowledge Me, I'll give you the right words to speak.

Today, the world is a violent place. Violence springs from the zealous followers of other gods, whose aim is to seize the kingdom of heaven by force. They cause great harm to many and incentivize people to doubt My goodness. But My true followers promote peace. Those who take up My yoke bring goodness and rest.

Blessed are those who are not offended by Me and those who love Me. They will not stumble or fall. When people seek the truth, they see things that are hidden from others. Often, it's not the most prestigious or learned people who accept My message of hope. Those who willingly receive, welcome, and accept you also receive, welcome, and accept Me.

Those who reject you are really rejecting Me, and they are rejected by Me in the end.

Day 265

Why Jesus spoke in parables

"This was in fulfillment of what was spoken by the prophet: I will open My mouth in parables; I will utter things that have been hidden since the foundation of the world."
—*Matthew 13:35*

Matthew 12-13

My Son taught with parables to fulfill the prophetic words in Psalm 78:2 and Ezekiel 20:49—that He'd give instruction by allegories to reveal truths hidden since the world began. Why were these truths hidden? Because the god of this world had deceived Adam and Eve and many who followed them. He'd obscured what I originally made clear.

Why did only some people understand Jesus's parables? Because the stories differentiated between Light and darkness, and their meaning would always be obscure to those who dwell in darkness. But those with "ears to hear" could understand. Secrets and mysteries are imbedded in His life examples. And only some will ever comprehend their meaning. Like His disciples, these are those who want to know. Four reactions always result from hearing My Word: Some immediately reject the truth they hear—it's stolen from them. Others receive the truth but quickly turn away because of life's pressures. Some hear My Word, receive it for a while, but are drawn away by the cares of the world—wealth, recognition, and power, which choke out any belief in Me. Finally, those who grasp its meaning, love what it represents, and yearn to know more are the fruitful seed that yield spiritual abundance. They are the "good wheat" sown to be gathered at the end harvest and given places of honor and favor. Often considered the least and lowliest of people, their capabilities and what lies within them are often overlooked. But, like the mustard plant's very tiny and insignificant beginning, they grow into magnificent trees that protect and harbor many others. So, never underestimate what I can do for and through you. People may try to disqualify you because of your beliefs and Who you represent, just as they did My Son. Just remember, I am training you for a greater purpose.

I want you to be able to understand My hidden truths so you can enjoy greater treasures later, and so you will have an honored seat in My Kingdom!

Day 266

Stop being afraid!

"For the Son of Man is going to come in the glory (majesty, splendor) of His Father with His angels, and then He will render account and reward every man in accordance with what he has done."
—Matthew 16:27

Matthew 14-16

People still don't get it! They see My miracles every day and yet they don't understand. I sent My Son to show them that, even when things seem hopeless, I can cause wonderful results to flow to them. I deliver goodness and fulfillment when others see no hope.

People came in droves to see Jesus, and His disciples panicked when He asked them to feed the crowds. They exclaimed, "There's no way!" Sometimes you'll respond the same way. What was Jesus's reaction? "Bring me the five loaves and two fish." Most people can't see what's right in front of them. They're used to trusting in their own ability and what they've known. But what I want them to see is that I am a God of fathomless ability with boundless resources! I can produce an abundance out of a little. When the disciples were in the boat tossed by a storm, they were filled with fear. Then, Jesus walked out to them! Their fear became panic, because they thought He was a ghost. How did He respond? He stopped the storm and shouted, "Take courage! I AM! Stop being afraid!" That is still My response, My message to you today.

Jesus wanted people to see the differences between what may be taught erroneously by religious leaders and others and what is My true intent for them. People like to create demands. They mutter, "Don't do this! Don't do that!" They take what I intended as good and make laws out of My teachings. But, My true heart was always to set people free from rules!

My Son came to build faith in My boundless ability to make something good out of every bad situation.

And I want to reward you, when My Son returns, for all the times you trusted Me, walked away from your fears, and displayed faith in how I could produce miracles in your life and others'!

Day 267

All things are possible with Me

*"Truly I say to you, if you have faith like a grain of mustard seed,
you can say to this mountain, Move from here to yonder place,
and it will move; and nothing will be impossible to you."*
—Matthew 17:20

Matthew 17-19

All things are possible with Me. Including forgiveness. How many times should you forgive? My Son's answer was 70 times seven.

Remember the king who forgave his attendant of all his great debt, yet the attendant turned and refused to pardon the small debt of his fellow servant? It's like this for you. I've forgiven all your shortcomings through My Son. He gave up everything so you could live forever, free from any "debts" to Me! How can you then not forgive others for what they've done or not done to or for you?

My Son sits now on the throne of glory I prepared for Him. One day, you'll stand before Him and see His face shining like the sun, with clothing white like light, just as Peter, James, and John beheld Him on the mountaintop. As you stand before Him, He'll acknowledge what you've done. If you trusted in Me as a little child and humbled your heart, if you left riches or honor, family or lands, for My sake, He will honor you and give you rewards for the sacrifices you made, the good things done. Those who are "first" in this world, who sought honor and glory and riches and the praise of many, will be "last" in My Kingdom. Those who put Me first now will be first in the kingdom.

Life with Me requires forgiveness. Through forgiving, you are freed from hurt, harm, sorrow, self-pity—all the things that burden the people around you. People often get divorced, because they can't forgive, when it would have been better for them to stay married. My intention was that "one flesh" could never be separated.

Freedom from the burdens of life also requires humility—a willingness to submit to Me and what I can do for and through you to bring others closer to Me.

This may seem difficult but, remember, "all things are possible with Me."

Day 268

They hated Him

"They said to Him, Do You hear what these are saying? And Jesus replied to them, Yes; have you never read, Out of the mouths of babes and unweaned infants You have made perfect praise."
—Matthew 21:16

Matthew 20-21

It's the same today! Leaders who say they represent Me often lead others away from Me. Those who are small in the eyes of the world, who have no title or honor, are often closest to Me and what I truly represent. Don't be fooled by those who seem to be weighty with knowledge and have the praise of others, who stand in high places and look down on the rest. Their hearts are far from Me. My Son came riding on a donkey through the city gates. He understood that "whoever wishes to be great in My kingdom must be your servant."

The leaders of His day disdained Him and His teachings. But He was not afraid to confront their hypocrisy. He did the outrageous. He over-turned the tables of the moneychangers, because they were taking advantage of those who'd traveled from far away and needed to buy items for sacrifice in My temple. They jacked up the prices, knowing the people had no other place to buy what they needed.

Why did He curse the fig tree? This was in fulfillment of Micah's prophecy that claimed that people were famished, not even able to find a first-ripe fig, because of the dearth of godly men on the earth (Micah 7:1-2). Jesus felt the same way. He was saddened by the lack of god-fearing leaders who would act as shepherds for My people and lead them to Me. With his whole heart, he showed the greatness of prayer and how faith in Me brought good things, even miraculous results. And it didn't matter how religious people were, how many good deeds they did, or how much respect they obtained from others. What mattered was the heart and how one ultimately came and followed Me.

His teachings upset the religious leaders of the day, who focused on actions, obedience to their laws, and the praise of people. They hated Him.

It was the lowly, humble, and simple ones who came and shouted, "Hosanna! Blessed is He Who comes in the name of the Lord!"

Day 269

Who is invited to the wedding banquet?

"He replied to him, You shall love the Lord your God with all your heart and with all your soul and with all your mind (intellect)."
—*Matthew 22:37*

Matthew 22-23

Who was originally invited to the wedding banquet, as described by Jesus? And who were the ones summoned when the first ones refused their invitation? Because of My love for Abraham and the promises I had made to him long ago—that I would bless him and his children forever because he trusted Me—My first love was always for the Israelites. These were the ones My Son came to bless primarily. He came from them, as promised to the prophets. He was their longed-for Messiah. And He offered them an invitation to His wedding feast first, because He desired to be their Bridegroom, as prophesied in the Old Testament. But they rejected Him, just as they'd shamefully handled and killed those who came before Him—the prophets whom I sent to foretell His coming. So, I turned to others and made it available for those outside Israel's flock to come and dine with My Son at His banquet—to be wedded with Him. And those who accept My invitation will be received with joy and will sit with Me at Our feast. But only those who "wear His robe"—the spirit from Me received when they believe—can enter.

Many are called, but few are chosen, because many do not accept My ways when they see how it differs from the world's ways. You see how hard it was for the Pharisees, the learned scholars of Jesus's day, to accept His simple, meaningful, and uncomplicated explanations of life and what is important. He was able to take very complex topics, like marriage in heaven, and make them easy to understand. This infuriated the Pharisees, who delighted in obscuring every issue so that others would think them more educated, experienced, and wise than they were. They burdened others with obligations that they themselves couldn't meet.

It's the same today. The most learned ones often try to belittle and bully others with their "knowledge and understanding." But what is most important to Me? To love Me with all your heart and mind and soul and to love others as yourself.

These sum up what is most important in life itself.

Day 270

When will He return?

"Watch therefore [give strict attention, be cautious and active], for you do not know in what kind of a day [whether a near or remote one] your Lord is coming."
—*Matthew 24:42*

Matthew 24-25

As Jesus explained to His disciples, no one knows when He will return. Before His return to earth to reign, He will call up those who've accepted Him as Lord and received My Holy Spirit. These will be gathered in the air and brought before Him at My throne. They will stand beside the risen Christ with My angels during the tribulation years, when the antichrist will deceive the nations and set up his throne in Israel—the abomination prophesied by Daniel.

False prophets will arise to cause many to distrust and desert Me and to betray others, even family members. They will perform signs and wonders to lead many astray. Nation will rise against nation, and the world will be filled with famines and earthquakes unlike any before. Lawlessness will increase and the love of many will grow cold. The days will be shortened to spare the few who still believe in Me. Those who endure will be given a place in My millennial and eternal kingdoms.

When all seems lost, and the world is so dark that even the stars can't shine, My Son will return to earth with His saints and angels, like lightning flashing from the east. Then He will gather to Him His chosen ones from the ends of the universe to stand and reign with Him in a place of honor. Many will lament and mourn, because they did not believe in Him.

No one knows when these things will occur. Until then, use the gifts you've been given with the power of the Holy Spirit within you. As you yearn for more of Me, I can give you greater ability and power. How you use your natural and spiritual abilities determines what I can offer you later.

Seek that day—when I will come for you.

Day 271

Always a Judas

"As they were eating, He said, Solemnly I say to you, one of you will betray Me!"
—Matthew 26:21

Matthew 26

Anyone who stands for Me and expresses My truth will be betrayed. David recalled in Psalm 41:9 how his good friend Ahithophel turned against him. Jesus experienced it with Judas, and you may be betrayed by someone close who disagrees with your message. What causes people to betray others? Usually, it's fear. It can be fear of "falling into the wrong hands," though often they've succumbed to this already. It can be the fear of submitting to Me and My will, instead of being self-directed, or of being coerced to give up the things that "prop them up." It also comes from hatred initiated by jealousy, anger, suspicion, false idols, or wrong teaching. Sometimes the betrayer feels betrayed. Judas did.

Judas's compulsion to break faith with Jesus stemmed from several seeds. He'd followed Jesus because of his own ideals and false expectations of what the Messiah was sent to do. He wanted the savior to be a "strong man," a warrior, someone who'd upset the establishment and overturn the Roman government. He imagined someone who'd set himself up to reign. And Judas wanted to rule with him. His idols were control and power. He wanted to have a title, to be acknowledged as a ruler on earth alongside the messiah. He wanted praise and glory now. What he didn't understand was that Jesus came this time, not to reign, but to prepare people for His return. Now, He came as a shepherd, calling My sheep to Him. He came to heal and teach and show by example My true heart. He came as Love to open their hearts to a new way and to lead them back to Me. Later, He'd come back to earth, after I'd established My flock and determined who were My sheep. Then, He'd come in power and glory. But first, it had to be accomplished through submission. And Judas wanted no part of it.

There will be other Judases who reject My message, because it doesn't fit with their agenda or ideology. They're the ones who want honor now and to hold onto their idols. But life is not about attaining power and control.

It's about giving of yourself so that you can receive My love and abundance later.

Day 272

No one can hide what was accomplished

"Go then and make disciples of all the nations, baptizing them into the name of the Father and of the Son and of the Holy Spirit."
—Matthew 28:19

Matthew 27-28

What was accomplished by My Son's trial, crucifixion, death, and resurrection? First, many Old Testament prophecies were fulfilled. This included the 30 pieces of silver offered—the price of someone without worth or value (Exodus 21:32)—and the purchase of the potter's field—a place to bury strangers with no heritage in Israel. Why was it called the potter's field? It was the area where potters dug clay to make pots. *Grammarphobia.com* says the word for "potter" during the 1500s meant an itinerant peddler or vagrant. By the 1700s, the term "potter's field" referred to a plot of land set aside to bury indigents. The significance of a field to bury indigents or foreigners? My Son's death and resurrection opened a door through which even those from outside of Israel were allowed into His kingdom. The veil torn from top to bottom at Jesus's death showed that the segregation between My Holy of Holies and the worshippers was finally ripped apart. Jesus unified what was once separated—My people from Me. Remember, I am the Great Potter, designing things as I choose, including My church, which I graciously fashion to be a complete and beautiful vessel made up of individuals formed from "clay" and filled with My Spirit.

Jesus didn't answer His inquisitors during His trial. This too was a fulfillment of prophecy. The betrayal by the Jews—their acceptance of His blood as a curse on their own heads and the heads of their children, the dividing of His garments, the mock trial and abuse by the guards, the offering of gall to drink, the malefactors crucified with Him, those who jeered and accused him, even His death, burial, and resurrection were all predicted and foretold in Psalm 22. Joseph of Arimathea had read the scriptures. He understood what Jesus was doing. Jesus's disciples only hoped what He'd promised would happen. But Joseph believed.

And when they all saw Him again, imagine their joy, though some still refused to believe and lied to hide His resurrection!

But no one can ever cover up what was accomplished.

Day 273

He was not afraid of people

"They were completely astonished at His teaching, for He was teaching as One Who possessed authority, and not as the scribes."
—Mark 1:22

Mark 1-2

What you see in Jesus is not the authority of a person with earthly power but My authority given through My Son. Jesus was not afraid to speak or to act with My power. And the results of this action are what amazed the people who observed Him. He understood what I desired Him to do, and He was not afraid to act on My instructions.

Did He heal everyone? No. He couldn't, because some didn't believe in His ability to act for Me. Only through a belief in My power can anyone receive what I can give. And those who believed in My power through Him partook of it.

Do you see how unafraid He was of people? This is rare. He didn't heed the judgmental words of the Pharisees, even when they accused Him of breaking the Sabbath, befriending sinners, and working for the prince of demons! He didn't care when they spoke against Him for pardoning the sins of a paralytic or when they asked why His disciples didn't fast and picked grain on the Sabbath. What He cared most about was following Me and helping people through difficult times by leading them to a greater understanding of Me.

It was all about forgiveness, and He knew it. He understood that perfect love, My love, casts out fear. He walked with Me continuously, even when he was threatened by extreme temptation and hardship for over 40 days. He sought only My will. And that made all the difference.

Because He didn't submit to the demands of the strongest, or the most prestigious and powerful people, I was able to work through Him to will and to do of My good pleasure.

And as a result, He was able to speak and act supernaturally with My authority in ways beyond anyone's comprehension.

Day 274

He had feelings

"He glanced around at them with vexation and anger,
grieved at the hardness of their hearts...."
—Mark 3:5

Mark 3-4

Jesus had feelings just like yours. He was vexed, angry, grieved, and sad. What upset Him the most? Fear and unbelief—the questioning of My will and My heart. He was upset when people misunderstood and misrepresented Who I am, especially the religious leaders, who said they stood for Me. To counter their lack of faith and trust in Me, He did outrageous things. He healed the sick people others discarded. He forgave sins. And He did these things on the religious leaders' forbidden days to show that it was always My will to make people whole.

I taught Him how to protect Himself. When people pressed in on Him, He knew when it was time to go. I always provided a way out of harm. I can still do this today for those who will listen. I can do it for you. Why did He tell people to refrain from revealing their healing to others? Because He knew people would come to Him in droves, only to have their physical needs met. His purpose was to teach and to reveal the spiritual side of life. And He needed time with His disciples to do this. They would be His future leaders and carry on His ministry. They must know how. Sometimes He'd go up to the top of a mountain or out in a boat to get away with the disciples. He'd go alone first to receive instructions from Me, then He could disseminate My power and authority to them so they could preach and heal and drive out demons. When they experienced the pressure of persecution from outsiders, insiders, family, or friends, He pulled them even closer. His teaching increased, and He explained more about the mysteries behind the parables He shared openly. He helped them understand that His power could only come from one source—Me. But any who misrepresented My Holy Spirit by accepting and worshipping falsehoods, and leading others astray, would not be forgiven. This was because they were led by adversarial spirits, whose purpose was to upend the things of Me. Whoever did My will was His brother, sister, or mother! This was His surprising revelation.

And to these He entrusted My true mysteries.

Day 275

What fear causes

"Take heart! I AM! Stop being alarmed and afraid!"
—Mark 6:50

Mark 5-6

Do you see what fear can do to people? It can cause them to lose any sense of humanity and reality. They can even relinquish their natural ability to care about another person's well-being, especially if that person changes too much and that change affects them. The people in the Gerasene region reacted very negatively when they heard that the man in the tombs was cured of his outrageous behavior. They'd always known him to be crazy and couldn't accept any change in him, even for the better. They couldn't focus on the miracle—how Jesus had set him free. They could only see how their lives were affected, and they were seized with alarm and fear. The man in the tombs knew it would be difficult to stay among these people and be accepted as a changed man. He wanted to go with Jesus. But Jesus knew better. The man could help other people by telling them of his miraculous deliverance. Many would marvel when they saw him and heard his story, especially in areas away from his own hometown.

One synagogue leader believed in Jesus's power. Not many leaders trusted like Jairus. Amid mockery and jeering, Jesus raised his daughter up because of his faith. Some received healing directly from Jesus, like the woman with the issue of blood. She believed He could heal her and tapped into His latent spiritual power by merely touching His garment.

Some didn't believe. So, they didn't receive. Many in His hometown of Nazareth would not accept His words or what He offered. They "knew too much" about Him. How could this man, who'd lived as a child among them, be the Messiah? They listened to lies and refused to acknowledge Who He really was.

Your own family and some close to you will doubt your words and what you can offer them. If they refuse to receive you, shake the dust from your feet and move on as Jesus instructed the disciples to do. Don't take it personally.

They are rejecting Me, after all.

Day 276

A few knew Who He was

"He asked them, But who do you yourselves say that I am? Peter replied to Him, You are the Christ (the Messiah, the Anointed One)."
—*Mark 8:29*

Mark 7-8

People often live for show. They see what they can gain here and now and forget about the next life. But, if you "lose yourself" by relying on Me to direct and show you how to follow Me, you will gain an abundance of life later. The religious leaders in Jesus's time focused on "show." They adhered to religious rituals rather than on what might please Me. Their hearts moved far from Me, because they were more devoted to customs. They honored Me with their lips but not with their hearts. They thwarted My will, and what I would have all people know and do, by burdening them with man-made rules and regulations. My heart was always that people be free to love Me and others. Some will follow their lead. They'll move away from Me, trying to please others, especially those in authority, by "acting the right way." Remember, the things that come out of a person are more important than what goes in. Evil purposes and desires come from within.

When My Son came the first time, it was to the children of Israel, as I promised His forefathers. Yet He was willing to heal some outside of Israel—those who came and asked and believed. His purpose was to teach and give guidance on Who I am. This was why He implored those He healed to tell no one. But the rumors and stories spread, and it became harder for Him to focus on teaching. After so much instruction and so many demonstrations of My power, why did His disciples still not understand what I could do for and through them? Isn't it the same today? Often people can only see what's in front of them: the obstacles and challenges of life. Jesus showed My limitless ability as Jehovah-Jireh, the "Lord who provides," by feeding the multitudes. He also demonstrated My ability to make whole as Jehovah-Rapha, "the Lord who heals." But, He grew tired of the demands of those who refused to see, even after He'd performed so many miracles. His desire was that they understand that *He* was My real miracle—their Messiah come among them! But their hearts were in a settled state of hardness.

A few knew Who He was and what He would do, but only a few.

Day 277

Why don't you see signs and wonders?

"Jesus glanced around at them and said, With men [it is] impossible,
but not with God; for all things are possible with God."
—Mark 10:27

Mark 9-10

When they're fearful, people become awkward. They say the wrong things. Peter was like this. But I loved how he tried so hard and was earnest and persistent. He wanted to please Me and Jesus but wasn't sure how. He often blurted out inappropriate things out of fear. Unlike him, I want you to take your time. Instead of allowing anxiety to reign, causing you to live in a world full of worry and disregard for others, listen for My guidance in every situation. Then, whatever you say or do will be right. And you, and those around you, will be blessed. If you don't know what I desire, be still until you do. Wait until it's clear to you through My Spirit in you.

The disciples often didn't understand. Jesus explained many things, but it wasn't until later that it all became clear. Then, they understood why He had to suffer and be rejected and die and how He fulfilled the scriptures. Later, they saw how He could have such amazing faith and how they could do the deeds He did. Through what He accomplished, they began to see how they could trust Me the way He did. And when they received My Spirit, they saw their own signs, miracles, and wonders with My help. Why don't people see the same marvels today? Because of what Jesus said: Sometimes healing requires prayer, trust, fasting, and patience. It's always harder for adults, who are hardened by the world's doubts and fears. "Whoever accepts and receives and welcomes a child accepts, receives, and welcomes Me," He said. Trust like little children. "With men [it is] impossible, but not with God."

I loved the rich man because of his heart. So did Jesus. Riches alone don't corrupt. It's reliance on them, instead of Me, that perverts a person. People can have a perfect heart and riches too. It's trust in things that causes them to move away from a firm reliance on Me. When people give up what takes them far from Me, I reward them for seeking Me first.

And then they begin to see the miracles.

Day 278

Which side do you stand on?

"They sent some of the Pharisees and of the Herodians to Him for the purpose of entrapping Him in His speech."
—Mark 12:13

Mark 11-12

It's never actions alone that matter most, but the heart with which they're done. When a scribe asked Jesus what was the most important of all the commandments, He answered, "The Lord our God is one Lord and His desire is that You love Him with your whole heart and soul and mind and strength. Then love your neighbor as yourself." Understanding a person's heart helps you comprehend that person's true motivation. If a person is Mine, and I am his or her central focus, then he or she can come from a place of perfect love.

How did Jesus answer the confrontational questions of the scribes and Pharisees, who tested Him continuously and questioned His sincerity? He always asked Me for the right words to say. He put them in their place—especially those who wouldn't accept Him for Who He was. It's the same for you today. You'll be questioned for what you believe, especially if it stems from My truth. Come to Me for the answers. Then none can defame you, and your answers will stun them.

When you know My Word and My power, and you apply them, you'll never wander from your true path or go the wrong way. And no one can entrap you in your words. Forgiveness is the answer. It's the key to your peace. It unlocks answered prayer. If you have anything against anyone, quickly forgive that person and let go of whatever hurt that person caused you. Then I can pardon you for your own shortcomings and failings.

Many will try to corrupt what I've said. They'll twist My words to suit themselves and their own agendas. But My Word will always prove true in the end. Trust in Me and My truth for good results.

Which side do you stand on?

Why not end up on the side of truth so you can stand forever by My side, where life is everlasting?

Day 279

How could I just watch what they did to Him?

"Then they will see the Son of Man coming in clouds
with great power and glory (majesty and splendor)."
—Mark 13:26

Mark 13-14

The spirit is often willing, but the flesh is weak. It's the same today. People have good intentions. They may recognize the truth and those who speak it. They may even believe what's spoken. But when push comes to shove, and the heat of persecution increases, they turn and flee. They may even deny they ever believed in the truth. The disciples fled when Jesus was taken. They acted out their fear. Jesus understood. Because He knew the flesh is weak, he predicted their turning away and their flight from Him. Peter denied he'd do this. But Jesus knew better.

Why was Jesus so upset before they came for him? What did He know? Why was He exceedingly sad and overwhelmed with grief? Wasn't He the Son of God? Couldn't He save Himself? He knew the ugliness of hate and revenge. He'd seen it in the Pharisees' eyes. And He would have to submit to their horrible and agonizing abuse. Even when He knew the truth and what would happen later—how I'd raise Him up—He also knew what He must suffer first at their hands.

He would've liked a way out. He begged Me for that. But I couldn't allow it, though I also knew what I would suffer while I watched Him go through these things. Though many would never appreciate what He'd gone through for them, He chose the only way for them to return to Me. And I had to watch what the princes of evil did to Him—My only Son.

Could He have saved Himself? Could I have spared Him? Yes. But We both knew what would come afterward—a resurrection, not just of His body, but of thousands more later, because He endured such suffering at the hands of evil ones.

Then We would rejoice. When all was said and done, many could come because of what He did.

Only by knowing this were We able to go through what We did.

Day 280

Why so much hatred toward Jesus?

"Let the Christ (the Messiah), the King of Israel, come down now from the cross, that we may see [it] and trust in and rely on Him and adhere to Him! Those who were crucified with Him also reviled and reproached Him [speaking abusively, harshly, and insolently]."
—Mark 15:32

Mark 15-16

Why didn't Jesus defend Himself? Because His life was a fulfillment of the prophecies, this one from Isaiah 53:7. He'd be tormented but would not speak up for Himself. Like a lamb brought to be slaughtered, He must dumbly submit to sacrifice for the atonement of sins. It was the only way.

Why so much hatred toward Him? Why so much animosity against the Jews, even now? Anyone who represents Me, and My plan for salvation, who is part of My determination to save mankind, will be rejected. Why? Because of the god of this world. Satan, with authority now on earth because Adam relinquished this to him, will continue to inspire hatred against My people. He will always promulgate lies against anyone who stands for, or has stood for, Me until My Son's return to earth.

Was Jesus abandoned by Me? No. I was there with Him during His ultimate sacrifice. But I could not help Him. He had to do this Himself as a man. His reciting of Psalm 22 reflected David's feelings about his own life and the Messiah to come. Like the sweet psalmist, Jesus felt forsaken by, or hidden from, Me during extreme suffering. Though neither could feel My presence, faith never failed them. Parents who watch a child suffer or die will also feel as they did—that I am not present. But I always am. And I want you to know that, although I may not be able to deliver you from all suffering now, one day I will because of what My Son endured. Though I may seem hidden at times, My mysteries will be understood by those who search for their meaning. Most people present at Jesus's death did not understand why He had to die. Some were touched, like the Roman centurion, who believed in His rise from death. Joseph of Arimathea had the courage to request His body. He remembered His words.

It wasn't until after Jesus's resurrection that the disciples understood what He'd done and recalled His promises.

Day 281

Why did I choose Mary?

*"For with God nothing is ever impossible and no word from
God shall be without power or impossible of fulfillment."*
—Luke 1:37

Luke 1

Why did I wait so long before My Son was born? And why did I choose Mary to bear Him? The woman I chose to bear the Messiah had to be a descendant of David, and her husband too must have this lineage. This was to fulfill My promises to Abraham and his descendants. The one who bore the Messiah must also accept this great responsibility and be willing to do it. Do you realize what an immense undertaking this was? She had to not only be willing to accept the assignment but be strong enough to withstand the persecution of many, who questioned that her child was Mine. Many would assume her Son was illegitimate. Can you imagine the whispers, taunts, and disapproval she must endure? She had to be strong in her belief to withstand all of this. She also had to be faithful. Throughout Jesus's childhood, He needed parents who'd listen to and follow My guidance. Raising My Son was an awesome and overwhelming responsibility. I needed parents who'd heed Me and persist in following My ways. I knew Mary and Joseph would faithfully do this.

Why was it important for Mary to know that her cousin Elizabeth also bore a son? First, she'd see that I am a miracle worker. Her cousin was older and barren, yet she bore a promised child. This substantiated My role in both their lives. Second, Mary gained support from Elizabeth when others doubted her veracity. Upon hearing Mary's voice, Elizabeth uttered a prophecy that supported My words to Mary. Her child was blessed, and she was blessed because she believed. Elizabeth also told her that this child fulfilled the long-held promises to Abraham and his descendants.

My hand was in every detail of these women's lives, as it is in yours. Through them, I was able to bring others an understanding of salvation and deliverance.

With them, I was able to awaken many with a Light that dawned through the ages.

Day 282

I prepared Mary's heart

"The Holy Spirit descended upon Him in a bodily form like a dove and a voice came from heaven, saying, You are My Son, My Beloved! In You I am well pleased and find delight!"
—Luke 3:22

Luke 2-3

What did Mary and Joseph think of this Child? They'd heard that He was My Son. The angel had told them so. But they must come to understand His purpose and what He would do. They'd read the Scriptures and listened to them spoken in the temple. They knew of the prophecies predicting the Messiah's coming. But they didn't really understand what it all meant until they saw them fulfilled before their eyes. It's the same today. People read the predictions about the latter days and His second coming. But until they happen, they won't fully understand. At His first coming, I revealed things to a few—those who'd receive the information. The shepherds heard of His birth from the angels. They were told that this was the Messiah—a Savior Who'd bring peace to people with whom I was pleased. And their presence made Mary consider and ponder what her Son would do and Who He really was. Simeon was an elderly man, filled with My Spirit, who'd waited patiently for the day when he'd behold My Son. I honored My promise to him. I always do this for people who continue in faith and expectation of My assurances. He was grateful to hold the promised Messiah in his arms, and he praised Me for this great blessing. He also revealed a little more to Mary about her Son: He would make a way to salvation for all people, be a Light to the Gentiles, disclose the unknown, and bring praise and honor and glory to My people. His parents marveled to hear this. Why? Not because they didn't know the prophecies in Isaiah about the Messiah. It just hadn't hit home for them yet that this truly *was* the Messiah until they heard someone pronounce these words over their Son. "A sword will pierce through your own soul also—that the secret thoughts and purposes of many hearts may be...disclosed," Simeon told Mary. Why would he utter such heart-wrenching words as she held her baby in her arms? To prepare her. I knew what she'd endure one day—the pain of watching her Son die. I wanted her to know what this would ultimately accomplish and how His death would open doors for many to believe and stand before Me in righteousness.

As with anyone I love, I prepared her heart to face future events.

Day 283

Why some gave up everything to follow Jesus

"Jesus went back full of and under the power of the Spirit into Galilee, and the fame of Him spread through the whole region round about."
—Luke 4:14

Luke 4-5

Jesus's disciples didn't decide to follow Him because of a sudden whim. He was well known in the communities and towns around Galilee. Many had heard of Him in the synagogues. He'd developed quite a reputation. Some heard Him teach and were amazed at the authority with which he spoke. He was unlike any they'd ever heard. But it wasn't until Peter experienced His power himself that he chose to follow Him. Jesus told him where to cast his nets, which at first baffled the fisherman, who'd toiled all night and caught nothing. He wondered how this Man could possibly know more than he did about the trade. When he saw the great load of fish, then he believed in Jesus and His ability! Matthew had heard and seen Him in action. But it wasn't until Jesus asked him to join His party that he thought someone like himself, a detested tax collector, could be accepted by Him.

Jesus had seen these men before. He'd watched them at work. I showed Him who to choose by revealing their hearts. But what about Judas? Why would I have My Son select a man who'd later betray Him? Because of My mercy. Everyone has shortcomings, like Peter. And even evil-hearted people serve My purposes.

Why did these men give up everything to follow Jesus? Because the lives of people in Israel at that time centered around teaching and understanding the Scriptures. They lived and breathed their beliefs. It was part of their culture. They were familiar with prophets, and following in the footsteps of a holy man was considered to be a privilege. Whole families would shadow and support a relative who gave up everything to live a life of teaching and preaching—a "rabbi."*

Today, most consider a person who gives up everything, especially the possibility of a lucrative career, a fool. Now, anyone who follows Me with their whole heart is considered a fanatic.

But then it was different!

Day 284

Jesus could see into peoples' hearts

"The upright man out of the good treasure in his heart produces what is upright, and the evil man out of the evil storehouse brings forth that which is depraved; for out of the abundance of the heart his mouth speaks."
—Luke 6:45

Luke 6-7

Jesus perceived matters of the heart. He never judged by outward appearances or one's standing in the community. He looked inside people through the eyes of My Spirit and could see their make-up. Why do you think He loved the centurion, a Gentile, but rejected the Pharisees, who were Jews? In the centurion, He saw a heart of mercy and trust when the man sent the elders to beg Jesus to heal his servant, because he felt himself unworthy to ask. "Not even in Israel have I found such great faith as this," Jesus told His disciples. Why did He allow the woman considered to be a great sinner to weep over Him and anoint Him with oil? "She's unacceptable!" the Pharisees shouted. And when the Pharisee Simon asked Him why He would allow her to do this, Jesus revealed both their hearts in His answer. "When I came into your house, you gave Me no water for My feet, but she has wet My feet with her tears and wiped them with her hair." He revered those who loved Him with their whole heart. And He forgave their faults.

"He who is forgiven little loves little," He said.

And those who see specks in others' eyes often hold beams in their own. Out of the good treasure stored in one's heart, a person can produce good things, and out of the abundance of the heart the mouth speaks.

Jesus had compassion, because His heart was filled with good treasure from His Spirit. That is why He recognized the treasure in others' hearts. It is also why healing power exuded from Him.

He knew that when you give from the fullness in your own heart by forgiving others and releasing any resentment, you will always receive back more than you gave so that you have even more to offer later.

Day 285

How people react determines so much

"Be careful therefore how you listen. For to him who has [spiritual knowledge] will more be given; and from him who does not have [spiritual knowledge], even what he thinks and guesses and supposes that he has will be taken away."
—Luke 8:18

Luke 8-9

The parable of the seeds sown shows four responses to hearing My Word. Each rejoinder shows a different way that people react to hearing it. In the first three examples, some sort of disruption prevents the seeds from taking root: displacement, dearth, distractions, and dread. Remember how the Gerasenes responded when they heard how Jesus freed the man possessed by demons? They saw their lives affected by what was done, and they were afraid. Their main source of livelihood—pigs—was destroyed. They didn't care about the man or that he was delivered. Jesus used incidents like this to show His disciples what trust in God looked like as opposed to life dominated by fear. He taught them how to discern between His Father's truth and the lies of the religious leaders. When the disciples doubted during a storm, weren't sure how to feed the crowds, or couldn't heal people, He showed them how things could be done through faith. As they observed, their lives changed. The seed that falls along a path and is immediately trampled represents people who hear but never heed My words. The seed that falls on stony ground never takes root, like people who hear and accept My Word but don't persist long enough to see their faith mature. Their hearts become hardened, like stones, when they are troubled or perplexed by circumstances, and they lack the patience and endurance to proceed. The seed that falls among thorns represents those who hear but allow anxieties, cares, riches, and pleasures to supersede the truth. As a result, their seed never develops into a mature plant that can produce fruit. The seed falling on good soil are people who hear My Word, patiently nurture a belief in it, and endure trials, because their hearts remain steadfast in Me. They hear and they continue in their belief.

Like Peter, they may not get it right the first or the second or even the third time, but, because they persist, they grow, mature, and eventually bear much good fruit.

Day 286

Don't be afraid to live outrageously

*"He who hears and heeds you hears and heeds Me; and he who slights
and rejects you slights and rejects Me; and he who slights
and rejects Me slights and rejects Him who sent Me."*
—Luke 10:16

Luke 10-11

How people treat you is determined by how they view Me. If My Son walked the earth today, He'd be treated the same way as when He was here the first time. When people defame and insult you for your faith, they also do this to Me. But those who hear My Word and do it are blessed now and later.

My Son reveals Himself to whomever He chooses. And often He shows up in the lives of the unskilled, less educated, and lowly ones in this world—those who are considered of little value to others. Why? Because often these are the ones who hold the keys to receiving an understanding of Me. They are humble and undaunted by the world's expectations. Many want to burden you with demands that you must comply with to be acceptable to them. These are never My burdens. My way is freeing. Remember the priest and the Levite, who were so encumbered by religious rules that they couldn't respond to a personal crisis? It was the Samaritan, despised by the Jews, who saw beyond the expectations to be able to help a person in need. Remember, your eye is the lamp to your soul. How you regard life is determined by whether you see things through the Light-filled eyes of My Spirit or through the darkened eyes of the world. The illumination of your soul is determined by how much Light you let in through your spirit. If you choose to view life through the world's perspective and accept its propaganda as truth, then you will be filled with hopelessness and desperation. Persist beyond the world's demands and receive My wonder. Keep seeking answers. I'll always respond to your requests. Don't let fear keep you from receiving what I have for you. And don't be afraid to be outrageous. Your trust in Me sets you free. My Son was not afraid to speak out for Me. And the religious leaders hated Him for this. But this did not prevent Him from bending their rules and healing on the Sabbath. Be like Him!

Don't be afraid to act on your beliefs or to respond to others in need, even if it means going against someone else's expectations.

Day 287

How to seek My kingdom

"For where your treasure is, there will your heart be also."
—Luke 12:34

Luke 12-13

Jesus talked a lot about seeking My kingdom first, above all else. He explained how you can do this, and he discussed how important it is to accumulate "treasure in heaven." What did He mean by this? Is it wrong to have things or to strive for a better life? Not if you do these with the right heart.

Having treasure in heaven involves the heart. It means making sure that your mind is focused more on Me than on yourself and others. "Loins girded" means being ready to do what I prompt you to do[1] by way of My Spirit in you. "Lamps burning" is simply making sure you are filled to overflowing with My oil—a symbol of My Spirit that guides you continuously.[2] Both involve listening to the spirit and heeding its promptings. Thinking My thoughts doesn't just increase your spiritual ability. It also helps your mind and body so you can work most effectively in this world, being mentally and physically able to help and encourage others. Live as though you expect My Son to return for you any minute. Remain alert to what is around you and whether things are from Me or the adversary. By My Spirit you can discern between good and evil and make right choices.

Be willing to use the abilities and talents I've given you for your own good and the benefit of others. Then you will receive rewards in the new kingdom.

Stand up for Me, even when others reject you for your stance. Ask forgiveness for your misdeeds, and amend your ways if they are wrong. Be just in dealing with others and willing to forgive their mistakes.

Who can enter My kingdom? Those in whom My seed was planted. Like a mustard seed, Mine may seem small and inadequate, yet it can produce mighty results. What I sow in you can grow into a mighty arbor that offers shelter to you and others from the storms of life.

It is a tree that can provide peace and protection to many.

Day 288

Have you lost your savor?

"Salt is good [an excellent thing], but if salt has lost its strength and has become saltless (insipid, flat), how shall its saltness be restored?"
—*Luke 14:34*

Luke 14-16

What does it mean to be salty? And how do you lose your saltiness? What did Jesus mean when He warned against losing your savor? Jesus often addressed the Pharisees. Why was it important to point out their ways? These religious leaders were teachers who were instructed in all matters of the Law of Moses. Many peoples' lives revolved around their teachings, and they placed them in highest regard because of this. To them, they were guides providing answers to questions about the best ways to follow the Judaic Law. Their job included showing people how to please Me so that they could enter My kingdom later.

But Jesus saw how they misled people. Instead of drawing them closer to Me, they drew them farther away from My heart into laborious and time-consuming traditions. My laws were meant to prepare people to live sound and healthy lives. Yet the Pharisees criticized Jesus for healing the sick on the Sabbath. They manipulated the meaning of the Law. Jesus saw how honor and recognition and power over people were more important to them than serving Me. He watched how they coveted the best seats at banquets and complained about how He sat with sinners—those they considered "unclean." They sought the company of the wealthy, because they coveted money. They had lost their saltiness or their love for Me. They'd replaced this with a desire for comfort, honor, praise, control, and material things. They'd become unworthy.

It was of them that Jesus spoke the parable of the prodigal son. They were like the older son, who bitterly complained when the forgiving father celebrated his brother's return home. Jesus wanted them to see that I rejoice when those who've strayed from Me come back to the fold. Through the parable about Lazarus, He wanted them to understand their dismal future. They needed to see how they'd be tormented later by neglecting those who suffer now, and how they were far too concerned about their status in this life. They had misplaced their purpose.

They had lost their savor.

Day 289

How can you activate faith?

"Then one of them, upon seeing that he was cured, turned back, recognizing and thanking and praising God with a loud voice."
—Luke 17:15

Luke 17-18

How can you activate your faith? What can cause a tiny mustard seed to grow and become mighty enough to move a mountain? The disciples wanted to know, because their faith never seemed like it was enough.

Jesus explained what was missing in the disciples' faith through His parables and the examples of the people they met along the way. Remember the 10 lepers, who asked Him for healing? When they did what Jesus asked them to do and went to the priests, they received what they requested. But only one saw the result of his obedience and returned to thank Him for what He'd done. And he got more than physical healing that day. He was made completely whole in his body and soul. This one action revealed the missing piece that the disciples were seeking—the thing that activated faith and made it supernatural. It's still the puzzle piece that most people miss today. What is it?

Praise.

Jesus explained that the kingdom of God was a matter of the heart. Those who received it fully were those who were persistent in prayer and praise. It wasn't the haughty and self-righteous, or the ones who proclaimed their own goodness, who would enter. It was those humble enough to recognize their own faults and ask for forgiveness. It was the ones who thanked Him and Me for what We had done and recognized Our greatness and ability. The blind man who shouted at Jesus as He walked by was a good example of what Jesus wanted them to see. He acknowledged the man's persistence, and the man was healed.

It's all about persistent prayer, or asking Me, and praise, or thanking Me, for what you've received.

These are the keys to activate supernatural faith, and they still hold true today.

Day 290

I love eager people

*"So he ran on ahead and climbed up in a sycamore tree in
order to see Him, for He was about to pass that way."*
—Luke 19:4

Luke 19-20

*Don't you love stories of underdogs, who rise above their situations, overcome their lacks,
surmount great obstacles, and end up winning the prize?* Jesus is like you in this. He especially
appreciates those who persist in trusting, even when others mock and belittle them for their
faith. He loves people bold enough to proclaim their devotion, especially when others try
to dissuade them and disapprove of them and Me. These "little ones" in others' eyes will
receive much more later.

For this reason, people love the story of Zacchaeus. Even today, people are drawn to this
little man's persistence and complete lack of concern about what others thought of him. He
was just too eager to see Jesus! He was small in stature, but he was mighty in courage and
perseverance. Though others looked down on him, literally and figuratively, and despised
him for his occupation, he "rose above it all" and did not succumb to their negativity.

And he was willing to amend his ways for this One he loved. He recognized his own faults
and declared his aim to restore four times as much to those he'd slighted. Jesus acknowledged
his desire to please Him and Me and blessed, not only him, but his entire household, who
also received Him. He even promised them salvation. What did this mean? They would be
"made whole" in body and soul, *and* they would be received into the kingdom later.

When you take a stand, or climb a tree, like Zacchaeus, just to be closer to Me, I will always
stand beside you. I will give you the right words to say, the best answers to tricky questions,
and show you the most appropriate choices. Especially when you address the naysayers, who
try to catch you in your words or actions to destroy your eager trust in Me. I did this for
Zacchaeus.

I will do this for you.

Day 291

What of wars and fighting?

"Keep awake then and watch at all times [be discreet, attentive, and ready],
praying that you may have the full strength and ability and be accounted
worthy to escape all these things [taken together] that will take
place, and to stand in the presence of the Son of Man."
—Luke 21:36

Luke 21-22

You will hear of wars, chaos, and confusion, but don't panic or become alarmed. These things will come long before the end. When earthquakes, famines, and infectious diseases devastate, when family and friends betray you, and even the heavens shake down in protest, remember that I am by your side. I will protect you as you trust in Me. By your steadfast endurance, you will win the true life. Know that, when Jerusalem is surrounded by armies, the desolation is near. When the city is trodden down by unbelievers, then the end times are being fulfilled. These are the days when things predicted will come to pass, including signs in the sun, moon, and stars and great anguish among the nations. Resources will diminish, and the seas will roar, and people will swoon with fear and dread. After this, My Son will return to earth in a cloud with power, majesty, and splendor.

Lift your eyes to Me now, because you will be redeemed if you believe in Him Who was sent to atone for you. Be on guard, lest your heart be overburdened by the stress of worldly worries, cares, and the busyness of life. Prepare now for the day when He will come for you. Always watch and pray for strength so you can stand in the presence of the glorified Son.

To prepare them as the future leaders, My Son instructed His disciples to be servants. They were not to be lords, deified and worshipped. They were to serve and support each other and those I called. And they would lack nothing. He also encouraged them to defend themselves—to fight for their lives if necessary. Not to murder indefensibly, but to "carry a sword." Even now, I stand with you when your life is threatened by those who would steal, kill, or destroy My followers. Know that I will always fight for you.

Remember, I am with you even when others hate and despise you.

Day 292

Only some eyes can see

"Now the centurion, having seen what had taken place, recognized God and thanked and praised Him, and said, Indeed, without question, this Man was upright (just and innocent)!"
—Luke 23:47

Luke 23-24

Why did only a few people see the risen Christ? And why did so many not understand what He had accomplished or why? Even with all the Old Testament prophecies and all the time spent with Him, His disciples didn't have a clue why He had come, suffered, or died! At the time of His trial and crucifixion, only a few people recognized Him for Who He was. Pontius Pilate, a Gentile, realized he was making a big mistake when he turned Jesus over to be crucified. He could see something in this man, though he wasn't sure what it was, while the religious leaders shouted louder to have him killed. One of the malefactors crucified with Him understood and asked Him to remember him when He came into His power. Only a few of the women who followed Him came to cry at His feet as He hung on the cross. They still didn't get why He must suffer this way, but they acknowledged Him as My Son. Joseph of Arimathea was alone among the religious leaders in understanding why Jesus must die and rise again, because he'd listened to Jesus as He tried to explain it all to the disciples.

When the women came to the tomb to mourn their loss, they realized His body was gone. They saw the angels, and they ran to tell the disciples. After hearing their witness, the disciples still doubted what Jesus had told them. Then they saw Him with their own eyes. When two followers walked alongside Him on the road to Emmaus, it wasn't until Jesus revealed Himself to them that their eyes were opened.

Even today, most people do not have eyes to see Me or My Son. When miracles happen right in front of them, they still refuse to acknowledge what I've done. Only some fully understand Who My Son is or why He died the way He did.

But, when He returns to earth to redeem and set many free, all will finally comprehend what He did and why He did it.

Day 293

How did Jesus choose His disciples?

*"To as many as did receive and welcome Him, He gave the authority
(power, privilege, right) to become the children of God, that is, to
those who believe in (adhere to, trust in, and rely on) His name."*
—John 1:12

John 1-2

How each disciple came to follow Jesus was different in each case. When John the Baptist acknowledged Jesus as the Son of God, two men began to pursue Him. When Jesus saw them following, He didn't immediately accept them as His disciples. His reaction was, "What are you looking for?" Did they really know what they were getting themselves into? He wondered. He wanted only those who'd persist in following Him. And Andrew did. He even went to get his brother, Simon, saying, "We have found the Messiah!" The next day, in Galilee, Jesus found Philip and told him to "Join Me." And Philip did. Then Philip found Nathanael and said, "We have found the One...the prophets wrote about!" Jesus told Nathanael things about himself no one else would know. And he was persuaded. Each calling was different. It's the same today. How you come to know Him is unique to you. Ultimately, Jesus chose each disciple at My direction. He was surrounded by family and friends early on in His ministry. Many of the disciples Jesus called were people He'd known. This was a testimony to the life He lived, even as a young man. He always understood His purpose. And many had heard Mary's stories—about the shepherds at the manger, the prophecies of Simeon and Anna at the temple, and how Jesus taught the elders when He was only 12 years old. They'd watched Him grow up. And He didn't want to start His ministry with a miracle. But, at Cana, He wanted to honor His mother's request. Most of His time would be spent teaching—explaining My heart to His followers. If He mostly performed miracles, many would follow, not to hear His words but to see His wonders. He didn't want followers as thrill-seekers. When He confronted the money changers with a whip in the temple, this may have discouraged some from following Him. Life with Him grew tougher as the religious leaders spoke evil of Him and conspired to kill Him. They expelled from the temple any who acknowledged a belief in Jesus. As a result of the pressure, fewer family members and friends continued to follow Him.

But the original 12 held on, at least for a while.

Day 294

Why your words make some people angry

"Whoever takes a drink of the water that I will give him shall never, no never, be thirsty any more. But the water that I will give him shall become a spring of water welling up (flowing, bubbling) [continually] within him unto (into, for) eternal life."
—John 4:14

John 3-4

Why do people get angry when you share the truth? Why do they move away when they see you coming? Isn't it because they dwell in darkness and don't want their lives exposed? Those who practice truth love My Light, because they aren't afraid that their works will be revealed. I loved the world—the people I made—so much that I gave My Son to and for it so that whoever believes in Him can receive My Spirit, be born again, and live forever. Because I love My Son, I entrusted everything into His hand, and He reigns with Me now. You will too one day if you trust in what He did. Those who don't believe will never experience real life—now or later.

Why did Jesus speak so much about water? Why did He use an analogy about living water with the woman at the well? Because water meant life to the people of Israel. It was, and still is, a land where the supply of food depended on its availability. He knew she would understand the preciousness of what He offered if He compared it to this commodity. Through His description, she knew He was the Messiah, and she realized how precious He was—even more than water. She even left her water jar at the well to go and tell others—something women would never do. Jesus also made a comparison to bread, because He knew how important it was for sustenance and survival. "I have food to eat of which you know nothing," He said. Besides using analogies to draw people to Him, Jesus also went to forbidden places to find followers. Though the Judeans rejected Samaria because of its past history, Jesus knew that some Samaritans would trust Him more than those in His own homeland. Often, He found complete strangers more willing to come to where He was than those with ample opportunity to hear. It's the same way today.

Strangers may be more inclined to listen than those familiar with you, because they desire the Light you offer.

Day 295

Do you want to be made whole?

"Jesus replied, I am the Bread of Life. He who comes to Me will never be hungry, and he who believes in and cleaves to and trusts in and relies on Me will never thirst any more (at any time)."
—John 6:35

John 5-6

The first thing Jesus said to the man who lay by the pool for 38 years was, "Do you want to become well?" Jesus asked this question because He knew that some people don't want to be made whole. Some want to remain in their ill state to gain sympathy or attention, or they fear change. They want to stay a victim of their circumstances. It becomes their identity. The man had ample opportunity to move to the pool if he wanted healing badly enough. So, Jesus asked him what it was he wanted. Apparently, he did want healing, because he received it willingly from Jesus. Do you want to be rid of your life-stagnating problems—whatever weighs you down? You can receive healing and wholeness if you want them.

When some sought to persecute and kill Jesus, because He healed on a holy day, He said, "My Father never ceases working and I must be at My work." In other words, "My Father never takes a break and neither do I!" Some hated Him, because He spoke of Me as His Father. This was considered a sacrilege by those who did not know or understand Me or what I was doing through My Son. Jesus lived to do My will and accomplish My purpose, to be My voice to those who'd never heard or seen Me. His role was not to please Himself or receive earthly glory. He came to seek My praise and to glorify Me. He explained that My role is not to judge. He was assigned this role by Me for Judgment Day. But now, He gives life to those who believe in Him, and, by their belief, they can escape judgment. Those who hear His voice can be made whole now and receive eternal life later. Why did He withdraw from crowds who sought to make Him a king? Because He knew that this was not His purpose. He came to magnify Me so that, one day, many could reign with Us. His message was this: "Don't spend your life worrying about what you will eat or how you will live. Spend time with Me. Develop trust in Me. Then you can see My power in your life. I am the true Bread of Life. Only through Me can you be fulfilled and made whole.

"Why not be nourished by Me now and live!"

Day 296

What makes a leader controversial?

"Be honest in your judgment and do not decide at a glance (superficially and by appearances); but judge fairly and righteously."
—*John 7:24*

John 7-8

It has always been the same. People decide others' intent by judging their words or actions. They argue against those with authority, thinking they know better about whether they and others are being misled. It was so with Jesus. Even His brothers questioned Him. When leaders seek My glory and honor and teach with My authority, there is no falsehood or deception in them. When disputes arise about the veracity of a true leader, like Jesus, it's because people don't seek the truth. Instead of looking into an accusation to discern its accuracy, they accept it blindly, because this makes them feel like they're "in the know." People of low degree and position do it to feel more important. People of high degree and position incite falsehoods to belittle those they want to demean. They may talk down to those who are "less" in society—"the rabble"—to gain greater control.

Sometimes there is one among "the elite" like Nicodemus. He refused to follow the rules, thought for himself, and endeavored to spare the innocent. "Does our law convict a man without giving him a hearing and finding out what he's done?" Nicodemus asked the Pharisees, who plotted against Jesus. Their answer? "Do you support this faker, who is not from the right background like us?" The Pharisees questioned Jesus to catch Him in His words. How did Jesus respond when they brought out a woman caught in adultery and thrust her in front of Him? He thought of His ancestors: Tamar who slept with her father-in-law while posing as a harlot, Rahab who was a harlot yet helped the Israelites, Bathsheba who slept with David while married to Uriah, and His own mother Mary who was thought to have conceived Him illegitimately. How could He convict this woman, when He saw how I forgave sinners and included them in His own ancestry? He knew My heart. Only with Me can one judge fairly. The Pharisees assessed by the flesh. He discerned by the heart. If you know Him, you know Me. If you abide in Him, you are My disciple.

Those who belong to Me hear His words, understand the truth, and minister with justice and mercy.

Day 297

How much Light is in your life?

"The thief comes only in order to steal and kill and destroy. I came that they may have and enjoy life, and have it in abundance (to the full, till it overflows)."
—John 10:10

John 9-10

Jesus provides the Light. It's His Light that keeps darkness at bay. How much you can live, enjoy your life, truly see, and help others, depends on the amount of His Light you allow into your life. People fall short and become needy when they lack Light spiritually, mentally, or physically. The Pharisees refused to allow His Light to penetrate their thinking. They blocked it out with rules that trapped and imprisoned people. They did not recognize Who Jesus was, because little Light pierced their thinking. Fear blocks the entry of Light. It prevents people from living or receiving My blessings. The parents of the man born blind lived in fear of the repercussions if they believed and spoke the truth. They could not receive what I wanted to give them, because they feared the Pharisees.

The man born blind acknowledged My Son and how He'd healed him. He came to know Jesus and received enough of His Light to be able to understand that He couldn't perform miracles if He weren't sent by Me. He saw Who He was and was not afraid to admit it.

Jesus came to separate. He came to make the sightless able to see, and those who "see," or think they know it all, to become blind, because they choose to live in darkness. He is the Door. If you choose to enter through Him, you can enjoy life fully, and He will recognize you and you Him, because your eyes are enlightened.

He came to gather His flock. Those who are blind and can't see Who He is deny Him, despite His miracles. They are not in His flock. His sheep hear His voice. They listen, and no one can snatch them from His hand or Mine. These are those who adhere to Him.

The thief comes to steal, kill, and destroy through darkness.

Jesus came to give Light and life abundantly.

Day 298

He cried

"Jesus wept."
—*John 11:35*

John 11-12

He cried when He saw their grief. His heart hurt to see the people He loved so distressed by death. He never wanted them to experience such painful sorrow and suffering. He wanted them to live forever, to be by His side, My side. This had always been His intent and Mine. He tried to explain it to them: "Didn't I tell you, even promise you, that if you trusted Me, you would see God's glory?" Then He shouted, "Hear us, Lord!" Out His friend came, still wrapped in burial cloths. Through their shock, some saw and believed. And they acknowledged that this was My Son. But some did not. Even after seeing Lazarus raised from death, some were intimidated by the religious leaders and what they would do to them if they admitted a belief in Him. The leaders themselves were afraid and had to react. Otherwise, what would happen if too many people began to follow Him? There could be an insurrection. "We must put a stop to this," they whispered as they conspired against Him. "He must die so our nation can stay united under us and live!" But little did they know. Their evil purpose was to control and maintain power, but My purpose was greater. It always is. Often people don't see until years later why something occurred and what it meant.

Judas criticized Jesus for allowing Mary to pour precious perfume over Him. "This ointment should have been sold and the money given to the poor!" he cried with disdain. He failed to recognize Mary's heart or her intent. Those who overly condemn others often conceal their own hidden darkness.

Jesus didn't want to die. Do you? But He knew He must. Only then could many be raised up, like Lazarus. Still, He foresaw the suffering He'd endure, and He shuddered blood. So, He prayed. He begged. He sweated. He bled some more. Because He was human. But He also saw the Pharisees, who burdened the people He loved by controlling them with outlandish rules. And this made Him angry.

He had to suffer death to show the people, Our people, My love and what I really wanted for them.

Day 299

Because He loved you

"By this shall all know that you are My disciples, if you love one another."
—John 13:35

John 13-14

Why did Jesus wash the disciples' feet? This was such a demeaning act! Was it just to show them how to be servants? No. There was much more to it. He wanted to show His great love for them and how I'm willing to go above and beyond for those who come to Me. When He said, "You don't understand now what I do, but you will later," He knew they wouldn't comprehend until they watched Him give His life for them.

Even when He knew Judas would betray Him, He entrusted him with a position of responsibility. He wanted people to see His willingness to receive them, even when they were imperfect, lacking, and did the unthinkable. His message was this: "I give you a new commandment to replace all the others, and it is this—love one another." Because He loved us, we can also love. And, by this love, others can know we are His.

Even when hate-filled people betray your trust, refuse your love, and reject you, you can still love them, because He did. This was His unique and powerful message.

But, really, how can you love people who spit in your face, treat you cruelly, and abuse your sense of self? Jesus had the answer. If you accept what He did for you, you have a Helper. This Comforter lives in you to guide and teach you. With this Holy Spirit, you can know My will in all situations. And this gift gives you the ability to do the same works He did, even when they seem impossible. And loving the unlovable is included in this.

The world will never understand His love or His Spirit of truth, but those with it can love fully, because they can have complete freedom from fear.

Even when you are intimidated and faced with hate, you can remain fearless and able to love, because this gift in you is mightier than anything the world can offer.

Day 300

Take comfort in this

"I have told you these things, so that in Me you may have [perfect] peace and confidence. In the world you have tribulation and trials and distress and frustration; but be of good cheer [take courage; be confident, certain, undaunted]! For I have overcome the world. [I have deprived it of power to harm you and have conquered it for you.]"
—John 16:33

John 15-16

Apart from My Son, you can do nothing of lasting value. The works that you do without Him will be burned up one day—dissolved! If you make Him a part of your life, He'll work in and through you to perform miracles. And your fruit will honor Me and bring Me joy. Live in His love. Then your joy will overflow. Love as He loves you. He laid down His life for you. He considers you to be His closest friend. He chose and appointed you to bear lasting fruit so that whatever you ask of Me in His name can be given to you.

The world will always hate you. This is because you belong to Him, and He belongs to Me. Like Him, you'll be persecuted for your belief. The world will never understand or want to know the One Who sent Him and you. Whoever hates you hates Him, and whoever hates Him hates Me. And they have seen Our works, so they have no excuse. But the Comforter will help you tell His story—My story. He'll give you what you need to live for Me. When you're rejected for your faith, this Holy Spirit Helper will strengthen you. He'll be a Witness of Who I am. With His aid, you can teach others about sin, righteousness, and judgment. He'll guide you to an understanding of Me and what I've planned for the future. His voice will be My voice coming through you. Your sorrow will be turned into joy when you ask and receive, so keep on asking. You'll see how I can make your joy full and complete.

The world and its rulers bring hardship, suffering, defeat, and frustration. But, through My Son, I overcame the world. I deprived it of any power to harm you. I conquered it. Remember that My Comforter resides in you to be your guide and to bring you peace.

Take comfort in this.

Day 301

What is truth?

"Pilate said to Him, Then You are a King? Jesus answered, You say it! [You speak correctly!] For I am a King....This is why I was born, and for this I have come into the world, to bear witness to the Truth. Everyone who is of the Truth [who is a friend of the Truth, who belongs to the Truth] hears and listens to My voice."
—John 18:37

John 17-18

What is truth? Pilate asked. He didn't recognize it in Jesus, because he didn't understand His purpose or Mine. Most political leaders don't, because they seek something else. They represent the world and its purposes: survival of the fittest, power over people, and a grasp of money and control. And these are not what Jesus came to bring. His kingdom is not of this world order, but of one to come. This is the truth of which He spoke. Before Jesus crossed the Kidron Valley to the garden, he prayed a long prayer. He lifted His eyes to Me. This prayer was not for the world. It was for those I gave Him, those who belong to Me. It was for these that He prayed, not for those who seek the world's ways. There will always be a difference between those who serve the world and its dark purposes and those who serve Me and walk in My Light. You will know them by their fruit.

I gave My Son power and authority over people so He could grant eternal life and access to the next kingdom to those I give Him. Who are they? Those who recognize Him and know that He came from Me. All things are His now, because He glorified Me by what He did. He is no more physically in the world, but you are. And you must endure its betrayals as He did. If you continue to believe in what My Son accomplished, you are one with Us. He came to Me so that His joy and Mine might be full, and Our delight is to see fullness of joy in your life. The world hates you, because you're Mine. Its ruler blinds the minds of those whose worship embraces the world. And he sets them on a course to fulfill his own purposes: to be lifted up above Me. But, through My Son, you can overcome the world, and be perfected by the truth. What is the truth?

That you can become one with Us and be separated out from this world.

Day 302

Do you worship Me in secret?

*"On that same first day of the week...though the disciples were behind closed doors
for fear of the Jews, Jesus came and stood among them and said, Peace to you!"*
—John 20:19

John 19-21

"Where are you from?" Pilate asked Jesus. He did not answer. When Pilate told Him he
could release Him, Jesus responded that any power he had was given to Him from above.
Pilate was alarmed. Who was this man? But the Jews shrieked louder, "You are no friend
of Caesar if you don't crucify Him!" And Pilate was afraid. They'd appealed to his political
fears—those of not being right and of losing his power. Who do you fear most? The world's
leaders or the Leader of the universe? Pilate sat down. He relinquished his responsibility. He
surrendered to the shouting and demanding rabble. He wrote a title to hang above Jesus's
head on the cross: "Jesus the Nazarene, the King of the Jews." He realized that he just didn't
understand the repercussions. Most don't. The women and one follower, John, stood by
Him as He died. Where were the other disciples? Fear plays tricks on people. The thing they
are most afraid of is often the very thing they need to do. Two men came secretly to bury
Him. Joseph and Nicodemus loved Him, but they were afraid of the Jewish leaders. Do you
worship Me in secret? Are you afraid of others' reactions to you? Will you assert Me openly
and side with My Son during severe persecution? If others surround you accusingly, will
you admit to knowing Him? If He speaks to you as a friend, will you acknowledge Him?
The disciples hid behind closed doors, because they were afraid. What did Jesus say when
He stood among them? "Have peace! Rest in My Father who sent Me and now sends you!"
They'd be fearless once they received My gift, Holy Spirit. Why? Because it gave them needed
strength, insight, and courage. Like Peter, you might be fishing, doing something other than
what I called you to do. But, without Me, you'll work hard but never catch what you seek. I
know where the fish are. I can lead you to them. Just get out of the boat. Set aside your fears
and follow Me! Come and sit with Me and be warmed by My fire. Eat and be satisfied.

Follow Me.

Day 303

You are not abandoned here

*"You have made known to me the ways of life; You will enrapture
me [diffusing my soul with joy] with and in Your presence."*
—Acts 2:28

Acts 1-2

My promise was that one day I'd restore and establish My kingdom on earth. That promise
has not yet been fulfilled, and the Jews still look forward to its realization. One day, My Son
will return to head this kingdom. Just as a cloud received Him up to heaven, He'll return
in a cloud. But another promise has already been fulfilled since His first coming. And by
acknowledging the fulfillment of this pledge, you can reign with Him when He does come
again. That assurance, made long ago by Jesus, was that He'd send a Comforter after He died
and rose again. This Comforter, My Holy Spirit, was made available on the day of Pentecost.
And you can receive it, just as the disciples did, if you believe that Jesus is your Lord and that
He rose from death (Romans 10: 9,10). Like the disciples, you can also be a witness to the
ends of the earth. Do you see what a few people accomplished after receiving My Holy Spirit
in the book of Acts? You can also accomplish great things if you will receive this Helper.

In the last days, I promised to pour out even more of My Spirit. Many will prophesy, see
visions, and dream dreams. People will see wonders in the sky and signs on earth—blood,
fire, and smoke. The sun will be darkened, and the moon will turn into blood before My
Son returns to earth with the saints. Now, whoever calls on His name can be saved from the
disruption and devastation to come.

He was killed by lawless and wicked men. But He was raised and freed from death. Now,
He sits at My right hand. Through Him, your heart can rejoice, and you can dwell in hope.
For you're not abandoned here. I diffuse your soul with joy in My presence. Now you can
benefit by receiving from Me the promised blessing of My Spirit in you. Acknowledge My
Son as Lord in your life. Accept My will for you. Be released from your past sins—the times
you "missed the mark," by receiving My forgiveness and My amazing gift of Holy Spirit.

Then watch as My signs and wonders are performed through your life and others.

Day 304

Heed Me instead of people

"Then Peter and the apostles replied, We must obey God rather than men."
—Acts 5:29

Acts 3-5

What was the message? What did Peter and John want others to know? People saw the lame man at the gate walking, leaping, and praising Me. Was it the apostles' own power that healed him? No. "It's simple," they said. "Our ability to heal comes from faith in the One who rose from death and gave us this power!" How can you see these results in your own life? "You must turn from your old ways—apart from God—and come to the One who loves you so much He gave His Son for you. Then you can be revived, made new, even healed, like this man!"

The political and religious leaders hated this message. It threatened their ability to control people. They plotted against the apostles, because they feared this movement might strip away their power. But they couldn't suppress the apostles' remarkable works and the resulting awe of people. This made them nervous and angry. They decided to use their influence to stop the activity. But Peter announced, after his arrest: "We believe in the Stone you rejected.... Only through belief in His name can anyone be saved." In other words, we get our power from Jesus, not you! This cut them to the core. It flew in the face of their ideologies and the rules they used to influence others. It could uproot and expose their deception. They despised this message and those who delivered it. They wanted to squash it and destroy those who spread it. But, one leader admitted, "If it is of God, we cannot contain it." Those who followed the apostles thrived, despite the persecution. They lived and prayed together. But communal living can only work if everyone adheres to honesty and equal sharing. When members manipulate the system, by taking advantage of it, the concept is corrupted and falls apart. Peter understood this.

If you're imprisoned or persecuted for your godly stance, remember how the apostles were delivered from imprisonment. They boldly announced that they "must obey God rather than men." They knew that I would back them up.

When you stand boldly for Me, I will always stand up for you.

Day 305

The adversary's primary tools

"So they [secretly] instigated and instructed men to say, We have heard this man speak, using slanderous and abusive and blasphemous language against Moses and God."
—Acts 6:11

Acts 6-7

Slander and lies are the most useful tools of the adversary. He uses them to discredit and shut down those he can't overwhelm through adversity. Those who work for him use these devices to suppress and undermine those who speak the truth. They accuse those they oppose of the very things they themselves do. Their shams and accusations are always birthed in secret, behind closed doors. But when charges are brought against people who represent Me, the grace and peace in their lives can't be denied. The Jewish leaders saw these attributes in Stephen as he reminded them of their history and of another adversarial tactic used against those who stand for Me: offense. Moses was so deeply offended by a fellow Jew, who shot accusations at him when he tried to intervene in a fight, that he was diverted from his mission for many years. But, like with Jonah, who ran away from Me, I always remind people of their purpose. I will do this for you too.

Stephen reminded the Jewish leaders how Moses was pushed away by the very people I sent him to deliver. And, in the same way many rejected Moses's message, they also spurned Another One I sent. Stephen's words infuriated these leaders, because they were directed at them, and they sought to kill this truth-bearer, just as they'd annihilated other messengers. Even today, those established in their thinking, whose belief systems are the gods they sacrifice themselves to please, resist Me and those I send to save them from themselves. It's easier for people to turn their backs on reports that disrupt their thinking or unearth a tendency to believe a lie or reveal a faulty ideology. For some, it's easier to get by without making waves. But why would you want to live such a mediocre life? What about your purpose, your mission? What about the people who could benefit from a hopeful message? Turn to Me. Heed the words of the One I sent to save you.

Receive My Holy Spirit to overflowing, like Stephen, and have the kind of rest and peace that no amount of adversity can ever take away from you.

Day 306

When light shines the brightest

*"Saul said, Who are You, Lord? And He said, I am Jesus, Whom you are persecuting.
It is dangerous and it will turn out badly for you to keep kicking
against the goad [to offer vain and perilous resistance]."*
—Acts 9:5

Acts 8-9

When does light shine the brightest? Isn't it when there's the greatest amount of darkness? As persecution ramped up against the church in Jerusalem, many Christ-followers were scattered abroad. As they went from place to place, their testimony was received by many, especially when people saw the power behind their teaching. People were amazed to see what could be done when the spirit overflowed. They watched others speaking with new tongues, prophesying, discerning spirits, healing the sick, even raising some from death! They couldn't deny the power. The apostles quickly realized that when people received their message, and were baptized in water, they didn't automatically receive the spirit to overflowing. Water baptism was symbolic of the washing away of sin, resultant forgiveness, and newness of life (I Peter 3:21). But the apostles realized that this physical act did not guarantee that a person would receive the fullness of the spirit. When new converts failed to speak in tongues or prophesy or discern spirits, as they had, seasoned apostles came to make sure this power and ability were received and manifested.

And they continued their work with and for Me, despite the rising persecution against them. Today, when you are persecuted for your beliefs by some who are "hell-bent" on ridding the world of people like you, because they don't believe as you do, remember the Apostle Paul and how he came to believe in spite of his past. I can reach into anyone's heart and disrupt a fervent determination against you and Me. I can reveal Myself and point them in the right direction, often in ways you can't even imagine!

Never give up on those who work against you and Me.

They might be the very ones I choose to work for Me later.

Day 307

Are all religions acceptable to Me?

"To Him all the prophets testify (bear witness) that everyone who believes in Him [who adheres to, trusts in, and relies on Him, giving himself up to Him] receives forgiveness of sins through His name."
—Acts 10:43

Acts 10-11

If all religions and beliefs are valid and acceptable, then why did Cornelius need to hear Peter's message about My Son? Why did I expend so much effort by having one of My angels appear to this devout man to show him that there was a better way to worship Me? And why did I need to give Peter the vision to prepare him for a meeting with Cornelius and his household? Wouldn't it have been fine for Me to leave Cornelius alone and continue to accept his prayers and alms? After all, he was a good man. When people tell you that every religion is as good as the next, that any belief in Me is acceptable, and that any way of praying brings access to Me, please refer them to this account of Cornelius. Do you see why a belief in My Son brings access to Me? Through what He alone did, you can receive forgiveness for your sins—your actions against Me—and you are no longer separated from Me! By making Jesus your Lord, you receive My Holy Spirit, and you have a direct line to Me. We can communicate!

I did not send My Son only for the benefit of the Jews. Though He came first to them to fulfill My promises to Abraham and David, My intention was always that His life would bring access to all who believed. Many Jewish Christians were appalled when they heard of Cornelius's conversion. They denied this possibility and rebuffed Peter for receiving a Gentile. Why? Because they thought Jesus came only for their benefit. It took convincing by Peter, and others who'd experienced and seen Gentile conversions, before some could accept this new revelation. Today, when I reveal something contrary to what you were taught, be prepared to face resistance from those who are set in their own beliefs. Rely on My Spirit for ways to answer them. They may not accept your message, but you can still stand your ground. Rely on Me to bring them around. Never be discouraged by others' unbelief or resistance. I am always working to will and to do of My good pleasure.

This includes wonderful blessings in your life.

Day 308

Your choices can bring life or death

"For the Lord has charged us, saying, I have set you to be a light for the Gentiles that you may bring (eternal) salvation to the uttermost parts of the earth."
—Acts 13:47

Acts 12-13

People always have choices. They can either stand with Me or against Me. There is no middle ground. In every word and action, there is power. That power can either promote Me and My purposes, or it can obscure and diminish them. Leaders are held to a higher standard, because they can guide or mislead so many—either to truth or to dishonesty. Corrupt leaders, like Herod, often oppose Me and try to set themselves up as gods. They cherish hostility, which they can use to further their ambitions. Counselors, like Elymas, who desire power "through the back door," try to influence leaders through unscrupulous methods. They oppose the upright and good, and they will always eventually be cut down and removed. Paul used My power to demonstrate that I could make deceiving ones blind and seeking ones see. He understood this, because he himself had experienced it. The disciples' message was always the same: All who acknowledge Jesus as their Savior and devote themselves to Him are given right standing with Me. What does this mean? It means that they can receive and release inner strength through the gift of Holy Spirit. It means they have an awareness of another dimension—a spiritual one. It also means that they have a supernatural ability to help others.

You may ask why some followers die young, while others live longer. The kind of life you live on earth is determined by your desires, beliefs, expectations, and submission to My will, or by others who have authority over you if you can't make your own choices. Either way, when a person believes in Jesus, they have eternal life beyond this one. People may or may not accept My help to overcome obstacles. It often depends on their determination. Some want life to end sooner. They may want to be free from burdens, like sickness, pain, worry, or fear. Some refuse My help and choose paths that lead to death, while others choose life. The disciples, when persecuted and imprisoned, were filled with joy despite it all.

This was because they leaned on the power of the Holy Spirit in them, and they depended on Me.

Day 309

Peter understood grace

"But we believe that we are saved through the grace (undeserved favor and mercy) of the Lord Jesus, just as they [are]."
—Acts 15:11

Acts 14-15

Even in the early church, there was dissension. That's because every person has his or her own views. Some of the Jewish Christians believed it was still important for believers to follow parts of the Law of Moses, like circumcision. It's the same today. Some in the church try to burden others with rules and requirements—things they think others must do to be saved.

It was Peter who understood My grace, maybe more than others. He'd failed Me before. He'd denied My Son in His hour of crisis. As a disciple, he was often the most outspoken. He was not afraid to express his views. And, sometimes, his opinions were wrong and needed My correction. Yet, he was always forgiven for his failings. And he understood the great importance of grace. Because he knew My divine favor—My willingness to give when it wasn't deserved, he also had unique insight into My heart and what I wanted the most. He knew My desire was to bring people into a life unburdened by the Law. I wanted to be able to watch people live with joy and freedom in My Spirit. As the disciples watched the Gentiles receive the good news of My Son, they saw that My grace supersedes the Law's dictates, which no one can bear. This includes circumcision.

Good works and compliance with the Law would never be enough to save a person. It could only be through My gift of Holy Spirit that people could truly live with Me. Yes, believers needed to follow the leading of the spirit and avoid things that pulled them away from Me. Anything detrimental to one's heart, soul, or spirit should be avoided. But, otherwise, there was freedom to live and move and serve with gladness and thankfulness as the spirit directs. Peter understood this. And Paul lived it. Along with Barnabas and Silas, he reached multitudes in many lands. When some tried to worship him, he wouldn't allow it. He knew that the glory should go to his Lord—My Son.

Your mission today is this: to live free of burdens imposed by others by receiving My gift and serving Me with gladness and thankfulness.

Day 310

What Paul accomplished

*"So the churches were strengthened and made firm in the
faith, and they increased in number day after day."*
—*Acts 16:5*

Acts 16-17

Paul did what I knew he would. He fulfilled My calling and boldly followed where I
led him. Because of his ministry throughout the Mediterranean region, a belief in Me still
survives today. There are Christians in places like Turkey, Greece, Macedonia, and Italy
whose belief originated with Paul. What a legacy! How he reached and taught and ministered is a lingering example. He went where My Spirit led him. But why did he experience
persecution and obstruction in these areas? That's to be expected when other peoples'
beliefs and thinking are disrupted. Remember what Paul said in Athens as he stood on Mars
Hill and faced the philosophers. Athens was like most cities—filled with many ideologies.
He exclaimed, "I perceive...you are most religious, reverent to demons!" He explained that
what they worshipped was a result of human imagination, made with human hands, and
inspired by demons! But his God was different. His God formed the world and all things in
it. His God is Lord of heaven and earth. How can such a God be invented, imagined, or even
fathomed? And, by the way, this God put up with their strange beliefs for many years and
wanted them to turn to Him now so they could be judged justly later by His Son, Who came
to save them! Seems like a pretty benign message. Yet people accused Paul of causing massive
disruptions and chaos. Why would what he said cause such an uproar in places like Philippi
and Thessalonica? In Philippi, it was their concern for loss of profit and the love of money.
When Paul helped a girl, led by a demon to soothsay, the ones using her for their own gain
were outraged. The second cause for commotion was jealousy. In Thessalonica, unbelievers
stirred up many against Paul and Silas when they saw their own power diminished.

Do you see how Paul cared for every individual and wanted each person to understand
his message? He even stopped to help his jailer, because he wanted to make sure that this
man had the opportunity to hear and receive My words.

*Many women, considered then to be second-class citizens, were reached by him and led to a
belief in Me.*

Day 311

I can overcome the unjust through the just

"Thus the Word of the Lord [concerning the attainment through Christ of eternal salvation in the kingdom of God] grew and spread and intensified, prevailing mightily."
—Acts 19:20

Acts 18-19

Mighty things happened when peoples' eyes were opened. What did they see? The latent power behind the Holy Spirit—available through a belief in Jesus Christ. As its power was demonstrated, more believed in Him, and the movement called The Way spread throughout the Mediterranean region. As the message of hope and a new life ushered in signs, miracles, and wonders, chaos and confusion grew, initiated by those who opposed this belief. The adversary worked by stirring up their fear of a loss of power or wealth. He works the same way today. Paul, Aquila, Priscilla, Silas, Timothy, and Apollos were instrumental in spreading the message of Jesus Christ and what He'd accomplished. Some who received the message were not fully informed of its power. Some were baptized in water but didn't receive the fullness of the spirit. They were saved by grace, but the spirit in them was not "fully activated." They had never manifested its power, by speaking in tongues, prophesying, discerning spirits, offering words of wisdom, and healing others. In the early church, these capabilities were expected from those who received My Spirit. When people believed, but didn't "overflow into manifestation," the apostles were called to help, because they knew these manifestations were the proof of reception. In Paul's day, there were some just judges and leaders among the Gentiles. The proconsul Gallio stood up for the apostle to the Jews, who attacked Paul in Corinth. When they brought him before the judge's seat, Gallio acknowledged that the Jews' beef with Paul was merely a matter of words, names, laws, and doctrine. What right did he have to judge between their beliefs or decide who was right and who was lawful? He drove them away. When the angry Ephesians raged against Paul, and accused him of disrupting their trade, they wanted to kill him. But the town clerk calmed them down, pointing out that if Paul had broken any laws, they should take him to the courts to be judged justly. I worked on Paul's behalf, using current rules and laws. Through just men I was able to spare his life.

I can still do this today.

Day 312

I always give you choices

"But none of these things move me; neither do I esteem my life dear to myself, if only I may finish my course with joy and the ministry which I have obtained from [which was entrusted to me by] the Lord Jesus, faithfully to attest to the good news of God's grace (His unmerited favor, spiritual blessing, and mercy)."
—Acts 20:24

Acts 20-21

How many times did I warn Paul not to go to Jerusalem? While he was determined to go, he himself acknowledged that everywhere he went the Holy Spirit emphatically affirmed that imprisonment and suffering awaited him there. The disciples in Tyre, prompted by the spirit, kept telling him not to go. A prophet named Agabus took Paul's belt, bound his own feet and hands, and said, "Thus says the Holy Spirit: The Jews at Jerusalem will bind like this the man who owns this belt and deliver him into the hands of the Gentiles." How did Paul answer their appeals? "None of these things move me [I cannot be dissuaded]; neither do I esteem my life dear to myself, if only I may finish my course with joy and the ministry which I obtained from the Lord Jesus, faithfully attesting to the good news of God's grace." Knowing they were right, and that he might never see them again, he chose to do things his own way. As they pleaded, he exclaimed, "What do you mean by weeping and breaking my heart like this? I hold myself ready, not only to be arrested and bound and imprisoned, but even to die for the name of the Lord Jesus!" These words sounded good, but what did I really want for him? Wouldn't it have been better if he weren't imprisoned? If he'd lived in freedom, he could have brought the news of My Son to more people. He could have strengthened the churches with more visits. Instead, he lived out his life in prison. One good thing that came from this was that he wrote the epistles—great guidance for the Church. When people decide to do "more" than what I've asked of them, and step outside My bounds, they are always constrained. I could use them in greater ways if they'd listen to Me, but I must work out what good I can from the catastrophes they create. People always have choices.

They can listen to Me or not.

Day 313

I can release you from your prisons

"For you will be His witness unto all men of everything that you have seen and heard."
—Acts 22:15

Acts 22-23

Even when you're outside of My will and your steps take you beyond My bounds of protection, I can work on your behalf. I did this for Paul. I can do this for you. I loved Paul and his willingness to serve Me. I wanted him to know that My calling for him would be fulfilled by his carrying My Word to people throughout the known world. This included Gentiles. Because he was adamant about going to Jerusalem, despite My warnings, I was unable to completely protect him from his accusers. When his enemies were intent on killing him, I had to provide extraordinary means to get him out of threatening situations. While his attackers prepared to assault him, I worked through a Gentile commandant to spare his life multiple times. First, the man brought Paul out from a killing crowd and placed him in barracks. When the commandant found out Paul was a Roman citizen, he spared him from flogging. He also searched to find out why Paul was accused of wrongdoing.

Paul appealed to the Sanhedrin, the Jewish ruling body, knowing that some of them were Pharisees, who believe in the resurrection, angels, and spirits, and some of them were Sadducees, who don't. He used these differences of opinion in his appeal to explain that any misunderstanding of him centered on his teaching about a resurrection. Disputes quickly arose among the leaders, and Paul was dismissed. When 40 Jews conspired to kill him, his nephew overheard their plot. He told Paul, and he sent him to the commandant, who secreted Paul's removal from Jerusalem. Do you see how I protected Paul's life? I sent My Son to him on more than one occasion to encourage him and tell him how I would use his situation for good and work through him as a witness for Me in Rome.

I will do this for you too.

When your choices take you to places you regret, you can always turn to Me and see how I work to release you in ways beyond your comprehension.

Day 314

The aim of politics then and now

"I stand here on trial [to be judged on the ground] of the hope of that promise made to our forefathers by God."
—Acts 26:6

Acts 24-26

Life in Paul's day, as today, was framed by politics. When the high priest, Ananias, brought his forensic advocate, Tertullus, to present evidence against Paul in Caesarea, Tertullus began his presentation in a very political way. He tried to flatter Felix the governor, who had power over Paul, because he wanted to hand him over to his clients, the Jews. Tertullus used propaganda, hearsay, and lies to vilify Paul. But Paul's defensive words worked, and Felix, familiar with the Christian belief, wisely adjourned the trial. Being astute, he saw through Tertullus and the Jews' complaints against Paul. He knew it was all about politics and power. And he wanted to hear Paul himself, so he called an audience with him. But, when Paul spoke of uprightness and purity, it cut through Felix's heart because of his own lackluster dealings, lack of integrity, and his hope that Paul would bribe him. Instead, Paul spoke about turning away from evil. And Felix, unwilling to comply with this message, left Paul in chains for another two years to please the Jews.

The succeeding governor, Festus, was also ambitious for power and recognition among the Jews. Instead of freeing Paul, he tried to get him to appear to the Sanhedrin in Jerusalem. Paul, knowing their aim to kill him, appealed to Caesar. At King Agrippa's bequest, Festus had Paul come forward to stand and speak to him. Agrippa heard his message and considered what he said, but he would not go so far as to accept Christ as the Messiah. Festus insulted Paul to make himself look politically savvy. He even accused Paul of being insane.

Politics then, as now, is often a matter of show, pretense, desire for power, lack of integrity, and corruption. Those in charge may be more concerned about appearances, and how they can maintain control and power, than in bringing true justice to those who are falsely accused, like Paul.

And so, Paul was caught between two governors in a prison after he had become, in reality, a free man through Christ.

Day 315

When people are placed strategically

"When they had set a day with him, they came in large numbers to his lodging. And he fully set forth and explained the matter to them from morning until night, testifying to the kingdom of God and trying to persuade them concerning Jesus both from the Law of Moses and from the Prophets."
—Acts 28:23

Acts 27-28

Often My people are placed strategically to save souls who would otherwise be lost. With the help of the Holy Spirit, Paul warned those in charge of the ship bound for Rome. He knew that the timing of their departure was fraught with disasters, and he tried to prepare them. But, like most people who don't recognize My power at work through believers, they ignored him. The centurion in charge of Paul and the other prisoners paid greater attention to the pilot and ship owner, because their positions were more "weighty" than Paul's. He didn't recognize that their motives were driven by profits, not the welfare of the passengers.

As a result, the ship was caught up in a terrible northeaster, and the passengers would have been destroyed with the ship had it not been for Paul. Boldly, he stood up and reprimanded those in charge of the ship for not listening to him. Then he encouraged them with a message he'd received from My angel. "Keep up your courage, for I have faith in God that it will be exactly as it was told me," he said. They would all survive.

Later, the centurion defended Paul and the other passengers, because he recognized Paul's faith and ability and saw that they were from Me. Though they were stranded on an island, their side-trip was not without purpose. When a viper bit Paul, and he flung it off and never suffered harm, the Maltese natives decided he must be a god. But Paul's ministry among them pointed to Me and a belief in My Son.

Once in Rome, Paul first appealed to the Jews. A few believed, but most were hard-hearted and could not accept My Word spoken by him.

So, as in other lands, Paul turned to the Gentiles, for this was his ministry and mission—to bring My Light to the Gentiles throughout the world.

Day 316

Live as I always intended

"Glory and honor and [heart] peace shall be awarded to everyone who [habitually] does good, the Jew first and also the Greek (Gentile)."
—*Romans 2:10*

Romans 1-2

In the letter to the Romans, Paul explains what makes for righteousness, or right living in accordance with My will and purpose, and what doesn't. He says that the Jewish Law must be written in your heart. Does this mean you must follow each jot and tittle? No. The essence of the Law is obedience to Me. Now, by heeding the spirit in you, you can live the way I always intended. Through belief in Jesus Christ, you can receive the grace needed to live a life acceptable to Me and be able to reach others. I invite everyone to belong to Him. What does this mean? That you can serve through your spirit from Him. It means that you have My power working in you. It means that you are made righteous and saved from the wrath that will come against those who choose to live apart from Me.

You'll see people who don't know who they are or what they are, who can't fathom why I made them or for what purpose. They choose to look away from Me and accept what the world, and its god, tells them about themselves. They choose to live a lie, instead of coming to Me to discover their purpose. Remember, I make all things good. Those who try to corrupt or change what I've made do so at their own peril. The result of their work is corrosion and devaluation of life, because it's done without understanding or faith. In the end, it results in heartlessness, discouragement, hopelessness, and a lack of love and mercy.

And they have no excuse. Even nature speaks of My existence. Though they judge others who try to live righteously, they condemn themselves.

Through My kindness and patience, I provide a way out of a degrading existence through My Son. I offer a way back to Me. Every person will be judged by their works, and to those who were persistent in seeking My honor and glory, I will give eternal life and peace. And I show no partiality.

All will be judged, or rewarded, by My Son according to their inner thoughts, whether good or evil, and how these played out in life.

Day 317

Can you fathom this gift?

"God's free gift is not at all to be compared to the trespass [His grace is out of all proportion to the fall of man]. For if many died through one man's falling away (his lapse, his offense), much more profusely did God's grace and the free gift [that comes] through undeserved favor of the one Man Jesus Christ abound and overflow to and for [the benefit of] many."
—Romans 5:15

Romans 3-5

Can you fathom what a gift My Son's life is to you? Do you understand what happened when He rose from death and came to sit beside Me? Or why I would allow My own Son to suffer and die in the way He did? Do you see what is available to you now because of what He accomplished? He made an unspeakable gift available to you. When you recognize what He accomplished, truly believe in Him with your whole heart, and accept His lordship in your life, you receive this unfathomable gift—Holy Spirit.

Before Jesus came, people like Abraham would give anything to have what's available to you now. They could trust in Me, but they could never be fully acceptable to Me. Even if they obeyed My Law perfectly, they could never gain access to Me, because they did not have My Spirit in them. The Law was given to help them recognize their sin and understand their separation from Me. When Adam walked away from Me, he lost the spirit I gave him, and all born after him came without this third part of their being. He brought separation, sin, and death to all who came after him. Only through what My Son accomplished, and an acceptance of it, can people once again have My Spirit in them. They become as I intended—three-part beings once again—with bodies, souls, and spirits. Now, all can gain access to Me because of this gift. How Abraham would have rejoiced to have this! To you, it's available when you believe. And My love is poured out in your heart through it! As you walk in this world, surrounded by people who are deceived and misled, because they don't understand, remember that you can rely on My Spirit to help you. It can guide you and bring positive results by issuing in patience, endurance, integrity, and joyful, confident hope, because you know who you are.

You are saved by grace!

Day 318

Two worlds

"For [the Spirit which] you have now received [is] not a spirit of slavery to put you once more in bondage to fear, but you have received the Spirit of adoption [the Spirit producing sonship] in [the bliss of] which we cry, Abba (Father)! Father!"
—Romans 8:15

Romans 6-8

There are two worlds. The material world constrains you to what you can see, feel, taste, touch, or hear. Every choice you make is determined by these senses and may result in misinformation. Though you want to choose what's good, you often make wrong choices. It's the best you can do. But, once you receive My Spirit, after believing in Him whom I sent, you have another way to discern between what's bad and what's good. By listening to the spirit, you can avoid being misled, because it sees beyond the material world. The choices made via the flesh lead to suffering and death, because they stem from fleshly leanings that can confuse you. The choices made via the spirit lead to wholeness, peace, and life, because they're made in accordance with how I meant life to be. When your choices are approved by the world, and the god of this world, you head down the wrong path to death. But the mind of the spirit always leads to life and peace.

What do I have in store for those destined to live eternally—the ones who choose Me and a life lived under My Spirit's direction? Those who follow My lead allow their flesh to "die" so that they can live by the spirit. They are no longer slaves to the flesh. They become truly free. And they can never be separated from Me. Though they may experience hardship now, in the next life they, along with all My creation, will experience great and glorious freedom from bondage. And all will rejoice at the unveiling of My children.

If you choose Me, you have hope for a future life. And I can work all things for good in your life now. No one can condemn you, because My Son works always on your behalf. Life now is imperfect, but if you select a spirit-led life, you'll become more than a conqueror in this life and the next.

And nothing can separate you from My love made real and alive through the power of My Son.

Day 319

What made the difference?

"If you acknowledge and confess with your lips that Jesus is Lord and in your heart believe (adhere to, trust in, and rely on the truth) that God raised Him from the dead, you will be saved."
—Romans 10:9

Romans 9-10

Do you see what made the difference between what Christ made accessible and what's available from the world's religions? Do you see how every other belief system is based on accomplishments, merits, and worthiness to earn eternity? In religions, works are what determine what type of "life" you have after death. Some even teach that you can come back to earth as a different entity, depending on how you live life now. But My Son, through His life and overcoming of death, made something entirely unique obtainable to all who believe in Him. Anyone can attain a more fulfilling life now and eternal life later simply by believing. What does this really mean? It means that you receive by grace, or divine favor, a gift that you could never earn by your own efforts. You can never be "good enough" to obtain salvation, even if you live out every precept of the Mosaic Law. But the judgment slate I reserve for those who live apart from My Son, which is based on obedience to My will, is wiped clean when you simply believe!

One day, I'll close the account of each person who lived on earth. Some will be deemed worthy to live in the new heaven and earth I create. Those who accepted My mercy, through My Son, will gain automatic entry through the gates of My new city, not because they deserved it, or were worthy enough, but because they accepted Jesus as Lord and believed I raised Him from death. By this, and living life with and through Us, they are prepared for the glory of a new world that is set apart for them. This is righteousness based on faith. It can never be attained by goodness or accomplishments. Everyone who calls on Him will be saved. What does this mean? It means you are chosen to live life as one of My elect. And your main purpose now is to worship Me through My Son with your whole heart and to bring My message of hope to others. Later, you will live next to Me in glory, when this world ends and I bring a new one into being.

Then, you'll worship in adoration, because you'll see all that I have done for you!

Day 320

You are always at war!

"Do not be conformed to this world (this age), [fashioned after and adapted to its external, superficial customs], but be transformed (changed) by the [entire] renewal of your mind [by its new ideals and its new attitude], so that you may prove [for yourselves] what is the good and acceptable and perfect will of God, even the thing which is good and acceptable and perfect [in His sight for you]."
—Romans 12:2

Romans 11-13

You are always at war. The battle is between the flesh, or darkness, and the spirit, or Light. Those who recognize this, and fight on the side of good by accepting My grace, mercy, and strength through the spirit, will win. When you don the armor of Light by believing in My Son and becoming grafted into My tree, you're nourished by My Son's life-giving blood. And you can see your way clear to fight on My side. Then, good can triumph over evil. You can move away from a rebellious life to a life that's burning with the spirit. You can bless those who persecute you, rejoice with those who rejoice, and weep with those who weep. You'll fulfill your calling, best use your gifts to bless others, and become an active part in the body of Christ.

One day, He'll come to fulfill My promises to the Jews and bring many others— those grafted into My tree—into total fulfillment. Now's the critical hour. It's time to wake up! Through Me you can truly love others. And true love applied through My Spirit can never do wrong. Salvation is near. So, clothe yourself with My Son-provided Light-armor. Make no further provisions to the flesh. Put a stop to thoughts driven by evil that produce self-indulgence, jealousy, and hatred. Instead of being self-driven, be spirit-driven. And let My Spirit glow through you!

Everything originates from Me and lives through Me. Be thankful for what I've given you, and accept My lead in your life—to fight evil. Live your gifts to the fullest. That way, you can bless others, especially those in the body of Christ.

And remember, only I can truly judge.

Day 321

I give patience and endurance

*"Now may the God Who gives the power of patient endurance (steadfastness)
and Who supplies encouragement, grant you to live in such mutual harmony
and such full sympathy with one another, in accord with Christ Jesus."*
—Romans 15:5

Romans 14-16

Only I can give you true patience and endurance. Others may seek these and wish they had them, but only through My Spirit can you attain them. People who impatiently reject My promises and dismiss Me and My Son's work, because they don't see results that please them, don't understand how My Spirit works. And those who continue to serve their own purposes and desires, and make excuses for their unbelief, don't work on My behalf, because they aren't Mine. Avoid them. Your call is not to judge them or anyone. Let Me do that. When others in the faith choose to eat or drink something you wouldn't touch, don't judge them. If they have faith and no qualms about doing something, who are you to criticize them? But if a thing is not done with faith, or without a conviction of My approval for it, then it is sin. But only I can judge this.

I made all things well. Whatever is unclean or impure is only this way to those who think it is. And your job is to love. It may feel good to pass judgment or criticize, but this is not My will. My will is for you to bear others' failings and frailties, to serve them with love in the Body—the Church—and to practice peace.

My Son didn't come to please Himself. It's written in Psalm 69:9: "The reproaches and abuses of those who reproach and abuse you fell on Me." I can give you patience, endurance, and encouragement because of what My Son suffered for you. These can only come from Me, and My mercy extends beyond the Jews to all people so that all can be saved by faith and receive My promises. Some are weaker in faith than others. Your job is to extend My encouragement to all. Bring them an understanding of how I answer prayer and how to wait for the responses. You know these things, because you yourself have seen how I work. And you can endure, because you've survived hardship and loss.

Encourage others as I have encouraged you.

Day 322

They will never understand

"The natural, unspiritual man does not accept or welcome or admit into his heart the gifts and teachings and revelations of the Spirit of God, for they are folly (meaningless, nonsense) to him; and he is incapable of knowing them (of progressively recognizing, understanding, and becoming better acquainted with them) because they are spiritually discerned and estimated and appreciated."
—I Corinthians 2:14

I Corinthians 1-3

Does it surprise you when people who don't know Me base their worldview on the things they can see? They do this because they can only understand what they feel, think, or experience based on what they're taught or can surmise from their surroundings. To a person without My Spirit, the teachings of Christ are foolishness. They're meaningless. They don't make sense. That's because what I show you can only be discerned—seen or understood—through My Spirit. Without spirit, people are incapable of knowing My revelations. They can't accept or acknowledge them. Because they can't touch, taste, hear, see, or feel them. So, they seem absurd to them. But those with My Spirit can examine and discern all things. Though some may read into the meaning of things, nothing can be properly appraised without it. Who can know My mind? Those with Christ's mind in them. If you have My Spirit, you have His understanding, and you can hold My thoughts, feelings, and purposes in your heart!

Those who are factious, siding with one party over another, cannot be on My side. Your mission is to represent Me and My views, not those of individuals or groups, who may or may not stand for Me. Your main aim is to side with My Church—the believers. This is where My Spirit dwells. And its foundation is Christ. Any work not based on Him will be burned up and shown for what it is. And you'll receive rewards for how you've honored Him and Me. You are Mine because you hold Me in affectionate reverence and recognize My benefits. Through My Son, I make you guiltless and irreproachable in the day of His return. And I am faithful to keep My promises. The world, because it doesn't know Me, will let you down.

I never will!

Day 323

Don't allow others to judge you

"Do not make any hasty or premature judgments before the time when the Lord comes [again], for He will both bring to light the secret things that are [now hidden] in darkness and disclose and expose the [secret] aims (motives and purposes) of hearts. Then every man will receive his [due] commendation from God."
—I Corinthians 4:5

I Corinthians 4-6
Don't allow people to judge you by their own standards. I am the ultimate judge. And I examine every heart, even those of people who never believed in Me or My Son. I bring to Light the secret things that are hidden, and I expose the motives behind each thought, word, or action. Every person will receive what is due to him or her. In My Body, the Church, My desire is that people act as My representatives. Lawsuits, sexual impurity, abuse, dishonesty, cheating, greed, slander, and stealing are all prevalent among unbelievers. But not you. I understand that, before you came to Christ, you might have been involved in these things, because you didn't know any better. But now, you are Mine, and My desire for you is that you walk in love. This means not taking advantage of others' weaknesses. I atoned for all sins through the body and blood of My Son. But if you continue doing what I've spoken against, with yourself at the center of your choices, you'll suffer consequences now and lose out on My rewards for a life well-lived later. With My Spirit, you're free to act any way you choose, but you must be careful not to become a slave to things or other people's agendas. I want to be a part of your life so that you can be fulfilled. This can only happen if you honor Me in all you do, and bring glory to Me and the One Who died for you. Those who want to be My stewards must be trustworthy. As My representative, your job is not to judge those outside the Body. That is My job.

Live your life openly, without hidden secrets and shameful habits. As a leader, don't be haughty or arrogant. With heart-simplicity, represent Me by showing others grace, mercy, and love. You may need to walk away from those who disdain Me. But don't shun all unbelievers. Some will come. For these I'll give you the right words so their hearts can be won over to a knowledge of the truth.

Watch for them!

Day 324

How to make good choices

"If one loves God truly [with affectionate reverence, prompt obedience, and grateful recognition of His blessing], he is known by God [recognized as worthy of His intimacy and love, and he is owned by Him]."
—I Corinthians 8:3

I Corinthians 7-8

Yours can be a great life when you act from a place of love and peace. This includes the words you choose to speak and the ones you don't. Whether you marry or not, do it with Me in mind. Be sure to ask for My guidance. If you know that it would be hard for you to remain unmarried, because you want children, and you believe you could fulfill My calling and utilize your gifts while married, then get married. But remember, marriage is a partnership, so choose someone you can effectively collaborate with to fulfill your life's mission. If you're already married, stay married if you can, even if your spouse doesn't believe as you do. Your faith sets him or her apart from the world, and your good example could turn your spouse toward a belief in Me. Did you know that even your children are set apart by Me because of your faith?

The main thing is that your life be an example of what I've invited you to experience—a life filled with love and peace. If your spouse chooses to leave, you're free to remain single or to reconcile. Just know that marriage and children bring greater responsibilities and make it harder to freely serve in the Body. And, as the world grows darker, it will become more challenging to serve Me with added obligations. But you must do whatever helps you fulfill My purposes for you. Some will try to weigh you down with requirements, things you "have to do" to please Me. My will is that you freely serve Me, not that you be loaded down with burdens. I want you to be free from anxieties, especially in the coming days. If your actions or words cause others to move away from Me, refrain from them. Remember, everything must be done out of love. People sometimes become "puffed up," because they think they know more than you and Me. But My love encourages.

Those who love Me are known by Me and worthy of My intimacy with them.

Day 325

Run the race to claim your prize

"No temptation (no trial regarded as enticing to sin, no matter how it comes or where it leads) has overtaken you and laid hold on you that is not common to man [that is, no temptation or trial has come to you that is beyond human resistance and that is not adjusted and adapted and belonging to human experience, and such as man can bear]. But God is faithful [to His Word and to His compassionate nature], and He [can be trusted] not to let you be tempted and tried and assayed beyond your ability and strength of resistance and power to endure, but with the temptation He will [always] also provide the way out (the means of escape to a landing place), that you may be capable and strong and powerful to bear up under it patiently."
—I Corinthians 10:13

I Corinthians 9-10

At the heart of every action is whether or not it glorifies and honors Me. Remember that some things may be permissible, but not profitable. Not all actions build character and a more spiritual life. You should always ask yourself, "Will this encourage others to see God more clearly through my life, or will it lead them farther away from Him?" Your goal shouldn't be to seek your own good, advantage, or profit, but the welfare of others. You know that the whole earth is Mine. And you are allowed to do whatever you want, as long as it venerates Me. Remember, not every effort helps those around you. Avoid anything that discourages a trust in Me or involves the worship of other gods. At the heart of every temptation is an appeal to gratify self or sensual desires that indulge in immorality. The greatest temptation is to complain. But with every temptation to move away from thankfulness, *I will provide a way out.* I understand human nature. I won't allow you to be swayed beyond your ability, strength of resistance, and power to endure. I will offer a way of escape, so you can bear up under it patiently. But you must listen to Me. If your ears are plugged up by complaining or self-indulging thoughts, you won't hear Me. Avoid anything that causes you to love something more than Me, like a habit you know you should stop but don't think you can. I will always provide a way out, but you must listen!

Run your race so that you can claim the prize I have in store for you!

How important is what you do?

*"Earnestly desire and zealously cultivate the greatest and best gifts and graces
(the highest gifts and the choicest graces). And yet I will show you a still more
excellent way [one that is better by far and the highest of them all—love]."*
—I Corinthians 12:31

I Corinthians 11-12

Look at your own body. When your sinuses are congested, and you have a hard time
breathing, how does it affect the rest of your body? When you have a corn on your toe, how
does it influence the way you walk? If one of your ribs cracks, does it cause pain to your entire
body? It's the same in My Body of believers. When one member suffers, all suffer. I give to
each one special talents, abilities, and gifts that can be used to bless and help everyone in the
Body. One person may be good at discerning between good and evil to warn and protect
others. Another may have faith to heal the sick. Someone else might give words of wisdom
to guide people through difficulties. But if any one of these can't function well, or is hurt or
missing, it affects everyone. It's senseless to think that some members are more important
than others. Some might say that the head of a church is more important than the others.
But a person who serves as My "feet," by bringing messages of hope and welcoming others
into the Body, is just as indispensable. Without them, the Church would die. Some might
belittle My "hands"— those who serve through hospitality. My Church would suffer greatly
and miss their service. I have never looked upon one member as being more important than
any other. Each one serves a unique function, which I honor and reward according to how
his or her ordained talents are used to bless the whole Body. In some churches, all members
are acknowledged. In others, the leader, or "voice," is held in greater esteem. Christ is the
only real Head of My Church, and He is under Me. No man or woman is above Him.
Remember, even if your talent is to bring cookies, I honor this gesture as much as any other
action done with care. And love is the bottom line. All efforts are pleasing to Me when they
are done with affection for Me. Traditions may differ from church to church, but the most
important thing is that all celebrate communion.

*Because, by this, everyone can be reminded of what My Son accomplished for all through
His body and blood.*

Day 327

What is true love?

"So faith, hope, love abide [faith—conviction and belief respecting man's relation to God and divine things; hope—joyful and confident expectation of eternal salvation; love—true affection for God and man, growing out of God's love for and in us], these three; but the greatest of these is love."
—I Corinthians 13:13

I Corinthians 13-14

What is love? Many have asked this question throughout the ages. So, what's the answer? People often think of it as passion—a strong desire for a thing or a person, like a lust. And when they no longer "feel" this passion, they "fall out" of love. This is one type of love, but not the love Paul refers to here. What he speaks of is a love that only I can give. It emanates from true affection between Me and those who know Me. It grows out of My love for and through you. It displays certain characteristics, and it can be easily recognized. It is patient and kind. It is never envious or jealous of others. It never displays boastfulness or haughtiness. It is not arrogant or prideful or rude. It does not insist on its own way or its rights over others. It is not self-seeking. It is never touchy, fretful, or resentful, and it does not account for evil done to it or seek revenge. It never rejoices in injustice but is thankful when truth prevails. It bears up under every trial and is ready to believe the best of others. It does not fade away. It endures without growing weak.

You can do things to please yourself or others and have good intentions. And the things you do may bring some benefits. But, without My love, your efforts will prove to be worthless. Through My love, your actions never return void or empty of meaning. Now, you can only see things through a "smoke-filled mirror." Even with Me in your heart, your vision is often clouded, and you can only see things vaguely reflected. You can't see what lies behind the mirror. You may have faith—a strong conviction about your relationship with Me—to help you muddle through. You may have hope—a confident expectation of what lies ahead for you. But you still can't see clearly without My help. The greatest thing you can give is love. Why? Because anything you do, if done with love, will bring ultimate benefit to yourself and others.

And, one day, your rewards will be based on how you acted with and through it.

Day 328

I reveal to you a mystery

"In a moment, in the twinkling of an eye, at the [sound of the] last trumpet call. For the trumpet will sound, and the dead [in Christ] will be raised imperishable (free and immune from decay), and we shall be changed (transformed)."
—I Corinthians 15:52

I Corinthians 15-16

Through a death, many people will receive eternal life! What do I mean by this? I mean that Jesus died to defeat death. Adam brought loss of life into the world when he shunned his relationship with Me. Jesus came from Me as a man to regain what Adam lost. By overcoming death, He brought eternal life. Some people say there is no resurrection or afterlife. They don't believe in what Jesus accomplished. If He never rose from death, then your belief in what He accomplished is null and void. Your faith is a delusion. And you must still live a broken life under the weight of separation from Me. And, when you die, life ends, and you're lost forever. You have hope only for this life, with no expectation for the next. But this is all a lie. Christ was the first to die and rise from death. He was your "first fruit." Like a seed, He died on the earth so that new life could spring up from Him.

I tell you a mystery, a secret—you who are in Christ shall be transformed one day. In a moment, in the twinkling of an eye, at the sound of the last trumpet call, those who died believing in Christ will be raised up first, free from decay. Then those who are still living will also be changed. What once was perishable will become imperishable. What once was mortal must put on immortality. Then, death will be swallowed up, and it will utterly vanish forever. After that will come the completion—when He delivers over My kingdom, after abolishing every rule and authority and power not subject to Me.

Then, Christ will reign as King of Kings, and He will put every enemy beneath His feet, including death. Then He will also subject Himself to Me. This was the plan all along—that mankind would live and reign once again with Us on earth. And what Adam once gave up to forces not subject to Me will be regained.

And people will again live free from the bondage of sin and its result—death.

Day 329

Where My Spirit dwells is liberty

"Now the Lord is the Spirit, and where the Spirit of the Lord is, there is liberty (emancipation from bondage, freedom)."
—II Corinthians 3:17

II Corinthians 1-3

Why do very analytical people have a hard time receiving Paul's message and Mine? Why are the workings of the spirit often unacceptable to them? When people can only understand things that "line up" in certain ways, like mathematics or calculus, with no variance in style or procedure, they will always struggle with anything spiritual. Why? Because spiritual things cannot be lined up in a row or dissected. What My Spirit denotes, and how it leads, is different with each person in whom it dwells. Though My Word has guidelines, like not stealing or coveting or murdering, how it works in each person is different.

Paul was moved by My Spirit to change his plans, as he explained to the Corinthians. Was the change a contradiction or a failed promise to them? No. He was following the guidance of My Spirit. The Holy Spirit in you may tell you to do something contrary to your plans. Then, you must decide which way to go. Always trust the spirit more than your mind. My gift of Holy Spirit is My promise to you of what will come later. It is also a fragrance from you to every person you meet. To those who are saved through a belief in Me, it emanates a sweet smell of hope and newness of life. To those who reject your message, it is an aroma of death and fatal doom, because they cannot accept it.

Do not despair when some turn away from you and your life-giving message. It's not you they turn against, but Me. Those who can only see the material world, which they can analyze, can't fathom what you are saying, because they can't take it apart or see it through a microscope. This frightens them.

Remember, your power and ability and sufficiency always come from Me. And My words written in your heart can be read and recognized by anyone who is searching. Where My Spirit dwells, there is liberty.

As you behold My Word through your spirit, you'll be transformed more and more into My image of increasing splendor.

Day 330

You are a new creation

*"Therefore if any person is [ingrafted] in Christ (the Messiah) he is a new creation
(a new creature altogether); the old [previous moral and spiritual condition]
has passed away. Behold, the fresh and new has come!"*
—*II Corinthians 5:17*

II Corinthians 4-6

I always respond to your requests. And I hear your voice. Your words to Me never return void. I will always extend a helping hand to you. But realize that I already offered a hand to you long ago. When I sent My Son, I gave you a way to deliverance. I presented a gracious welcome of acceptance into My kingdom. Now is the day of salvation, and all can come freely and receive what I made available. Many looked forward to this day. It is here now!

The world will not recognize you if you are a believer. That's because you emanate Light, and worldly people can only see darkness. But those seeking Light will see you. The world may ignore you, but you will always be welcomed into My kingdom. Avoid hooking up with those who reject you and your faith. They will only discourage and lead you away from your desire to know Me. How can Light fellowship with darkness? It can't. Separate yourself from worldly depravity. Review your words and actions and, remember, you have a special place in My Body. I want to abide in and through you.

Those in the world pride themselves on surface appearances. You are no longer like this. You're a new creation. You resemble Me more and more as you live in harmony with Me. As you "put on" My Light, you are more and more able to attract others away from lawlessness and into an acceptance of Me. Your goal should be to unveil people's secret thoughts, feelings, desires, and underhandedness. You do not, as some, practice trickery and deceit, handling My Word dishonestly. But, working together with others in the Body, you can receive My merciful kindness, and extend it to others so they can know Me as you do. Then they can understand more fully how I hear and respond to their requests.

Never be afraid to speak the truth to those who want to know Me and be a part of My living temple.

Day 331

I replace pain with a promise

*"Godly grief and the pain God is permitted to direct, produce a repentance that leads
and contributes to salvation and deliverance from evil, and it never brings
regret; but worldly grief (the hopeless sorrow that is characteristic
of the pagan world) is deadly [breeding and ending in death]."*
—II Corinthians 7:10

II Corinthians 7-10

All grief and pain offered to Me is redirected to ultimate good. And any regret is absolved—washed away—because, when you commit faults, failings, lacks, or losses to Me, I make them "whole." Without Me, any shortcomings result in regret. Only I can repair things that are broken and make them right. I can even go above and beyond and restore them by doubling back to you what was lost. Think of Job, who lost his children, his home, and almost everything he had. When he turned to Me, and acknowledged My greatness, I restored everything he lost by double. Remember, no religion can offer you what I can. No man-made belief system can make up for your losses and bring ultimate good from them. My Son gave up all, even a life of fulfillment, so that you could be filled with My grace and live an abundant life. But the amount of grace and fullness you receive depends on you! When you give of yourself to others, you reap much in return. If you sow sparingly with a stingy heart, you also reap little. I treasure a cheerful and willing giver—one who gives from the heart.

As you lead every thought captive to Me and refuse to think evil or judge or compare yourself to others, then I can help you to succeed in life's battles. Remember, your daily battles may seem like they're "in the flesh," but they never are. They're always spiritual, and only with My help can you win!

The power resident in you cannot be measured by you or anyone else. It does no good to compare yourself to others. And don't accept their comparisons! People who lift themselves up are never the ones who are approved and acceptable to Me. I Myself commend the ones I choose.

I can make all grace abound to you as you give of yourself in the best way you can by using all your God-given abilities to glorify Me.

Day 332

I love your weakness

"He said to me, My grace (My favor and loving-kindness and mercy) is enough for you [sufficient against any danger and enables you to bear the trouble manfully]; for My strength and power are made perfect (fulfilled and completed) and show themselves most effective in [your] weakness. Therefore, I will all the more gladly glory in my weaknesses and infirmities, that the strength and power of Christ (the Messiah) may rest (yes, may pitch a tent over and dwell) upon me!"
—II Corinthians 12:9

II Corinthians 11-13

I never perceive weakness as you do. For Me, real strength isn't attained in the way people think it is. I allow people to become "weak," so they'll turn to Me for strength and depend on My sufficiency. I look at weakness as something good. Human imperfection was a part of My design from the beginning , because I want people to come to Me to fill the places where they're empty and find in Me the wholeness and perfection they lack. People rush to "fix" others. They try to patch up the broken places. They become anxious when others are sick, especially people they care about, because they fear death. Their anxiety stems from their uncertainty of what lies beyond this life. Never fear your brokenness. Bring it to Me! I will use it! I'll work it into the unique and beautiful pattern of your life. I'll make it into a masterpiece. But I can only do this if you trust Me! When you're sick, turn to Me for healing. I'll make you whole again. If it can't be accomplished in this life, it will be fulfilled in the next. When you're burdened with worry, bring your distressing thoughts to Me. I'll show you ways to overcome. A large part of your mental healing involves replacing destructive thoughts with the convictions that only I can give you—thoughts based on reality regarding yourself and your situation. When you are financially broken, come to Me with your hands open. I will fill them. It may take time to unwind past failures, choices, and habits. But I will help you if you trust Me. When others harass or hurt you, I will make it all good. And I'll deal with those who try to harm you. Leave them to Me.

My strength is made perfect and shows itself most effective through weakness.

Day 333

Who are Abraham's children?

"If you belong to Christ [are in Him Who is Abraham's Seed], then you are
Abraham's offspring and [spiritual] heirs according to the promise."
—Galatians 3:29

Galatians 1-3

Who are the real children of Abraham? When I promised Abraham that his Seed would live forever, what did I mean? Who did I refer to? It was Abraham's unique faith in Me that I considered when I made this promise. Above all the people on earth, only he believed in and knew Who I was. I gave the Law to Moses as a temporary means to spare Abraham's descendants. This was a way for them to survive until the Promised Seed came. But it also helped them to see their lacks and disparities and their need for a Savior.

Who was the promised Seed? None other than My Son, Who'd come from Abraham's descendants. Was it Abraham's perfect submission to the Law that caused Me to give him such a unique promise? No, because the Law had not been given yet. It was his faith alone that drew My attention. Remember, it is never your perfect submission to laws or rules that can save you. But, because of My Son's love and willingness to give His life for you, you can now live by faith in Him and have a relationship with Me. Because He became a curse for you, you no longer must live under the curse of the Law to appease or be worthy of Me.

Titles and positions will never impress Me. What gets My attention is your faith in Me and in My Son as Lord and Savior. Because of what He did, all who believe are made one in Him and in Me. No matter your background, or how many times you've fallen short, you become acceptable through your acceptance of what He accomplished for you. Remember, Paul murdered Christians, yet I drew him to Me through his belief in My Son. I will never be awed by your works. I am drawn by your faith in Me and in the perfect work of My Son. He purchased your freedom so that you no longer must earn it. Abraham looked forward to the coming of a Messiah. Who are the real children of Abraham?

They are those who, like Abraham, live by faith in that Promised Seed.

Day 334

What does walking by the spirit look like?

"The fruit of the [Holy] Spirit [the work which His presence within accomplishes] is love, joy (gladness), peace, patience (an even temper, forbearance), kindness, goodness (benevolence), faithfulness, gentleness (meekness, humility), self-control (self-restraint, continence). Against such things there is no law [that can bring a charge]."
—Galatians 5:22-23

Galatians 4-6

How do you know when you are living by the spirit? Here's the answer: by your fruit! The fruit of those who walk by the spirit are identified as: love, joy, peace, patience, kindness, goodness, faithfulness, humility, and self-control. Strict observance of religious rules can't produce these. Only by submitting to the Holy Spirit can you manifest these characteristics. This means you must listen to what the spirit tells you in every situation, then follow its lead. What's the fruit of those who walk by their godless nature? Immorality, indecency, hostility, strife, divisions, jealousy, bad temper, selfishness, devotion to one's own way of thinking, envy, and drunkenness. When people are "hell-bent" on living apart from Me, even if they have My Spirit in them, they won't receive the rewards intended for them in the kingdom later. Every person is responsible for his or her own behavior. And everyone can deal with faults and shortcomings by bringing them to Me. Through My Spirit, anyone can overcome these with the supernatural ability I give them to live selflessly and help others bear their burdens.

Following manmade rules, even when done perfectly, can never lead to perfection. My will was always that you have freedom from compliance with laws to try to please Me. Other religions depend on rules to gain favor with their gods. But My design is that My children become new creations through faith in My Son. And the spirit they receive as a result allows them to put on new natures filled with peace, mercy, and all the other fruit of the spirit. Only those who belong to Him can crucify the old godless nature and live by His Spirit in them.

Who is the true Israel now? Those who become one with Me and inherit what My Son gave—sonship!

And only My true children can manifest My real nature, which culminates in love.

$\mathcal{D}ay$ 335

You can be joyful in sorrow

*"Now to Him Who, by (in consequence of) the [action of His] power that is at
work within us, is able to [carry out His purpose and] do superabundantly,
far over and above all that we [dare] ask or think [infinitely beyond
our highest prayers, desires, thoughts, hopes, or dreams]."
—Ephesians 3:20*

Ephesians 1-3

How could Paul, while imprisoned, encourage others? How could he, while suffering, rejoice? Because of what he knew. He'd seen the revelation of a mystery that was hidden since time began. Seeing what I revealed gave him joy, because he saw what I had in store for him and for all who believed in what My Son had done. He realized the fulfillment of this mystery in his lifetime, as you can see it in yours. For centuries, only the called-out Jews could look forward to a life beyond this one through their belief in Me and observance of My Law. Now, all can approach Me when they believe in Christ. Not only can anyone have direct access to Me, and never have to go again to a priest to repent of their sins, they can be an integral part of My unique creation—My masterpiece, which I've been preparing since the world began. As a result of their belief, all can be raised up from a temporary, earthly life controlled by the prince of the power of the air, to an eternal life of peace. They can be seated in a heavenly sphere, awaiting the return of My Son to earth.

Though once you had no hope for a life beyond this one, now you can live a fulfilling life in preparation for one later, which I've prearranged for you. Through what I've done, you can be free from strife and anxiety. As you accept My destiny for you, I can work on your behalf to prepare you for your inheritance. The spirit you received is a powerful down-payment of what you will receive later in My kingdom. Why could Paul rejoice in suffering? Because he knew what lay ahead for him. He understood the masterpiece I was creating through the Body of Christ, and he knew he was an integral part of it. What is your inheritance? It depends on you. Your life in the spirit, and how much you allow Me to prepare you, determine your assignment in the new heaven and earth. Just as I showed Paul what I had in store for him, I can also show you what I have planned for you.

And you can be joyful, even in sorrow.

Day 336

How can My armor protect you?

"Therefore put on God's complete armor, that you may be able to resist and stand your ground on the evil day [of danger], and, having done all [the crisis demands], to stand [firmly in your place]."
—*Ephesians 6:13*

Ephesians 4-6

What is My armor, and what does it mean to you? Why is it important? One day, you will face a crisis, and how well you are armed with My protection will determine whether you can overcome or be overcome. How much of My armor you put on now will determine the outcome. What is My armor? First, I give you a belt of truth. There are two ways to buckle My belt: through My Word, either written or spoken, or by My Spirit in you. The more you "belt on" My truth, the more power you can wield and the more protection you will have physically, mentally, and spiritually. Next, I give you a breastplate of integrity, or right standing with Me. What is this? It's a determination to live by My Word and My Spirit, not making excuses for wrong behavior but having the fortitude and strength to live morally before Me, basing every choice on what you know from Me. With this breastplate, you not only prepare yourself for crises, you also protect your heart from hurt.

I equip you with the best "shoes" to help you stand firm-footed against the attacks of the enemy. With them, you'll always walk with stability, never moved, tripped up, or pushed aside by anyone or anything that steps up to harm you. The shield of faith is another gift that protects you from flaming missiles aimed at you by the wicked one, who seeks to destroy you by attacking your heart and mind. With faith in Me, you can thwart each ill-aimed missile. I fit you with the helmet of salvation, which gives you wholeness and soundness of mind when you are born-again of My Spirit. This helmet protects your thoughts. The more of My Word you put on in your mind, the more it can protect you. The sword you wield is a spiritual one and can only be grasped by knowing My words. Remember, Jesus's only defense against the devil was his understanding and use of My Word.

If you freely and willingly put on and use this armor, you will be able to live purposefully, worthily, and accurately, not as unwise, but as wise and able to overcome all the fiery darts of the wicked.

Day 337

When love abounds

"This I pray: that your love may abound yet more and more and extend to its fullest development in knowledge and all keen insight [that your love may display itself in greater depth of acquaintance and more comprehensive discernment]."
—Philippians 1:9

Philippians 1-2

How can your love abound more and more? Remember, your love can only thrive or grow through the spirit in you. It's My Spirit that makes your love supernatural. And the results of this love? First, you have a more developed understanding and keener insight, and you display greater depth and discernment. You have more ability to sense what is vital, excellent, and of real value. You also become untainted by the world—pure, unerring, blameless, and unadulterated, so that, as the day of Christ's return approaches, you're prepared and ready. You stumble less, and you can help others to stand firm in their own belief.

What's the fruit of this love? Righteousness or right standing with Me through Christ and a greater ability to spread My message of hope. Others also become emboldened by your stand. They see you working courageously because of your love and dependence on the spirit, and then they can grow more fearless of suffering and death. They also see your desire to help people. You're more concerned for others, because you put on His mind through His love. You become more affectionate and compassionate, and you live more harmoniously with those around you. Like Christ, you think more highly of others, because you have His servant spirit. You're stronger in your stand, and you're more unified with others, who also desire what you have—spirit and purpose. You're more confident in your deliverance because of your greater participation with the inner workings of the spirit. You're more able to hold your own against the world's temptations, and I am more able to will and to do of My good pleasure through you. You grow uncontaminated by darkness, and you shine more brightly as a Light in the world.

Your Light, like your love, brought forth by your willingness to lean on My Spirit in you, attracts others, like moths to light, because they see how you shine through the darkness around t hem.

343

Day 338

The secret to being constantly content

"Do not fear or have any anxiety about anything, but in every circumstance and in everything, by prayer and petition (definite requests), with thanksgiving, continue to make your wants known to God."
—Philippians 4:6

Philippians 3-4

What's the secret to being content in every situation? What did Paul know that you should know? He understood that, whether he was full or empty, had plenty or nothing at all, he still had the most important thing—Christ. And he was empowered by Him to face every situation. It was Christ Who infused him with inner strength and gave him sufficiency. When you know He is always there for you, you also know that you can rely on his ever-present strength to face any event, even death, without becoming anxious. You never fear any outcome, because you know I'll work everything out through Him Who is in you. And, knowing He will return for you, you need never be afraid for yourself or your loved ones.

My peace can infuse you. What is peace? It's a tranquil state of your soul, or mind, where you're assured of your salvation through Christ, fearing nothing and being content with your earthly lot—of whatever sort it is. The result is a peace that transcends all understanding. It actually "mounts guard" over your heart and mind. With it, you can focus on the things that are most important—whatever is honorable, just, pure, lovely, kind, gracious, and excellent. And you are free to praise and thank Me for everything! What do I want for you? A life of contentment that is filled with My peace and joy. And for you to know that you need never compare yourself to others, whose lives center on what they have or who they are, because you know that only through My Son can you have what I intended for you. Forget what lies behind you! Press forward into a deeper life with My Son. Be filled with what is crucial—love, joy, peace, and contentment. Know that, as you press into Me, I reserve a prize for you—an amazing life beyond this one. Rejoice in Me always! Be glad in Me and in what I've done for you. See where I can take you and what I can do for you, both now and later!

Never fret over your circumstances, for they are temporary and will change as you press into Me.

Day 339

What is My desire for you?

"[For my concern is] that their hearts may be braced (comforted, cheered, and encouraged) as they are knit together in love, that they may come to have all the abounding wealth and blessings of assured conviction of understanding, and that they may become progressively more intimately acquainted with and may know more definitely and accurately and thoroughly that mystic secret of God, [which is] Christ (the Anointed One)."
—Colossians 2:2

Colossians 1-2

What is the mystic secret that I want you to know? Kept hidden for ages, it is now revealed to you, and it is important that you understand it so you can partake of its benefits! It is this: in Christ lies all the treasures of divine wisdom—insight into My ways and purposes—and all the riches of spiritual enlightenment. With Him, you have access to these treasures, and you have everything you need to lead a fulfilling, meaningful, and powerful life! What is My desire for you? To be steadfast in your faith, leaning entirely on Him in absolute trust and having confidence in His power, wisdom, and goodness. And that you have the roots of your being firmly and deeply planted in Him so that you are continually built up through Him. I want you to become more and more established in your faith, so you are overflowing with thanksgiving. Knowing what's laid up for your benefit, you can be filled with a clear knowledge of My will so that you're able to discern all spiritual things. Then you can walk in a manner worthy of My Son, pleasing Him and Me in all things. I want you to bear fruit and grow in a knowledge of Me, having deeper insight. And that you to be strengthened with all My power, having endurance and patience with joy and thanksgiving, knowing that I enable you to share your inheritance with all My saints. I draw you out of the control and dominion of darkness, and I transfer you into the kingdom of my Son by His love. Through Him, all things in heaven and earth were created and exist. Through Him, all things are held together, and He is the Head of the Body, the Church, and the Firstborn from the dead. Through Him, you are reconciled to Me. And when you relinquish any hostility, and accept Him as your Lord, you receive My mystery—My complete fullness. It includes Me, My Son, and My Holy Spirit.

And no one can take this amazing gift away from you!

How to live your life to the fullest

"Clothe yourselves therefore, as God's own chosen ones (His own picked representatives), [who are] purified and holy and well-beloved [by God Himself, by putting on behavior marked by] tenderhearted pity and mercy, kind feeling, a lowly opinion of yourselves, gentle ways, [and] patience [which is tireless and long-suffering, and has the power to endure whatever comes, with good temper]."
—Colossians 3:12

Colossians 3-4

Do everything as if you were doing it for Me so I can reward you for all your efforts. Remember, it's from Me, not from people, that you will receive your inheritance later. What does working for Me look like? It looks like this: In everything you do, you seek the eternal treasure that is above, where Christ is seated at My right hand. You realize that you've died to this world and its ways, and your new life is hidden in Him. You understand that your eternal rewards come from Him, and, when He appears, you'll appear with Him in glory! As a new creation, you are tenderhearted. You have greater pity, mercy, kindness, humility, gentleness, tireless patience, and a good temper. You're forbearing of others' faults, and you're always ready to pardon them when they offend or hurt you, because you remember how much I forgave you! Above all, you put on My love in your heart, and you enfold yourself with this bond of perfectness, which binds together everything in complete harmony and promotes peace. When you allow Christ to rule in your heart, He settles all questions that arise in your mind. He allows you to remain in a peaceful state within the Body of Christ. And He reminds you to be thankful. Allow Christ's words to live in your heart. Let Him dwell in you richly so you can give guidance and grace to others by helping them acquire His insight and wisdom. Do everything in His name, and work with your whole heart, because you live for Him. Remember that your acceptance by Me is never dependent on how the world sees you. Pray steadfastly, because you are still in the world, surrounded by people who don't know Me.

Season your prayer with thankfulness and your speech with graciousness, so that, when you address others' questions about Me, they will listen and hear you, because they see how you live for Me!

Day 341

How to prepare for His return

"Thank [God] in everything [no matter what the circumstances may be, be thankful and give thanks], for this is the will of God for you [who are] in Christ Jesus [the Revealer and Mediator of that will]."
—I Thessalonians 5:18

I Thessalonians

Here's your hope: that one day My Son will return for you. When? No one, not even My angels, knows. It's hidden in Me. Who will be affected? Those who believe in Christ. How will it happen? The day will come unexpectedly, like a thief in the night. When people are saying, "Everything's great! We're secure and have peace and safety!" then destruction and death will come suddenly. And there will be no escape for those who never believed in Me. But you need not be afraid. Why? Because I've given you hope. As a child of Light, you won't be overtaken by darkness. I'll provide you with plenty of warning. But you must prepare for this day by being vigilant and by putting on My breastplate of faith and My helmet of hope for salvation. You're not appointed for judgment, because your faith is in Christ. He will call you up in a moment, and you will be with Him forever. And you'll be spared from the earth's devastation and destruction.

In the meantime, here are ways to prepare yourself for the coming day. First, stand firm in your belief in My Son. Refrain from the corrupt practices of the world. Control your body and mind, and avoid passions that block your thoughts and your heart from My Spirit. Live peaceably with all people, and mind your own affairs. Never defraud others by taking what is justly theirs. I will avenge such behavior, especially if it involves My believers. What is My desire? That you love others and command their respect and that you recognize others' gifts and callings. Heed the warnings, but test what people say by checking with your spirit to discern what is good and profitable and right. Be patient with everyone and manage your temper. Never repay evil for evil. Remember, it's My job to provide justice and judgment, and I will always follow through. Seek only to do good to others, then you'll be happy in your faith. Thank Me, no matter what circumstance you find yourself in, because I will make all things right.

Shrink away from evil, then My peace can permeate your whole spirit, soul, and body until My Son returns for you.

Day 342

When will He return to earth?

"When He comes to be glorified in His saints [on that day He will be made more glorious in His consecrated people], and [He will] be marveled at and admired [in His glory reflected] in all who have believed [who have adhered to, trusted in, and relied on Him], because our witnessing among you was confidently accepted and believed [and confirmed in your lives]."
—II Thessalonians 1:10

II Thessalonians

What will His coming to earth look like? When Christ returns to earth, after He calls us up to Him, He'll be revealed from heaven with His angels in a flame of fire. Some will think He's an asteroid or a burning star, and they will be afraid. He will mete out justice and retribution for the wrong done to My people by those who followed the antichrist, who will be exposed for what he is—a liar and deceiver. My Son will be glorified in His people, and many will marvel at His glory reflected in those who believed. I want you to be one of these through your faith and absolute trust in My power, wisdom, and goodness. That the name of Jesus Christ become more glorious through you, and that you be glorified in Him.

When will He come to earth? Many will see signs beforehand. His reign will be preceded by a period of great lawlessness when many will oppose authority. A "falling away" will occur, and many who say they believe in Me will be deceived by the antichrist, who will oppose all that is godly by exalting himself on My temple throne. He will call himself God and be attended by great power, miracles, signs, and deluding marvels. His goal? To seduce and deceive as many as possible, to mislead and make the world believe what is false, and to turn everyone against Me. Why? Because he works for My archenemy, Satan, the one who seeks to destroy and lead astray as many as possible before his time ends. But the full revelation of the antichrist's reign cannot occur until after the children of Light are removed. What can you do now? Be strengthened in Me by setting yourself on a firm foundation—My Word.

Let Me guard you from evil and direct your heart to My love and the steadfastness of Christ within you until His return for you.

Day 343

What is this hidden truth?

"Who wishes all men [and women] to be saved and [increasingly] to perceive and recognize and discern and know precisely and correctly the [divine] Truth."
—*I Timothy 2:4*

I Timothy 1-3

What is the truth that is hidden from the world? It is that I was made visible through a man—Jesus. I justify and vindicate all who believe in Him through My Holy Spirit. Because of Jesus, My purpose has been seen by angels, preached among nations, believed on in the world, and even glorified. And, through what He did, all can come to Me now. But, sadly, that truth is still hidden from many. What is My desire? That all be saved and able to discern, recognize, and know this truth. I am the only true God, and there is only one mediator between people and Me—the man, Jesus. He gave Himself as a ransom for all, so that anyone could come to Me. I also desire that, in every place, people would pray. Through prayer, they can intercede for others, and prayer prevents resentment, anger, quarreling, even doubt. It promotes good leadership, within and outside the Church. It is extremely important to intercede for worldly leaders, so that all people can live peaceful lives, free from the world's disturbances. Can women be leaders in the church? Of course. Any person who leads a godly life, centered on Me and My Son, who is not combative or showy, but temperate and self-controlled in all things, sensible and orderly, having love for believers and strangers, who is gentle and considerate, not given to slander, who promotes Christ in all things and displays patience, makes a good leader. My concern, and Paul's, was a false teaching being promoted at that time where some believed that life originated with the goddess Artemis and that women should dominate men.* Paul pointed out that Adam was made first, then Eve. He encouraged women, like Priscilla and Nympha, who led or hosted churches in their homes and taught against a belief that women were superior to men. I am not a respecter of persons, whether they be male or female, slave or free, Jew or Gentile—all are one in Christ. And My original intent was for men and women to be equal before Me.

Why would I want to reinvent rules regarding this, setting one sex above another, when the Law, with its inherent prejudices to deal with incumbent customs, was fulfilled and overcome through My Son?

Day 344

Is it wrong to be rich?

"As for you...aim at and pursue righteousness (right standing with God and true goodness), godliness (which is the loving fear of God and being Christlike), faith, love, steadfastness (patience), and gentleness of heart."
—*I Timothy 6:11*

I Timothy 4-6

Is it wrong to be rich? No. But isn't money the root of all evil? No. The LOVE of money is the root of all evils. Craving gain causes some to wander away from their faith and be pierced with many mental stresses. How do they end up this way? By listening to stories and being lured into a lifestyle by those who seem to "have it all." By being seduced by deluding spirits and by heeding demonic doctrines that lead them away from the truth. They salivate over hypocrisy and the pretensions of liars, who have no conscience. Is it wrong to have money? No. Remember the scriptures: "You shall not muzzle an ox when it is treading out the grain," and, "The laborer is worthy of his hire." (Deuteronomy 25:4 and Luke 10:7.) My desire is for all to live abundantly (John 10:10), but, even more, to be content in all situations. The greatest profit is godliness with contentment—having a sense of inward sufficiency. This brings the most abundant gain.

If you have more than enough, don't let your "richness" cause you to be proud, arrogant, and contemptuous of others. Don't put all your hope in what you have. Continue to trust in Me. Be rich in good works and ready to share! The main thing is that you, no matter what your circumstances, remain irreproachable until My Son comes for you. Pursue righteousness and godliness. Become more and more like Christ, having faith, love, patience, and gentleness. Turn away from godless chatter, including slander and the reproach of godly people. The sins of some are conspicuous enough to identify. Other sins may not be so easy to recognize. The telltale signs for sinful habits to avoid are that they usher in a morbid fondness for strife, and they result in envy, jealousy, quarrels, dissension, abuse, insults, and slander. Avoid these! Treat older men like fathers, younger men like brothers, older women like mothers, and younger women like sisters. And help widows. Above all, never neglect your gift, and persevere with the leading of the Holy Spirit. Fight the good fight of faith, and lay hold on the eternal life.

And remember, I will preserve and keep you.

Day 345

I know those who are Mine

"The firm foundation of (laid by) God stands, sure and unshaken, bearing this seal (inscription): The Lord knows those who are His, and Let everyone who names [himself by] the name of the Lord give up all iniquity and stand aloof from it."
—II Timothy 2:19

II Timothy

I know those who are Mine. They are the ones with My Spirit in them—a spirit of power and love that works to produce a calm, well-balanced, and self-controlled mind. They are not ashamed of Me; they are eager to testify about Me fearlessly. They know that I am the One Who delivered and saved them, the One Who called them to a life in Me, not because of anything they did, but because of My grace made available through Christ Jesus before the world began. My Son annulled death and brought you immunity from eternal demise. And He appointed you as a messenger of life to those who are dying in this world. Though you may suffer because of this calling, you need never be ashamed of who you are, or what you are called to do, because you're assured that I will keep and guard what I entrusted to you until the day you're called up to Me. Guard with care the precious truth entrusted to you by the Holy Spirit. Be strong in My grace and willing to transmit My instructions to those who are trustworthy and will teach others. Diligently study My Word so you can be ready to accurately present it to others. This will help you avoid empty, strife-filled conversations and controversies that breed quarrels. It will also help you reach others with courtesy and gentleness. My desire is that all come to know Who I am and understand My truth.

In the last days, before His appearing, times will become more perilous and filled with distress and trouble. People outside of My Word will become more self-focused. They will love money and be driven by greed and lust for material things. They will be proud, arrogant, boastful, abusive, and ungrateful, even to their own parents and children. Lacking affection, they will speak slander, falsely accuse others, and love evil more than good. They will seek pleasure and amusement more than Me. Those who are weak will be easily swayed.

But you must be determined to live worthy of My crown of righteousness, which I hold in store for you, because you love and welcome My Son's appearing.

Day 346

Who are you now?

"Awaiting and looking for the [fulfillment, the realization of our] blessed hope, even the glorious appearing of our great God and Savior Christ Jesus (the Messiah, the Anointed One), Who gave Himself on our behalf that He might redeem us (purchase our freedom) from all iniquity and purify for Himself a people [to be peculiarly His own, people who are] eager and enthusiastic about [living a life that is good and filled with] beneficial deeds."
—Titus 2:13-14

Titus and Philemon

What can keep you going, no matter what happens? Only hope. What I promised before the world began will be fulfilled one day. With anticipation, you can expect this blessed hope, which will be fulfilled in the glorious appearing of your Savior Christ Jesus, Who redeemed you by purchasing your freedom. He chose you and continues to create in you an enthusiasm for life. He inspires you to perform deeds that benefit you and others. He prepares you. You need never feel badly about yourself, or disparaged by others, who don't recognize your capabilities and calling. Why? Because you're Mine—a glorious ornament of worth and value.

As My chosen gem, be prepared to do My work. Don't be lured into other purposes. Apply your efforts to what is beneficial and worthy of your special calling. This application will bring greater good to yourself and others. Avoid foolish controversies, dissensions, and wranglings, for these are unprofitable and hurtful. Do what is honest and honorable. Be ready for His coming. At one time, you were thoughtless, disobedient, and misled. You were a slave to your cravings, and you wasted your time with jealousy, malice, envy, even hatred. But, when you saw My goodness and loving-kindness and understood how I'd set you apart, not because of how great you were but because of My great mercy, you were made new by My Holy Spirit. You changed. Now, you are no longer conformed to this world, but to My purposes, thoughts, and actions, which are all good. Who are you now? You are My amazing ambassador for Christ. You are no longer a slave or a prisoner to the world. Your life has meaning. And you are My partner in all you do, because you are one with Me.

Your life now has meaning as you wait with anticipation for My Son's return.

Day 347

Who is My Son?

"He is the sole expression of the glory of God [the Light-being, the out-raying or radiance of the divine], and He is the perfect imprint and very image of [God's] nature, upholding and maintaining and guiding and propelling the universe by His mighty word of power. When He had by offering Himself accomplished our cleansing of sins and riddance of guilt, He sat down at the right hand of the divine Majesty on high."
—Hebrews 1:3

Hebrews 1-3

Who is My Son, really? And where did He come from? He came as Light emanating from Me. He is the out-raying of My radiance. He is the sole expression of My glory. He is the perfect image of My nature. I appointed Him as My heir and the owner of all things. By and through Him, the worlds, the reaches of space, and the ages of time were created. He laid the foundation of the earth, and the heavens are the work of His hands. He upholds and maintains and propels the universe by His mighty word of power. Why did I give Him so much authority? Because of what He was willing to do to honor Me. He gave of Himself. By offering His body as a living sacrifice—tested and tried through suffering—and by dying to save you from death, He brought you the ability to be His brother or sister. He set His trust in Me and said, "Here I am and the children you gave Me." And I cried, because I saw His great love for Me and for you. I saw His willingness to leave His post in heaven and live and suffer among people, because He was faithful to Me. And, because of what He did, you can believe He is trustworthy. You can know that you're set apart as My daughter or son when you believe in Him. You can call Him your brother, because He is not ashamed to call you His sibling. And He assists you when you're tried, tested, or suffer. Do you realize what He did for you by sharing in your own flesh and blood? He overcame death for you. He didn't do this for any other beings, not even for My angels. What drove Him to do this? His passion and love for you. Like Me, He always wanted people to live as part of our family, with Me as father and He as brother, for eternity. He wanted others to share in His inheritance in a beautiful new heaven and earth.

Now, that is finally available because of what He did.

Day 348

He had to learn obedience

"Although He was a Son, He learned [active, special] obedience through what He suffered."
—Hebrews 5:8

Hebrews 4-6

Though He was My son, Jesus had to learn obedience. Just like you, He had to learn how to live and survive and obey. Remember when He left His parents to sit with the teachers at the temple in Jerusalem? They searched for Him for days! And, though they were astonished by His understanding and replies to the teachers, they still admonished Him for leaving them in the way He did. Like you, He had to master obedience through life-experiences, often through suffering and seeing others endure agony. Why was this necessary? Because He was born into this world as a person of flesh and blood, and he had to grow up. As a child, he had to learn how to comply with those over Him while still living in My will.

He was your forerunner. He ran ahead to make a way for you. He dove deep below the surface of life as an anchor to penetrate the depths of a veil. What veil? The thing that separated you from My presence. Under the Old Testament Law, only the high priest could enter this curtain to go into the Holy of Holies that represented My presence in the temple. But Jesus became your great High Priest through His pain and death, and He tore through this separating shroud so you could enter His Father's presence with Him for the first time! He didn't do this by exalting Himself, but by revering and obeying Me. During His life on earth, He was sometimes overwhelmed with sorrow. He watched others suffer, and He didn't want to experience the death I asked of Him. He shrank from the horror of separation from My bright presence. He wanted to live, but He chose death, because I asked Him to, and His completed experience equipped Him for the position I gave Him. I made Him the source of eternal life for all who heed and obey Him. And, because of what He did, you can now fearlessly and boldly draw near to My throne and receive mercy for your failures and grace to help in time of need. Now, you can enter a rest set aside for you. And later, you'll enter My special, profoundly peaceful place for eternity.

It's a place prepared and waiting for you from the foundation of the world, because you believed.

Day 349

A more excellent way

"Therefore He is able also to save to the uttermost (completely, perfectly, finally, and for all time and eternity) those who come to God through Him, since He is always living to make petition to God and intercede with him and intervene for them."
—*Hebrews 7:25*

Hebrews 7-9

Do you understand what Jesus did for you when He died and shed His blood? Most people will never understand. Why would He give His life like this, in such a horrible way? Because He loved you and chose to become your negotiator and mediator. He wanted to be My last High Priest forever, even though He didn't fit the Law's requirement for a high priest, who must be descended from Levi. I went against My own Law and picked Him out as the perfect High Priest to completely fulfill the Law. Why? Because only He could satisfy this role. Do you see how I broke My own rules when it came to this and accepting the Gentiles into My Family later? Why did I do this? Because I wanted people to see that no one could live by the Law *and* have a real relationship with Me. Access to Me could never be accomplished by perfecting the flesh or being "good enough." People are made of imperfect flesh, and I am perfect Spirit, and flesh will always be separate from spirit. I needed a way to live among My people, and the Law could just bring the Jews to the point of issuing forth My Son. Jesus was the only One Who could accomplish what was needed to bring My Spirit to those who chose Me and wanted to approach Me. I needed a way to reconcile people back to Me so they could know Me. I wanted My love to be imprinted in their thoughts and engraved in their hearts. I wanted to be their God and they to be My people. And only He could do this through His sacrifice of blood. Remember, every year a high priest had to sacrifice blood for the removal of sins. A life for a life. This was the Law. But I needed a way to permanently remove sin forever. It had to be done by someone I could work through so others could come to Me. And, although He wasn't a Levite, only He was willing to do this for Me. And so, I broke My own Law, because only Jesus was able to save to the uttermost.

He became your guarantee of a more excellent way that would demolish the barrier between Me and you.

Day 350

What is faith?

"Now faith is the assurance (the confirmation, the title deed) of the things [we] hope for, being the proof of things [we] do not see and the conviction of their reality [faith perceiving as real fact what is not revealed to the senses]."
—Hebrews 11:1

Hebrews 10-11

I always had something better in mind for you than what you must endure today. This world, though once perfect, was corrupted by people who turned away from Me. It's no longer the sacred and beloved place I intended for you. But, I have something else in mind. If you yearn for and aspire to a better place, and you are not ashamed to call Me your God, I've prepared something very special for you.

Do you know how many lived with faith, but never saw the fulfillment of My promise for a more-wonderful home? Think of Abel, Enoch, Noah, Abraham, and Moses. Think of Paul, Peter, John, and Timothy. They died still looking forward to the "fatherland" I promised—a place where they could freely, without persecution and torment, worship Me. My promise still endures. If you live with faith, and have steadfast patience and endurance through trials, you will fully enjoy what I have in store for you. Remember, without faith it is impossible to please Me. It is possible for you to come near Me now because of what My Son offered—His own body as a sacrifice to give you access to Me. But you must believe that I exist and that I reward those who earnestly and diligently seek Me.

Faith is the assurance of this. It is the confirmation, or title deed, of the things you hope for. It is the proof of things you can't see. It perceives as real what has not yet been revealed. I have something far better in mind for you, as a hero of faith. But it can't come to perfection until all who will believe do so. Then, all with faith will join Me and My Son.

The Coming One will come for you. So, never be afraid. Live by faith with strong persuasion in your relationship with Me. Have passionate zeal born of an excitement for My Son's return and the holy city that awaits you.

Then, you will have a supernatural delight born of faith.

Day 351

You ask, Why me?

"So we take comfort and are encouraged and confidently and boldly say,
The Lord is my Helper; I will not be seized with alarm [I will not
fear or dread or be terrified]. What can man do to me?"
—Hebrews 13:6

Hebrews 12-13

I will ask you to give of yourself when you don't feel like serving. I will ask you to "be there" for someone who's hurting or alone, and you will sigh and groan, because this person has never been there for you. And you will ask, "Why me?" My answer will be, "Because I love and I chose you." Remember, the people I choose, I also "bring along" with Me. This means that, when you stray from My path, I will endeavor to guide you back so you can walk in My steps. My path will always lead you to Me and to greater good. But, in this world, it's easy to wander from it. When you stray, you become weak, confused, and disheartened. Only I can cut through the clutter, help you up, reinvigorate you, set you right again, and pave your way so that it's smooth and straight.

I want you to strive to live in peace with everyone and to encourage others to thrive in My grace, as you do. Avoid roots of resentment, which can shoot out their tentacles, become entwined in your thoughts and actions, and cause mental torment. Protect your heart by tapping into My thoughts. Never be seized with fear. I am your helper. People cannot destroy you because of what My Son did for you. When you feel alone or deserted, turn to Me. Remember what Jesus did for you. He endured bitter hostility and terrible opposition so that you might never grow weary, lose heart, or be faint in your mind. He is your leader and the source of your faith. He is the finisher, because He lived through suffering and abuse for you, knowing what awaited Him, and you, later. Realizing that many others have believed and await your presence, you can have great joy! Understand that what you endure now is but for a moment. One day, you'll step into My heavenly city and be joined by countless others to celebrate together for eternity. So don't lose heart, even though life seems fruitless, unfair, and unkind. Remember, Jesus is the same yesterday, today and forever. His promises never cease, and He will never leave you helpless or let you down. *Never!*

Day 352

Does evil come from Me?

"Let no one say when he is tempted, I am tempted from God; for God is incapable of being tempted by [what is] evil and He Himself tempts no one."
—James 1:13

James 1-2

Am I ever the source of evil? Do I cause people hardship, suffering, and death? Never! When you encounter trials of any kind, never think that I initiated the evil, because I'm incapable of being tempted or of tempting others. Where does distress come from? The true source is always the father of lies—the devil. Once known as Lucifer, he rebelled against Me and now poses as the god of this world. He lures those who will follow him down paths of corruption. And every person who is drawn away from Me is baited by passions that he inspires.

So why would I allow the father of lies to try you with temptations that can cause you to fall? Isn't it his lures that prompt you to hesitate, doubt, and waver in your beliefs? Why do I let him do this? Remember, it was Adam who gave to him the authority to rule this world and use these tactics until My Son returns. But I can use every one of his ploys for My good.

I observe life now as an ultimate test, and I watch carefully to see how you react to each new trial. Do you respond with faith by relying on Me for wisdom and insight? Or do you assume you are in good stead because of your religious observances or beneficial actions? Yet you waver in your belief like a billowing surge of the sea blown hither and thither and tossed by the wind? Do you stand steadfast in your faith, or do you give in to each new temptation and watch to see where it leads you?

You may think your responses are acceptable, because they're done with religious or pious or good intent, but what I look at is your determination to do what's right in My eyes, according to My will. I always see the heart behind your choices.

How you respond, including your words, determines whether or not you receive what I want to give you later: a victor's crown of life, which I promise to those who love Me.

Day 353

What does My wisdom look like?

"But the wisdom from above is first of all pure (undefiled); then it is peace-loving, courteous (considerate, gentle). [It is willing to] yield to reason, full of compassion and good fruits; it is wholehearted and straight-forward, impartial and unfeigned (free from doubts, wavering, and insincerity)."
—James 3:17

James 3-5

My wisdom is peace-loving, considerate, and gentle. It's reasonable and compassionate. It has heart. It's straight-forward, impartial, and free from insincerity. It leads to a plentiful harvest, because it's sown by those who work for and make peace. It ushers in a serene mind free from fear, agitating passions, and conflicts. It leads to deeds that bless others, including the poor. And it issues forth encouraging words, because it's rooted in love. Remember, the essence of all that I am is love. Evil desires birth sins that lead to death. From Me comes only good. I am the Father of Light, and My Light never casts shadows. My children, birthed in truth, bring Light to My creation. And My hope for them is that they avoid strife, which comes from ungodly passions, and that they never hate like people of darkness. Remember what hatred leads to—murder and death. When you burn with anger, you can't have contentment or happiness. You can't receive what you truly desire, because you can't see My Light or follow it. When you're a friend of the world, you can't be My friend, because you're enveloped in its darkness. The world's ways lead to jealousy and contention. They're birthed by those inspired by a superficial wisdom based on pride, defiance, and lies. The result is rivalry and selfish ambition, which lead to confusion and unrest.

What is My desire? That you be patient as you wait for His coming. That you establish your heart by strengthening and confirming it with My Word as you wait. That you earnestly pray for others, because this is powerful. That you understand that I can richly bless you if you are steadfast like Job. And that you praise Me for what I've done for you, knowing that I am full of pity and compassion.

Remember that I am tenderhearted and merciful, and I will bear with you until the day of His coming.

Day 354

You will never be disappointed

"For thus it stands in Scripture: Behold, I am laying in Zion a chosen (honored), precious chief Cornerstone, and he who believes in Him [who adheres to, trusts in, and relies on Him] shall never be disappointed or put to shame."
—*I Peter 2:6*

I Peter 1-2

Why do I call Jesus My Cornerstone? What does this mean? Remember how I refer to you as part of My temple and how your body is a living piece of what I'm building? Jesus Christ is the Head of this temple—the Church—and His life was laid down as its foundation, its Cornerstone, upon which it could be built. He is a living Stone because, even though He died, He still lives on. He was rejected by some on earth, and, even now, many throw away His message and stumble over it, as over a stone, because they don't understand what He was sent to build. His mission was and still is to establish a new temple from the ground up to heaven. This temple can never be torn down. And it will last forever.

Angels and prophets sought to understand how the Messiah would come and what He would accomplish. They wanted to see how He could save people from the degradation they'd fallen into, after other gods had drawn them away from Me. They knew He had to suffer, and they wanted to understand how this could possibly bring redemption to My people. They knew that their worship and service would help to lay a foundation for something I would build later. Now, all can see how I laid in Zion a chosen and precious chief Cornerstone and how anyone who believes in Him will never be disappointed or put to shame. When you come to My living Stone, you are made precious like Him. You become another living stone—a gem that cannot be destroyed or crushed. What you do with your life helps to lay the foundational walls of My temple. And when He appears to you, He'll reveal your true identity. He'll show you how you truly served and contributed, and He'll reward you for your work. He'll present you with your own stone that represents who you are and demonstrates how you were part of building this eternal temple. Remember, your origin was not born of human intent, because it originated in an immortal source, My Living Word.

My Word endures forever, and, as one of My redeemed, you can now live with Me in My marvelous light and never be disappointed.

Day 355

No one can hurt you

"Casting the whole of your care [all your anxieties, all your worries, all your concerns, once and for all] on Him, for He cares for you affectionately and cares about you watchfully."
—*I Peter 5:7*

I Peter 3-5

Never be afraid of threats or opposition to you or your beliefs. Why? Because, when you endure hardship due to your faith, you're blessed now and later. How can I say this? Because I know the great rewards you'll receive when you stand before My Son. Know that everyone with faith in Me will experience pain in this life. But only I, the God of grace, can use any affliction for good by completing and making you what you ought to be. Only I can establish, strengthen, and ground you securely. And I will never leave you. Be ready always to give a logical defense to anyone who asks you to account for the hope that is in you. I will help you with this. I'll remind you that you have a real expectation, because you know My Son will return for you. Others who have no hope will lash out at you defensively. They may even threaten and revile you for what you believe. But you can answer them with love and respect, because you know that, one day, you, and they, will answer to My Son. It's always better to suffer unjustly for doing what's right than to endure pain for doing what's wrong. Christ gave His life for all people so He could bring some to Me, and, though His body died, His Spirit lives on. He now sits at My right hand, interceding for you. So why be anxious? Why spend your time trying to be good enough, or acceptable to others who really don't care for you, when I've made you lovely and acceptable through My Son. I even made you a joint-heir with Him of all that I have. Don't be overcome with anxieties. Instead, turn your thoughts to Me. Allow My peace to permeate you, because your peacefulness is precious to Me. Live by My Spirit in you. Let it guide you. When you have an unfailing love for others, this covers a multitude of sins. It forgives and disregards offenses. Live this love by utilizing your special talents and gifts to bring glory to Me. But never be surprised when you're tested and tried for your faith. Everyone with faith will be.

Just remember to cast your cares onto Me, and I will always watch over and give you what you need to live in peace and hope.

Day 356

Will He ever come?

"The Lord does not delay and is not tardy or slow about what He promises, according to some people's conception of slowness, but He is long-suffering (extraordinarily patient) toward you, not desiring that any should perish, but that all should turn to repentance."
—II Peter 3:9

II Peter

Some say, "Where is the promise of His coming?" They scoff at your hope, because they don't see its realization. They try to dissuade you from your faith, and they mock the leaders I send. They lay charges and accusations at their feet. They promise greater freedom if you walk away from Me and My plans, but they themselves are slaves to their ideologies. My desire is that you be completely free from the world's fears, agitations, and conflicts. This can only happen if you come closer to Me. Then I can give you what you need to live a full and peaceful life, and I am able to fulfill in you all My precious promises. When you study My scriptures, adhere to what you read, discover new things about Me, and develop a trust in Me, then you can truly understand Who I am. And I can help you to be steadfast in Me as you lean on My Spirit to guide you. It takes discipline to reject the evil inclinations of the world. Only by consistently coming to Me can you grow in love. Only then can your words and actions become fruitful and beneficial. Then you can grow in your understanding of Me and My Son and in what He's done for you. Keep in mind what's in store for you. Some are impatient and ignore the prophecies that have already come to pass. But, one day, My Son will come suddenly, like a thief in the night. My promises will come to pass in My own special timing. Because I want as many as possible to be part of what I've planned, I move slowly so I can include those who will one day believe. When My Son returns to earth, all will stand before Him and give an account of their lives. This earth will be burned up, the heavens will dissolve, and I will make a new heaven and earth. I want you to be part of this new world. I want you to sit with Me and sing songs of praise. I want you to eagerly stand before Him and be at peace, free from the world's fears and conflicts.

My slowness in bringing these things to pass gives you precious time to receive more from Me so that you can jump for joy at His coming!

Day 357

How do you tell true believers from false ones?

"He who keeps (treasures) His Word [who bears in mind His precepts, who observes His message in its entirety], truly in him has the love of and for God been perfected (completed, reached maturity). By this we may perceive (know, recognize, and be sure) that we are in Him."
—I John 2:5

I John 1-2

People who look for excuses not to believe in Me or participate in My Church will say that many Christians are hypocrites. And they are right! Many who say they believe in Me and My Son are not really Mine at all in their hearts. So how can you tell the real believers from the false ones? It's easy. The main test to prove if I abide in a person via My Spirit is this: does the person love others? Or does he or she hate and dislike other people, including believers? If a person abides in Me, My love will pervade their every thought and action, especially toward My own. The only way a person can truly love people, all of whom are broken, is if that person loves and serves Me. How can a person serve Me? By practicing My teachings. And what is the thrust of what I teach? To love.

In your lifetime, you'll see deceivers. They say they believe in Me and may even tell you they represent Me. But if they don't acknowledge My Son or His teachings, they can't really know Me, because My Son came from Me and stands for all that I am. And those who truly live and walk by My Light will have unbroken fellowship, not only with Me, but with their fellow believers. If they say they have no sin, be wary. They delude themselves and cannot know the truth. Every person falls short. Only through a belief in My Son can anyone be made whole through forgiveness. How do you discern what's true and what's false? You have a guide inside you. The spirit in you shows you the truth in a real way. But you must listen. With the spirit's help, you can abide safely in Me. And the more you live through the One in you, the more I'm made visible in your life. A life lived via My Spirit will not fear His coming but will welcome it. Remember, those who live by My teachings conform to My will. This makes them My own.

And the test for those who are really Mine is always "Do they love?"

Day 358

Nothing to fear

*"Beloved, we are [even here and] now God's children; it is not yet disclosed
(made clear) what we shall be [hereafter], but we know that when He
comes and is manifested, we shall [as God's children] resemble
and be like Him, for we shall see Him just as He [really] is."*
—*I John 3:2*

I John 3-5

John answers many questions for those who seek My truth. First, he explains "What is sin?"
It's lawlessness, he says. It's the violation of My laws, which I set in place when I created the
heavens and the earth. It's being unwilling to accept My will in your life. When you abide
in Me, and live in communion with Me, you never deliberately, knowingly, or habitually
practice sin. Those who continue to "break fellowship with Me" don't understand or know
Me. All wrongdoing is sin. Worship of idols or what is false—anything that occupies My
rightful place in your heart—is sin. Where did sin come from? It came from My enemy, the
devil, who continues to violate My divine law of love. What are the results of sin? Hatred
and death—what My Son came into this world to overturn.

How do you know what is from Me? How do you avoid being deceived? Watch for a
desire to understand My ways. Does the speaker seek truth? Does he or she acknowledge
that Jesus came from Me? Or love his or her fellowmen? Remember, love springs from Me.
People who don't love don't know Me, for I am love. How much do I love you? I sent My
only Son to give His life for your sins, so you could live in My love. How can you tell if My
Son dwells in you? When you acknowledge Him as your Lord, you receive My Spirit, and we
make our home in you and you in Us. Through this bond, My love is perfected. And you
have confidence in your standing with Me. You need never be afraid, because My love in
you expels all fear, which brings anxiety. When you live in My love, you're never concerned
about where you stand with Me. With My Spirit in you, you're always victorious. In what
way? You have eternal life, and death has no more hold over you. With My Son in you,
you have a forever life. And, because you know He hears you, you have clearer insight and
understanding of all things.

And you realize there is nothing to fear.

Day 359

My hope for you

"Guard and keep yourselves in the love of God; expect and patiently wait for the mercy of our Lord Jesus Christ (the Messiah)—[which will bring you] unto life eternal."
—Jude 21

II John, III John, Jude

What is My hope for you? First, that you prosper and have health. Contrary to false teachings, I *do* want these things for you. And, beyond these, I want you to look forward to My Son's return! You will, if you abide in what you've learned—My truth. With My love in you, you can welcome strangers—those who seek My message of hope. You can imitate My goodness by working closely with those who contend for the faith and seek My will in their lives. Don't pay attention to those who pervert My message by spreading lies about Me. You can recognize them. They reject My power, scoff at what they don't understand, rebel against those I've set in authority, promote lawlessness, immorality, and perverseness, and deny My Son and His teachings. Walk away from them, for their efforts are fruitless and will come to nothing. Though they flatter themselves to gain advantage, their works will eventually be destroyed.

One day, My Son will return with myriads of saints—those who believed in Him—to execute judgment on the earth. In the meantime, pray in the spirit. Guard yourself with My love and patiently wait for My mercy to be unveiled by the amazing revelation of My guarantee to you—eternal life. Bring along with you those with doubts about My promises by affirming your faith with them. You can help "snatch them from the fire" so that their lives and works are never burned up. Behold Him Who can keep you from stumbling and falling. One day, He will present you without fault before My glorious presence in triumphant joy and unspeakable delight!

Look forward to His coming as you would an extra-special, beyond-amazing, death-defying, and awe-inspiring event.

Then you can have unspeakable joy!

Day 360

What can you expect?

"Behold, I stand at the door and knock; if anyone hears and listens and heeds My voice and opens the door, I will come in to him and will eat with him, and he [will eat] with Me."
—Revelation 3:20

Revelation 1-3

John saw into My world—the world of the spirit. What exactly did he see? He saw My Son, the risen Christ. He viewed the faithful and trustworthy Witness, the Firstborn of the dead, the Ruler of the kings of the earth, the Alpha and the Omega, and the Almighty Ruler of all. He saw One Who possesses the keys of death and searches all minds and hearts—the Origin and Author of My creation. Why is this significant? Because He offers you grace and peace through the Holy Spirit, along with seven other things: wisdom, understanding, good judgment, power, knowledge, God-reverence, and righteousness that ushers in faithfulness. These were long-awaited promises of what the Messiah would bring recorded in Isaiah 11:2-5. What does this mean to you now? That when you accept My Son as Lord, you are brought into His kingdom. You now belong to a royal race and priesthood. What can you expect? You can look forward to His return, when He'll present you with a crown of life—eternal life. Then, He'll give you hidden manna and a white stone bearing your new name, which only you will recognize and understand. He'll reward you for what you've done, and He'll give you power and authority over nations. He'll set you as a pillar in My sanctuary and write My Name upon you. Your name will be written in the Book of Life and He'll acknowledge you before Me and the angels. He'll set you beside Him on His throne. Until then, He'll protect you in the hour of trial. He'll come to you when you call. What does He desire of you? To be your First Love. When He corrects you, it's because He loves you and wants you to repent of wrongdoing so you can receive more rewards in the next life. He wants you to overcome in every situation. He wants you to be loyal until death, but to never fear what lies ahead. He desires your love, faithful service, and patient endurance. He wants you to hold fast to what He's given you and to what you've learned until He comes for you. He wants you to walk beside Him and to share His inheritance with you.

He wants grace and peace for you and, most of all, that you burn with zeal and enthusiasm for Him now, so you can sing with Him in glory later.

Day 361

Why you should adore Him

"For the Lamb Who is in the midst of the throne will be their Shepherd,
and He will guide them to the springs of the waters of life;
and God will wipe away every tear from their eyes."
—Revelation 7:17

Revelation 4-8

Why do all who know My Son love and adore Him? My angels sing songs of adoration for Him continually. Why? Because they know the tremendous power and authority He holds for good. And He was willing to set all this aside to live and suffer and die among the people He'd made, because He wanted them to have what We have. John wept, because there seemed to be no one worthy in all the universe to open the scroll bound with seven seals. This document revealed future events leading up to the revelation of a kingdom in a new heaven and earth. But then, an elder of the heavenly Sanhedrin showed John One Who was worthy to open the seals. It was the Lamb Who was slain. The Lion of Judah. Only He could do it. Because of what He'd done, the heavenly host sang a new song. By His blood, He'd purchased a people for Me from every tribe and language and nation. He'd made them into a royal race and priesthood for Me. And they would reign with Him as kings over the earth. One day, they'd sing this new song with Him. Who are the four creatures who serve Me? They're a special order of angelic beings. They hold in their hands the prophecies and prayers of the saints. They lead My worship and call forth My justice. They stand for what I will do for My people.[1] The lion face of one represents the overcoming of sin to set up and advance the kingdom of God on earth. The ox or calf face represents the sacrifice of a servant willing to suffer. The man's face shows intercession to remove sin and bring forth fruits of righteousness in God's people. The eagle represents the judgment time when truth is revealed, decisions made, rewards and punishments given, and I am vindicated.[2] Who are the 24 elders? They are people who lived, believed, and won the victory in life. So, they wear crowns of victory and robes of righteousness. Representing the raptured Church, they rule with My Son after being drawn from earth.[3] The 144,000 are the Jews who believe in Me and proclaim My message on earth during the tribulation in the end times.[4] As I will do for you, I guide them to the springs of the water of life.

And I wipe away every tear from their eyes.

Day 362

Why do I allow such death and destruction?

"The seventh angel then blew [his] trumpet, and there were mighty voices in heaven, shouting, The dominion (kingdom, sovereignty, rule) of the world has now come into the possession and become the kingdom of our Lord and of His Christ (the Messiah), and He shall reign forever and ever (for the eternities of the eternities)!"
—Revelation 11:15

Revelation 9-12

I am Light, and in Me is no darkness at all. So why would I allow death and destruction on the earth? It's a good question. Let Me explain. Death and disease were not initiated by Me. I created life and wanted people to live eternally. That was always My intent. If you look closely, you realize that the devil, once Lucifer, a shining star, was thrown from heaven, after being defeated by Michael and two-thirds of My angels. It was he and his angel-followers who brought evil to this world. It's he who deceives people. And he continues to bring accusations against My people, pursuing destruction for all mankind. When people become consumed with evil, and there is no Light left in this planet, one third of the earth will be burned up, but two-thirds will remain. Even as the devil pursues My people through lies and accusations, those who continue to heed Me and bear witness to My Son will be hidden in a safe place during trials and devastation. Before My Son is revealed on earth, there will be plagues, fires, and cataclysmic events. I'll send witnesses to warn people and bring them back to Me for safekeeping. But many will turn away and celebrate the death of My witnesses, who'll be brought back to life. And those who embraced their death will be terrified. When an earthquake destroys one tenth of Jerusalem, many will come to Me. But many will not. Before My Son comes, and My secret design is made known, numerous nations will rage against Me. For three-and-a-half years, their leaders, led by an antichrist, will reign as deceivers. And those who believe in Me will be persecuted. My goal is to rid the earth of evil, which causes the degradation of what I made. Remember the flood during Noah's time? Why did I allow this? Because when evil causes all that is good to be distorted and disrupted, it must be stopped. When evil spreads, My time for justice grows closer.

And I will fight for what is just and good to finally rid the world of all that is evil—all that causes death and destruction.

Day 363

Who are the beasts?

"And they sang the song of Moses the servant of God and the song of the Lamb, saying, Mighty and marvelous are Your works, O Lord God the Omnipotent! Righteous (just) and true are Your ways, O Sovereign of the ages (King of the nations)!"
—Revelation 15:3

Revelation 13-16

Who are the beasts described in Revelation? The first beast is a coalition of nations. Its 10 horns represent 10 kingdoms. Its seven heads stand for seven leaders. The beast itself is like a leopard, who has authority and power over the earth. Its feet are represented by a bear—a nation with authority to initiate aggression against any who won't bow down to the beast. The mouth of the beast is lion-like—a kingdom that leads as spokesman. One head will emerge as the overarching leader, who survives a mortal wound and miraculously recovers. This is the antichrist. Because he pays homage to the dragon, the devil, he is given authority overall, and many will worship him for his supernatural abilities. The beast will wage war against My people, who will require great patience and endurance to withstand its evil attacks. Another beast will emerge from the first beast, made up of two kingdoms, represented by horns. The antichrist will direct it and attract followers by appearing to be just and godly. Many will be deceived by his lying signs, which include a talking statue of himself that will demand worship. During his reign, his true nature will be revealed, and he will exert power and control over the former beast and demand obedience from all people, compelling them to be inscribed with his sign. The number of the beast is 666. This number was used before in II Chronicles 9:13, when Solomon received 666 talents of gold. Why is this significant? Because the beast will be viewed as one like Solomon, having great "wisdom" and "tolerance." He'll attract many to him by accepting all religions and allowing "gods on every hill," just as Solomon did. Gold as a standard will be significant. Those who can withstand his domination through faith in Me will be saved later, when all are harvested from the earth. At the end of the antichrist's reign, before the last battle, seven calamities will darken the earth: terrible body sores, bloody seas, tainted rivers and streams, burning sunlight, darkness, dried up rivers, and a great earthquake.

Then there will be terrible hailstones—all before the Mighty One is revealed.

Who is the Great Harlot?

*"Let us rejoice and shout for joy [exulting and triumphant]! Let us celebrate
and ascribe to Him glory and honor, for the marriage of the Lamb
[at last] has come, and His bride has prepared herself."*
—Revelation 19:7

Revelation 17-19

Who is the Great Harlot in Revelation? She is a great city seated on many waters that represent the races, languages, and nations of the earth. With her power, she controls rulers and leaders. Businesspeople will adore her, because she's made them wealthy. The demand for luxury that brings extravagant spending enables people to grow rich through her. Idolatry abounds, and the souls of many are bought and sold through her. Though she boasts that, because of her, none will see suffering or experience lack, crime and corruption abound in her. As people treasure what they've made more than what I've created, she becomes more degraded and corrupt. Those who speak against her excesses and lack of concern for Me and the people I've made are severely persecuted by those who serve her. My servants are denied a voice and martyred by her. Their blood lies within her walls. Not everyone likes the Great Harlot. The rulers and leaders led by the 10 horns and seven heads of the beast hate her. Why? Because she holds more power than they do. So, in her hour of destruction, they celebrate. Those who profited from her are devastated. They beat their breasts as they watch smoke rise from her and fire burn up all their goods and profits. They've lost their power to trade with her. And the souls of those sold into slavery can no more be enslaved by them. After this, there is great rejoicing in heaven. Why? Because something greater is being revealed. My Son's Bride, made up of those who've stood for Me, is about to be presented, and she is being adorned with radiant robes. My Son appears on a white horse, and He is recognized for What He is: Faithful and True, because He revealed My Spirit of Truth and inspired the teaching of My divine will and purpose. With fire-flaming eyes, He bears many crowns on His head. He wears a red robe, dyed with the martyred blood of My saints. And His true name is The Word of God. His robe and thigh are inscribed with these words: King of Kings and Lord of Lords. He is followed by troops of saints. Clothed in dazzling linen and riding white horses, they accompany Him.

They fly to earth with Him to fight for justice and declare His might.

Day 365

What will the end and beginning look like?

"The [Holy] Spirit and the bride (the church, the true Christians) say, Come! And let him who is listening say, Come! And let everyone come who is thirsty [who is painfully conscious of his need of those things by which the soul is refreshed, supported, and strengthened]; and whoever [earnestly] desires to do it, let him come, take, appropriate, and drink the water of Life without cost."
—Revelation 22:17

Revelation 20-22

To those with eyes to see and ears to hear, I reveal the final events on earth. The dragon, the devil, will be bound for 1,000 years. Some will be brought forth in a first resurrection—those who believed in Me and My Son during the tribulation. Martyred for their belief, they're given special authority as judges to reign. After 1,000 years, Satan will be released for a final battle. He'll muster forces against My Son and His kingdom, and they will surround the camp of My people, but My fire from heaven will consume them. After this, the devil will be thrown into a lake of fire. In a final resurrection, many will stand before My Son. He'll open the Book of Life, and all whose names are written inside will live on with Him. Others will be thrown into the lake of fire. Every case in this resurrection is determined by what the person accomplished, including motives and aims. Those in the gathering together and first resurrection are spared this judgment by their belief in My Son. They receive only rewards for what they've done. Earth and sky will flee away. Then I will create a new heaven and earth. My holy city will descend from heaven and be placed on a high mountain. With 1,500 miles on each of four sides, her 12 gates will be made of large pearls, labeled with the names of each of the 12 tribes. The city's wall will be made of jasper. Its foundations will be precious stones representing the 12 apostles. The city will be translucent gold and will hold no temple. The Lamb and I will reign there and lighten the earth. The city gates will be open, and those who are worthy may enter. A river through it will give healing to all who drink of it. Death and suffering will no longer exist.

Blessed are you if you heed My Word so you may partake of My bounty in this life and the next and be able to enter My gates with joy in that day.

Read other books by Lele Beutel, sign up for
her newsletter, and follow on social media by
scanning the QR code or going to the URL below:

linktr.ee/authorlelebeutel

Notes

Day 1: Once there was another earth
*"Satan, Sin and Death in Deep-Time"—www. kjvbible.com

Day 3: I didn't want to start over again
*"Who were the sons of God and daughters of men in Genesis 6:1-4?"—www.gotquesti-ons.org

Day 5: Be patient with My promises
*"The Letter Hey"—www.hebrew4christians.com and "Biblical numerology-Number
  5"— www.numerology.center

Day 7: Abraham understood My promise
  1. "Call of Abraham, Excavation of Ur, Child Sacrifice, Transfiguration"—stmary-
    yvalleybloom.org

  2. "97-lesson-22-genesis-22-23"—www.torahclass.com

Day 10: I will always come through for you
  1. "10 Unbelievable Facts About The Mandrake Root"—strangeago.com

  2. "Did Jacob placing branches in front of his flock really result in the offspring being
    speckled and spotted?"—www.gotquestions.org

Day 25: I love to work within the details of life!
  1. "Is there any significance to colors in the Bible?"—www.gotquestions.org

  2. "Bible Numerology"—www.bbclandrum.com

Day 26: What the priests wore and why
1. "Saul Camped under a Pomegranate Tree"—godasagardener.com

2. "Onyx Definition and Meaning"—www.biblestudytools.com

3. "Hidden Message in the Names of the 12 Tribes"—hoshanarabbah.org

Day 28: Special gifts for special purposes
1. "Bezalel"—wikipedia.org

2. "Aholiab Son of Ahisamach's Art in the Tabernacle"—www.angelfire.com

3. "Tin Definition and Meaning-Bible Dictionary"—Bible Study Tools

4. "Gold in the Bible"—www.biblestudy.org

5. "Biblical numerology"—Wikipedia, en.m.wikipedia.org

Day 29: What was it like to enter My tabernacle?
1. "What Does the Tabernacle Symbolize?"—www.thegospelcoalition.org

2. "The Door of the Tabernacle"—www.bible-history.com

3. "The Entrance Gate to the Outer Court of the Tabernacle of Moses"—www.bible-history.com

4. "The Tabernacle-The Walls and Gate"—magazine.thewarcry.org

5. "Brass Definition and Meaning"—www.biblestudytools.com

6. "Acacia Wood in the Tabernacle"—godasagarden.com

7. "The Meaning of Bronze in the Bible"—www.oneforisrael.org

8. "The Significance of Numbers in Scripture"—www.agapebiblestudy.com

9. "What is the prophetic significance of the four horns of the altar?"—hoshanarabbah.org

10. "What was the significance of the bronze laver?—www.gotquestions.org

11. "Golden Lampstand of the Tabernacle Symbolism"—www.learnreligions.com

12. "Spiritual Meaning of Frankincense"—www.biblemeanings.info

13. "Shewbread, The Definition and Meaning"—www.biblestudytools

14. "What was the significance of the altar of incense?"—www.gotquestions.org

15. "What are cherubim?"—www.gotquestions.org

16. "What is the Ark of the Covenant?"—www.gotquestions.org

17. "The Symbolism of the Ark of the Covenant"—feedingonchrist.com

Day 30: What were the different sacrifices?
*"What were the various sacrifices in the Old Testament?"—www.gotquestions.org

Day 32: What was the significance of the offerings?
*"What were the various sacrifices in the Old Testament"—www.gotquestions.org

Day 33: How does the law about leprosy apply to you?
1. "The Ancient Ritual of Two Doves...and Yeshua??"—hoshanarabbah.org

2. "Dove Definition and Meaning"—biblestudytools.com

3. "What is the significance of a scarlet thread?"—www.gotquestions.org

4. "What is hyssop?"—www.gotquestions.org

5. "What is the significance of cedar in the Bible?"—kathrynwarmstrong.wordpress.com

Day 34: The significance of the Day of Atonement
1. "Christ as Burnt Offering"—christianity201.wordpress.com

2. "Strongs's #5930: 'olah-Greek/Hebrew Definitions"—www.bibletools.org

3. "Why would the aroma of a sacrifice be important to God?"—www.gotquestions.org

4. "Why were non-Israelites allowed to participate in the sacrificial system?"—www.gotquestions.org

5. "Benson Commentary, Leviticus 16:21 Commentaries"—biblehub.com

Day 35: What does it mean to be "holy"?
*"The Meaning of Holiness"—www.ligonier.org

Day 40: What were the Levites' responsibilities?
*"What are the Colors of God?"—www.purposebydesigns.com

Day 45: Why are My words so exacting?
*"What is the significance of a red heifer in the Bible?"—www.gotquestions.org

Day 46: The symbolism of the serpent and the well...
    1. "Why is a bronze serpent used to save the Israelites in Numbers 21:8-9?"—www.gotquestions.org

    2. "The Symbolism of Metals in the Old Testament"—standardbearer.rfpa.org

Day 48: What were the Israelites' special feast days?
*"A Concise Overview of the Seven Feasts of Israel"—www.hebrew4christians.com

Day 50: Boundaries and vows...
*"The Biblical Boundaries of Israel-Taking it Literally"—www.chosenpeople.com

Day 54: When two mountains never meet...
    1. "What is the significance of left and right in the Bible?"—carm.org

    2. "Why was Mount Gerizim chosen for the blessing ceremony"—jbqnew.jewish-bible.org

Day 58: Why they had to use unhewn stones
    1. "End Time Kingdoms-The Feet and Toes of Nebuchadnezzar's Image"—www.end-times-prophecy.org

    2. "Spiritual Meaning of Hewn, Unhewn"—www.biblemeanings.org

Day 64: Who were the Canaanite people?
    1. "Who were the Perizzites in the Bible?"—www.gotquestions.org

    2. "Who were the Rephaim?'—www.gotquestions.org

    3. 3"Fertility Cults of Canaan"—www.thattheworldmayknow.com

Day 69: A tale of two women
    1. "What is the significance of the palm tree in the Bible?"—en.m.wikipedia.org

    2. "What does the oak tree symbolize in the Bible?"—https://urnabios.com

Day 70: What if I asked you to fight against all odds?
    1. "Ram Christian Dream Symbol"—m.dream-interpretation.org.uk

    2. "A Trumpet, A Jar, A Lamp"—www.walkingintruth.org

Day 71: A leader's vow and a daughter's life
*"Did Jephthah Actually Kill his Daughter?"—TheTorah.com

Day 72: The substance of Samson's strength
*"Samson"—www.sheknows.com

Day 75: What Ruth represented
*"The Feast of Firstfruits (First Fruits)"—truthnet.org

Day 76: Hannah's heart
*"What was the significance of weaning a child in the Bible (Genesis 21:8)?"—www.got-questions.org

Day 78: They demanded a king
*"Samuel"—https://en.m.wikipedia.org

Day 79: All Saul's fears
*"Saul Camped under a Pomegranate Tree"—godasagardener.com

Day 81: Why Saul sat under a tamarisk tree
*"Wanted: Dead and Alive, The Tamarisk Tree"—www.misterchad.com

Day 85: David's zeal and humility
*"Moving a Mulberry Tree"—godasagardener.com

Day 88: When people turn against you
*"David & Goliath in the Terebinth Valley"—godasgardener.com

Day 91: The significance of Gihon Springs...
  1. "The Valleys of Jerusalem"—land-of-the-bible.com

  2. "Ellicott's Commentary for English Readers," I Kings1:9 Commentaries—biblehub.com

  3. "Cambridge Bible for Schools and Colleges," I Kings 1:9 Commentaries—biblehub.com

  4. "Cherethites Definition and Meaning"—www.biblestudytools.com

Day 93: Each part of the temple meant something
  1. "What is the significance of cedar in the Bible?"—kathrynwarmstrong.wordpress.com

  2. "Pulpit Commentary," I Kings 6:29 Commentaries—biblehub.com

  3. "The Gourd in Biblical Symbolism"—biblicalanthropology.blogspot.com

4. "Matthew Poole's Commentary, I Kings 6:29 Commentaries"—biblehub.com

5. "International Standard Bible Encyclopedia, Topical Bible: Gold"—biblehub.com

6. "What is the significance of the olive tree in the Bible?"—gotquestions.org

Day 95: Solomon's "Camelot" years...
1. "Queen of Sheba"—www.ancient.eu

2. "What does the word sheba mean?"—www.behindthename.com

Day 98: I am in the stillness...
1. "limp"—www.dictionary.com

2. "Elijah under the Broom Tree"—godasagardener.com

Day 108: The zeal of a leader who lives My Word...
1. "Who was Asherah/Ashtoreth?"—www.gotquestions.org

2. "Topheth Definition and Meaning"—www.biblestudytools.com

Day 109: What you teach your family matters...
1. "Map of the Origin of Nations in Genesis 10"—www.bible-history.com

2. "Who were the Kenites?"—www.gotquestions.org

3. "From Jabez to Othniel"—www.skywatchministries.org

Day 117: The difference between David and Solomon...
1. "The Laver and the Molten Sea"—www.stempublishing.com

2. "Symbolism of the Pomegranate"—jewishgiftplace.com

Day 119: When a king's focus moves away from Me...
1. "Algum Wood for Temple Musical Instruments"—godasagardener

2. "Almug or Algum Definition and Meaning"—www.biblestudytools.com

3. "House of the Forest of Lebanon"—encyclopedia.com

Day 128: A timeline for reigns and events...
*"Bible Timeline, Persian Kings Period"—bradbeaman.wordpress.com

Day 129: Ezra's dilemma...
*Taken from THE AMPLIFIED BIBLE, Copyright © 1954,1958, 1962, 1964, 1965, 1987 by The Lockman Foundation. All rights reserved. Used by permission. (www.Lockman.org), page 543.

Day 134: How offense creates havoc and hatred...
*"Ahasuerus"—https://en.m.wikipedia.org

Day 184: About when does Isaiah really speak?
1. "Isaiah 21:1-10 The Desert by the Sea (Babylon): the fall of the gods"—www.theseedchristianfellowship.com

2. "Isaiah 22: The Valley of Vision Prophecy Jerusalem's Leadership is Judged"—thewritelife.tech

Day 209: I hate slavery and love commitment...
*"Slavery/Definition of Slavery"—www.merriam-webster.com

Day 212: What was the Healing Balm of Gilead?
*"Who is the Queen of Heaven?"—www.gotquestions.org

Day 213: Why have lands and people been destroyed?
*"Who was Chemosh?"—www.gotquestions.org

Day 219: Are you an "adamant?"
*"Who are the four living creatures in Revelation?" and "What were the wheels in Ezekiel 1?"—www.gotquestions.org

Day 221: What are cherubim and what is their purpose?
1. "What are cherubim?"—www.gotquestions.org

2. "The Cherubim and The Gospels...Rev 4"—billrandles.wordpress.com

3. "Who was Tammuz?"—www.gotquestions.org

4. "What does 'put the branch to their nose' in Ezekiel 8:17 mean?"—hermeneutics.stackexchange.com

Day 233: I care about every little thing...
*"Palm tree, Definition and Meaning"—www.biblestudytools.com

Day 234: Like the sound of many waters...
*"Will there be animal sacrifices during the millennial kingdom?"—www.gotquestions.org

Day 235: Your promised inheritance...
*"Who is the prince in Ezekiel 46?"—www.gotquestions.org

Day 283: Why some gave up everything to follow Jesus...
*"Follow Me"—preservingbibletimes.org

Day 287: How to seek My kingdom...

    1. "Gird one's loins"—www.dictionary.com

    2. "Oil as Symbol (Forerunner Commentary)"—www.bibletools.org

Day 343: What is this hidden truth?

*"Artemis worship instigated the restrictions of I Timothy 2:9-15"—kbonikowsky.word-press.com

Day 361: Why you should adore Him...

    1. "Who are the four living creatures in Revelation"—www.gotquestions.org

    2. "The Four Faces of Jesus"—myplace.frontier.com

    3. "Who are the twenty-four (24) elders in Revelation?"—www.gotquestions.org

    4. "Who are the 144,000?"—www.gotquestions.org

About the Author

Lele Beutel and her husband, Mike, enjoy traveling to new places and have found that, with each excursion, come opportunities to make a difference in people's lives. They consider themselves to be "secret agents" for God because of how He often leads them into unexpected situations where they're able to minister to others. With a degree in business communications, she spent 25 years as a financial advisor and was able to encourage many people mentally, spiritually, and financially through her faith-based advice. Now retired, she and her husband spend time with their two dogs, Andey and Barney, with their grandkids, and as volunteers at their church. They also share experiences with their life group members and the neighbors they meet while walking the dogs.

Other books she has written include *The Camino Connection*, which describes her healing journey across the Camino de Santiago, *God Answers*, a daily devotional with deeply sought-out questions and answers to and from God. Her poetry books include *Lele's Selah: Prayerful Poems that Inspire Hope,* a compilation of God-inspired poems written over a lifetime, *Lele's Lovesongs: Words of Hope for the Ones We Love,* and *Lele's Sighs: Reflections and Recollections.*

To reach her, you can find her on Facebook or at her website: www.lelebeutel.com